Advances in Pattern Recognition

For other titles published in this series, go to
www.springer.com/series/4205

Ling Shao · Caifeng Shan · Jiebo Luo ·
Minoru Etoh

Editors

Multimedia Interaction and Intelligent User Interfaces

Principles, Methods and Applications

 Springer

Editors
Dr. Ling Shao
Department of Electronic and Electrical
Engineering
University of Sheffield
Mappin Street
Sheffield, S1 3JD
UK
ling.shao@sheffield.ac.uk

Dr. Caifeng Shan
Philips Research
High Tech Campus 36
5656 AE Eindhoven
Netherlands
caifeng.shan@philips.com

Dr. Jiebo Luo
Kodak Research Laboratories
Lake Avenue 1999
Rochester, 14650 NY
USA
jiebo.luo@kodak.com

Dr. Minoru Etoh
Service & Solution Development
Department
NTT DoCoMo, Inc.
Hikarinooka 3-6
Yokosuka Kanagawa, 239-8536
Japan
etoh@ieee.org

Series Editor
Professor Sameer Singh, PhD
Research School of Informatics
Loughborough University
Loughborough, UK

ISSN 1617-7916
ISBN 978-1-84996-506-4   e-ISBN 978-1-84996-507-1
DOI 10.1007/978-1-84996-507-1
Springer London Dordrecht Heidelberg New York

British Library Cataloguing in Publication Data
A catalogue record for this book is available from the British Library

Library of Congress Control Number: 2010936504

Cover design: VTEX, Vilnius

Printed on acid-free paper

Springer is part of Springer Science+Business Media (www.springer.com)

Preface

With the development of silicon technologies, consumer electronics devices, such as personal computers, HDTV, mobile phones, digital cameras, and game consoles, have become ubiquitous for people's daily life. These devices can provide multimedia sources for entertainment, communication, and so on. To interact with these equipments, consumers currently rely on devices such as remote controls, keyboards, or control panels, which are often inconvenient, ambiguous, and noninteractive. How to design user interfaces of CE products that enable natural, intuitive and fun interaction is one of the main challenges the CE industry is facing. Many companies and institutes are working on the advanced user interfaces.

User interface technologies have been studied in various disciplines for decades. Considering that modern CE products are usually supplied with both microphones and cameras, how to employ both audio and visual information for interactive multimedia has recently received much attention in both academia and industry. But interactive multimedia is still an under-explored field. Many challenges exist when moving to multimodal interaction. For example, how to annotate and search huge data acquired by using multiple sensors, especially in the unconstrained end-user environments? How to effectively extract and select representative multimedia features for human behavior recognition? And how to select the fusion strategy of multimodal data for a given application? To address these challenges, we must adapt the existing approaches or find new solutions suitable for multimedia interaction.

This book brings together high-quality and recent research advances on multimedia interaction, user interfaces, and particularly applications on consumer electronics. The targeted readers are researchers and practitioners working in the areas of multimedia analysis, human–computer interaction, and interactive user interfaces from both academia and industry. It can also be used as a reference book for graduate students studying computer vision, pattern recognition, or multimedia. In the following we summarize all the chapters.

In *"Retrieving Human Actions Using Spatio-Temporal Features and Relevance Feedback"*, Jin and Shao present the solution of human action retrieval with local spatio-temporal features based on the bag-of-words model. Brightness gradient and 3D shape context are combined to increase the discriminative power of feature descriptors. Relevance feedback is then applied to refine retrieved action sequences and is demonstrated to be effective in highly complex scenarios, such as actions in movies.

In "*Computationally Efficient Clustering of Audio-Visual Meeting Data*", Hung et al. present novel computationally efficient algorithms to extract semantically meaningful acoustic and visual events related to each of the participants in a group discussion. Their methods can be used as a principal component that enables many higher-level semantic analysis tasks needed in search, retrieval, and navigation.

In "*Cognitive-Aware Modality Allocation in Intelligent Multimodal Information Presentation*", Cao et al. emphasize that modality allocation in intelligent multimodal presentation systems should also take into account the cognitive impacts of modality on human information processing. After presenting a user study, they show a possible way to integrate cognitive theories into a computational model that can predict the suitability of a modality choice for a given presentation task.

In "*Natural Human–Computer Interaction*", D'Amico et al. introduce the theorization and development of natural human–computer interaction systems. After reviewing the state of the art, a case study, a Smart Room with Tangible Natural Interaction, was discussed.

In "*Gesture Control for Consumer Electronics*", Shan presents an overview on gesture control technologies for Consumer Electronics. Different sensing technologies are discussed; existing researches on vision-based gesture recognition are extensively reviewed, covering face/hand detection, tracking, and gesture recognition. The latest developments on gesture control products and applications are also introduced.

In "*Empirical Study of a Complete System for Real-Time Face Pose Estimation*", Gritti focuses on the task of fully automatic real-time face 3D pose estimation. A complete system is developed, which is capable of self-initializing, estimating the pose robustly, and detecting failures of tracking. A robust tracking methodology is also introduced.

In "*Evolution-Based Virtual Content Insertion with Visually Virtual Interactions in Videos*", Chang and Wu present an evolution-based virtual content insertion system which can insert virtual contents into videos with evolved animations according to predefined behaviors emulating the characteristics of evolutionary biology. The system would bring a new opportunity to increase the advertising revenue for video assets of the media industry and online video-sharing websites.

In "*Physical Activity Recognition with Mobile Phones: Challenges, Methods, and Applications*", Yang et al. introduce a novel system that recognizes and records the physical activity of a person using a mobile phone. With the data collected by a built-in accelerometer, the system recognizes five everyday activities in real-time, i.e., stationary, walking, running, bicycling, and in vehicle.

In "*Gestures in an Intelligent User Interface*", Fikkert et al. investigate which hand gestures are intuitive to control a large display multimedia interface from a user's perspective. Numerous gesture possibilities are evaluated for a set of commands that can be issued to the interface. A working prototype is then implemented with which the users could interact with both hands and the preferred hand gestures with 2D and 3D visualizations of biochemical structures.

As video summarization techniques have attracted increasing attention for efficient multimedia data management, quality evaluation of video summary is required. In "*Video Summary Quality Evaluation Based on 4C Assessment and User Interaction*", Ren et al. propose a novel full-reference evaluation framework to assess the quality of the video summary according to various user requirements.

In "*Multimedia Experience on Web-Connected CE Devices*", Tretter et al. discuss the features that characterize the new generation of CE and illustrate this new paradigm through an examination of how web services can be integrated with CE products to deliver an improved user experience. Choosing digital photography as a case study, they introduce AutoPhotobook, an automatic photobook creation service, and show how the collection of technologies is integrated into a larger ecosystem with other web services and web-connected CE devices to deliver an enhanced user experience.

Sheffield, UK   Ling Shao
Eindhoven, The Netherlands   Caifeng Shan
Rochester, NY, USA   Jiebo Luo
Kanagawa, Japan   Minoru Etoh

Contents

Retrieving Human Actions Using Spatio-Temporal Features and Relevance Feedback

Rui Jin and Ling Shao

Abstract In this paper, we extend the idea of 2D objects retrieval to 3D human action retrieval and present the solution of action retrieval with spatio-temporal features. The framework of this action retrieval engine is based on the spatio-temporal interest point detector and the bag-of-words representation. For description of action features, we observe that appearance feature and structural feature from interest points can provide complementary information to each other. Then, we propose to combine brightness gradient and 3D shape context together to increase the discriminative power of descriptors. The experiments carried on the KTH dataset prove the advantage of this method. The extension of this work is applying the interest points based action retrieval technique to realistic actions in movies. As actions in movies are very complex due to the background variation, scale difference and performers' appearance, etc., it is a difficult target to localize and describe the actions. The results show that our method is very efficient computationally and achieves a reasonable accuracy for those challenging scenarios. We believe that our work is helpful for further research on action retrieval techniques.

1 Introduction

Visual information interpretation is an active research field, becoming a key technique in different applications, such as visual information indexing and retrieval, object and behavior recognition, video surveillance and human–computer interaction. As the demand of digital multimedia retrieval on the Internet and in large databases significantly increases these years, the traditional text-based retrieval is not satis-

R. Jin
Department of Electrical Engineering, Eindhoven University of Technology, Eindhoven, The Netherlands

L. Shao (✉)
Department of Electronic & Electrical Engineering, The University of Sheffield, Sheffield, UK
e-mail: ling.shao@sheffield.ac.uk

L. Shao et al. (eds.), *Multimedia Interaction and Intelligent User Interfaces,*
Advances in Pattern Recognition,
DOI 10.1007/978-1-84996-507-1_1, © Springer-Verlag London Limited 2010

Fig. 1 Examples of actions 'handclapping', 'running' in the KTH dataset and 'stand up', 'kissing' in the Hollywood dataset

fying for human beings who want to search for certain particular information. Recently, content-based retrieval is becoming the focus of academic research and has been successfully applied in both image and video retrieval. The advanced image retrieval methods extract features on local invariant regions [1] that are detected by specific interest point detectors [2, 3, 6] and use these features for retrieval. In [4], Sivic extended the local regions based image retrieval techniques and proposed a search engine based on the SIFT descriptor and Harris affine detector. This work enables video shots containing the same object as the query to be retrieved efficiently. James Philbin et al. [5] developed a similar system, which used SIFT features and adopted the technology of text retrieval architecture to retrieve specific buildings in image databases.

In this work, we attempt to extend the idea of 2D object retrieval to 3D action retrieval. Video retrieval techniques mentioned above only use spatial information and treat a video sequence as a set of images. Consequently, these methods are not able to capture the motion patterns which are critical for classifying human actions. In general, human actions can be considered as a set of features distributed over several frames, and the task to classify actions has been studied for several years. Some samples of recent studied action datasets are shown in Fig. 1. The traditional approach to action classification is based on the holistic analysis of spatio-temporal volumes [7–9]. This holistic approach focuses on exploring characteristics of the whole human body such as contours and poses as well as computing the correlation between two spatio-temporal volumes. Although this method is easy to implement and to utilize the geometrical consistency effectively, it cannot handle large geometric variation between intra-class samples, moving cameras and nonstationary backgrounds, etc. Instead of performing a holistic analysis, many researchers have adopted an alternative, part-based approach which is frequently combined with the 'bag-of-words' representation. This approach only analyses the 'interesting' parts of the whole spatio-temporal volume and thus avoids problems such as nonstationary backgrounds.

We adopt the solution of part-based action classification approach which extends the two-dimensional interest point detection and patch description to three dimensions and utilizes the spatio-temporal features to capture appearance and motion patterns for action classification and retrieval. Similar to ours, several recent works explore the part-based approach and the bag-of-words representation. Dollar et al. [10] proposed a novel interest point detector with separable linear filters in order to extend the feature response to constant and fluent motions and also analysed different cuboid descriptors. Nieble et al. [11] classified actions by applying an unsupervised learning method in form of probabilistic Latent Semantic Analysis (pLSA) model. Nieble and Fei-Fei [12] built a hierarchical model for action recognition using Dollar et al.'s feature detector [10] and static features represented by edge-based shape context [13]. In [14], Wong et al. presented a novel generative model called pLSA-ISM to capture both semantic and structural information for motion category recognition. Most recently, Jhuang et al. [15] developed a biologically inspired system based on hierarchical feedforward architectures for action recognition. Laptev et al. [16] presented a new method for action classification which extends several recent ideas including the HOGHOF descriptor, space-time pyramids and multichannel nonlinear SVM and applied this method to learning and classifying challenging action classes in movies.

Different to the above papers, our aim focuses on action retrieval which is a new direction of action analysis and also satisfies the demand of people for handling increasingly large video collections. That means given a specific action shot, the corresponding actions in a dataset or in movies can be retrieved or located automatically and efficiently. It should be noticed that our method cannot rely on advanced classification methods like SVM and pLSA used in action recognition, because the action data is unlabeled and the training stage is not practical in our action retrieval scheme. Instead, we focus on exploring the discriminative power of descriptors and the similarity learning within the same action class. The action data adopted in our work include both simple action datasets such as the KTH human action dataset [17] and more complex and realistic datasets such as the Hollywood dataset [16] (see Fig. 1). Our main contribution can be summarized as follows:

(1) We adopt spatio-temporal features and the bag-of-words representation to extend the retrieval technique from 2D object retrieval to 3D action retrieval.
(2) We propose to utilize both appearance information (content of cuboids) and structural information (layout of interest points) to form the action descriptor. The proposed descriptor which combines gradient and shape context shows more discriminative power in action retrieval.

(3) We explore the challenging task of retrieving actions in real movies. Our search engine is effective to capture some simple actions appeared in complex backgrounds.

The rest of this paper is organized as follows. Section 2 elaborates the action retrieval scheme. In Sect. 3, we evaluate and analyse the experiments carried out on the KTH dataset. The methods and results for action retrieval in real movies are presented in Sect. 4. Finally, we conclude the paper in Sect. 5.

2 Action Retrieval Scheme

2.1 Action Retrieval Framework

Given a query video with a specific action, the aim of this work is to retrieve similar action videos in the dataset. Our action retrieval scheme is illustrated in Fig. 2. The framework includes two stages, i.e. the off-line stage for dataset processing and

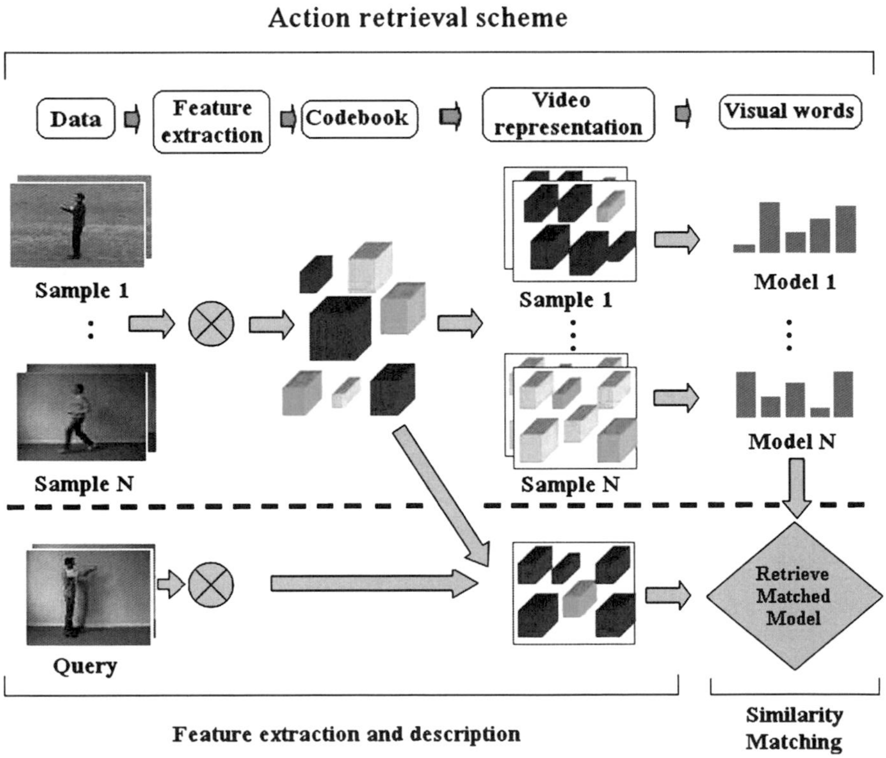

Fig. 2 The framework of action retrieval scheme

the on-line stage for querying. The off-line stage includes feature extraction, codebook formation and video representation. The feature extraction step is based on the spatio-temporal interest point detection and cuboid description techniques [10]. The detector first scans all the action videos in the dataset and locates the interest points. Then, cuboids are extracted around each interest point and contain spatio-temporally windowed pixel values. The extracted cuboids are further described with specific descriptors to form unique features. After processing feature extraction in the entire dataset, all extracted feature vectors are clustered into a set of spatio-temporal 'words', from which the codebook is built. Thus, each video in the dataset can be represented by a histogram of visual word occurrence. During the querying stage, the query video is also represented by the visual words. Then, we use a simple similarity matching scheme to find matched action videos corresponding to the query video. The details of this action retrieval scheme are introduced in the following.

2.2 Spatio-Temporal Interest Point Detection

An action video can be represented as a collection of spatio-temporal words by extracting spatio-temporal interest points. This method provides a reasonable feature space to build action models and also eliminates the need of common processing steps in holistic approaches such as background subtraction. Among the available interest point detectors, we observed that the interest points obtained by the generalized space-time detector [18] are too sensitive to noise in complex backgrounds. Here, we choose to use the separable linear filter method proposed in [10] for interest point detection. This spatio-temporal interest point detector is operated on a stack of images denoted by $I(x, y, t)$. A response function is calculated at every location in the video, and feature points correspond to local maxima. The response function has the following form:

$$R = (I * g * h_{ev})^2 + (I * g * h_{od})^2 \qquad (1)$$

where $g(x, y; \sigma)$ is the 2D Gaussian smoothing kernel, applied only along the spatial dimensions, and h_{ev}, h_{od} are a quadrature pair of 1D Gabor filters applied temporally, which are defined as $h_{ev}(t; \tau, \omega) = -\cos(2\pi t\omega) \times e^{-t^2/\tau^2}$ and $h_{od}(t; \tau, \omega) = -\sin(2\pi t\omega) \times e^{-t^2/\tau^2}$. The two parameters σ and τ correspond to the spatial and temporal scales of the detector, respectively. It is necessary to run the detector with different parameter sets to handle multiple scales. But for simplicity, we use one scale in our experiments and rely on the codebook to encode limited scale changes. In practice, any region with spatially distinguishing characteristics undergoing a complex motion can induce a strong response, especially for periodic motions. However, regions undergoing pure translational motion or without spatially distinguishing features will in general not induce a response. The space–time interest points are extracted according to the local maxima of the response function and could be regarded as low-level action features. Figure 3 shows examples of interest point detection in the KTH action dataset.

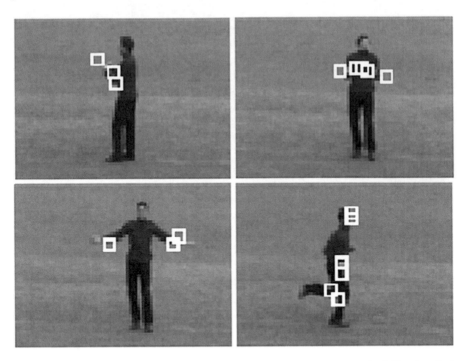

Fig. 3 Examples of Interest point detection over actions 'boxing', 'handclapping', 'handwaving', 'running'

2.3 Feature Description

After getting the locations of interest points, the next step is to describe the extracted cuboids in a certain way to form the feature vectors. The size of the cuboid is set to contain most of the volume data that contributed to the response function; specifically, cuboids have a size of approximately six times the scale at which they were detected.

A common way in [10] for feature description is using brightness gradient applied on three dimensions of cuboids. The spatio-temporal cuboid is first smoothed at different scales. Then the brightness gradient is calculated at each spatio-temporal location (x, y, t), giving rise to three channels (G_x, G_y, G_t), each of which has the same size as the cuboid. The feature vector is formed by concatenating the gradient values of each pixel in the cuboid. Additionally, we apply the Principal Component Analysis (PCA) [24] dimensionality reduction technique to project the feature vector to a lower-dimensional space.

Another feature descriptor involved in this work is interest points based 3D shape context (3DSC). The original 2D shape context proposed by Belongie et al. [19] has already shown its advantage in shape matching and objects recognition. In [20], Grundmann et al. extended 2D shape context to three dimensions and applied on 3D points cloud extracted by sampling 2D silhouettes over time for human action

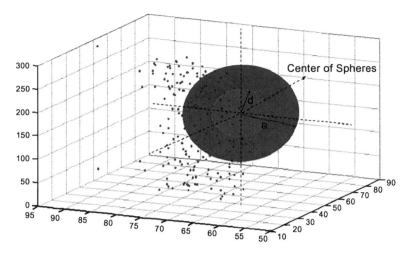

Fig. 4 Demonstration of 3D shape context applied on detected interest points

recognition. Recently, Shao and Du [21] proposed to use the combination of spatio-temporal interest points and 3DSC to represent the spatio-temporal correlation of extracted interest points. This method focuses on the geometric information of interest points and uses this information to build up action descriptors. Thus, we adopt this method in our framework to enhance the discriminative power of feature vectors. Given the locations of spatio-temporal interest points, this approach builds a histogram $H(S)$ as a vector function which captures the number of occurrences of spatio-temporal interest points in relative to a reference point within a sphere kernel $S(\delta, \theta, r)$. For each interest point location p, a set of K kernels centered on p and with different angles, δ and θ, and radius r is formed. In order to deal with scale changes, maximum distance between any two interest points is used as the maximum radius and the radius of each kernel increase linearly. The demonstration of sphere for 3DSC is shown in Fig. 4. The step of radius can be set as $1/10$ of the maximum radius, and the step of angles δ and θ can be set as $\pi/4$. In our experiments, the effect of different radius step and angular step is evaluated as shown in Fig. 7.

Theoretically, the gradient descriptor focuses on the appearance information of each cuboid, while the 3DSC descriptor captures the structural information, i.e. the spatio-temporal distribution of interest points. As the information provided by two descriptors is complementary, we propose to combine these two descriptors together, namely GRAD plus 3DSC, in order to increase the discriminative power of features. It is worth noting that there are also other advanced descriptors, e.g. HOGHOF [16]. The efficiency and relatively good performance of gradient and 3DSC enable us to choose them as the descriptor of our proposed system.

2.4 Codebook Formation and Action Video Representation

In order to distinguish different actions, we adopt the codebook method in our scheme. The codebook is constructed by clustering the descriptors with the k-means algorithm, and Euclidean distance is used as the distance metric. The centre of each resulting cluster is defined to be a spatio-temporal word in the codebook. Thus, each detected interest point can be assigned a unique cluster membership such that a video can be represented as a collection of spatio-temporal words from the codebook. To distinguish action classes, we use histograms of occurrences of spatio-temporal words.

2.5 Similarity Matching Scheme

At the retrieval stage, the common way to rank the action videos in a dataset is computing the Euclidean distance of visual words between query and each video. However, we observe that the performance of this method decreases as the number of retrieved samples increases, because this method also boosts the difference between similar action videos performed by different subjects. Thus, we use a simple similarity voting method in our implementation. Suppose we have a query with a visual word representation $Q(q_1, q_2, \ldots, q_m)$ and a sample in the dataset with $V(v_1, v_2, \ldots, v_m)$, where m is the total cluster number, and q_i, v_i represent the time of occurrence of cluster i, the similarity voting score between these two videos can be calculated as

$$S_{q,v} = \sum_{i=1}^{m} \min(q_i, v_i). \tag{2}$$

Each sequence in the dataset can be ranked by this matching score. This method only emphasizes the coexisting features between similar actions and will rely on the discriminative power of the descriptor to achieve high accuracy.

3 Action Retrieval on the KTH Dataset

3.1 Dataset Processing

We first test our action retrieval scheme on the KTH dataset [18] which is the largest available video sequence dataset of human actions. In this dataset, each video sequence has only one action. The whole dataset contains six types of human actions (boxing, handclapping, handwaving, walking, running and jogging) performed several times by 25 subjects. This dataset is considered to be very challenging because it contains different scenarios of outdoor and indoor environments as well as scale

	Boxing	Hand-clapping	Hand-waving	Running	Walking	Jogging
1						
2						
3						
4						

Fig. 5 Samples of the KTH dataset and actions performed in different scenarios

variations. The dataset contains 599 short sequences. Some sample images of this dataset are shown in Fig. 5.

To increase the computational efficiency of the dataset processing step, we first down-sample all sequences into half resolution and only adopt the first 200 frames of each sequence in our experiments. Then, we extract interest points and describe the corresponding spatio-temporal cuboids with the methods described in Sect. 2. The detector parameters are set to $\sigma = 0.4$ and $\tau = 1.5$ to fit the scale of down-sampled videos. It should be noticed that in this step, both gradient and 3DSC descriptors are stored for further processing. Then, the two types of descriptors are projected to a lower-dimensional space using PCA, 200 dimensions for the gradient descriptor and 100 dimensions for 3DSC. We directly concatenate these two PCA-reduced descriptors to form the proposed descriptor.

In order to build the codebook, we need to cluster the feature descriptors of all video sequences in the dataset. However, since the total number of features from all videos is very large, we use only a subset of sequences to learn the codebook, in order to accommodate the requirements of memory. Thus, we build the spatio-temporal codewords using only $1/5$ of the entire dataset.

To test the accuracy and efficiency of our method, we use each action video as query to get a retrieval response. The samples in the dataset are ranked according to their voting scores to query sequence. The final retrieval result is formed by averaging the accuracy obtained from videos for each action class. Additionally, in order to get a particular feedback of the retrieval performance, we evaluate the retrieval accuracy in different levels according to the number of top ranked samples. As there are 100 videos for each action, we set the range of retrieved number from 1 to 100 with a step up to 20.

3.2 Performance Evaluation

In this subsection, we will present a detailed evaluation of the proposed retrieval system and also of the effect of some parameter settings. The tests include the effect

Fig. 6 Evaluation of the effect for codebook size

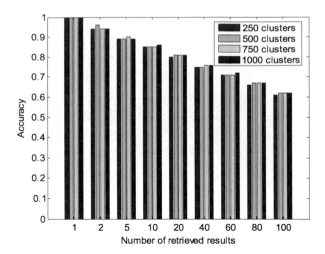

of different codebook sizes, parameter setting of spatio-temporal shape context and the performance of combined descriptors. Furthermore, we adopt Laptev's descriptor (HOGHOF) [16] as the state-of-the-art for comparison.

(1) Evaluation of different codebook sizes

The effect of codebook size is explored in our experiments and the result is shown in Fig. 6. In this test, we use the combination of gradient and 3DSC descriptors and set the codebook size from 250 to 1000 with a step of 250. It shows that the dependency of the retrieval accuracy on codebook size is very small. While the number of retrieved samples increases, a larger codebook size slightly improves the retrieval accuracy. A codebook size from 500 to 1000 provides almost the same performance. Thus, in further experiments, we choose the codebook size as 500.

(2) Evaluation of 3DSC parameter setting

As 3DSC can be configured with different radius steps and different angle steps, we need to find the proper setting to meet the demand of high retrieval accuracy. There are three settings included in our experiments as shown in Fig. 7. In this figure, setting A contains 8 angular bins and 5 radius bins, while setting C contains 16 angular bins and 10 radius bins. We can see that setting C performs better comparing to the other two. It proves that the increased bin number provides higher discriminative power. The remaining tests use the radius step $(\pi/8)$ and angular step $(1/10$ of the max distance) as in setting C.

(3) Performance of the proposed method

We evaluate different descriptors on our action retrieval scheme as shown in Fig. 8. The descriptors include gradient, 3DSC, GRAD plus 3DSC and HOGHOF proposed by Laptev [16]. It should be noted that for Laptev's method, we use the original implementation which combines the multiscale spatio-temporal corner detector and the HOGHOF descriptor. For all methods, we choose the number of interest points as 150 due to the consideration of efficiency. Actually, the performance varies slightly, while the number of interest points increases from 100 to 200.

For different action classes in Fig. 8, we can see the result of retrieving the 'jogging' action, which shows the lowest accuracy for all description methods because

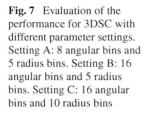

Fig. 7 Evaluation of the performance for 3DSC with different parameter settings. Setting A: 8 angular bins and 5 radius bins. Setting B: 16 angular bins and 5 radius bins. Setting C: 16 angular bins and 10 radius bins

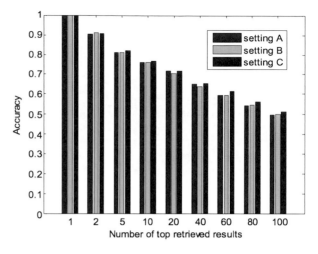

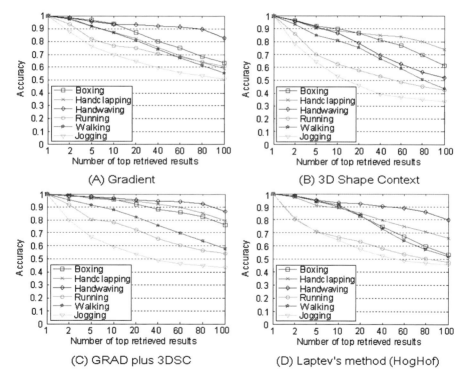

Fig. 8 Evaluation of performance for deferent descriptors with (**A**) brightness gradient, (**B**) 3D shape context, (**C**) gradient plus 3D shape context, (**D**) Hoghof from Laptev's method

'jogging' and 'running' in this dataset are essentially difficult to distinguish. In addition, Figs. 8(B) and (C) show the lowest accuracy for 'jogging'. This demonstrates that the 3DSC descriptor shows weak performance in handling actions that have

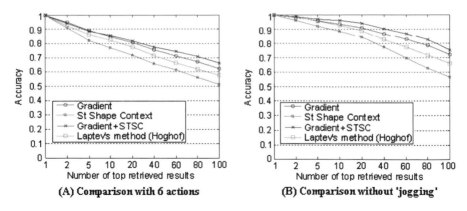

(A) Comparison with 6 actions   (B) Comparison without 'jogging'

Fig. 9 Comparison of average performance for different descriptors

similar layout of interest points. Furthermore, the retrieval accuracy for actions with whole body movements such as 'running', 'jogging', 'walking' are lower comparing to accuracy obtained from actions with arm movements such as 'handwaving', 'handclapping', 'boxing'. The similar results can also be found in [10] and [12]. The gradient descriptor and the HOGHOF descriptor provide high accuracy on action 'handwaving' but relatively lower result for 'boxing' and 'handclapping'. On the contrary, 3DSC keeps high performance on retrieving actions 'handclapping' and 'boxing' as 3DSC can emphasize the geometric information of actions. We observe that when we increase the number of top retrieved samples, the lower ranked samples have less matched cuboids with the query. As the descriptor with only appearance information such as gradient is not discriminative enough, different actions performed with similar appearance will be frequently misclassified. Thus, the proposed descriptor which combines appearance information and structural information shows great advantages to distinguish actions such as 'handclapping' and 'boxing' which have some similar features on arm's movements but different interest points layouts. It can be seen in Fig. 8 that the proposed descriptor gives a rise of about 15% to the accuracy on retrieving 100 samples of these two actions. The disadvantage of the proposed descriptor is its low performance on retrieving actions with similar appearances and layouts.

The overall performance comparison is illustrated in Fig. 9(A). Our combined descriptor performs the best (66% with 100 retrieved samples) and provides 5% improvement comparing to the gradient descriptor (61%) and Laptev's method (58%). The 3DSC descriptor performs the worst (51%), which proved that the discriminative power of pure structural information is not sufficient in action retrieval. Additionally, we also evaluated the performance of four descriptors in the situation without action 'jogging' in Fig. 9(B). Apparently, the retrieval accuracy significantly increased, and the proposed GRAD plus 3DSC also performs the best and achieves accuracy of 75%. The curve in Fig. 9 also illustrates that the performance gain of the proposed descriptor is less with a small number of retrieved samples and it increases while with a larger number.

Fig. 10 Confusion matrix of top 100 retrieved samples with GRAD plus 3DSC

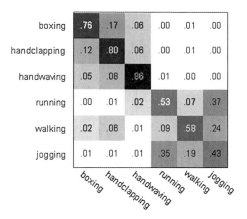

To demonstrate detailed information of inter-class error, Fig. 10 shows the confusion matrix on 100 retrieved samples only for the proposed method. The percentage in this figure visualizes the proportion of correctly retrieved samples over the total retrieved action videos. Specifically, we take the 'boxing' action in Fig. 10 as an example. The average rates for retrieving 'boxing' include 76% correct results, 17% 'handclapping' and 6% 'handwaving'. The confusion matrix illustrates the main retrieval errors come from actions with similar characteristics, especially for actions 'jogging', 'running' and 'walking'.

(4) Efficiency of our method

Our action retrieval scheme includes two stages. During the off-line stage, to process each video in dataset is a time-consuming task. We found that most of the processing time is elapsed on interest point detection and descriptor generation. The computational complexity for brightness gradient and 3D shape context is very low comparing to other advanced algorithms such as HOGHOF. We roughly calculated that it takes only 6 seconds for processing one action video using our method (implemented with Matlab 7.0, P4 2 GHz CPU and 2G memory), which is almost three times faster than Laptev' method. At the online stage, because the visual word model of each action video is already stored in memory, the action matching step takes only 1 second for processing a certain query.

3.3 Summary for Experiments on the KTH Dataset

In this section, we described our action retrieval scheme applied on retrieving actions in the KTH dataset. Although this dataset is challenging, our method shows competitive accuracy and great efficiency for action retrieval. The proposed descriptor can capture the appearance information of extracted cuboids and structural information, which shows improved discriminative power in our experiments. We show an example of our retrieved results in Fig. 11. We can see that the action performed by different subjects and in different backgrounds can be successfully retrieved.

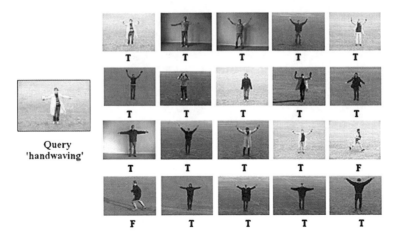

Query
'handwaving'

Fig. 11 Examples of top 20 retrieved results for query action 'handwaving'. The samples with 'T' are positive results, while the samples with 'F' are negative

4 Realistic Action Retrieval in Movies

As the work on the KTH dataset proved that the part-based action analysis method is very effective in retrieving actions, we extend our work on more realistic situations, i.e. retrieving actions in movies. This task can be briefly described as retrieving similar actions appeared in movies corresponding to a given query.

4.1 Challenges of This Task

How to describe an action in movies is a very difficult problem. When we watch a movie and we see a man holding a gun and pulling the trigger, we can easily say that this action is 'shooting'. If we see this man taking out his gun from the pocket and raising his arm with the gun, we can also recognize this action as 'shooting'. The difference is that the former one can be judged with a static frame and the latter is identified by body language distributed over several frames, i.e. the motion pattern. Thus, we categorize the actions into two classes, shape-based and motion-based. In this work, we focus on the study of the latter, because our interest point detector is highly relying on motion responses.

Another difficulty of analysing actions in movies is the variation of intra-class samples. This problem includes the variation of background, scale, viewpoint and subjects. In movies, the background could be very complex comparing to simpler scenarios in the KTH dataset. This will cause the error of interest point detection and inappropriate cuboids' description. Then different subjects usually perform the same action in different styles with different appearances. This will give different feature representations for similar actions, which leads to unexpected matching. Furthermore, scale variation, view point variation and camera motion induce more troubles for action description and action matching. Shown in Fig. 12, a simple action

Fig. 12 Examples of action 'stand up' in different scenario with different performers

'standup' is performed by different subjects in different scenarios. Although these actions can all be considered as 'standup', we can see that the styles of the performers and backgrounds are significantly different.

To our knowledge, realistic action analysis in movies is rarely studied in previous work. The only reported work can be seen in [16] and [18]. In [18], Laptev and Perez proposed to use Keyframe Priming technique combined with boosted space–time window classifiers for human action recognition and localization. They apply this method for recognizing the action 'drinking' in real movies. Furthermore, they studied the action recognition in the Hollywood dataset and proposed the HOGHOF descriptor [16]. In this work, we expect to design an efficient system which can rapidly localize the actions corresponding to the query.

We adopt the Hollywood dataset [16] for action retrieval experiments in movies. This dataset contains a large amount of shots from different movies. These shots are not clearly defined as there is usually more than one action in one shot. The actions involved in this dataset include 'handshaking', 'kissing', 'stand up', 'sit down' and 'hugging', etc. The examples of 'stand up' can be seen in Fig. 12. For our experiments, we use shots from three movies which are 'It's a wonderful life', 'Double indemnity' and 'Casablanca'.

4.2 Implementation

To retrieve actions in movies, we modified our action retrieval scheme used for the KTH dataset. The framework of our implementation is illustrated in Fig. 13. We first observe that hard cuts in real movies will cause inappropriate interest point detection and even wrong results in the retrieval stage. A hard cut is the change from one scene to another without any transition effects in between. Apparently, the hand cut part will frequently induce a high response for the interest point detector which cannot be ignored. Our treatment to this problem is applying a cut detector before further processing. This cut detector calculates the difference of pixel grey values between two neighborhood frames, and a predefined threshold is used to identify whether it is a hard cut or not. It should be noted that in our experiments there are still soft cuts such as 'fade in', 'fade out' and other undetected hard cuts. For the next step, we divide the movie shots into segments according to the information from cut detection. The size of each segment is limited with a maximum length of 100 frames. Then, we run the interest point detector on each segment; and the detected interest point number is set as two times the length of segment. To improve

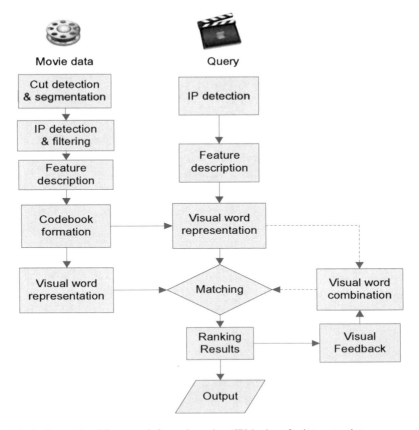

Fig. 13 Action retrieval framework for real movies. 'IP' is short for interest points

the efficiency of the detector, we apply an interest point filter to remove the isolated interest points without neighborhood supporting.

The descriptor we used in this engine is brightness gradient which is very computationally efficient. The previous experiments on the KTH dataset already proved that this descriptor can capture the motion pattern by describing the appearance information of cuboids. Here, we do not apply shape context as the structural information varies too much in real movies. Then, the codebook is formed by clustering the features as introduced before. Additionally, we adopt the idea of stop list [22] to suppress the most frequent visual words. The common features appeared in different actions will increase the number of meaningless matching pairs and also lead to unexpected ranking results.

The matching stage is slightly different with the former experiments. Because actions in movies are not performed periodically as in the KTH dataset, we use a sliding window to localize the action. The sliding window further divides the segment into small clips and can be represented with the collection of visual words inside this clip. Then, we use the similarity voting method to get the voting score for each clip. In our implementation, we set the window size as 20 frames with an overlap of 5 frames.

With a single query, we can get only a small number of similar scenes retrieved because of the variation of background and subjects. To improve the performance of our retrieving scheme, we adopt the visual feedback method [23] in our work. This

Query: stand up

Fig. 14 Top 20 results for 'stand up'

idea for improving the query process is to visualize the query results including a set of approximate answers. In our action retrieval engine, we can select several true positive samples among the top ranked results and combine their features with those of the original input query. For each visual word in the combined representation, the largest number between feedbacks and query is taken in order to increase the likelihood for matching.

4.3 Result Demonstration

In this subsection, we will demonstrate the retrieval results obtained by our action retrieval engine for real movies. It should be noticed that for the original input query, we only select the part of desired action instead of the entire volume in the interest point detection step. Further to improve the matching performance, we also inverse each frame horizontally as in a mirror to generate more features. For the Hollywood dataset, we specifically analyse the actions 'stand up', 'sit down', 'kiss & hug'(we consider 'kiss' and 'hug' to be in the same class). As introduced before, we only take three movies of the Hollywood dataset for simplicity. There are more than 100 sequences in these three movies, and these sequences can be further segmented into 277 clips by a sliding window. The example of retrieving the action

Query: kiss & hug

Fig. 15 Top 20 results for 'kiss & hug'

Query

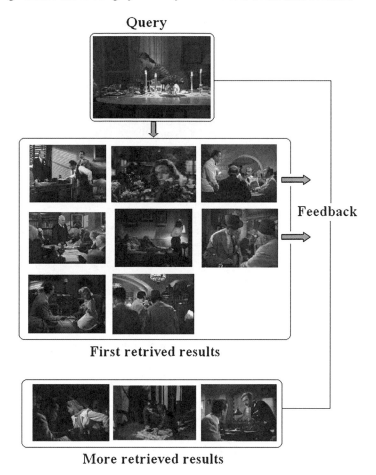

Feedback

First retrived results

More retrieved results

Fig. 16 Demonstration of results with visual feedback for action 'stand up'. This result is based on the top 40 ranked results

'stand up' is shown in Fig. 14. There are 6 correct results in top 20 retrieved results. Figure 15 demonstrates the result of retrieving 'kiss & hug', and there are 5 results correctly retrieved. All of these displayed frames are snapshots of actual retrieved action shots. We can see from the above figures that the relevant actions to the query are not always ranked on top of the list. Then, we apply the visual feedback method to improve the performance. The result of applying visual feedback for retrieving action 'stand up' is demonstrated in Fig. 16. In this example for the top 40 ranked results, the visual feedback can improve the results as we expected. It should be noted that the action 'kiss & hug' generates less matching pairs comparing to action 'stand up' as the motion response for 'kiss & hug' is very low.

4.4 Discussion

In general, our action retrieval engine can successfully retrieve a part of corresponding action shots in movies. Although the performance as we can see is not robust, this method can be considered effective as the computational complexity is very low. In our experiments, we observe that the matching errors are mainly from two aspects. The first one is inappropriate interest point detection as the detector cannot always accurately localize the interest regions to represent the action. Because the detector is sensitive to temporal variation, the background with motion will cause strong responses which cannot be averted. Additionally, the interest points are distributed around the action region with high response. These regions are easily matched to irrelevant query, and some nearby actions with weak response are frequently ignored. Furthermore, we have also tested the performance of 3D corner detector proposed by Laptev [16]. This method shows even weaker tolerance to background variation. The result obtained by Laptev's method for action 'standup' is shown in Fig. 17. Most of retrieved results are irrelevant to the query.

Another aspect is due to the appearance of different action performers. This appearance information includes performer's dress, action style, scale and viewpoint, etc., which are crucial for action matching in our scheme. We observe that different actions performed by actors with similar appearance will also generate a lot of

Query: stand up

Fig. 17 Retrieval results with Laptev's 3D corner detector and HOGHOF descriptor

Query: run

Fig. 18 Result demonstration for movie 'Run Lola Run'

matched pairs in the matching stage. These irrelevant matches will lead to unexpected retrieval results.

4.5 Application

In this subsection, we demonstrate an application of our action retrieval engine in the movie 'Run Lola Run'. This movie contains a large number of running scenes performed by the same actor. Due to the limitation of memory, we use only a segmentation of approximately 20 minutes in this movie. The query volume is the front view of action 'running' defined by user. The retrieved results are shown in Fig. 18. We can observe that our retrieval engine can effectively retrieve similar actions in this movie.

5 Conclusions

This paper seeks to extend the task of 2D object retrieval to 3D action retrieval. We adopt the recently studied part-based action analysis method and introduce an action retrieval model using spatio-temporal features and bag-of-words representation. We discussed actions in videos that can be effectively represented with spatio-temporal cuboids which are detected by interest point detector. For simple actions in static backgrounds such as the KTH dataset, we propose a descriptor combining gradient with shape context to capture both appearance information (content of cuboids) and structural information (layout of interest points). The experimental results show that our action retrieval model can effectively retrieve actions with competitive accuracy and high computational efficiency. The proposed descriptor also performs better in our model than other descriptors such as the recently reported HOGHOF descriptor in our comparison. The remaining problem for these experiments is distinguishing similar generated actions, e.g. running and jogging.

The extension of this work addresses on action retrieval in real movies. This task is very challenging as the scenarios in movies are much more complex than simple action datasets. Thus, we modify our retrieval scheme to meet the high requirements for movies. The results demonstrated in this paper show that our model can successfully retrieve action shots corresponding to the query, but the performance is not robust in complex situations. For further work, we consider the improvement of interest point detection for handling background variation as well as multiscale detection. We also expect to adopt the face detection and human body detection to serve for action detection and retrieval.

References

1. Schmid, C., Mohr, R.: Local grayvalue invariants for image retrieval. IEEE Trans. Pattern Anal. Mach. Intell. **19**, 530–535 (1997)
2. Harris, C., Stephens, M.: A combined corner and edge detector. In: Proceedings of the 4th Alvey Vision Conference, pp. 147–151 (1988)
3. Canny, J.: A computational approach to edge detection. IEEE Trans. Pattern Anal. Mach. Intell. **8**, 679–714 (1986)
4. Sivic, J., Schaffalitzky, F., Zisserman, A.: Efficient object retrieval from videos. In: The 12th European Signal Processing Conference, Vienna, Austria, September 2004
5. Philbin, J., Chum, O., Isard, M., Sivic, J., Zisserman, A.: Object retrieval with large vocabularies and fast spatial matching. In: IEEE Conference on Computer Vision and Pattern Recognition, June 2007, pp. 1–8 (2007)
6. Mikolajczyk, K., Schmid, C.: Scale & affine invariant interest point detectors. Int. J. Comput. Vis. **60**, 63–86 (2004)
7. Bobick, A.F., Davis, J.W.: The recognition of human movement using temporal templates. IEEE Trans. Pattern Anal. Mach. Intell. **23**(3), 257–267 (2001)
8. Blank, M., Gorelick, L., Shechtman, E., Irani, M., Basri, R.: Actions as space-time shapes. In: IEEE International Conference of Computer Vision, vol. 2, October 2005, pp. 1395–1402 (2005)
9. Wang, L., Suter, D.: Recognizing human activities from silhouettes: motion subspace and factorial discriminative graphical model. In: IEEE Conference on Computer Vision and Pattern Recognition, pp. 1–8 (2007)
10. Dollar, P., Rabaud, V., Cottrell, G., Belongie, S.: Behavior recognition via sparse spatio-temporal features. In: 2nd Joint IEEE International Workshop on Visual Surveillance and Performance Evaluation of Tracking and Surveillance, October 2005

11. Niebles, J.C., Wang, H., Fei-Fei, L.: Unsupervised learning of human action categories using spatial-temporal words. Int. J. Comput. Vis. **78**, 299–318 (2008)
12. Niebles, J.C., Fei-Fei, L.: A hierarchical model of shape and appearance for human action classification. In: IEEE Conference on Computer Vision and Pattern Recognition, pp. 1–8 (2007)
13. Belongie, S., Malik, J., Puzicha, J.: Shape matching and object recognition using shape contexts. IEEE Trans. Pattern Anal. Mach. Intell. **24**, 509–522 (2002)
14. Wong, S., Kim, T., Cipolla, R.: Learning motion categories using both semantic and structural information. In: IEEE Conference on Computer Vision and Pattern Recognition (2007)
15. Jhuang, H., Serre, T., Wolf, L., Poggio, T.: A biologically inspired system for action recognition. In: IEEE International Conference of Computer Vision (2007)
16. Laptev, I., Marszałek, M., Schmid, C., Rozenfeld, B.: Learning realistic human actions from movies. In: IEEE Conference on Computer Vision and Pattern Recognition (2008)
17. Schuldt, C., Laptev, I., Caputo, B.: Recognizing human actions: a local svm approach. In: International Conference on Pattern Recognition, pp. 32–36 (2004)
18. Laptev, I.: On space-time interest points. Int. J. Comput. Vis. **64**, 107–123 (2005)
19. Belongie, S., Malik, J., Puzicha, J.: Shape matching and object recognition using shape contexts. IEEE Trans. Pattern Anal. Mach. Intell. **24**, 509–522 (2002)
20. Grundmann, F., Meier, M., Essa, I.: 3D shape context and distance transform for action recognition. In: 19th 1–4 (2008)
21. Shao, L., Du, Y.: Spatio-temporal shape contexts for human action retrieval. In: Proceedings of the ACM International Workshop on Interactive Multimedia for Consumer Electronics, in Conjunction with ACM Multimedia, Beijing, China, October 2009
22. Sivic, J., Zisserman, A.: Video Google: a text retrieval approach to object matching in videos. In: Ninth IEEE International Conference on Computer Vision, vol. 2, p. 1470 (2003)
23. Keim, D.A., Kriegel, H.-P., Seidl, T.: Visual feedback in querying large databases. In: IEEE Conference on Visualization, pp. 158–185 (1993)
24. Turk, M.A., Pentland, A.P.: Face recognition using eigenfaces. In: IEEE Conference on Computer Vision and Pattern Recognition, pp. 586–591 (1991)

Computationally Efficient Clustering of Audio-Visual Meeting Data

Hayley Hung, Gerald Friedland,
and Chuohao Yeo

Abstract This chapter presents novel computationally efficient algorithms to extract semantically meaningful acoustic and visual events related to each of the participants in a group discussion using the example of business meeting recordings.
The recording setup involves relatively few audio-visual sensors, comprising a limited number of cameras and microphones. We first demonstrate computationally
efficient algorithms that can identify who spoke and when, a problem in speech
processing known as speaker diarization. We also extract visual activity features efficiently from MPEG4 video by taking advantage of the processing that was already
done for video compression. Then, we present a method of associating the audio-
visual data together so that the content of each participant can be managed individually. The methods presented in this article can be used as a principal component
that enables many higher-level semantic analysis tasks needed in search, retrieval,
and navigation.

1 Introduction

With the decreasing cost of audio-visual sensors and the development of many
video-conferencing systems, a growing trend for creating instrumented meeting
rooms could be observed. As well as aiding teleconferencing, such meeting rooms
could be used to record all meetings as a tool for staff training and development or
to remind them of certain agenda items that were discussed. Given the number of

H. Hung (✉)
University of Amsterdam, Amsterdam, Netherlands
e-mail: hayleyhung@gmail.com

G. Friedland
International Computer Science Institute (ICSI), Berkeley, USA

C. Yeo
Institute for Infocomm Research, Singapore, Singapore

L. Shao et al. (eds.), *Multimedia Interaction and Intelligent User Interfaces,*
Advances in Pattern Recognition,
DOI 10.1007/978-1-84996-507-1_2, © Springer-Verlag London Limited 2010

meetings that occur for a single person or even a work group, recording and storing meetings alone would not be useful unless they could be searched and browsed easily later.

In this chapter, we discuss ways in which we can move toward the use of instrumented meeting rooms while also minimizing the amount of audio-visual sensors, thus enabling fast setup and portability; We show experiments to cluster the audio and visual data of each person where only one microphone and two cameras are used to record the group meetings. From this, we present computationally efficient algorithms for extracting low-level audio and video features. The chapter is divided into sections describing firstly the general challenges of the meeting room scenario and what types of applications have been proposed. Then, we describe the related work on audio-visual speaker segmentation and localization in Sect. 2. In Sect. 3, we describe the overall approach that is presented in this chapter. Then, we describe the audio-visual sensor setup that we used in evaluating our algorithms in Sect. 4. Next, we describe how speakers and their turn-taking patterns are extracted using an online speaker diarization algorithm (Sect. 5). Then, in Sect. 6, we describe how visual activity from individuals can be extracted from compressed-domain features and compare this to conventional pixel-domain processing. In Sect. 7, we describe a method of associating audio-visual data and present bench-marking results. We conclude in Sect. 9 and discuss the future challenges.

2 Background

Clustering audio-visual meeting data can involve the grouping of events on different levels. From the coarsest level, we may want to group them based on date, location, or which work-group participated. If we increase the granularity, we observe events within a single meeting such as the types of activities that took place. Increasing the granularity further, each activity consists of a conversation type (ranging from monologue to discussion) where speech turn-taking events occurs. For each speech event, there are also accompanying motion features, such as a nod of the head, that might accompany a statement of agreement. We can go further in granularity by observing each speech utterance such as separation into phonemes. The motion can be organized based on the types of motion that occur such as whether it is an upward or downward motion.

Like any data mining task, our ultimate obstacle in creating a system that can cater completely to our searching and browsing needs is the problem of the *Semantic Gap*. The semantic gap is defined as the difference between the cognitive representation of some data compared to what can be extracted in terms of its digital representation. In this chapter, we concentrate on discussing how audio-visual meeting data can be clustered by who spoke when and where. The approach we present here consists of two tasks. The first clusters audio data based on how many speakers there are and when they speak. Semantically, this is not so meaningful since we only know that there are N speakers and when they spoke but we do not know who each speaker was. The second task takes these speaker clusters and identifies where they are in a set of video streams by associating the clustered audio with video features, which can then be used to show the corresponding speakers at the relevant time. This step already closes the semantic gap in terms of finding speakers and when they spoke and provides audio and video footage of how a speaker delivered a line.

Historically, speaker diarization has been a useful tool for the speech processing community since once the speakers have been identified, automatic speech recognition (ASR) can be applied to the utterances and attributed to a particular person. There are many who believe that closing the semantic gap has involved processing speech in terms of its verbal content. From a linguistic viewpoint, this seems to be the natural choice if we wish to extract the verbal content of what is being said so that interactions can be analyzed semantically. However, while semantics are closely related to verbal cues, meaning can also be extracted from nonverbal features. In some cases, the nonverbal cues can be a better indicator of the sentiment of the delivery of a phrase. A common example would be the use of sarcasm where someone may say "yes" when they actually mean "no". Analyzing the verbal content alone would provide us with the incorrect interpretation of the message but looking at the nonverbal cues, we might see that the delivery contained audio features that are more highly correlated with disagreement.

Practically speaking, systems that can automatically analyze audio-visual data using ASR and computational linguistics face many challenges. In natural speech, people do not always speak in perfect sentences and may correct themselves, change topic, talk over each other or complete each other's sentences. Typically ASR algorithms are plagued with challenges such as variations in accent, overlapping speech, and differences in delivery of the same word from the same person (which can depend on the preceding and following words), errors from detected words which are out of vocabulary, or inaccurate language models. The state-of-the art word error rate (WER) using distant microphones is around 25% using close-talk head-set microphones and around 40% using a distant (0.5 m) microphone source [29]. In terms of computational linguistics, analyzing dialog acts (the aim of the utterance e.g. agreement, disagreement, knowledge transfer), summarization, topic detection or the sentiment of what was said based on the ASR output can introduce further errors into the system chain. This is particularly problematic if the content of the exchanges are to be used for the analysis of higher semantic concepts from the data.

Analyzing or identifying these higher semantic concepts goes beyond the traditional meeting browsing technologies that can be used to navigate between changes in topic in a conversation or simple functions just as skipping through a video every 5 minutes. Being able to analyze a meeting by its social nonverbal content takes the potential of meeting browsing technology to a more intuitive level for users. Much of data mining and audio-visual clustering has been treated as a data-driven problem but perhaps in the context of recorded meetings and in particular where conversations are concerned, we must not overlook the stable nature of the nonverbal behavior that is exhibited during these interactions. For example, it is known that we move more than our mouths when we talk; we gesticulate for emphasis or to help us get our point across [43]. If our final goal is to browse meeting data in terms of social memory triggers, can the patterns of nonverbal behavior seen in social interactions be used to cluster the data too? That is, could aspects of nonverbal behavior during conversations provide us a simple and practical solution to this problem? Recent work on estimating behavioral constructs such as find who is dominant [35], the personality of participants [52] or what roles people have [20] suggest that using automatically extracted nonverbal cues can be effective.

For meetings in a natural setting, we expect to see mostly unconstrained conversations. Natural conversation in meetings involve many factors that are generally unwanted in a clean test scenario. The first is overlaps or interruptions in speech. Traditional data-sets [50] that are used to test audio-visual synchrony algorithms assume that only one person speaks at a time. In more complex cases, one person mouths words not corresponding to the associated audio sequence in order to confound simpler synchrony algorithms. Others contain subjects reciting digits simultaneously. However, in all cases, the speech is not natural and test data in such conditions do not reflect the majority of circumstances in which people find themselves talking.

Other aspects of real conversations involves natural body movements. In natural conversations, people move to aid emphasis of what they are saying, provide feedback for others and regulate their gaze patterns to encourage a smooth flow of conversation between conversants [30, 43]. Promising work has been presented to take advantage of the correlation between more holistic body motion and speech [31, 32, 59, 60]. Such methods have shown a relationship between global body motion and speech over longer term sequences. The experiments presented in this chapter, continues in this direction, exploring the extent to which we can use findings in the psychology literature to address the audio-visual clustering problem in meetings more directly for constructing a plausible practical approach to the problem of speaker localization. For the remainder of this section, we will discuss firstly the general challenges faced with organizing meeting data. Then we will concentrate the discussion on related work on speaker diarization and on audio-visual synchrony, related to speech and finally some background on the findings in psychology on audio-visual synchrony during conversations.

2.1 Challenges in Meeting Analysis

Organizing audio-visual meeting data involves using many different sorting criteria. For now, let us concentrate on scenarios where all the conversants are co-located so that interactions can occur face-to-face. Even under such circumstances where acoustic and lighting conditions can be controlled, there are still considerable challenges that can be addressed in a multi-disciplinary domain from signal processing, to computer vision, linguistics, and human–computer interaction.

Activities in meetings consist mainly of conversations or interactions between the participants. Within meetings, people can communicate with each other in different permutations and at different times. They can talk over each other, have sub-conversations, be involved in multiple conversations at the same time, and can provide verbal as well as nonverbal signals to others. In some cases the verbal and nonverbal delivery of a message can be contradictory.

As well as investigating group conversational dynamics in the work place from a psychological perspective [6, 17, 49], work has been done in the domain of computational modeling [2, 40, 48, 54]. Due to European project initiatives, the computational modeling of meetings has been considered in terms of either visual or audio-visual segmentation of the group activities as discussions, monologues, note-taking, presentations or writing on a white board from the Multi-Modal Meeting Manager Corpus (M4) (http://www.idiap.ch/mmm/corpora/m4-corpus/) [2, 40, 54] where the meetings were scripted so each meeting activity and the times of execution were predetermined. The main problem with approaching meeting analysis from this perspective is that in reality, it is very difficult to objectively label monologues, dialogues, discussions, or presentations. For example, if someone is giving a presentation and someone else asks a question, which ultimately leads to a discussion, then is the current scenario a presentation or a discussion? The answer lies in the interval over which the judgment is made or the temporal context which is applied. Therefore, depending on whether the judgment is made on a fine-grained time scale or a longer time scale, the judgment of the scenario can also be different. Since the M4 corpus, new audio-visual meeting data (Augmented MultiParty Interaction (AMI) corpus http://www.idiap.ch/mmm/corpora/ami) has been recorded, where the scripting part of the scenario was removed. In more natural meeting scenarios, people do not cut from doing a presentation to a discussion or a monologue necessarily so annotating these meetings in terms of meeting actions is not practical.

With this in mind, it is probably easier to extract semantically meaningful features which are easier to evaluate. The problem with analyzing meeting actions is that labeling is strongly dependent on the temporal context. Rather than examining temporal intervals of time, we can also segment based on events such as a change of speaker or when someone starts or stops speaking. Such instantaneous events are much less ambiguous to label. This can be done by either speech/nonspeech detection for cases where each person has their own microphone [66] or using speaker diarization if a single microphone cannot be directly associated with a single speaker.

If we are able to cluster the audio and video information of a speaker, we can begin to analyze more complex behaviors such as who responds to whom. Analysis of turn-taking patterns in discussions can be quite powerful for indicating who is dominant [35] or what roles people play in a meeting [20, 34]. With an audio-visual clustering method we could automatically obtain both the audio and video information for the project manager for a meeting, for example. Given that the discussion above has established that it is easier to analyze meetings in terms of these turn-taking events, we provide a background review of speaker diarization. In addition, we provide a review of work on the audio-visual association of speakers so that some semantic meaning can be associated with the speakers that are identified. Finally, we provide some background information about how human body motions are related to speech during conversations.

2.2 Background on Speaker Diarization

The goal of speaker diarization is to segment audio into speaker-homogeneous regions with the ultimate goal of answering the question "who spoke when?" [55].
While for the related task of speaker recognition, models are trained for a specific set
of target speakers which are applied to an unknown test speaker for acceptance (the
target and test speaker match) or rejection (mismatch), in speaker diarization there
is no prior information about the identity or number of the speakers in the recording. Conceptually, a speaker diarization system therefore performs three tasks: First,
discriminate between speech and nonspeech regions (speech activity detection); second, detect speaker changes to segment the audio data; third, group the segmented
regions together into speaker-homogeneous clusters.

Some systems combine the two last steps into a single one, i.e., segmentation
and clustering is performed in one step. In the speech community, different speaker
diarization approaches have been developed over the years. They can be organized
into either one-stage or two-stage algorithms, metric-based, and probabilistic systems, and either model-based or non-model-based systems.

Many state-of-the-art speaker diarization systems use a one-stage approach, i.e.,
the combination of agglomerative clustering with Bayesian Information Criterion
(BIC) [12] and Gaussian Mixture Models (GMMs) of frame-based cepstral features
(MFCCs) [55] (see Sect. 5). Recently, a new speaker clustering approach, which
applies the Ng–Jordan–Weiss (NJW) spectral clustering algorithm to speaker diarization is reported [45].

In two-stage speaker diarization approaches, the first step (speaker segmentation) aims to detect speaker change points and is essentially a two-way classifi-
cation/decision problem, i.e., at each point, a decision on whether it is a speaker
change point or not needs to be made. After the speaker change detection, the speech
segments, each of which contains only one speaker, are then clustered using either
top-down or bottom-up clustering.

In model-based approaches, pretrained speech and silence models are used for
segmentation. The decision about speaker change is made based on frame assignment, i.e., the detected silence gaps are considered to be the speaker change points.
Metric-based approaches are more often used for speaker segmentation. Usually, a
metric between probabilistic models of two contiguous speech segments, such as
GMMs, is defined, and the decision is made via a simple thresholding procedure.

Over the years, research has concentrated on finding metrics for speaker change
detection. Examples are the Bayesian Information Criterion (BIC) [12], cross
BIC (XBIC) [4, 36], Generalised Likelihood Ratio (GLR) [18], Gish distance
[26], Kullback–Leibler distance (KL) [9], Divergence Shape Distance (DSD) [39].
A more detailed overview can be found in [3]. Newer trends include the investigation of new features for speaker diarization, such as [24, 61], and novel initialization
methods.

2.3 Background on Audio-Visual Synchrony

So far, the speaker diarization system provides some intervals of speech associated with a single person, but we do not have information about what they look like or how the message was delivered nonverbally. This can be done by associating the audio streams with the correct video stream by identifying or exploiting the synchrony between the two modalities. Alternatively, sound source localization from video can be used to tackle a similar problem. Most computational modeling has involved identifying one or two people in a single video camera only where short-term synchrony of lip motion and speech are the basis for audio-visual localization. Audio-visual synchrony or sound source localization can be considered a task in itself. However, both these tasks could be combined, and recent work has started to consider both speaker diarization and localization as a single audio-visual task.

Common approaches to audio-visual speaker identification involve identifying lip motion from frontal faces [13, 21, 22, 46, 47, 53, 57, 58]. Therefore, the underlying assumption is that motion from a speaker comes predominantly from the motion of the lower half of their face. This is further enforced by artificial audio-visual data of short duration, where only one person speaks. In these scenarios, natural conversation is not possible, and so problems with overlapping speech are not considered. In addition, gestural or other nonverbal behaviors associated with natural body motion during conversations are artificially suppressed [50].

Nock et al. [46] presents an empirical study to review definitions of audio-visual synchrony and examine their empirical behavior. The results provide justifications for the application of audio-visual synchrony techniques to the problem of active speaker localization in the more natural scenario of broadcast video. Zhang et al. [69] presented a multimodal speaker localization method using a specialized satellite microphone and omni-directional camera. Though the results seem comparable to the state-of-the-art, the solution requires specialized hardware, which is not desirable in practice. Noulas et al. [47] integrated audio-visual features for online audio-visual speaker diarization using a dynamic Bayesian network (DBN), but tests were limited to two-person camera views. Tamura et al. [58] demonstrate that the different shapes the mouth can take when speaking facilitates word recognition under tightly constrained test conditions (e.g., frontal position of the subject with respect to the camera while reading digits).

The approaches discussed above were often tested on very limited data sets (which are not always publicly available) and were often recorded in highly constrained scenarios where individuals were unable to move or talk naturally. In general, the speakers face the camera frontally and do not talk over or interrupt each other. In contrast to previous methods which combine audio and video sources in the early stages of the speaker diarization process, we present a late fusion approach where noisy video streams are associated with estimated speaker channels.

In terms of finding speakers in conversational settings where video data does not capture high-resolution faces, Vajaria et al. [59, 60] were the first to consider the global body motion could be synchronous with speech. They presented a system that combines audio and video on a feature-level using eigenvector decomposition of global body motion. Hung et al. [31] developed this notion further by considering how simple motion features could be used to identify speakers in video streams for group discussions. Finally Campbell and Suzuki [10] analyzed speech and upper torso motion behavior in meetings to study participation levels but did not go further into evaluating how well speech and motion could be correlated.

2.4 Human Body Motions in Conversations

In contrast to much previous work in this area, we have found that relying on lip motion to identify speakers is not always necessary and is not always possible [31, 32]. In the psychology literature, it has been shown on many occasions that speaker and also listener movements are directly related to the role they play in a conversation [37, 43]. We will explore this in more detail here to show that such nonverbal cues play a huge role in understanding and inferring behavior types in conversations.

In social psychology, human body movements in conversations have been studied from different perspectives. The first looks at the movements of speakers, the second looks at the movement of listeners, and the final considers the synchrony between the movements of speakers and listeners. The first two are important for understanding what differentiates speakers from listeners in terms of kinesic behavior, while the third is used more to measure the degree of mutual engagement between conversants. The latter is beyond the scope of this paper, but more details can be found in a critique of work on interactional synchrony by Gatewood and Rosenwein [25].

The first aspect involving the movement of speakers suggests that speakers accompany their speech with gestures [37, 43]. Gestures accompanying speech themselves have been classified in many different ways. Adam Kendon defined gesture as a

> "range of visible bodily actions that are ... generally regarded as part of a person's willing expression" (p. 49).

The reason for gesturing has been explained as a means of increasing precision [27, 43], an evolutionary origin of language [38], or as an aid to speaking to facilitate lexical retrieval [42, 43]. Whatever the reason for moving when speaking, psychologists are in agreement that we definitely move a number of body parts when we speak. Moreover, it was noted by Gatewood and Rosenwein that "normal human beings exhibit remarkable integration of speech and body motion at the subsecond time scale" (p. 13, [25]). Such a phenomenon was labeled as "self synchrony" by Condon and Ogston [15], who later elaborated that,

> "As a normal person speaks, his body 'dances' in precise and ordered cadence with the speech as it is articulated. The body moves in patterns of change which are directly proportional to the articulated pattern of the speech stream .... There are no sharp boundary points but on-going, ordered variations of change in the body which are isomorphic with the ordered variations of speech" (p. 153) [16].

Gestures that accompany speech can be divided into a number of different categories involving manipulation of facial features, head pose, the trunk (or upper torso), arms, shoulders, and hands. Hadar et al. found that short and rapid head movements can accompany points of stress in a sentence as a person speaks [27]. In addition, Hadar et al. also found that the frequency of large linear movements of the head was correlated with a person's speaking time in a conversation [28]. In larger groups, speakers can also move their head to address all the participants. Depending on the person's status within the group, their level of conversant monitoring can vary [19].

Hand motions have been shown to be very related to the content of what is being said; it has been suggested by Armstrong et al. that

> "Most gestures are one to a clause, but when there are successive features within a clause, each corresponds to an idea unit in and of itself .... Each gesture is created at the moment of speaking and highlights what is relevant... " (p. 40–41) [5].

McNeill called such gestures "spontaneous" where "their meaning is determined on-line with each performance" (p. 67) [43] and identified four types of relationships between spontaneous gestures and speech: iconic, metaphoric, beat, and abstract deictic. Iconic gestures represent objects and events in terms of resemblance; metaphoric gestures represent an abstraction; beat features are rhythmic movements of the hand such as for counting or indexing a list; and abstract deictics represent locations of objects within a gesture space [43].

The listener in a conversation can provide feedback to the speaker, indicate that they wish to claim the floor, or indicate their interest in a conversation. It was found by Hadar et al. [27] that listener's head movements tended to involve more "linear and expansive" movements when indicating that they wanted to speak, "symmetric and cyclic" when providing simple feedback such as "yes" or "no" responses, and "linear but with shorter movements" during pauses in the other's speech, which could be attributed to "synchrony" behavior between conversants. While speaker's movements tend to be more pronounced, the movements of listeners are less pronounced but still observable. Harrigan found that body movements occurred more frequently when a person was requesting a turn than during the middle of someone else's speaking turn [30], showing that listeners tend to move less. She also found that hand gestures tended to precede a turn compared to feedback responses that were observed from motion from the head such as nods, shakes and tilts, facial expressions, and shoulder shrugs. In particular, gestures from the hands were related to speech, serving to accent or emphasize what was being said.

3 Approach

Figure 1 shows a flow diagram of the approach that we have taken for clustering the audio-visual meeting data in terms of who spoke when and where they are. The goal of the presented system is to identify speakers and their approximate locations in multiple camera streams, in an online and real-time fashion. We perform experiments with four-participant meetings for cases where there are either four cameras (one for each person) or two cameras (two people are shown per camera). A summary of the approach is listed below.

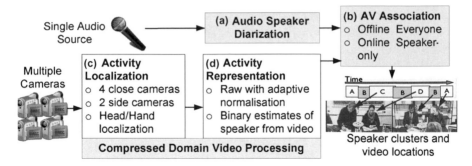

Fig. 1 Figure showing our approach. The work consists of two stages: (**a**) solving the task of "who is speaking now?" based on audio information only; (**b**) associating speakers with video streams. Different types of video features (**c–d**) are used to enhance the practicality and performance of the system

(a) *Online real-time speaker diarization*: Speaker clusters are generated using the audio data to represent each speaker and when they speak. From this unsupervised data-driven method, a set of speaker clusters are generated where it is assumed that one speaker corresponds to one cluster.

(b) *Audio-visual association of speakers streams and video*: Using these speaker clusters, audio-visual association with a set of video streams is performed so that the video or approximate spatio-temporal location of a speaker can be found from multiple cameras. We carried out experiments showing whether it is possible to associate *all* participants to their audio source correctly in a batch manner and how the performance degrades as the length of the meeting is shortened. As the window size gets smaller, the likelihood of more than one person speaking within the same time interval is greatly reduced, so we finally carried out experiments on selecting and evaluating whether *just the speaker* was associated with the correct video stream.

(c–d) *Extraction of visual activity features*: The video features themselves are computed in the compressed domain to take advantage of processing that is already required for the video compression process. Using these features, it is possible to do some spatial video-processing in order to identify the locations of two participants in video streams. We try using different sets of cameras to both represent and localize speakers in the meeting. Finally, to improve localization performance, we tried creating a binary representation of each person's visual activity, which generated a cleaner signal than the original raw features used.

4 The Augmented MultiParty Interaction (AMI) Corpus

One of the largest corpora of meeting room data has been recorded by the Augmented MultiParty Interaction (AMI) corpus which was created out of a European

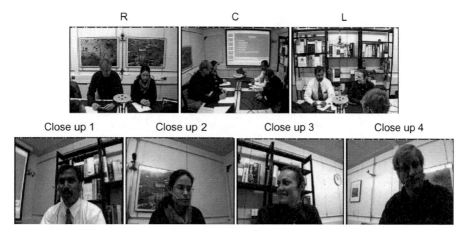

Fig. 2 All available views in the data set

Fig. 3 Plan of the
experimental meeting room

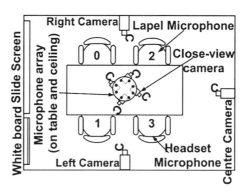

Union funded project [11]. This initiative generated a corpus that contains both 100 hours of audio-visual data and annotations from semantically low-level features, such as who is speaking to, more semantically meaningful concepts, such as dialogue acts or who is looking at whom. In each meeting, four participants were grouped together, and were asked to design a remote control device over a series of sessions. Each person was assigned a role such as "Project Manager", "Marketing Expert", or "Industrial Designer". A microphone array and four cameras were set in the center of the room. Side and rear cameras were also mounted to capture different angles of the meeting room and its participants, as shown in Fig. 2.

Each camera captures the visual activity of a single seated participant, who is assigned a seat at the start of each meeting session. Participants are requested not to change seats during the session. No other people enter or leave the meeting during the session, so there are always only four interacting participants. Each person also wore a headset and a lapel microphone. A plan view of the meeting room is shown in Fig. 3.

5 Audio Speaker Diarization

5.1 Traditional Offline Speaker Diarization

As previously explained in Sect. 2, the goal of speaker diarization is answering the
question "who spoke when?". The following section outlines the traditional audio-
only speaker diarization approach as shown in Fig. 4.

Feature Extraction   Wiener filtering is first performed on the audio channel for
noise reduction. The HTK toolkit[1] is used to convert the audio stream into 19-dim-
ensional Mel-Frequency Cepstral Coefficients (MFCCs) which are used as features
for diarization. A frame period of 10 ms with an analysis window of 30 ms is used
in the feature extraction.

Speech/Nonspeech Detection   The speech/nonspeech segmentation [64] proceeds
in three steps. At each step, feature vectors consisting of 12 MFCC components,
their deltas and delta-deltas (approximations of first- and second-order derivatives),
and zero-crossings are used.

In the first step, an initial segmentation is created by running the Viterbi algorithm on a Hidden Markov Model (HMM) with Gaussian Mixture Model (GMM)
emissions that have been trained on Dutch broadcast news data to segment speech
and silence. In the second step, the nonspeech regions are split into two clusters:
regions with low energy and regions with high energy. A new and separate GMM is
then trained on each of the two new clusters and on the speech region. The number
of Gaussians used in the GMM is increased iteratively, and resegmentation is performed in each iteration. The model that is trained on audio with high energy levels

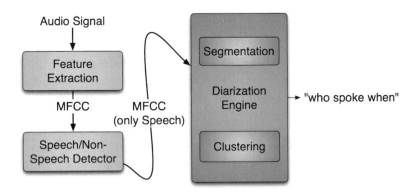

Fig. 4 Block diagram illustrating the traditional speaker diarization approach: as described in
Sect. 5, an agglomerative clustering approach combines speaker segmentation and clustering in
one step

---

[1] http://htk.eng.cam.ac.uk/.

is added to the nonspeech model to capture non-speech-like sounds such as music, slamming doors, paper rustling, etc. In the final step, the speech model is compared to all other models using the Bayesian Information Criterion (BIC). If the BIC score is positive, the models are added to the speech model.

Speaker Segmentation and Clustering   In the segmentation and clustering stage of speaker diarization, an initial segmentation is first generated by randomly partitioning the audio track into k segments of the same length. k is chosen to be much larger than the assumed number of speakers in the audio track. For meetings data, we use $k = 16$. The procedure for segmenting the audio data takes the following steps:

1. Train a set of GMMs for each initial cluster.
2. Resegmentation: Run a Viterbi decoder using the current set of GMMs to segment the audio track.
3. Retraining: Retrain the models using the current segmentation as input.
4. Select the closest pair of clusters and merge them. This is done by going over all possible pairs of clusters and computing the difference between the sum of the Bayesian Information Criterion (BIC) scores of each of the models and the BIC score of a new GMM trained on the merged cluster pair. The clusters from the pair with the largest positive difference are merged, the new GMM is used, and the algorithm repeats from the resegmentation step.
5. If no pair with a positive difference is found, the algorithm stops, otherwise the algorithm repeats from step 2.

A more detailed description can be found in [64].

The result of the algorithm consists of a segmentation of the audio track with n clusters and an audio GMM for each cluster, where n is assumed to be the number of speakers.

The computational load of such a system can be decomposed into three components: (1) find the best merge pair and merge; (2) model retraining and realignment; (3) other costs. After profiling the run-time distribution of an existing speaker diarization system, we find that the BIC score calculation takes 62% of the total run-time.

Analyzing how the best merge hypothesis is found, the reason for the high cost of the BIC score calculation can be identified. Let D_a and D_b represent the data belonging to cluster a and cluster b, which are modeled by θ_a and θ_b, respectively. D represents the data after merging a and b, i.e., $D = D_a \cup D_b$, which is parameterized by θ. The Merge Score (MS) is calculated as (1) [1]:

$$MS(\theta_a, \theta_b) = \log p(D|\theta) - \big(\log p(D_a|\theta_a) + \log p(D_b|\theta_b)\big). \qquad (1)$$

For each merge hypothesis a and b, a new GMM (θ) needs to be trained. When the system is configured to use more initial clusters, which is preferable for better initial cluster purity, the computational load can become prohibitive.

The speaker diarization output consists of meta-data describing speech segments in terms of starting time, ending time, and speaker cluster name. This output is usually evaluated against manually annotated ground truth segments. A dynamic programming procedure is used to find the optimal one-to-one mapping between the hypothesis and the ground truth segments so that the total overlap between the reference speaker and the corresponding mapped hypothesized speaker cluster is maximized. The difference is expressed as Diarization Error Rate (DER), which is defined by NIST.[2] The DER can be decomposed into three components: misses (speaker in reference, but not in hypothesis), false alarms (speaker in hypothesis, but not in reference), and speaker errors (mapped reference is not the same as hypothesized speaker).

This Speaker Diarization System has competed in the NIST evaluations of the past several years and established itself well among state-of-the-art systems.[3]

The current official score is 21.74% DER for the single-microphone case (RT07 evaluation set). This error is composed of 6.8% speech/nonspeech error and 14.9% speaker clustering error. The total speaker error includes all incorrectly classified segments, including overlapped speech. NIST distinguishes between recordings with multiple distant microphones (MDM) and recordings with one single distant microphone (SDM). In the case of MDM, beam-forming is typically performed to produce a single channel out of all available ones.

For our approach, the various experimental conditions that we used can be categorized into a single distant microphone case and an individual close-talk microphone. For the first case, a single audio stream was created by mixing individual close-talk microphone data, i.e., "Mixed Headset" or "Mixed Lapel" using a summation. For the latter condition, a single microphone was selected from a microphone array from either the table or ceiling sources.

5.2 Online Speaker Diarization

Our first goal is to segment live-recorded audio into speaker-homogeneous regions to answer the question "who is speaking now?". For the system to work live and online, the question must be answered on intervals of captured audio that are as small as possible and performed in at least real-time. The online speaker diarization system has been described in detail in [62] and has two steps: (i) training and (ii) recognition, which will be described in more detail in the subsequent sections. Figure 5 shows a summary of the on-line audio diarization algorithm.

Unsupervised Bootstrapping of Speaker Models To bootstrap the creation of models, we use the speaker diarization system proposed by Wooters et al. [64] which was presented in Sect. 5.1 in the first meeting of each session. This also results in an estimation of the number of speakers and their associated speaker models. Once models have been created, they are added to the pool of speaker models and can be

---

[2]http://nist.gov/speech/tests/rt/rt2004/fall.

[3]NIST rules prohibit publication of results other than our own. Please refer to the NIST website for further information: http://www.nist.gov/speech/tests/rt/rt2007.

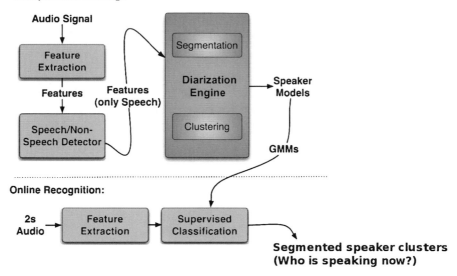

Fig. 5 Summary of the on-line audio diarization algorithm

reused for all subsequent meetings. The speaker diarization system used for training is explained as follows.

Speaker Recognition   In recognition mode, the system records and processes chunks of audio as follows. First, Cepstral Mean Subtraction (CMS) is implemented to reduce stationary channel effects [56]. While some speaker-dependent information is lost, according to our experiments performed, the major part of the discriminant information remains in the temporally varying signal. In the classification step, the likelihood for each audio frame is computed against each set of Gaussian Mixtures obtained in the training step. From our previous experiments on larger meeting corpora, [62], we decided to use two-second chunks of audio. This introduces a latency of about 2.2 seconds after the person has started talking (recording 200 audio frames at 10-ms intervals plus a processing time of $0.1 \times$ real time).

The decision on whether a segment belongs to a certain speaker or the nonspeech model is reached using majority vote on the likelihoods of an audio frame belonging to a GMM. If the audio segment is classified as speech, we compare the winning speaker model against the second best model by computing the likelihood ratio. We use this as an indicator of the confidence level. In our experiments, we assume that there are speaker models for all possible speakers, so we used the highest confidence level to indicate the most likely speaker. For a more realistic case, it is possible to apply a threshold to the confidence level to detect an unknown speaker, but this currently requires manual intervention.

A Note on Model Order Selection   Offline audio speaker diarization can lead to more clusters than speakers since the method is data-driven, and therefore cluster merging stops depending on whether the BIC score is improved or worsened by merging two candidate clusters. Due to the robustness of our online speaker diarization algorithm, while more clusters than participants can be generated in the offline training phase, in the online stage, noisy or extraneous clusters have much lower likelihoods, so they are never selected as likely speaker models. We found in our experiments that the number of recognized clusters and that of actual participants were always equal.

It is also important to note that the data we use includes overlapping speech. These periods are automatically ignored when the speaker models are generated to ensure they remain as clean as possible. Work has been carried out to address overlapping speech in offline diarization systems but involve a second pass over the diarized audio signal, which would not be feasible for an on-line and real-time system [8].

5.3 Summary of the Diarization Performance

As described earlier, the output of a speaker diarization system consists of metadata describing speech segments in terms of start and end times, and speaker cluster labels. NIST provides a measurement tool that uses a dynamic programming procedure to find the optimal one-to-one mapping between the hypothesis and the ground truth segments so that the total overlap between the reference speaker and the corresponding mapped hypothesized speaker cluster is maximized. The difference is expressed as Diarization Error Rate, which is also defined by NIST.[4] The Diarization Error Rate (DER) can be decomposed into three components: misses (speaker in reference, but not in hypothesis), false alarms (speaker in hypothesis, but not in reference), and speaker errors (mapped reference is not the same as hypothesized speaker). It is expressed as a percentage relative to the total length of the meeting.

To characterize the algorithm under increasingly noisy input conditions, three different sources were used. Two signals were obtained by mixing the four individual headset microphones (MH) or lapel microphones (ML) using a direct summation. Also a real far-field case (F) where a single microphone from the array on the table was used. Table 1 shows the results for the online audio diarization system where the average, best, and worse performances are shown for 12 meeting sessions that were used. As expected, one can observe a decrease in performance as the SNR decreases. It was interesting to observe a high variation in performance where in one case the error rate fell to 4.53% for the mixed headset condition. If we observe the variation in performance more closely, as shown in Fig. 6, we see that there is one particular meeting session which has a consistently better performance than the rest. This is because in this meeting, everyone stays seated (and therefore maintains equidistance from the far-field microphone). In addition, the meeting is mostly a discussion, and there is little use of the other equipment in the room such as the slide

---

[4]http://nist.gov/speech/tests/rt/rt2004/fall.

Table 1 Diarization results in terms of the Diarization Error Rate (DER) using both offline and on-line methods. Note that the offline results were computed using meetings of 5-minute length, while the online results were bootstrapped using longer meetings but speaker models were produced from just 60 s of speech from each person. Results are also presented using different microphone sources where the associated signal-to-noise ratio for each source is shown in brackets

Input	Offline results			Online results		
Video Methods	F (21 dB)	ML (22 dB)	MH (31 dB)	F (21 dB)	ML (22 dB)	MH (31 dB)
Average DER (%)	33.16	36.35	36.16	18.26	26.18	28.57

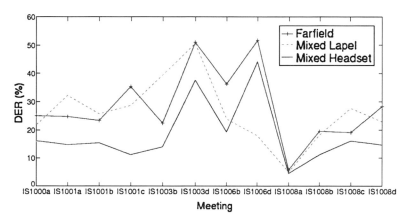

Fig. 6 Comparison of the online speaker diarization performance across different input conditions and over the different meetings that were considered

screen or white board. In contrast, meeting IS1006d is one of the worst perform-ing meetings because people are often presenting at the whiteboard or slide screen. It is also interesting to observe that while the relative performance when using the far-field and headset microphones remain fairly consistent (the far-field case always performs worse), the mixed lapel condition does not. This could be explained by additional noise generated by shifting of the body or touching the microphone by accident, particularly when participants were moving around the meeting room.

6 Extracting Computationally Efficient Video Features

With the increased need for recording and storing video data, many modern day video cameras have hardware to encode the signal at the source. In order to capture visual activity efficiently, we leverage the fact that meeting videos are already in compressed form so that we can extract visual activity features at a much lower computational cost.

These features are generated from compressed-domain information such as mo-tion vectors and block discrete-cosine transform coefficients that are accessible with

(a)   (b)   (c)   (d)

Fig. 7 Compressed domain video feature extraction. (**a**) Original image, (**b**) Motion vectors, (**c**) Residual coding bitrate, (**d**) skin-colored regions

almost zero cost from compressed video [63]. As compared to extracting similar higher resolution pixel-based features such as optical flow, compressed domain features are much faster to extract, with a run-time reduction of 95% [67].

Video streams that have been compressed using MPEG4 encoding contain a collection of group-of-picture (GOP) which is structured with an Intra-coded frame or I-frame, while the rest are predicted frames or P-frames. Figure 7 summarizes the various compressed domain features which can be extracted cheaply from compressed video as the *motion vector magnitude* (see Fig. 7(b)) and the *residual coding bitrate* (see Fig. 7(c)) to estimate visual activity level. Motion vectors, illustrated in Fig. 7(d), are generated from motion compensation during video encoding; for each source block that is encoded in a predictive fashion, its motion vectors indicate which predictor block from the reference frame (in this case the previous frame for our compressed video data) is to be used. Typically, a predictor block is highly correlated with the source block and hence similar to the block to be encoded. Therefore, motion vectors are usually a good approximation of optical flow, which in turn is a proxy for the underlying motion of objects in the video [14].

After motion compensation, the DCT-transform coefficients of the residual signal (the difference between the block to be encoded and its prediction from the reference frame) are quantized and entropy coded. The *residual coding bitrate*, illustrated in Fig. 7(c), is the number of bits used to encode this transformed residual signal. While the motion vector captures gross block translation, it fails to fully account for nonrigid motion such as lips moving. On the other hand, the residual coding bitrate is able to capture the level of such motion, since a temporal change that is not well modeled by the block translational model will result in a residual with higher energy and hence require more bits to entropy encode.

6.1 Estimating Personal Activity Levels in the Compressed Domain

Even when personal close-view cameras are used, the distance from the camera causes scale and pose issues, as shown in some example shots in Fig. 8. By averaging activity measures over detected skin-color blocks, we hope to mitigate some of these issues. Therefore we implement a block-level skin-color detector that works

Fig. 8 Possible pose variations and ambiguities captured from the video streams

mostly in the compressed domain which can detect head and hand regions as illustrated in Fig. 7. This is also useful for detecting when each meeting participant is in view. To do this, we use a GMM to model the distribution of chrominance coefficients [41] in the YUV color-space. Specifically, we model the chrominance coefficients, (U, V), as a mixture of Gaussians, where each Gaussian component is assumed to have a diagonal covariance matrix. In the Intra-frames of the video, we compute the likelihood of observed chrominance DCT DC coefficients according to the GMM and threshold it to determine skin-color blocks. Skin blocks in the Inter-frames are inferred by using motion vector information to propagate skin-color blocks through the duration of the group-of-picture (GOP).

We threshold the number of skin-colored blocks in the close-up view to detect when a participant is seated. If a participant is not detected in an image frame of the close-up video stream, he is assumed to be presenting at the projection screen, which is a reasonable assumption in the meeting data. Since they are assumed to be presenting at the slide screen or whiteboard, they are more likely to be active and also speaking. Therefore, a simple assumption was to set periods where the person was detected as not seated to the maximum value seen so far. While this is a simple rule, it was found to be effective in previous experiments [31].

6.2 Finding Personal Head and Hand Activity Levels

While previous work has concentrated on extracting personal visual activity from gross head motion, here we go a step further by trying to understand how head and hand motion might play a part in human discourse, at a holistic level. The importance of this can be highlighted in Fig. 9, where we observe three seconds of a meeting discussion. There are four participants in the discussion, in the configuration shown in Fig. 3. Here we see just two participants where the person on the right is speaking. The top two rows of Fig. 9 shows a breakdown of the gross head and hand motion that is observed for the two observed meeting participants, illustrated in the bottom row of the figure. To illustrate the change in motion over time more clearly, the average motion vector magnitudes over the head and hand skin regions are shown (further details about how these are calculated will be provided in the remainder of this section). The visual head and hand activity for the silent participant on the left is shown in grey, while the speaker's visual activity is shown in black.

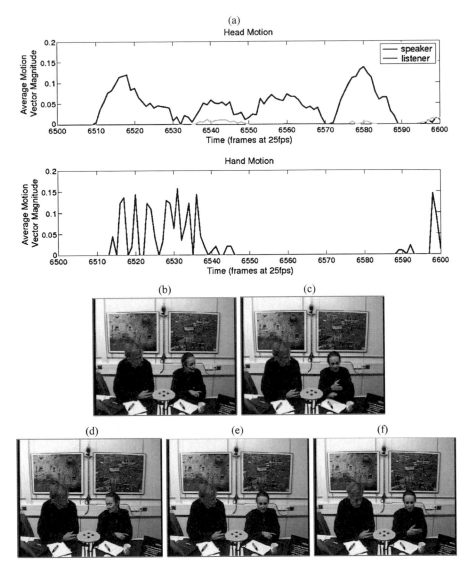

Fig. 9 Illustration of the difference in head and hand motions between speaker and listener. The *black lines* show the head and hand motions of the speaker, while those in *grey* show the motions of the listener. The *two rows below* shows key image frames from this 3-s interval where the person on the right is speaking the entire time

The bottom two rows of the figure shows some key image frames within the three-second interval where the person on the right is speaking. She starts off addressing those on the other side of the table and then directly addresses the participant to the left half way through the observed interval. When he realizes that he is being addressed directly, he moves his head to face her directly but then lowers it again when attention is shifted away from him. In terms of hand motion, we see that the speaker is the only person of the two that moves during this interval. Note that in this paper, we describe head motion to be observed from skin-color regions, which captures visual activity inside the face as well as some translations and deformations of the face region.

The example in Fig. 9 shows that a speaker and an attentive listener can have very different behavior types if we simply observe the head and hand motions separately. It is also interesting to observe that partial occlusion of one of the hands does not affect the discrimination between the roles of these two meeting participants. Of course, the data is not always as clean and depends on how involved the participants were. Note also that the motion vector magnitudes were shown for illustrative purposes only; in our experiments, we use the residual coding bitrate, which we found to produce better results since it tends to smooth out large and fast variations in the visual activity, and can also detect small motions from the lips if they are visible.

The features extraction method described in Sect. 6.1 were for gross body motion, and can include both head and hand motions where the hands are only sporadically visible in the close-up views (see bottom row of Fig. 2). Therefore, we focus on extracting the desired features from the side views (see images L and R of the top row of Fig. 2) where two people's head and hands are captured.

We first need to find the boundary between the two persons in each side view. The method we employ was inspired by the work of Jaimes on studying body postures of office workers [33]. For each image frame, we construct a horizontal profile of the number of detected skin-color blocks in each column, as shown by the accumulated profile at the bottom of the image in Fig. 10. Suppose $S(x, y)$ is an indicator function of skin color blocks for the (x, y) block in the image frame. The horizontal profile is simply $S_h(x) = \sum_y S(x, y)$. Since we expect the horizontal location of each person's head to result in a strong peak in $S_h(x)$, we use a K-means clustering algorithm (with $K = 2$) to find the locations of the two peaks. To ensure continuity between image frames, K-means is initialized with the locations of the peaks from the previous image frame. The boundary is simply the midpoint between the two peaks. Once the left and right regions of each camera-view are separated, we treated the two portions of the image frame as two video streams, representing the individual visual activity of each person in the same way as described in Sect. 6.1.

Next, we needed to find the boundary between the head and hands for each person. This time, for each person (i.e., the left half or right half of the view, separated by the estimated boundary), we constructed a vertical profile of the number of detected skin-color blocks in each row as shown in Fig. 10. Again, since we expect the vertical locations of the head and hands to result in strong peaks in the vertical profile, we use a K-means algorithm to find the two peaks. As before, K-means is initialized with the locations of the peaks from the previous image frame, and the boundary between the head and hands is just the midpoint. Note that the vertical profile is only considered below a certain height to remove spurious detections of skin color in the background.

Now, we can compute head and hands activity levels using the same approach as in Sect. 6.1, except that the area of interest is the estimated quadrant of the side-view

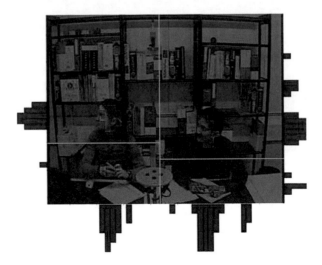

Fig. 10 Example of the horizontal and vertical profiles of the skin blocks and the located boundaries between the two people and their respective head and hand regions. The accumulated horizontal of the skin-color blocks is shown at the bottom of the example snap-shot. The vertical profiles of the skin-color blocks for each corresponding person are shown to the left and right of the image frame. The detected skin color regions are highlighted in *red*, and the estimated boundaries using the horizontal and vertical profiles are shown in *green*

that contains the subject of interest, i.e., left person's head, left person's hands, right person's head, and right person's hands.

We evaluated the boundary estimation described above on one meeting session, where bounding boxes of speakers' heads had been annotated. The error rate of finding the boundary between two persons was 0.4%, where an error is defined as the estimated boundary not cleanly separating the bounding boxes of the two persons. The error rate of finding the boundary between the head and hands is 0.5%, where the error is defined as the estimated boundary not being below the head bounding boxes of the respective person. We found that errors occurred mostly when the hands touched the face or moved above the shoulders or when a person reached across the table to their neighbor's table area. From this two-camera setup, four different personal activity features were generated; head activity; hand activity; the average activity of the head and hand blobs; and the maximum of the average head and average hand motion after the features were normalized.

6.3 Estimating Speakers Using Video Only

From previous experiments, we have found that speech and the visual activity of the speaker are better correlated over long-term intervals [31, 32]. We know that people who move are not necessarily talking, but we know that people who talk will tend to move. This is further illustrated by the distributions in Fig. 11(a) where we

Fig. 11 The accumulated visual activity histograms over our data-set during speaking (*dashed line*) and silence (*solid line*) for all participants for both the average residual coding bitrate features in (**a**) and also the average motion vector magnitude in (**b**)

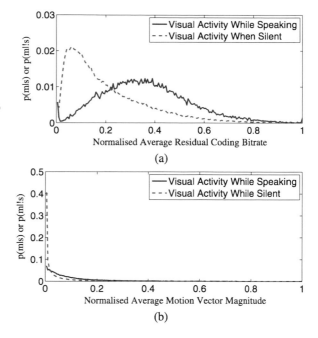

(a)

(b)

see accumulated histograms of the distribution of visual activity as measured using the residual coding bitrate with the close-up cameras, when people were seated and speaking or silent. This shows that people who talk tend to move more but that people who are silent can sometimes move a lot too. As mentioned in Sect. 6.1, when a person is detected as standing, their visual activity level is set to the highest value for that person that has been observed so far. Note also that previously [32] we found that using the motion vectors to associate audio and video streams led to worse performance. This is further illustrated in Fig. 11(b) where the same distributions as (a) are shown but using the average motion vector magnitude instead.

To estimate the speaker based on observing the meeting participant with the most motion, it is important to first normalize the visual activity features for each person. The normalization allows us to compare the speaking and silent behavior of each participant in the meeting across all participants. For our meetings, there are no participants who remain inactive for the entire meeting; therefore, we apply the normalization assuming that all participants will be relatively engaged in the meeting activities. Since the method is online, the normalization needed to be adaptive, and so each new visual activity value was divided by the maximum value that was observed until that point.

Once the values have been normalized, each person's visual activity stream is considered to be comparable across individuals. Using this assumption and also that we know that speakers tend to move more than listeners, binary versions of each person's speaking activity was estimated. This was done by making the person who had the highest visual activity over the previous time window the estimated speaker, as described in Algorithm 1. This makes the same assumption as the speaker di-

1 Computationally Efficient Clustering of Audio-Visual Meeting Data
   foreach *p in Participants* **do**
   | $Votes[p] = 0$;
   end
   foreach *t in Window* **do**
   | $i = argmax_p(VisualActivity[t, p])$, $\forall p \in Participants$;
   | $Votes[i] = Votes[i] + 1$;
   end
   $j = argmax_p(Votes[p])$, $\forall p \in Participants$;
   BinaryVisualActivity[j]=1;

Algorithm 1: Estimating speakers using visual activity only.

arization system, that the speech is not overlapped, though in reality overlapping regions of speech exist in our test data and are usually the periods in which correct estimates are more difficult to make. As discussed previously, it would have been interesting to account for cases of overlapping speech, but previous work has shown that this would require a second pass over the data in order to find regions where the likelihood of a particular person speaking becomes much lower than during periods of clean speech [8].

7 Associating Speaker Clusters with Video Channels

To begin with, let us consider how well speech and audio streams can be associated together if clean audio signals are used. We used speaker segmentations from the audio signal taken from personal headset microphones as a simple automated speaker segmentation method. These were associated with the two real-valued visual activity features using the residual coding bitrate or motion vector magnitudes. The headset segmentations were generated by extracting the speaker energy from each headset and then thresholding this value to create a binary signal where 1 represents speaking and 0 is silence.

For each pair-wise combination of speaking and visual activity channels, their corresponding normalized correlation was calculated. We then matched the channels by using an ordered one-to-one mapping based on associating the best correlated channels first. Figure 12 shows the algorithm in more detail.

(a) *Quantifying the distance between audio-visual streams*: the pair-wise correlation between each video, v_i, and audio stream, a_j, is calculated:

$$\rho_{v_i,a_j} = \frac{\sum_{t=0}^{T} v(t) \cdot a(t)}{\sum_{t=0}^{T} v(t) \sum_{t=0}^{T} a(t)} \quad \forall \{i, j\} \tag{2}$$

where T is the total length of the meeting, and in our experiments, t indexes the feature value at each frame. For our experiments, the frame rate used was 5 frames per second.

(b) *Selecting the closest audio-visual streams*: the pair of audio and video streams with the highest correlation are selected.

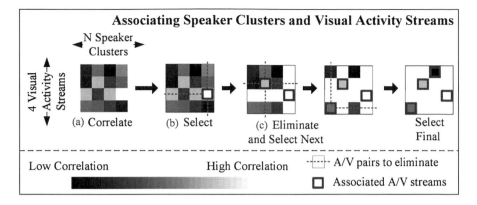

Fig. 12 Greedy Algorithm for ordered and discriminative pairwise associations between audio and video streams. (i) All pairwise combinations of the audio and video streams are correlated. (ii) The pair with the highest correlation is associated first and then eliminated from the correlation matrix

Table 2 Proportion of correctly associated meetings using speech segmentations generated from individual headset microphones that were then associated with visqual activity from the close-view cameras. *EvH*: Hard evaluation strategy where all audio-visual streams in the meeting must be associated correctly; *EvM* Medium evaluation strategy where at least two of the audio-visual streams in the meeting must be associated correctly; *EvS* Soft evaluation strategy where at least one of the audio-visual streams in the meeting must be associated correctly

	EvS	*EvM*	*EvH*
Residue	1.00	1.00	0.90
Vector	1.00	0.95	0.81

(c) *Selection of the next closest audio-visual streams*: the next best correlated pair of audio and video streams is selected.

(d) *Full assignment of audio and video streams*: step (c) is repeated until all audio-visual streams are associated.

Since the association is performed on a meeting basis, it is important to evaluate the performance similarly. Three evaluation criteria are used to observe the difficulty in associating more channels correctly in each meeting. Hard (*EvH*), medium (*EvM*), and soft (*EvS*) criteria are used that assign respectively a score of 1 for each meeting only when all, at least two, or at least one of the pairs of associated audio and visual streams is correct for each meeting. We refrain from evaluating on a participant basis since the meeting-based ordered mapping procedure, by definition, discriminates pairs that are easier to distinguish, as a means of improving the association from noisier channels which may have less observable activity.

The proportion of correctly associated meetings using both visual activity feature types are shown in Table 2. Correlating the headset segmentations and Residue visual activity channels performed best. Also, it was also encouraging to see that even for the hard evaluation strategy, the performance remained high for this case.

For the online association method, the association method described above was modified so that after all streams were associated within a 2-s sliding window. Then, only the person who spoke for the longest time was assigned their associated video stream for that window.

8 Audio-Visual Clustering Results

Speaker localization experiments were run on the same meeting data that was used in the previous section. The outputs from the online speaker diarization were used as a reference to determine which video stream contained the relevant speaker. As described in Sect. 6, the visual activity of each individual could be represented by a number of features. These are summarized in Table 3. In addition, a binary feature can be derived from each of these using the method described in Sect. 6.3.

For the 4-camera and 2-camera case, the location of each stream was known so evaluation was straightforward. For the 2-camera case, it was assumed that each half of the frame would be treated as a single stream, leading to four possible video candidates. An analysis window of 2 s was used with a 40-ms shift.

8.1 Using Raw Visual Activity

As an initial extension to the method presented in the previous subsection, we applied the online association algorithm to the real-valued average residual coding bitrate in the five video forms described in Table 3. The results are summarized in Table 4, where evaluation was done using the same scoring as for the online diarization. Rather than comparing the speaker reference with the speaker clusters, which was done for the speaker diarization evaluation, we compare the speaker reference with the estimated video stream labels. For clarity, we refer to this measure as the association error rate (AER), but the mechanics of the performance measure are the same as the DER. We see that the error is quite high in all cases but note that the results are still better than random, where the error would be closer to 80% since the associated video could be one of the four participants or none of them. Comparing the performance more carefully across the different input audio conditions, we see that there is again a slight improvement in performance when the mixed headset signal is used rather than the far-field microphone. Comparing across the different video features that were tried, using the mean residual coding bitrate for the estimated hand regions from the 2-camera set-up for each person gave the best results, but there was not a significant difference between the best and worse average results.

Table 3 Summary of video features that were used

4 close-up cameras	Head Close-up			
2 mid-view cameras	Head+Hands	Head	Hands	Max(Head,Hands)

Table 4 Audio-visual speaker localization with the real-valued average residual coding bitrate for each person, using the different video feature methods. The signal-to-noise ratio for each audio type is shown in brackets for each input audio source. The results show the average AER over all the meetings for each experimental condition, where the bracketed number shows the lowest AER that was achieved

Input video methods	Input audio conditions					
	F (21 dB)		ML (22 dB)		MH (31 dB)	
	AER (%)	(Min)	AER (%)	(Min)	AER (%)	(Min)
Head(Closeup)	68.39	(64.92)	68.42	(65.45)	68.04	(64.82)
Max(Head,Hands)	68.05	(62.75)	67.91	(62.09)	68	(60.62)
Heads	68.1	(64.25)	67.84	(63.79)	67.98	(63.03)
Head+Hands	67.67	(61.54)	67.58	(61.87)	67.54	(61.31)
Hands	67.92	(61.41)	67.65	(61.29)	67.64	(61.13)

8.2 Using Estimates of Speaking Activity from Video

We then conducted similar experiments with each video feature type replaced by its binarized version using the method described in Sect. 6.3. These binarized video streams were then associated with the relevant audio stream as described in Sect. 7. The results are summarized in terms of AER again in Table 5. Here we see a significant increase in performance when these binarized visual activity values are used. This indicates that our hypothesis that people who talk tend to move more is quite successful at finding speakers from video only. Overall, the best speaker and video association performance was observed when the motion from the close-up cameras was used. This is not surprising since the head is represented at a higher resolution and therefore lip motion is better captured. It is encouraging to see that even when using the 2-camera set-up, where the size of the heads was about half of those in the close-view cameras, the performance is slightly worse but still comparable. Of the 2-camera features, the one using head activity alone gave the best average performance, but the best performance for any session used the Max(Head,Hands) feature. This indicates that hand motion can still be effective for discriminating speakers from listeners and is complementary to head motion. The worse average AER of the Max(Head,Hands) case compared to the Heads is likely to be due to how much body motion was attributed to meeting activities such as using a laptop, writing, or manipulating the remote control prototype they were designing.

Since the AER is not a widely used performance measure, in multimodal processing tasks, we also provide the average precision, recall, and F-measure when using the far-field microphone and binary estimates of speaking activity in Table 6. Here the boldened values show the best achieved performance for a single meeting, while the number on the left shows the average. Using these measures, similar differences in performance are observed, although here, using the maximum of the head and hand motion appears to give the best overall performance for the 2-camera case. Again, the 4-camera case performs the best. It is also interesting to observe that the head-only and the Max(Head,Hands) features perform similarly, while the

Table 5 Audio-visual speaker localization results using binary estimates of speaking status from each person's visual activity. The signal-to-noise ratio for each audio type is shown in brackets for each input audio source. The results show the average AER for each experimental condition, and the accompanying bracketed number shows the minimum AER that was achieved from one of the 12 sessions that were used

Input video methods	Input audio conditions					
	F (21 dB)		ML (22 dB)		MH (31 dB)	
	AER (%)	(Min)	AER (%)	(Min)	AER (%)	(Min)
Head(Close-up)	41.89	(20.19)	41.91	(19.71)	41.55	(19.71)
Max(Head,Hands)	42.38	(22.24)	42.82	(22.37)	42.83	(22.39)
Heads	42.3	(26.27)	42.75	(26.42)	42.62	(26.4)
Head+Hands	46	(33.3)	46.83	(33.41)	46.24	(33.31)
Hands	53.83	(34.48)	54.79	(34.55)	54.18	(34.67)

Table 6 Summary of the average precision, recall, and F-measure for the different video feature types. Results for using the far-field microphone are shown and the binary estimates of speaking status from visual activity. For each video feature, the highest performance is shown boldened

Input video methods	Prec.		Recall		F-meas.	
Head(Close-up)	52.74	**72.93**	41.64	**62.53**	44.72	**66.18**
Max(Heads,Hands)	50.64	**68.62**	41.58	**62.26**	43.59	**63.1**
Head	51.01	**66.41**	41.95	**58.18**	43.93	**60.2**
Head+Hands	39.63	**56.51**	34.17	**54.21**	34.68	**49.44**
Hands	37.17	**56.91**	31.33	**48.12**	31.64	**43.28**

Head+Hands and hands-only features perform similarly badly compared to the rest. This indicates that for both listeners and speakers, observing head motion is more discriminative in most situations. However, the success of the feature which takes the maximum of the head and hand motion indicates that the head and hand features should be treated independently since they are complementary.

From the results we have presented, it seems that using the binary estimates of speaking activity from video is effective. However, the performance is not as high as estimating speakers from the audio alone. We can observe the locations of failure modes by looking more closely at an example meeting, which is shown in Fig. 13. Here the binary segmentations of the estimated speaker are shown using the association method described in Sect. 7 (first row); the binary estimates of speaking activity from video (second row); and the speaker clusters generated from the online speaker diarization algorithm (third row). The final row shows the ground truth speaker segmentations. We can see that there are occasions (e.g., between 150–200 s and 600–700 s) when the binary estimates of speaking activity fail since the person who moves the most is not talking. This is not surprising since there is still a considerable overlap observed in the speaker and listener activity shown in Fig. 11 previously. Furthermore, we observed that there are occasions where nonspeakers

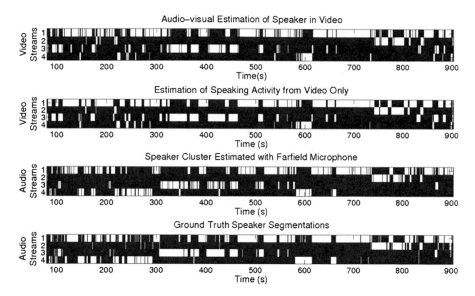

Fig. 13 Graphical comparison of different feature representations and estimates. *White areas* indicate either that someone is speaking. The *first row* shows the estimated associated video stream, given the diarized speaker clusters in the *third row*; the *second* row shows the estimate of speaker status from just the motion activity taken from the maximum of the head and hand motion; and the *final row* shows the ground-truth speaker segmentations

were involved in other activities while someone was speaking (e.g., working on a laptop). However, there are also observed cases where speaker diarization fails and the speaker estimates from video was successful (between 350–450 s). The failure in the speaker diarization could be caused by speaker models being confused due to either short utterances or because the speaker models were only generated from 60 s of speech for each speaker in the training phase. This example of complementary failure modes suggests that combining the audio and video features at an earlier stage may also improve the speaker diarization performance.

9 Discussion

In this chapter, we have discussed offline systems which can be used for post-processing of previously recorded data. However, audio-visual mining of the data could also happen in real-time. A system that can work online and in real-time is useful for remote meeting scenarios where subtle information about an interaction can be lost through transmission. These could relate to transmission failure of one or more modalities but could also be due to the inherent time delay between sending and receiving data. In terms of more complex immersion problems within the remote meeting scenario, it is also difficult for remote participants to know when to interrupt in a conversation or judge the mood or atmosphere of the group they are interacting with. For colocated meetings, live-recording and summary may be useful for a quick recap if someone missed what was said (e.g., a phone call interruption) but does not want to interrupt the conversation flow in order to catch up on information they missed. Aside from this, live processing also aids post-meeting browsing since a live capability could be used to enable live tagging of automatically segmented events such as how an issue on the agenda was received by other meeting participants. Of course, some of the tags could be substituted by automated event identification methods, but when certain technologies are not available, tagging is an extremely useful way of labeling information. In particular, tagging has been used extensively for mining image data with the emergence of social networking sites where photos are organized amongst self-organized groups. It has been demonstrated that imagery data itself need not be used for mining the data if tags are available [44].

Moving away from the online and real-time problems, there are other ways in which the performance of the speaker diarization and audio-visual association task can be improved. In particular, while the approach presented in this chapter demonstrated a late fusion approach, given that we know that speech and body motion it correlated, there is also motivation to make the task into a speaker diarization and localization task by fusing the modalities early on in the clustering process. This is particularly interesting since clustering video data alone into speakers tends to require a priori knowledge of the number or participants. Of course, techniques such as face detection can be employed to identify the speakers, but this may not be practical if the resolution of faces is in the video and nonfrontal faces tend to be difficult to detect robustly. Research on fusing audio and visual features for speaker diarization or speaker localization as discussed in Sect. 2 has shown an improvement in performance over single-modality methods. However most work performs experiments on data where two talking heads are visible and remain relatively stationary with fully frontal faces. Few consider more global body movements [10, 31, 32, 59, 60]. Vajaria et al. [59, 60] was one of the first to use gross body movement for speaker diarization and localization but suffer from the need to cluster spatially separated noisy visual features. Recently some preliminary success by using just a single camera and microphone [23] to perform speaker diarization where the audio and visual features are fused early on in the agglomerative clustering process. Results for the speaker diarization task show improvement, despite the low resolution of each participant in the captured video. In both cases, the correlation of speech and motion from different body parts was not considered for the diarization task. Also, finding a suitable way to evaluate the locations of speakers in the video in a similar way to the diarization performance is yet to be found.

With the success of multimodal speaker diarization methods, it is clear that the trend is moving toward using multiple sensors and multiple modalities to solve data-mining problems, certainly in the domain of meeting analysis. The importance of multimodal data mining when capturing human behavior is further emphasized since psychologically, both modalities are used differently when we communicate socially and communicate very different messages. It is sometimes these differences and in particular unusual events which trigger memories for us about a particular conversation. It could be said that these are the events which are the most difficult to find again once they have been archived. This brings us to the application of estimating dominance, which was demonstrated at the end of this chapter. It showed that even with computationally efficient methods for clustering the data where the estimates of the raw outputs was degraded, the performance of the semantically higher level dominance task was not necessarily affected. This addresses some interesting questions about how the problem of the semantic gap should be addressed in data mining. From a cognitive perspective, perhaps we would expect that the verbal content of each speaker would need to be analyzed. However, experiments have shown that using speaking time alone is quite robust, even if the estimates of the speaker turns are not as accurate. Given these results, one might ask the question of whether other semantically high-level behavioral types or affiliations can be characterized using equally simple features such as the excitement levels in a meeting [65], roles [68], or personality [52].

Ultimately, one could argue that to address the semantic gap in mining meeting data, we must start from the questions we ask ourselves when trying to search through meeting data such as in terms of what happened, what were the conclusions, and how people interacted with each other. From a functional perspective, knowing the meeting agenda and the final outcomes are useful, but from a social perspective knowing about the subtle nonverbal behavior tells us more about relationships between colleagues or clients. For example, knowing how a person usually behaves can help us to detect unusual behavior, which could be indications of stress, if, for example, the person has been delegated too much work. These are ultimately useful tools to ensure that teams in organizations work effectively and that staff are not overworked or under-utilized. From an individual perspective, there are those that argue that success is well correlated with "emotional intelligence" which is defined as the ability to monitor both one's own and the other's feelings and emotions in order to guide one's thinking and actions [51]. Automatically estimating the feelings and emotions of others are topics of interest currently [7, 65]. In particular, recent work on distinguishing real from fake facial expressions of pain has shown that automated systems perform significantly better than human observers [7]. Such research shows the potential of using machines to help us understand how we interact and in particular how this could potentially be used to help individuals in becoming more aware of social interactions around them. Ultimately, such knowledge should lead to more efficient team-working where perhaps the easiest failure mode in teams occurs through a break-down in communication between members.

Acknowledgements   This research was partly funded by the US VACE program, the EU project AMIDA (pub. AMIDA-103), the Swiss NCCR IM2, and the Institute for Infocomm Research, Singapore.

References

1. Ajmera, J., Wooters, C.: A robust speaker clustering algorithm. In: Proc. IEEE Automatic Speech Recognition Understanding Workshop (2003)

2. Al-Hames, M., Dielmann, A., Gatica-Perez, D., Reiter, S., Renals, S., Rigoll, G., Zhang, D.: Multimodal integration for meeting group action segmentation and recognition. In: Proc. Multimodal Interaction and Related Machine Learning Algorithms Workshop (MLMI–05), pp. 52–63. Springer, Berlin (2006)
3. Anguera, X.: Robust speaker diarization for meetings. PhD thesis, Technical University of Catalonia, Barcelona, Spain, December 2006
4. Anguera, X., Peskin, B., Aguilo, M.: Robust speaker segmentation for meetings: the ICSI-SRI spring 2005 diarization system. In: Proc. of NIST MLMI Meeting Recognition Workshop, Edinburgh (2005)
5. Armstrong, D.F., Stokoe, W.C., Wilcox, S.: What is gesture? In: Gesture and the Nature of Language pp. 40–41. Cambridge University Press, Cambridge (1995)
6. Bales, R.F.: Interaction Process Analysis: A Method for the Study of Small Groups. Addison-Wesley, Cambridge (1950)
7. Bartlett, M., Littlewort, G., Vural, E., Lee, K., Cetin, M., Ercil, A., Movellan, J.: Data mining spontaneous facial behavior with automatic expression coding. In: Verbal and Nonverbal Features of Human–Human and Human–Machine Interaction, pp. 1–20 (2008)
8. Boakye, K., Trueba-Hornero, B., Vinyals, O., Friedland, G.: Overlapped speech detection for improved speaker diarization in multiparty meetings. In: IEEE International Conference on Acoustics, Speech and Signal Processing (ICASSP), pp. 4353–4356 (2008)
9. Campbell, J.P.: Speaker recognition: a tutorial. In: Proceedings of the IEEE, pp. 1437–1462 (1997)
10. Campbell, N., Suzuki, N.: Working with very sparse data to detect speaker and listener participation in a meetings corpus. In: Workshop Programme, vol. 10, May 2006
11. Carletta, J.C., Ashby, S., Bourban, S., Flynn, M., Guillemot, M., Hain, T., Kadlec, J., Karaiskos, V., Kraiij, W., Kronenthal, M., Lathoud, G., Lincoln, M., Lisowska, A., McCowan, M., Post, W., Reidsma, D., Wellner, P.: The AMI meeting corpus: a pre-announcement. In: Joint Workshop on Machine Learning and Multimodal Interaction (MLMI) (2005)
12. Chen, S., Gopalakrishnan, P.: Speaker, environment and channel change detection and clustering via the Bayesian information criterion. In: Proceedings of DARPA Speech Recognition Workshop (1998)
13. Chen, T., Rao, R.R.: Cross-modal prediction in audio-visual communication. In: International Conference on Acoustics, Speech and Signal Processing (ICASSP), vol. 4, pp. 2056–2059 (1996)
14. Coimbra, M.T., Davies, M.: Approximating optical flow within the MPEG-2 compressed domain. IEEE Trans. Circuits Syst. Video Technol. **15**(1), 103–107 (2005)
15. Condon, W.S., Ogston, W.D.: Sound film analysis of normal and pathological behavior patterns. J. Nerv. Ment. Dis. **143**(4), 338 (1966)
16. Condon, W.S., Osgton, W.D.: Speech and body motion synchrony of the speaker–hearer. In: The Perception of Language, pp. 150–184 (1971)
17. DABBS, J.M.J.R., Ruback, R.B.: Dimensions of group process: amount and structure of vocal interaction. Adv. Exp. Soc. Psychol. **20**, 123–169 (1987)
18. Delacourt, P., Wellekens, C.J.: Distbic: a speaker-based segmentation for audio data indexing. In: Speech Communication: Special Issue in Accessing Information in Spoken Audio, pp. 111–126 (2000)
19. Dovidio, J.F., Ellyson, S.L.: Decoding visual dominance: attributions of power based on relative percentages of looking while speaking and looking while listening. Soc. Psychol. Q. **45**(2), 106–113 (1982)
20. Favre, S., Salamin, H., Dines, J., Vinciarelli, A.: Role recognition in multiparty recordings using social affiliation networks and discrete distributions. In: IMCI '08: Proceedings of the 10th International Conference on Multimodal Interfaces, pp. 29–36. ACM, New York (2008)
21. Fisher, J.W., Darrell, T.: Speaker association with signal-level audiovisual fusion. IEEE Trans. Multimed. **6**(3), 406–413 (2004)
22. Fisher, J.W., Darrell, T., Freeman, W.T., Viola, P.A.: Learning joint statistical models for audio-visual fusion and segregation. In: Conference on Neural Information Processing Systems (NIPS), pp. 772–778 (2000)

23. Friedland, G., Hung, H., Yeo, C.: Multi-modal speaker diarization of real-world meetings using compressed-domain video features. In: Proceedings of IEEE ICASSP, April 2009
24. Friedland, G., Vinyals, O., Huang, Y., Mueller, C.: Prosodic and other long-term features for speaker diarization. Trans. Audio Speech Lang. Process. **17** (2009)
25. Gatewood, J.B., Rosenwein, R.: Interactional synchrony: genuine or spurious? A critique of recent research. J. Nonverbal Behav. **6**(1), 12–29 (1981)
26. Gish, H., Schmidt, M.: Text-independent speaker identification. IEEE Signal Process. Mag. 18–32 (1994)
27. Hadar, U., Steiner, T.J., Clifford Rose, F.: Head movement during listening turns in conversation. J. Nonverbal Behav. **9**(4), 214–228 (1985)
28. Hadar, U., Steiner, T.J., Grant, E.C., Clifford Rose, F.: The timing of shifts of head postures during conversation. Hum. Mov. Sci. **3**, 237–245 (1984)
29. Hain, T., Burget, L., Dines, J., Garau, G., Karafiat, M., van Leeuwen, D., Lincoln, M., Wan, V.: The 2007 AMI(DA) system for meeting transcription. In: Multimodal Technologies for Perception of Humans. Lecture Notes in Computer Science, vol. 4625, pp. 414–428. Springer, Berlin (2008). International Evaluation Workshops CLEAR 2007 and RT 2007, Baltimore, MD, USA, May 8–11, 2007, Revised Selected Papers
30. Harrigan, J.A.: Listener's body movements and speaking turns. Commun. Res. **12**, 233–250 (1985)
31. Hung, H., Friedland, G.: Towards audio-visual on-line diarization of participants in group meetings. In: Workshop on Multi-Camera and Multi-Modal Sensor Fusion Algorithms and Applications in Conjunction with ECCV, Marseille, France, October 2008
32. Hung, H., Huang, Y., Yeo, C., Gatica-Perez, D.: Associating audio-visual activity cues in a dominance estimation framework. In: IEEE Computer Society Conference on Computer Vision and Pattern Recognition Workshop on Human Communicative Behavior, Alaska (2008)
33. Jaimes, A.: Posture and activity silhouettes for self-reporting, interruption management, and attentive interfaces. In: International Conference on Intelligent User Interfaces, pp. 24–31. ACM, New York (2006)
34. Jayagopi, D.B., Ba, S.O., Odobez, J.-M., Gatica-Perez, D.: Predicting two facets of social verticality in meetings from five-minute time slices and nonverbal cues. In: Proceedings ICMI (2008)
35. Jayagopi, D.B., Hung, H., Yeo, C., Gatica-Perez, D.: Modeling dominance in group conversations using nonverbal activity cues. IEEE Trans. Audio Speech Lang. Process. (2008)
36. Juang, B., Rabiner, L.: A probabilistic distance measure for hidden Markov models (1985)
37. Kendon, A.: Conducting Interaction: Patterns of Behavior in Focused Encounters. Cambridge University Press, Cambridge (1990)
38. Kendon, A.: Some considerations for a theory of language origins. Man, New Ser. **26**(2), 199–221 (1991)
39. Kim, H.-G., Sikora, T.: Hybrid speaker-based segmentation system using model-level clustering. In: Proceedings of the IEEE International Conference on Audio and Speech Signal Processing (2005)
40. McCowan, L., Gatica-Perez, D., Bengio, S., Lathoud, G., Barnard, M., Zhang, D.: Automatic analysis of multimodal group actions in meetings. IEEE Trans. Pattern Anal. Mach. Intell. **27**(3), 305–317 (2005)
41. McKenna, S.J., Gong, S., Raja, Y.: Modelling facial colour and identity with Gaussian mixtures. Pattern Recognit. **31**(12), 1883–1892 (1998)
42. McNeill, D.: Hand and Mind. What Gestures Reveal About Thought. University of Chicago Press, Chicago (1992)
43. McNeill, D.: Language and Gesture. Cambridge University Press, New York (2000)
44. Negoescu, R.-A., Gatica-Perez, D.: Topickr: Flickr groups and users reloaded. In: MM '08: Proc. of the 16th ACM International Conference on Multimedia, Vancouver, Canada, October 2008. ACM, New York (2008)
45. Ning, H., Liu, M., Tang, H., Huang, T.: A spectral clustering approach to speaker diarization In: The Ninth International Conference on Spoken Language Processing, Proceedings of Interspeech (2006)

46. Nock, H.J., Iyengar, G., Neti, C.: Speaker localisation using audio-visual synchrony: an empirical study. In: ACM International Conference on Image and Video Retrieval, pp. 488–499 (2003)
47. Noulas, A., Krose, B.J.A.: On-line multi-modal speaker diarization. In: International Conference on Multimodal Interfaces, pp. 350–357. ACM, New York (2007)
48. Otsuka, K., Yamato, J., Takemae, Y., Murase, H.: Quantifying interpersonal influence in face-to-face conversations based on visual attention patterns. In: Proc. ACM CHI Extended Abstract, Montreal, April 2006
49. Parker, K.C.H.: Speaking turns in small group interaction: a context-sensitive event sequence model. J. Pers. Soc. Psychol. **54**(6), 965–971 (1988)
50. Patterson, E.K., Gurbuz, S., Tufekci, Z., Gowdy, J.N.: CUAVE: a new audio-visual database for multimodal human–computer interface research. In: International Conference on Acoustics, Speech, and Signal Processing, pp. 2017–2020 (2002)
51. Petrides, K.V., Frederickson, N., Furnham, A.: The role of trait emotional intelligence in academic performance and deviant behavior at school. Pers. Individ. Differ. **36**(2), 277–293 (2004)
52. Pianesi, F., Mana, N., Cappelletti, A., Lepri, B., Zancanaro, M.: Multimodal recognition of personality traits in social interactions. In: International Conference on Multimodal interfaces, pp. 53–60. ACM, New York (2008)
53. Rao, R., Chen, T.: Exploiting audio-visual correlation in coding of talking head sequences. In: International Picture Coding Symposium, March 1996
54. Reiter, S., Schuller, B., Rigoll, G.: Hidden conditional random fields for meeting segmentation. In: 2007 IEEE International Conference on Multimedia and Expo, pp. 639–642 (2007)
55. Reynolds, D.A., Torres-Carrasquillo, P.: Approaches and applications of audio diarization. In: Proc. of International Conference on Audio and Speech Signal Processing, 2005
56. Reynolds, D.A.: Speaker identification and verification using Gaussian mixture speaker models. Speech Commun. **17**(1–2), 91–108 (1995)
57. Siracusa, M.R., Fisher, J.W.: Dynamic dependency tests for audio-visual speaker association. In: International Conference on Acoustics, Speech and Signal Processing, April 2007
58. Tamura, S., Iwano, K., Furui, S.: Multi-modal speech recognition using optical-flow analysis for lip images. In: Real World Speech Processing (2004)
59. Vajaria, H., Islam, T., Sarkar, S., Sankar, R., Kasturi, R.: Audio segmentation and speaker localization in meeting videos. Proc. Int. Conf. Pattern Recognit. **2**, 1150–1153 (2006)
60. Vajaria, H., Sarkar, S., Kasturi, R.: Exploring co-occurrence between speech and body movement for audio-guided video localization. IEEE Trans. Circuits Syst. Video Technol. **18**, 1608–1617 (2008)
61. Vinyals, O., Friedland, G.: Modulation spectrogram features for speaker diarization. In: Proceedings of Interspeech, September 2008, pp. 630–633 (2008)
62. Vinyals, O., Friedland, G.: Towards semantic analysis of conversations: a system for the live identification of speakers in meetings. In: Proceedings of IEEE International Conference on Semantic Computing, August 2008, pp. 456–459 (2008)
63. Wang, H., Divakaran, A., Vetro, A., Chang, S.F., Sun, H.: Survey of compressed-domain features used in audio-visual indexing and analysis. J. Vis. Commun. Image Represent. **14**(2), 150–183 (2003)
64. Wooters, C., Huijbregts, M.: The ICSI RT07s speaker diarization system. In: Proceedings of the NIST RT07 Meeting Recognition Evaluation Workshop. Springer, Berlin (2007)
65. Wrede, B., Shriberg, E.: Spotting "hot spots" in meetings: human judgments and prosodic cues. In: Proc. Eurospeech, pp. 2805–2808 (2003)
66. Wrigley, S.J., Brown, G.J., Wan, V., Renals, S.: Speech and crosstalk detection in multichannel audio. IEEE Trans. Speech Audio Process. **13**, 84–91 (2005)
67. Yeo, C., Ramchandran, K.: Compressed domain video processing of meetings for activity estimation in dominance classification and slide transition detection. Technical Report UCB/EECS-2008-79, EECS Department. University of California, Berkeley, June 2008

68. Zancanaro, M., Lepri, B., Pianesi, F.: Automatic detection of group functional roles in face to face interactions. In: International Conference on Multimodal interfaces, pp. 28–34. ACM, New York (2006)
69. Zhang, C., Yin, P., Rui, Y., Cutler, R., Viola, P.: Boosting-based multimodal speaker detection for distributed meetings. IEEE International Workshop on Multimedia Signal Processing (MMSP) (2006)

Cognitive-Aware Modality Allocation in Intelligent Multimodal Information Presentation

Yujia Cao, Mariët Theune, and Anton Nijholt

Abstract Intelligent multimodal presentation (IMMP) systems are able to generate multimodal presentations adaptively, based on the run-time requirements of user–computer interaction. Modality allocation in IMMP system needs to adapt the modality choice to changes in various relevant factors, such as the type of information to be conveyed, the presentation goal, the characteristics of the available modalities, the user profile, the condition of the environment, and the type of user task. In this study, we emphasize that modality allocation in IMMP systems should also take into account the cognitive impacts of modality on human information processing. We first describe several modality-related cognitive and neuropsychological findings. Then a user study is presented to demonstrate the effects of modality on performance, cognitive load and stress, using a high-load and time-critical user task. Finally, we show a possible way to integrate relevant cognitive theories into a computational model that can systematically predict the suitability of a modality choice for a given presentation task.

1 Introduction

The development of intelligent multimodal presentation (IMMP) systems has received much attention during the past two decades. The application domain of IMMP is very broad, including home entertainment [19], technical document generation [58], medical training [29], crisis management support [22], and much more. IMMP systems have been defined as knowledge-based systems, which exploit their

Y. Cao (✉) · M. Theune · A. Nijholt
Human Media Interaction, University of Twente, P.O. Box 217, 7500 AE Enschede, Netherlands
e-mail: y.cao@utwente.nl

M. Theune
e-mail: m.theune@utwente.nl

A. Nijholt
e-mail: a.nijholt@utwente.nl

L. Shao et al. (eds.), *Multimedia Interaction and Intelligent User Interfaces,*
Advances in Pattern Recognition,
DOI 10.1007/978-1-84996-507-1_3, © Springer-Verlag London Limited 2010

knowledge base in order to dynamically *adapt* their design decisions to the run-time requirements of user–computer interaction, such as the user profile, task character-istics, nature of the information to be conveyed, etc. [8, 28]. They are *intelligent* in the sense that they are able to generate multimodal presentations *adaptively* at run-time. A key issue in this process is to automate modality allocation—a process that chooses one or more modalities to present a certain information content for achiev-ing a certain presentation goal [8]. Modality allocation can also be considered as making the most suitable mappings between a set of information items and a set of modalities, constrained by certain factors [1]. The factors can be the type of in-formation to be conveyed, the presentation goal, the characteristics of the available modalities, the user profile, the condition of the environment, the type of user task, or any other factors that are identified to be relevant to a specific application. In IMMP systems, modality needs to be allocated on the fly, adapting to changes in the selected factors.

In existing IMMP studies, modality allocation is commonly rule-based [2, 20, 28, 29, 33, 43, 44, 56, 57, 59]. Modality allocation rules typically associate factors with preferred modality choices. They are usually predefined and embedded in the knowledge base of the system. They are the core of the intelligence in the sense that they define what (factors) the system should adapt to and how it should adapt. To demonstrate modality allocation rules, several examples associated with various factors are listed as follows.

- *The type of information to be conveyed*: for location and physical attributes, use graphics; for abstract actions and relationships between actions (such as causal-ity), use text; for compound actions, use both text and graphics (in [20] for tech-nical document generation).
- *Presentation goal*: to inform the user about TV programs, use the text in a list (in [57] for home digital guide).
- *State of the environment*: if the noise level is greater than 80 Db, use visual or tactile modalities (in [44] for phone call reception announcement).
- *Application specific factor*: when the needle is outside the patient's body, use only sound to present the distance to the target; when the needle is inserted into the body, use both sound and color gauge; when the needle tip is very near the target point (<10 mm), use only color gauge (in [29] for surgery training).

In order to be inferred by the system, modality allocation rules need to be trans-lated into the representation language of the system, such as M3L used in [57] and MOXML used in [43]. For each presentation task, modalities can be allocated on the fly by searching the rule base for rules associated with the factor values at that spe-cific point of presentation. Alternatively, some studies quantify the rules by translat-ing them into numerical metrics of weights or appropriateness and then apply com-putational models for an overall optimization, such as the graph matching method used in [64] and the weighed additive utility model used in [28]. These computa-tional methods were not often named as rule-based. However, the input metrics are still derived from rules. What differs is the way in which the rules are encoded and inferred by the system.

When viewing the modality allocation rules used in existing IMMP systems, it appears that most of them are disassociated from knowledge of human information processing. In other words, they do not seem to consider how information carried by different modalities is perceived and processed by the human cognitive system. Consequently, the efficiency of interaction might be affected due to the unnecessary cognitive load that the multimodal presentations impose on the user. As technology advances, computer systems are increasingly able to assist users in data-rich and time-critical applications, such as crisis management and stock monitoring. The cognitive compatibility issue could be particularly important in these applications, because users are very likely to work under high cognitive load and stress. The need to integrate relevant cognitive knowledge into IMMP has gained awareness in recent years and has been addressed in several articles providing design guidelines [41, 45, 54].

In this chapter, we first describe several findings from the field of cognitive psychology and neuropsychology on the relevance of modality to human information processing. These findings reveal the necessity of considering the cognitive impacts of modality and can serve as a theoretical foundation of cognitive-aware modality allocation. Then, we present a user study to further demonstrate the effects of modality on user performance and cognitive load, using a high-load and time-critical scenario. The experimental results are interpreted in the light of relevant cognitive theories. Based on the consistency of the results and the theories, we go one step further to construct a computational model for predicting the suitability of the modality variants that were not investigated in the experiment. This model also demonstrates a way to integrate relevant cognitive knowledge into the modality allocation for this specific presentation task. Lastly, several suggestions on adapting this model to other applications are given.

2 Modality and Human Information Processing

First, we present a conceptual model of human information processing proposed by Wickens [60]. This model provides a useful framework for further discussing the relation between modality and several stages of human information processing. The model, as shown in Fig. 1 represents human information processing as a series of stages. In the *sensory processing* stage, information from the environment is received by the brain as raw sensory data that can be processed by the brain. Then, attention is needed to select certain raw sensory data to be interpreted and given meaning in the *perception* stage. Afterwards, more complex cognitive operations (reasoning, comprehension, etc.) are conducted in the *working memory* stage. Working memory also has access to the long-term memory system. Based on the outcome of cognitive processing, decisions are reached on how to respond in the *response selection* stage. Finally, the selected response is executed. The feedback loop at the bottom of the model indicates that the human response to the environment can be observed again. This feedback loop makes it possible to keep adjusting

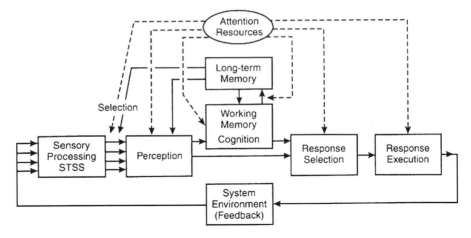

Fig. 1 A model of human information precessing stages proposed by C.D. Wickens (reproduced from [60], p. 11)

the response to reach a certain goal. This is important for many real-world tasks, such as walking and driving.

From the perspective of a system (in the bottom block), output modalities[1] mostly influence three stages of information processing: sensory processing, perception, and working memory. The response selection stage has not been explicitly related to the use of modalities in the literature, because the response to an event is mostly based on the output of cognition rather than the modality of information presentation. However, in multimodal interaction, users might choose to respond to the system with modalities that are consistent with the output modalities, such as speech response to speech outputs. The response execution stage is modality-specific because different modalities are generated by different parts of the body, such as hands for tactile response and vocal organs for speech response. These modalities are input modalities[2] from the perspective of a system, thus are outside the focus of multimodal information presentation. In the remainder of this section, we describe the role of modality in sensory processing, perception (selective attention from sensory processing to perception), and working memory (cognition).

2.1 Modality and Sensory Processing

At the very first sensory processing stage, the distinction of modalities is physically determined, because the five human senses are realized by different sensory receptors. The receptors for visual, auditory, tactile, olfactory, and gustatory signals are

---

[1] Output modalities refer to modalities a system uses to present information to users.

[2] Input modalities refer to modalities users use to interact with a system.

found in the eyes, ears, skin, nose, and tongue, respectively. Each sensory receptor is sensitive to only one form of energy. The function of these receptors is to transduce the physical energy into electrochemical energy that can be processed by the brain.

2.2 Modality and Perception

Sensed stimuli do not have to be consciously attended to and actively interpreted. Instead, attention is needed to select certain raw sensory data to be perceived, given meaning and further processed by the brain [42, 60]. This selection process is referred to as "selective attention" [27]. Modality plays a role in selective attention, because different modalities vary in their abilities to attract attention, mostly based on their sensory properties. Here, we focus on visual and auditory modalities.

2.2.1 Visual Attention

Visual attention guides what we are looking at. The visual field is divided into foveal and peripheral fields. Only foveal vision is able to observe details of objects, but it has a very limited angle of only about two degrees. Therefore, without foveal visual attention, people often have surprising difficulty in detecting large changes in visual scenes—a phenomenon known as "change blindness" [46, 47]. Peripheral vision is sensitive to motion and luminance changes. Visual attention can be directed in a top-down manner or a bottom-up manner [14]. The top-down manner means that visual attention is consciously directed by top-down knowledge, such as task-dependent goals [36], contextual cues [12, 40], current items in the working memory [15, 25], and expectations of what to see [53]. In contrast, the bottom-up manner is saliency driven, meaning that the visual stimuli which win the competition for saliency will *automatically* be attended. When an object in a visual field contains some unique features, this object seems to "pop out" and captures the attention [26]. Through the bottom-up mechanism, attention shifts can be influenced by how the visual information is presented. Items that have higher priority should be presented with a unique (compared with surrounding) color, shape, intensity, orientation, depth, size, or curvature [39, 63].

2.2.2 Auditory Attention

The auditory modalities are different from the visual ones in three aspects regarding attention attraction. First, auditory modalities are more salient than visual modalities. Usually, attention is promptly directed to an auditory signal upon the onset of its presentation [53]. This feature makes auditory modalities a preferred choice to present information with high priorities, such as warnings and alerts [55]. The risk of using auditory modalities is that they might interrupt an ongoing task by pulling full attention away from it, referred to as "auditory preemption" [62]. Second, unlike visual information which needs to be in the visual field in order to be attended to, auditory information can grab attention no matter which direction it comes from, and its direction can be distinguished if perceived by both ears. This feature makes it possible to assist visual search by providing location cues via auditory modalities. For example, it was demonstrated in [6] that 3D audio information could indeed assist pilots to locate outside-the-window visual targets faster. Third, auditory information is transient if no repeat mechanism is added to it. Therefore, it is force-paced, meaning that in order to be fully perceived, attention needs to be held on to an auditory stream during its presentation. In contrast, static visual information tends to be more continuously available and thus offers more freedom of perception in terms of time [60].

2.2.3 Cross-Modal Attention

In real-life situations, attention often must be simultaneously coordinated between different senses—a fact that motivated the development of a relatively new research topic, crossmodal attention [52]. It has been proved that a shift of attention in one modality toward a certain spatial location tends to be accompanied by corresponding shifts in other modalities toward the same location [16, 21]. Such crossmodal links can operate in a reflexive (automatic) manner or a voluntary (controlled) manner. The reflexive manner means that an irrelevant but salient event in one modality tends to attract attention toward it in other modalities as well. Such reflexive links have been found for many modality combinations. For example, a salient auditory event (e.g., a loud bang) can generate rapid shifts of visual attention towards its direction; a tactile event on one hand (e.g., being touched) can generate shifts of visual and auditory attention toward the location of the touch. Crossmodal links can also direct attention voluntarily. When a person strongly expects an event in one modality at a particular location, his/her sensory sensitivity improves at that location not only for the expected modality but also for other modalities, even if there is no motivation to expect events from other modalities to occur at that location [51]. The crossmodal attention shifts have been supported by electrophysiological evidences from event-related brain potential (ERP) studies [17, 18]. There might be a single crossmodal attentional system that operates independently of sensory modality and controls shifts of spatial attention for all senses. In summary, spatial attention toward a location typically spreads across modalities, and this finding has implications for multimodal information presentation to better support attention management in complex and data-rich interface applications.

2.3 Modality and Working Memory

The working memory stage following the perception stage also works in a modality-specific manner. Two theories about this are discussed below.

Fig. 2 The working memory
model from Baddeley and
Hitch [5]

2.3.1 Working Memory Theory

In 1974, Baddeley and Hitch proposed a three-component model of working memory, which has been well supported by scientific evidence from cognitive psychology, neuroimaging, and anatomy [4, 5]. According to this model, working memory contains a central executive system aided by two subsidiary systems, a visual-spatial sketch pad and a phonological loop (Fig. 2). The phonological loop has a phonological store for temporarily storing auditory information. It also includes a rehearsal system. Auditory traces within the store are assumed to decay over a period of about two seconds unless being refreshed by the rehearsal system. Particularly, the rehearsal system relies on speech coding to maintain the memory trace, meaning that information is usually rehearsed in the mind via subvocal speech [3]. The visual-spatial sketch pad is assumed to temporarily maintain visual information and to form a relation between visual and spatial information. The information stored in the two subsidiary systems is retrieved by the central executive system, which is assumed to be an attentional system whose role extends beyond memory functions. As the name indicates, it is believed to be a processing and control system which is involved in attention management, learning, comprehension, decision making, reasoning, judgement, and planning. Neuroimaging and anatomical studies have indicated that these three components of working memory are localized in different brain regions. There is clear evidence of the phonological loop being on the left temporoparietal region. The visual-spatial pad is identified to be primarily localized in the right hemisphere [34, 50]. There is the least agreement among research findings on the anatomical location of the center executive. It seems possible that different executive processes are implemented by different brain components. It can be inferred from this theory that the visual and auditory channels consume separated perceptional resources. Therefore, two perception tasks can be better performed in parallel when they make use of different channels, compared to when they compete for resources in the same channel [61].

2.3.2 Dual Coding Theory

At about the same time when the working memory theory was proposed, Paivio proposed a dual coding theory which addresses another modality-specific feature of human cognition [37]. This theory assumes that cognition is served by two separate symbolic systems, one specialized for dealing with verbal information and the other with nonverbal information (Fig. 3). The two systems are presumed to be interconnected but capable of functioning independently. The verbal system processes

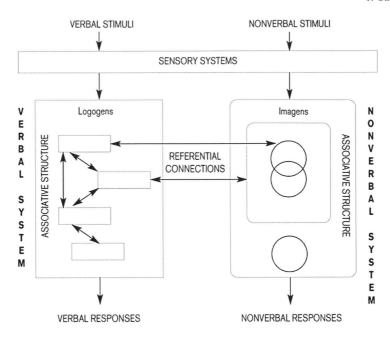

Fig. 3 Verbal and nonverbal symbolic systems of Dual Coding Theory [38]. Logogens and imagens refer to verbal and nonverbal representational units, respectively

visual, auditory, and other modality-specific verbal codes. The nonverbal system processes images, environmental sounds, actions, and other nonverbal objects and events. The two systems are linked into a dynamic network through referential connections. The referential connections convert information between two systems and join corresponding verbal and nonverbal codes into knowledge that can be acted upon, stored, and retrieved for subsequent use. It has been demonstrated that the referential connections play major roles in various educational domains, such as knowledge comprehension, memorization, the learning of motor skills, etc. [13]. Neuroimaging studies have provided support for the dual coding theory by showing that different parts of the brain are responsible for the passive storage and active maintenance of verbal, spatial, and object information [48, 49].

2.3.3 Relating the Two Theories

The aforementioned two theories have not been explicitly related to each other by their founders. However, they are complementary instead of contradictory. It seems reasonable to assume that the center executive selectively retrieves information from modality-specific mental systems, integrates them into a unified percept, and then implements executive processes (reasoning, decision making, etc.). The center executive may also be responsible for the transfer of information between modalities. Since the rehearsal of information in the working memory is based on subvocal speech [3], rehearsing written materials during reading is an example of modality transfer from visual to auditory system. Moreover, mental imagination of the appearance of an object upon hearing its name is an example of modality transfer from verbal to nonverbal system.

In the educational psychology domain, multimedia learning studies have applied both theories to understand the impacts of various learning material designs on the learning performance. Regarding the dual coding theory, it was found that it was more beneficial to present knowledge both verbally and nonverbally than only verbally or only nonverbally [30, 31]. This is because the mental processes of associating related verbal and nonverbal information can help deepen the understanding of the knowledge and thus lead to better problem-solving transformation. Regarding the dual coding theory, it was found that when nonverbal information (illustration, animation, diagram, etc.) was provided visually (on paper or on screen), the associated verbal explanation was better presented in speech than in text [9, 32, 35]. When all information was presented visually, perceptional resources in the visual channel had to be divided for verbal and nonverbal items, causing a so-called split-attention effect. By replacing text with well-synchronized narration, related verbal and nonverbal units could be concurrently perceived via two channels. As a result, more cognitive resources are available for further processing of the knowledge.

In the study presented here, we intended to apply these two cognitive theories together with findings on attention (Sect. 2.2) to a high-load and time-critical user task rather than learning. Our goal was twofold. The first was to investigate/validate the modality effects on user performance, cognitive load and stress, with our high-load and time-critical task setting. Second, we intended to interpret the experimental results in association with relevant cognitive findings. By doing so, we could also investigate whether these theories could be used to predict how suitable a certain modality choice is for this presentation task.

3 Experiment on Modality Effects in High-Load HCI

A user study was conducted, using an earthquake rescue scenario, where the locations of wounded and dead people are continuously reported to the crisis response center and displayed on a computer screen. Based on these reports, a crisis manager directs a doctor to reach all wounded people and save their lives. In this experiment, the subject plays the role of the crisis manager, and his/her task is to save as many wounded victims as possible. Note that it was not our goal to make the crisis scenario realistic, and subjects were not required to have any experience in crisis management. The choice of scenario was made to better motivate a high-load and time-critical user task.

3.1 Presentation Material

For each victim report, two types of information could be provided: basic information and additional aid. The basic information included the type of the victims (wounded or dead) and their location. The additional aid reduced the searching area by indicating which half of the screen (left or right) contained the victim.

To convey these two types of information, four modalities were selected based on their visual/auditory and verbal/nonverbal properties, namely text (visual, verbal), image (visual, nonverbal), speech (auditory, verbal), and sound (auditory, nonverbal). The basic information could be efficiently conveyed by locating a visual object on a map. Therefore, we selected text and image to present the victim type (Fig. 4, left), and the location on a grid-based map indicated the location of the victim (Fig. 4, right). Three modalities were selected to present the additional aid. They were image (a large-size left arrow or right arrow right below the map area), speech ("left" or "right"), and sound (an ambulance sound coming from the left or the right speaker).

Finally, five experimental conditions were chosen, two without additional aids and three with aids (see Table 1). We predicted that image would be better than text for presenting victim types, because it has been found that the categorization and understanding of concrete objects are faster when they are presented by image

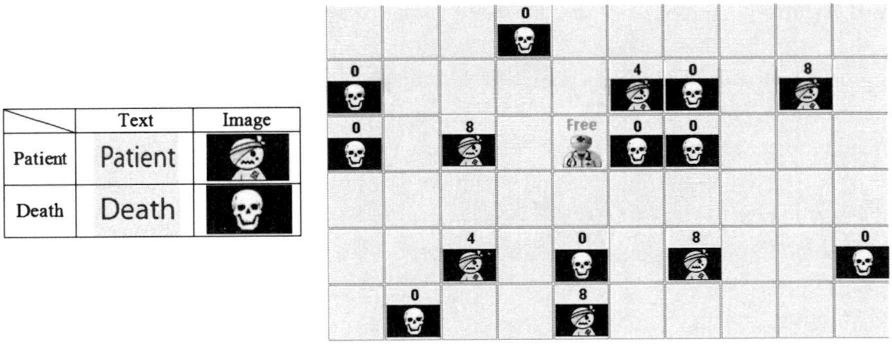

Fig. 4 Presentations used in the experiment. *Left*: text and image presentations of the victim types. Wounded and dead victims are named "patient" and "death," respectively. *Right*: a part of the grid-based map (the full size is 20 grids by 13 grids)

Table 1 Five experimental presentation conditions

Index	Basic Information	Additional Aid	Modality Properties
1	Text	None	Visual, verbal
2	Image	None	Visual, nonverbal
3	Text	Image	Visual + visual, verbal + nonverbal
4	Text	Speech	Visual + auditory, verbal + verbal
5	Text	Sound	Visual + auditory, verbal + nonverbal

than by text [7]. Therefore, in order to better observe the benefit of the additional aid, basic information was always presented by text when additional aids were provided.

3.2 Task and Procedure

The subject played the role of the crisis manager, whose task was to send the doctor to each patient by mouse-clicking on the presentation (text or image). New patients appeared at random intervals of 2 to 5 seconds, usually at the same time as one or more dead victims. A patient had a lifetime of 10 seconds and would turn into a dead victim without a timely treatment. A number above the presentation of a patient indicated his remaining lifetime. When timely treated, patients disappeared from the screen. In each trial, 100 patients were presented in about 5 minutes. Dead victims served as distracters that required no reaction.

The difficulty of the task could be regulated by the number of distracters (dead victims). At the beginning of a trial, there were no any objects on the grid map, and the task was relatively easy. As the number of dead victims grew, it became more and more difficult to identify a patient in the crowded surroundings. The task difficulty reached the maximum (about 40% of the cells contained objects) after about 150 seconds and remained unchanged for the rest of the trial.

Twenty university students (bachelor, master, or Ph.D.) volunteered to participate in this experiment. A participant first received an introduction to the experiment and then performed a training session in order to get familiar with the task and presentation conditions. Afterwards, the participant performed all five experimental trials with a counterbalanced order. Short breaks were placed between trials, during which the questionnaires were filled in. At the end of the experiment, an informal interview was carried out to obtain additional feedback from the participant. The whole experimental procedure lasted for about 80 minutes.

3.3 Measurements

The performance was assessed by three measurements. *Reaction time* (RT) measured the time interval between the moment when a patient was presented and the moment when the doctor was sent (in seconds). *Number of patients died* (ND) referred to the number of patients that were not treated within 10 seconds and died. *Time of the first patient death* (TF) measured the time interval between the start of a trial and the moment when the first patient died in the trial (in seconds). Since the number of distracters increased gradually in the first half of a trial, TF actually reflected how tolerant the performance was against the increase of task difficulty.

Besides performance, we also obtained subjective assessments on cognitive load (SCL) and stress (SS). Based on the Task Load Index from NASA [23], the rating scale was designed to have 20 levels, from 1 (very low) to 20 (very high).

3.4 Hypotheses

We constructed the following four hypotheses.

1. The image (nonverbal) condition is superior to the text (verbal) condition in terms of better performance, lower cognitive load, and lower stress, because image is better than text for presenting concrete objects.
2. The auditory (speech and sound) aids are superior to the visual (image) aid, because they can be better time-shared with the visual rescue task.
3. The nonverbal (image and sound) aids are superior to the verbal (speech) aid, because the location information is nonverbal in nature, so that verbal presentations require additional mental resources to be converted.
4. Additional aids lead to benefits in terms of performance, cognitive load and stress, because they carry useful information and are meant to assist the user.

4 Results on Performance, Cognitive Load and Stress

Due to the within-subject design, we applied repeated-measure one-way ANOVAs on the five dependent measurements, using modality as the independent factor. Results are presented in this section.

4.1 Performance

RT. The average reaction time of all trials is shown in Fig. 5 (left). On average, it took subjects between 1.9 seconds and 3.1 seconds to react to a patient. The reactions were the fastest in the "text + speech aid" condition and the slowest in the text condition.

ANOVA results revealed a significant modality effect on reaction time, $F(4, 16) = 12.76$, $p < 0.001$. Post-hoc tests (Bonferroni tests) were then conducted for pair-wise comparisons. Significant differences in reaction time were found between the five condition pairs. The reaction was faster in the "text + speech aid" condition than in the text, "text + image aid," and "text + sound" conditions. The reaction was faster in the image condition than in the text and "text + image aid" conditions.

ND. On average, the number of dead patients in each condition was between 2 and 12 (see Fig. 5, right). As 100 patients were presented in each trial, the percentage of saved patients was between 88% and 98%. The most patients were saved in the "text + speech aid" condition, and the least were saved in the text condition.

ANOVA results indicated that there was a significant modality effect on the number of dead patients, $F(4, 16) = 16.81$, $p < 0.001$. Pairwise comparisons showed five significant effects. More patients died in the text condition than in the image,

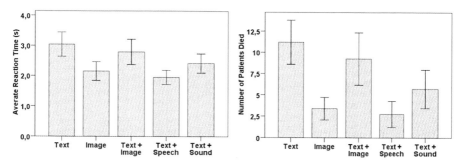

Fig. 5 Average reaction time (*left*) and number of patients that died (*right*) in five modality conditions. *Error bars* represent standard errors

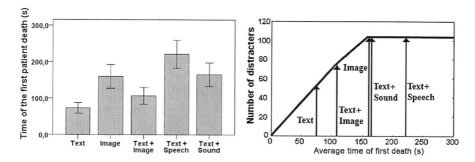

Fig. 6 Time of the first patient death. *Left*: average TF in all modality conditions. *Error bars* represent standard errors. *Right*: average TF shown on the curve of task difficulty over time

"text + speech aid" and "text + sound aid" conditions. More patients died in the "text + image aid" condition than in the image and "text + speech aid" conditions.

TF. As Fig. 6 shows, the first dead patient occurred the earliest in the text condition (at the 73th second on average), and the latest in the "text + speech aid" condition (at the 221th second on average). Again, ANOVA revealed a significant modality effect on this measurement, $F(4, 15) = 17.71$, $p < 0.001$. According to post-hoc tests, the first patient death occurred significantly earlier in the text condition than in the image, "text + speech aid" and "text + sound aid" condition. The first patient death also occurred significantly earlier in the "text + image aid" condition than in the "text + speech aid" condition.

The effects found from this measurement actually indicate that the use of modality significantly affected how tolerant the performance was against the increase of task difficulty. As Fig. 6 (right) shows, in the text condition, the performance dropped when the task difficulty increased to about half of the maximum. In contrast, in the "text + speech aid" condition, the good performance was maintained for more than 50 seconds after the task difficulty reached the maximum.

4.2 Cognitive Load and Stress

SCL. The average rating scores on subjective cognitive load mostly fell in the higher half (10–20) of the rating scale (see Fig. 7, left). Subjects considered the text condition as the most difficult one and the "text + speech aid" condition as the easiest. The cognitive load ratings were significantly affected by the use of modality, $F(4, 16) = 17.06$, $p < 0.001$. Generally, two groups could be identified among the five modality conditions. The image and the "text + speech aid" conditions formed a group of higher ratings. The remaining three conditions formed a group of lower ratings. Results of post-hoc tests showed that there were significant differences in rating scores between any two conditions taken from different groups (six condition pairs in total).

SS. As shown in Fig. 7 (right), the text condition was rated the most stressful, and the "text + speech aid" condition was rated the least stressful. ANOVA results show a significant subjective stress ($F(4, 16) = 9.379$, $p < 0.001$). According to post-hoc tests, the stress level was significantly higher in the text condition than in the image, "text + speech aid" and "text + sound aid" conditions. The "text + image aid" condition was also rated significantly more stressful than the "text + speech aid" condition.

A very similar pattern can be seen when comparing the two graphs in Fig. 7. Indeed, there is a strong positive correlation between ratings on cognitive load and stress (Corr. $= 0.855$), suggesting that subjects felt more stressed when they devoted more cognitive efforts to the task. Moreover, the subjective measurements were also found to be positively correlated with the performance measurements RT and ND. There are positive correlations at the 0.01 confidence level between ND-SCL, ND-SS, RT-SCL, and RT-SS. In combination, these correlations indicate that when the task was more difficult (due to a suboptimal use of modalities), subjects devoted more cognitive effort, felt more stressed, and performed worse.

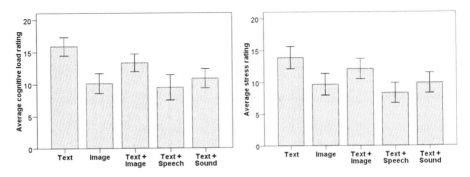

Fig. 7 Average subjective rating scores on cognitive load (*left*) and stress (*right*) in five modality conditions. *Error bars* represent standard errors

5 Discussion

The experimental results clearly showed that the use of modality affected the performance of the task, as well as the experienced cognitive load and stress. In this section, the experimental results are discussed in association with the hypotheses and the cognitive theories.

5.1 Text vs. Image

Comparing the two conditions without performance aid, the five measurements all suggested that image had advantage over text in this scenario. Thus the first hypothesis has been clearly confirmed. Image, as a nonverbal and analogue modality, is better for presenting concrete concepts [7, 24], such as wounded and dead victims in this experiment. For this task, image made it easier to distinguish between the two types of objects and thus led to faster and better performance, lower cognitive load, and lower stress. In contrast, text, as a verbal modality, is known to be less suitable for presenting concrete information but more suitable for abstract concepts, logic, quantitative values, relations [7, 24]. In this study, as the two words in text had the same font, size, and color, the two icon images were also designed to have similar shapes and colors. We believe that the advantage of image over text would become even more notable if the two images showed larger contrasts in color, shape, and size. These findings stand in line with the dual-coding theory, because they show that verbal and nonverbal presentations of the same information indeed have different impacts on how well the information can be processed. This in turn suggests that the verbal/nonverbal property needs to be taken as one dimension of modality selection in IMMP system design.

5.2 Visual Aid vs. Auditory Aid

Here, we compare the "text + image aid" condition to the "text + speech aid" and the "text + sound aid" conditions. The results from all five measurements consistently showed that the speech aid was significantly more appropriate than the image aid. In terms of average values, the sound aid was also superior to the image aid in all five measurements. However, this advantage only reached a statistical significance in the cognitive load measurement. Overall, we could conclude that the auditory aids were more beneficial than the visual aid in this experiment. The second hypothesis is confirmed.

The explanation of this finding is twofold. First, auditory signals are more able to attract attention than visual signals, especially when the eyes are occupied with another task (Sect. 2.2.2). Therefore, while busy searching for patients, visual aids displayed at the bottom of the display were more likely to be missed than speech aids. Besides conveying the search area for a patient, a performance aid also indicated that a patient was newly added onto the map. If a visual aid was missed, the arrival of that patient could be missed as well. Therefore, in the "text + image aid" condition, subjects were likely to lose track of the number of patients remaining unattended.

Second, even when being attended to, visual aids still have drawbacks due to cognitive resource competition. According to the working memory theory from Baddeley (Sect. 2.3.1), separated perceptional resources are used for visual and auditory information. Therefore, auditory aids could be perceived in parallel with the ongoing rescue task. In contrast, the perception of visual aids cannot be time-shared with the rescue task. Limited visual perceptional resources needed to be shared between the rescue map and the aids. When the rescue task was already demanding, visual aids were more likely to cause overload than to be of help. Not surprisingly, many subjects mentioned during the interview at the end that they sometimes had to consciously ignore the image aids in order to concentrate on the rescue task.

5.3 Verbal Aid vs. Nonverbal Aid

Although the image aid is nonverbal, it has been identified as inappropriate for this task (Sect. 5.2). Therefore, we focus the comparison on the speech aid and the sound aid. In terms of average values, all five measurements showed an advantage of the speech aid over the sound aid. The difference in reaction time was significant. When asked to compare these two conditions, the majority of subjects preferred the speech aid. These results clearly contradict the third hypothesis. The understanding of words "left" and "right" is highly automatic for most people. So the additional load associated with it (if any) was probably too little to harm the task performance. Then, why were speech aids better than sound aids? Subjects provided two explanations. First, it was commonly mentioned that speech aids made it easier to maintain a short queue of newly reported patients ("left"s and "right"s) in mind, while solving a current one. It was however harder to do the same with the sound aids. Baddeley's working memory theory states that the working memory usually relies on subvocal speech to maintain a memory trace (Sect. 2.3.1). That is to say speech aid "left" and "right" could be directly rehearsed, but the direction of a sound, as a nonverbal information, had to be converted into a verbal form in order to be maintained. This conversion (via referential connections) consumed additional cognitive resources, and this was probably why subjects found it harder to maintain a queue of untreated patients with sound aids than with speech aids. Second, a few subjects disliked the ambulance sound. They found it disturbing when used at a high frequency, and they could not concentrate well on the rescue task.

Interestingly, the dual coding theory (Sect. 2.3.2) leads to a different suggestion for our task than for learning material design. A learning task requires comprehension and long-term memorization of presented knowledge. The combined use of verbal and nonverbal presentation invokes referential connections which have been shown to be essential to a deeper understanding and a better memorization [13]. In contrast, our task required short-term memorization and did not involve comprehension of complex information. In this case, the additional cognitive effort spent on building referential connections was less useful and more harmful.

5.4 Additional Aid vs. No Aid

Of the five conditions, the text condition was the worst one, shown by all measurements. However, when text was combined with speech aid, the condition became the best of the five. This comparison seems to suggest that providing additional aids is beneficial compared to not providing them. However, the benefit of additional aid was only conditional, because it could be influenced by the modality used to present the aid.

When comparing the image condition with the "text + image aid" condition, one can see that the former led to shorter reaction times (RT), better rescue performance (ND), and lower cognitive load (SCL) than the latter. Considering average values, time of the first patient death (TF) and subjective stress (SS) also showed an advantage of the image condition over the "text + image aid" condition. However, the differences did not reach statistical significance. This comparison shows that presenting less information using an appropriate single modality (image) could be more beneficial than presenting more information using an inappropriate modality combination (text + image aid). Therefore, the additional aids can be of real help only when they are presented via an appropriate modality. The fourth hypothesis is only partially confirmed.

5.5 Low Load vs. High Load

We further investigated whether the modality effects reported above would also occur without the high-load condition. At the beginning of each trial, no objects were on the grid map, and thus the rescue task was relatively easy. As more and more objects were presented, it got more and more difficult to identify a patient in the crowded surroundings. According to the data from the TF measurement, the first patient death occurred after 60 seconds in all trials of all subjects. Therefore, we considered the first 60 seconds as a relatively low-load period. The average reaction time was recalculated with this period (see Fig. 8). Comparing Fig. 8 to Fig. 5 (left), a similar up-and-down trend can be recognized, suggesting that the relative difference in task difficulty between conditions remain unchanged. However, the differences in reaction time between conditions were much smaller during the first 60 seconds. On average, reactions in the fastest condition ("text + speech aid") was about 0.15 seconds faster than in the slowest condition (text)—a difference that was only about 14% of the value calculated from the whole trial (1.09 s, Fig. 5, left).

Fig. 8 Average reaction time from the first 60 seconds in five modality conditions. *Error bars* represent standard errors

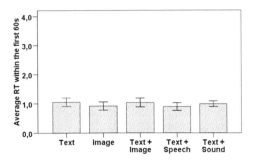

Furthermore, ANOVA analysis did not reveal any modality effect on the reaction time during the first 60 seconds ($F(4, 16) = 1.61$, n.s.). These results suggest that in the low-load period, the use of modality influenced the task performance to a smaller extent, compared to in a high-load condition in which this influence became significant. Therefore, it is particularly important for IMMP systems with high-load applications to integrate modality-related cognitive principles into the modality allocation processes.

6 A Modality Suitability Prediction Model

The discussion of experimental results showed that cognitive theories of working memory and attention, together with the expressive feature of modalities, accounted for variations in user performance and experienced cognitive load and stress. In this section, we demonstrate a possible way of integrating these theoretical foundations into a model that can systematically predict the suitability of a certain modality choice for this presentation task. Several suggestions on adapting this model to other applications are also given.

Again, we assume that the set of available modalities consists of text, image, speech, and sound. Regarding the two basic information elements, all four modalities are suitable to present the victim types, but only text and image are suitable to present the victim locations. Speech can refer to a location by a row index and a column index, or a zone index. Sound can use variations in tone, pitch, or direction to convey location. However, since the grid-map used for this task contains 260 location units (grids), using only auditory modalities without any visual hint actually locating a point on the map would be much too inefficient to convey the locations. It would be particularly hard or even impossible for users to distinguish between 260 sound variations. Therefore, only text and image are chosen as candidates for presenting basic information. The additional aid, if provided, can be presented by all four modality candidates. A total of 10 possible modality choices are identified to be evaluated (Table 2).

A weighted additive utility model (Eq. 1) has been constructed which takes modalities as inputs and outputs a numerical value describing the level of suitability

Table 2 Predicted suitability of 10 possible modality usages

Index	Modality for basic info.	Modality for additional aid	B (0.5)	P (0.3)	M (0.2)	Suitability score
1[a]	text	none	1	0	0	0.5
2	text	text	1	−1	2	0.6
3[a]	text	image	1	−1	1	0.4
4[a]	text	speech	1	1	2	1.2
5[a]	text	sound	1	1	1	1.0
6[a]	image	none	2	0	0	1.0
7	image	text	2	−1	2	1.1
8	image	image	2	−1	1	0.9
9	image	speech	2	1	2	**1.7**
10	image	sound	2	1	1	1.5

[a]Experimental conditions

of the input modality choice. The higher the output value is, the more suitable the input modality choice is:

$$Suitability = f_b \times B + f_p \times P + f_m \times M. \tag{1}$$

The model contains three attributes. For each of them, suitability values are assigned to all modality candidates, based on predictions from relevant theories.

1. **B:** the expressive feature of the modality that presents the basic information. Modality candidates are image and text. Image is more suitable than text to present concrete objects such as victim types (see Sect. 5.1), and thus a 2 is assigned to image and a 1 to text.
2. **P:** the perception property of the modality that presents the additional aid. Four modality candidates are either visual or auditory. Based on the attention and working memory theory, visual aids harm the rescue task and auditory aids benefit the task (see Sect. 5.2). Therefore, a −1 is assigned to the visual modalities and a 1 to the auditory modalities.
3. **M:** the verbal/nonverbal property of the modality that presents the additional aid. Two modality candidates are verbal, and two are nonverbal. According to the working memory theory and the dual-coding theory, verbal aids are more beneficial than nonverbal aids (see Sect. 5.3). Thus, a 2 is assigned to verbal modalities and a 1 to nonverbal modalities.

Furthermore, a weight f is assigned to each attribute, determining how much the attribute contributes to the final suitability score. The summary of the three weights is 1. The basic information and the additional aid are considered equally important, and therefore attribute B gets a weight of 0.5, and P and M get 0.5 in total. Comparing P and M, our experimental results suggest that the difference between visual and auditory aids was more notable than the difference between verbal and nonverbal aids, which in turn suggests that P may have a larger influence on the suitability evaluation than M. Therefore, f_p is set to 0.3, and f_m is set to 0.2.

Finally, the suitability predictions for 10 possible modality choices are shown in Table 2. The outcomes for the five investigated conditions are consistent with the experimental results, indicating the validity of this model. The "image + speech aid" combination is predicted to be the best modality choice for this specific presentation task.

This suitability prediction model demonstrates the possibility of quantitatively evaluating the cognitive effects of modalities and systematically selecting the best modality usage for a specific presentation task. To adapt this model to other applications, the following aspects need to be reconsidered: (1) the input: what are the available modalities and possible allocation choices; (2) the output: how to define suitability based on the presentation goal (performance, cognitive load and stress in our case); (3) the attributes: which factors have an influence on the suitability assessment and which criteria can be used to predict the influence; (4) the weights: how large is the relative influence of each attribute.

7 Conclusions

In this study, we emphasized that modality allocation in IMMP system needs to consider the cognitive impact of modalities, especially for high-load and time-critical applications. A user experiment was conducted, the results of which confirmed that the use of modality significantly affected the performance and experienced cognitive load and stress. The experimental findings were well explained by relevant cognitive theories and the expressive features of modalities. Furthermore, a suitability prediction model was constructed to predict the suitability of other uninvestigated modality choices for this specific task. This model demonstrated a possible way of integrating cognitive theories into the modality allocation process in IMMP systems. Further work is needed to evaluate and extend this model for more complex user tasks and a larger set of modalities.

Acknowledgements   The user experiment and results presented in this paper have been published previously in [10] and [11].

References

1. André, E.: The generation of multimedia presentations. In: Handbook of Natural Language Processing, pp. 305–327 (2000)
2. Arens, Y., Hovy, E., Vossers, M.: On the knowledge underlying multimedia presentations. In: Intelligent Multimedia Interfaces, pp. 280–306 (1993)
3. Baddeley, A.D.: Essentials of Human Memory. Taylor & Francis, London (1999)
4. Baddeley, A.D.: Working memory: Looking back and looking forward. Nat. Rev., Neurosci. **4**, 829–839 (2003)

5. Baddeley, A.D., Hitch, G.J.: Working memory. Psychol. Learn. Motiv. Adv. Res. Theory **8**, 47–89 (1974)
6. Begault, D.R.: Head-up auditory displays for traffic collision avoidance system advisories: a preliminary investigation. Hum. Factors **35**(4), 707–717 (1993)
7. Bernsen, N.O.: Multimodality in language and speech systems—from theory to design support tool. In: Multimodality in Language and Speech Systems, pp. 93–148 (2002)
8. Bordegoni, M., Faconti, G., Feiner, S., Maybury, M.T., Rist, T., Ruggieri, S., Trahanias, P., Wilson, M.: A standard reference model for intelligent multimedia presentation systems. Comput. Stand. Interfaces **18**(6), 477–496 (1997)
9. Brünken, R., Steinbacher, S., Plass, J.L., Leutner, D.: Assessment of cognitive load in multimedia learning with dual-task methodology: auditory load and modality effect. Instr. Sci. **32**, 115–132 (2004)
10. Cao, Y., Theune, M., Nijholt, A.: Modality effects on cognitive load and performance in high-load information presentation. In: Proceedings of the 13th International Conference on Intelligent User Interfaces (IUI'09), pp. 335–344. ACM, New York (2009)
11. Cao, Y., Theune, M., Nijholt, A.: Towards cognitive-aware multimodal presentation: the modality effects in high-load HCI. In: Proceedings of the 8th International Conference on Engineering Psychology and Cognitive Ergonomics: Held as Part of HCI International 2009, pp. 12–21. Springer, Berlin (2009)
12. Chun, M.M., Jiang, Y.: Top-down attentional guidance based on implicit learning of visual covariation. Psychol. Sci. **10**(4), 360–365 (1999)
13. Clark, J.M., Paivio, A.: Dual coding theory and education. Educ. Psychol. Rev. **3**(3), 149–210 (1991)
14. Connor, C.E., Egeth, H.E., Yantis, S.: Visual attention: bottom-up versus top-down. Curr. Biol. **14**(19), 850–852 (2004)
15. Downing, P.E.: Interactions between visual working memory and selective attention. Psychol. Sci. **11**(6), 467–473 (2000)
16. Driver, J., Spence, C.: Cross-modal links in spatial attention. Philos. Trans. R. Soc. Lond. B, Biol. Sci. **353**(1373), 1319–1331 (1998)
17. Eimer, M.: Can attention be directed to opposite locations in different modalities? An ERP study. Clin. Neurophysiol. **110**(7), 1252–1259 (1999)
18. Eimer, M., van Velzen, J., Forster, B., Driver, J.: Shifts of attention in light and in darkness: an ERP study of supramodal attentional control and crossmodal links in spatial attention. Cogn. Brain Res. **15**(3), 308–323 (2003)
19. Elting, C., Michelitsch, G.: A multimodal presentation planner for a home entertainment environment. In: Proceedings of the Perceptive User Interfaces (PUI'01), pp. 1–5. ACM, New York (2001)
20. Feiner, S.K., McKeown, K.R.: Automating the generation of coordinated multimedia explanations. Computer **24**(10), 33–41 (1991)
21. Ferris, T.K., Sarter, N.B.: Cross-modal links among vision, audition, and touch in complex environments. Hum. Factors **50**(1), 17–26 (2008)
22. Fitrianie, S., Poppe, R., Bui, T.H., Chitu, A.G., Datcu, D., Hofs, D.H.W., Willems, D.J.M., Poel, M., Rothkrantz, L.J.M., Vuurpijl, L.G., Zwiers, J.: Multimodal human–computer interaction in crisis environments. In: The 4th International ISCRAM Conference, Delft, The Netherlands (2007)
23. Hart, S.G., Staveland, L.E.: Development of NASA-TLX (Task Load Index): results of empirical and theoretical research. Hum. Ment. Workload **1**, 139–183 (1988)
24. Heller, R.S., Martin, C.D., Haneef, N., Gievska-Krliu, S.: Using a theoretical multimedia taxonomy framework. J. Educ. Resour. Comput. **1**, 1–22 (2001)
25. Huang, L., Pashler, H.: Working memory and the guidance of visual attention: consonance-driven orienting. Psychon. Bull. Rev. **14**(1), 148–153 (2007)
26. Itti, L., Koch, C.: A saliency-based search mechanism for overt and covert shifts of visual attention. Vis. Res. **40**, 1489–1506 (2000)
27. Johnston, W.A., Dark, V.J.: Selective attention. Annu. Rev. Psychol. **37**, 43–75 (1986)

28. Karagiannidis, C., Koumpis, A., Stephanidis, C.: Adaptation in IMMPS as a decision making process. Comput. Stand. Interfaces **18**(6), 509–514 (1997)
29. Mansoux, B., Nigay, L., Troccaz, J.: Output multimodal interaction: the case of augmented surgery. People Comput. **20**, 177–192 (2007)
30. Mayer, R.E., Anderson, R.B.: The instructive animation: helping students build connections between words and pictures in multimedia learning. J. Educ. Psychol. **84**(4), 444–452 (1992)
31. Mayer, R.E., Gallini, J.K.: When is an illustration worth ten thousand words. J. Educ. Psychol. **82**(4), 715–726 (1990)
32. Mayer, R.E., Moreno, R.: A split-attention effect in multimedia learning: evidence for dual processing systems in working memory. J. Educ. Psychol. **90**, 312–320 (1998)
33. McRoy, S.W., Channarukul, S., Ali, S.S.: Multimodal content adaptations for heterogeneous devices. J. Digit. Inf. **7**(1), 1–34 (2006)
34. Mishkin, M., Ungerleider, L.G., Macko, K.A.: Object vision and spatial vision: two cortical pathways. In: Philosophy and the Neurosciences: A Reader, pp. 199–208 (2001)
35. Moreno, R., Mayer, R.E.: Learning science in virtual reality multimedia environments: role of methods and media. J. Educ. Psychol. **94**(3), 598–610 (2002)
36. Navalpakkam, V., Itti, L.: A goal oriented attention guidance model. Lect. Notes Comput. Sci. **2525**, 453–461 (2002)
37. Paivio, A.: Coding distinctions and repetition effects in memory. Psychol. Learn. Motiv. Adv. Res. Theory **9**, 179–211 (1975)
38. Paivio, A.: Mental Representations: A Dual Coding Approach. Oxford University Press, Oxford (1986)
39. Parkhurst, D., Law, K., Niebur, E.: Modeling the role of salience in the allocation of overt visual attention. Vis. Res. **42**, 107–123 (2002)
40. Peterson, M.S., Kramer, A.F.: Attentional guidance of the eyes by contextual information and abrupt onsets. Percept. Psychophys. **63**(7), 1239–1249 (2001)
41. Reeves, L.M., Lai, J., Larson, J.A., Oviatt, S., Balaji, T.S., Buisine, S., Collings, P., Cohen, P., Kraal, B., Martin, J.C., McTear, M., Raman, T.V., Stanney, K.M., Su, H., Wang, Q.Y.: Guidelines for multimodal user interface design. Commun. ACM **47**(1), 57–69 (2004)
42. Rensink, R.A., O'Regan, J.K., Clark, J.J.: To see or not to see: the need for attention to perceive changes in scenes. In: Psychological Science, pp. 368–373 (1997)
43. Rousseau, C., Bellik, Y., Vernier, F., Bazalgette, D.: Architecture framework for output multimodal systems design. In: Proceedings of OZCHI'04 (2004)
44. Rousseau, C., Bellik, Y., Vernier, F., Bazalgette, D.: A framework for the intelligent multimodal presentation of information. Signal Process. **86**(12), 3696–3713 (2006)
45. Sarter, N.B.: Multimodal information presentation: design guidance and research challenges. Int. J. Ind. Ergon. **36**(5), 439–445 (2006)
46. Simons, D.J., Chabris, C.F.: Gorillas in our midst: sustained inattentional blindness for dynamic events. Perception **28**, 1059–1074 (1999)
47. Simons, D.J., Rensink, R.A.: Change blindness: past, present, and future. Trends Cogn. Sci. **9**(1), 16–20 (2005)
48. Smith, E.E., Jonides, J.: Working memory: a view from neuroimaging. Cogn. Psychol. **33**(1), 5–42 (1997)
49. Smith, E.E., Jonides, J., Koeppe, R.A.: Dissociating verbal and spatial working memory using PET. Cereb. Cortex **6**(1), 11–20 (1996)
50. Smith, E.E., Jonides, J., Koeppe, R.A., Awh, E., Schumacher, E.H., Minoshima, S.: Spatial versus object working memory: PET investigations. J. Cogn. Neurosci. **7**(3), 337–356 (1995)
51. Spence, C., Driver, J.: Audiovisual links in endogenous covert spatial attention. J. Exp. Psychol. Hum. Percept. Perform. **22**(4), 1005–1030 (1996)
52. Spence, C., Driver, J. (eds.): Crossmodal Space and Crossmodal Attention. Oxford University Press, Oxford (2004)
53. Spence, C., Nicholls, M.E.R., Driver, J.: The cost of expecting events in the wrong sensory modality. Percept. Psychophys. **63**(2), 330–336 (2001)

54. Stanney, K., Samman, S., Reeves, L., Hale, K., Buff, W., Bowers, C., Goldiez, B., Nicholson, D., Lackey, S.: A paradigm shift in interactive computing: deriving multimodal design principles from behavioral and neurological foundations. Int. J. Hum.-Comput. Interact. **17**(2), 229–257 (2004)
55. Stanton, N. (ed.): Human Factors in Alarm Design. CRC Press, Boca Raton (1994)
56. Sutcliffe, A.G., Kurniawan, S., Shin, J.E.: A method and advisor tool for multimedia user interface design. Int. J. Hum.-Comput. Stud. **64**(4), 375–392 (2006)
57. Wahlster, W.: Smartkom: symmetric multimodality in an adaptive and reusable dialogue shell. In: Proceedings of the Human Computer Interaction Status Conference, vol. 3, pp. 47–62 (2003)
58. Wahlster, W., Andre, E., Bandyopadhyay, S., Graf, W., Rist, T.: WIP: the coordinated generation of multimodal presentations from a common representation. Communication from an Artificial Intelligence Perspective: Theoretical and Applied Issues, pp. 121–144 (1992)
59. Wahlster, W., André, E., Finkler, W., Profitlich, H.J., Rist, T.: Plan-based integration of natural language and graphics generation. Artif. Intell. **63**(1), 387–427 (1993)
60. Wickens, C.D.: Engineering Psychology and Human Performance, 3rd edn. Prentice Hall, New York (1999)
61. Wickens, C.D.: Multiple resources and performance prediction. Theor. Issues Ergon. Sci. **3**(2), 159–177 (2002)
62. Wickens, C.D., Dixon, S.R., Seppelt, B.: Auditory preemption versus multiple resources: who wins in interruption management. In: Proceedings of Human Factors and Ergonomics Society Annual Meeting, vol. 49, pp. 463–467. Human Factors and Ergonomics Society, 2005
63. Wolfe, J.M.: Visual attention. Seeing **2**, 335–386 (2000)
64. Zhou, M.X., Wen, Z., Aggarwal, V.: A graph-matching approach to dynamic media allocation in intelligent multimedia interfaces. In: Proceedings of the 10th International Conference on Intelligent User Interfaces, pp. 114–121. ACM, New York (2005)

Natural Human–Computer Interaction

Gianpaolo D'Amico, Alberto Del Bimbo,
Fabrizio Dini, Lea Landucci, and Nicola Torpei

Abstract Research work in relation to Natural Human–Computer Interaction concerns the theorization and development of systems that understand and recognize human communicative actions in order to engage people in a dialogue between them and their surroundings.

Natural interaction is defined in terms of "experience": people communicate in a natural way through vocal, gestural, and emotional expressions, exploring the environments through the vision and manipulation of physical objects. The key is then to allow them to interact with technology in the same way they interact with each other in everyday life.

1 Introduction

Natural interaction research involves multidisciplinary fields of study such as Interaction Design and HCI (Human–Computer Interaction), ergonomics, computer science, cognitive science and communication, and visual art and creativity.

1.1 From Ergonomics to Human–Computer Interaction

In 1949 Murrell used for the first time the term "Ergonomics" derived from the Greek "ergon" (work) and "nomos" (law), and founded the first American company on its inspiration. The International Ergonomics Association (IEA) has approved the following definition:

> "Ergonomics (or human factors) is the scientific discipline concerned with the understanding of the interactions among humans and other elements of a system, and the profession that applies theoretical principles, data and methods to design in order to optimize human well being and overall system performance."

G. D'Amico · A. Del Bimbo (✉) · F. Dini · L. Landucci · N. Torpei
MICC—Media Integration and Communication Center, University of Florence, Florence, Italy
e-mail: delbimbo@dsi.unifi.it

L. Shao et al. (eds.), *Multimedia Interaction and Intelligent User Interfaces,*
Advances in Pattern Recognition,
DOI 10.1007/978-1-84996-507-1_4, © Springer-Verlag London Limited 2010

In the first half of the 1970s, the main task of ergonomics became the study of interfaces between the Human Being and the Interacting Event. In order to describe the relationship between man and machine, the research community started to talk about interaction instead of human adaptation to systems: the user is no longer the "weak factor" of the system design, but rather the strength, the main character of the project. This innovative approach allowed a new concept of *human-centered design*.

The research community initially focused on the physical characteristics of the interaction: the way in which controls were designed, the environmental conditions in which the interaction took place, the layout and the physical qualities of the screen, and so on. Then, they started to evaluate the software in "ergonomic" terms: quality depends not only on purely technical parameters, but it is also closely related to the psychology of the user including ease of use and speed of learning. For this reasons, in the late 1970s, they developed a rich field of studies known as HCI (Human–Computer Interaction) based on principles of ergonomics, psychology, and computer science. The ACM Special Interest Group on Computer–Human Interaction (SIGCHI) in [1] offers a working definition that is very similar to the ergonomics one:

> "Human–computer interaction is a discipline concerned with the design, evaluation and implementation of interactive computing systems for human use and with the study of major phenomena surrounding them."

The difference between the two disciplines concerns purely the scope of application: ergonomics ranges over objects, services, living environments and work, and HCI focuses specifically on interactive systems. Current objectives for Human–Computer Interaction [2] are to build computer systems that are useful, safe, usable, and functional: the system's task is to support the user in achieving his goal, meeting the criteria of usability. In the early 1990s, HCI was integrated within the Computer Science, and its continuous growth soon brought to the development of approaches and technologies able to overcome the limited user/computer paradigm of communication trying to get closer to a new kind of natural interaction. Researchers once more focused on system suitable for users, instead of requiring the adaptation of people to the latter technology:

> "The same technology that simplifies life by providing more functions in each device also complicates life by making the device harder to learn, harder to use. This is the paradox of technology." [3]

1.2 Multimodal Interfaces

For a long time the, Human–Computer Interaction has been limited to the use of a graphical display, a keyboard, and a mouse. The metaphor of desk is still based on the concept of indirect manipulation: through the movement of the mouse on a horizontal surface, we can move, explore, and interact with data on a vertical surface (the computer display).

Recently, the availability of techniques for computer visual and sound recognition, along with projection systems and other multimedia devices, have suggested the development of a richer interaction. These techniques are often referred as multimodal interaction, focusing on how machines can understand commands coming from different channels of human communication [4]. Among those, speech recognition, natural language understanding, and gesture recognition have been applied in different mixtures with roles ranging from active (the system observes the user and is proactive in interacting with him) to passive (the system expects some kind of command, often through a device that is worn by the user).

We can talk about multimodality when a type of interaction involves more than one perception channel (or inputs of communication); the most typical example is undoubtedly the human communication: during a conversation sight, hearing, touch, and even smell are stimulated simultaneously. From a human–computer point of view, this concept encourages the development of systems in which the communication with computer exploits the perceptual input commonly used by humans to interact with the world.

1.3 Natural Human–Computer Interaction

The concept of Natural Human–Computer Interaction (NHCI) was born in the late 1990s as a possible solution to fill the gap between humans and computerized systems. It claims for interfaces that can be used in a natural and intuitive way, exploiting results and developments in the field of pattern recognition and image and speech understanding. Recent examples of such systems use the integration of methodologies based on artificial vision for eye tracking, lip reading, or gesture recognition.

The massive marketing and promotion of new technologies are generating lively criticism for the supposed "cognitive prosthesis" addiction. This is the major criticism to those systems exploiting helmets, data suites, gloves, or other exoskeleton tools for virtual reality: they undermine the naturalness of the interaction by introducing intrusive features. Such reflections can be also applied to simple tools such as traditional interactive phones, PDAs and even mouse and keyboard. The solution is not to step back to less performing technologies, but rather to study new paradigms of communication starting from human-centered design.

2 Natural Interaction Systems

The advent of new technology means that we are continuously offered high-tech devices that should make our life more agreeable, safe, and pleasant. Actually, users deal with the *technology paradox*: innovation technology risks making our life more complex every day [3]. The intention of this warning is to make us conscious of the importance of "human-centred design", particularly when we talk about Human–Computer Interaction.

2.1 Human-Centered Design

Human-centered design may be considered as a developmental process that is influenced by the user and his needs rather than by technology. As first step we can identify the principles for a good system design [5]:

- *Visibility.* The user can recognize the state of the system and the alternatives for action just by looking at the system itself.
- *A good conceptual model.* Every human being has mental models helpful to understand and interact with the environment: designers must provide a coherent system, able to encourage clear and consistent mental models, with no contradictions in the presentation and results of operations.
- *Good mapping.* A natural mapping exploits cultural patterns and spatial analogies. Exploiting a natural mapping means ensuring that the user can determine the relationships between intentions and possible actions, actions and their effects on the system, and the real state of the system and what is perceived.
- *Feedback.* The user receives a complete and continuous feedback about the results of his actions; in complex systems that may cause appreciable latency between a command and its realization, sound or visual feedback makes the user aware that the system has registered his request, thus promoting a confident expectation.
- *Good affordance.* Affordance can be defined in terms of relationship between an object in the world and the intentions, perceptions, and capabilities of its user. The idea of affordance, powerful as it is, tends to describe the surface of a design [6]. A system has a good affordance if it has the real or perceived property to "suggest" its functioning.

2.2 Intuitive Interaction

As mentioned before, natural interaction means intuitive interaction: providing a system a good affordance gives possibilities for users to use it in a simple and intuitive way.

In order to understand which kind of process can be considered intuitive, let us consider the flow of information in the human memory. One of the most influential models was the *Modal Model of Memory* proposed by Atkinson and Shiffrin in 1968 (see Fig. 1).

From this model it is easy to argue that the only factor that can be "guided" by the interface of an interactive system is the external stimulus (environmental input) which is the triggering event of the whole cognitive process. The response provided by the interactive system will be intuitive if it fits the cognitive model selected by the user during the perceptual recognition. The point is to activate the correct models through the correct stimulus. Otherwise, the effect will be the increase of the cognitive load that is the amount of activity imposed to the short-term memory.

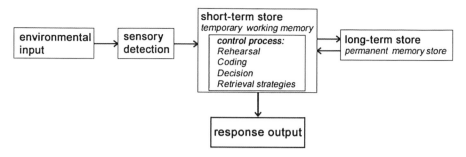

Fig. 1 The model of human memory proposed by Atkinson & Shiffrin (1968)

As we approach the Human–Computer Interaction exploiting natural human channel of communication, we can activate the prior knowledge of the users (cognitive models) in order to minimize the cognitive load: that is what we call Natural Human–Computer Interaction.

2.3 Natural Language and Tangible User Interfaces

Human expressions that can be used to create a natural interaction language are those considered innate or those which do not need to be learned because they belong to our cultural/social background. We can include vocal and gestural expressions used by humans to explore the surrounding space with their body, such as touching, pointing, moving in an area, move objects, etc. The problem is then to develop systems able to "sense" and understand such actions associating them to system actions in a consistent way.

Exploratory applications may be implemented using simple innate gestures, but in the case of more complicated applications (with a variety of content and actions), such spontaneous gestures are not enough. A solution would be to enrich the interaction language by adding new hinged gestures mapping them to different actions: this could undermine the naturalness of the interaction forcing users to learn unnatural gestures. Alternatively, we could introduce another display layer using standard interface elements such as menus, icons, etc. This could reduce the intuitiveness of the interaction causing conflict between digital content and interface elements, both sharing the same visualization area.

Both solutions seems to increase the cognitive load of the system users.

Tangible User Interfaces (TUIs [7]) can be an alternative to those mentioned. The idea is to introduce physical, tangible objects that the system interprets as embodiment [8] of different elements of the interaction language. Users can manipulate these objects inspired by their affordance having simple and direct access to the features mapped on the objects themselves [9].

3 Sensing Human Behavior

The design of a Natural Human–Computer Interaction (NHCI) system is focused on recognizing innate and instinctive *human expressions* in relation to some object, and returning the user a corresponding feedback that has the characteristics of being both *expected* and *inspiring*. All the technology and intelligence has to be built inside the digital artifacts so that users are not asked to use external complicated devices, wear anything, or learn particular commands or procedures. Instead, the first interactions with the systems should be enough expressive to guide the user through the exploration of the rest of the interface.

NHCI systems use human communication channels instead of those artificial:

- Vocal commands (speech recognition).
- Body and hand gesture analysis.
- Face expressions recognition.

Moreover, it utilizes metaphors that preserve the analogy with the natural laws:

- Basic physical principles.
- Fluidity in movements, transformations, transitions.

In the last years, studies have been following the concept of Natural Interaction as a conjunction of different technologies and design principles, with a more radical view about the user freedom in using interactive artifacts.

3.1 Sensed Spaces and Sensors Categories

From a technological point of view, *sensing* mechanisms involve the use of various sensors that provide data regarding physical dimensions. In the market, there are a large number of electronic sensors that are commonly used in various industrial fields such as robotics, automation, and automatic controls (cameras and corresponding Computer Vision algorithm, capacitive sensors for the detection of touch or pressure, accelerometers for the recognition of gestures and body movements). Each sensor can provide these types of data in different ways in terms of resolution, range, tolerance, and error. Some of these are capable of providing discrete data with high accuracy, while others (such as cameras) provide only a large amount of data, and to obtain useful information, they must first be processed by Computer Vision algorithms.

A logic processing layer must be applied to abstract all data from individual sensors and create a uniform model for the Human–Computer Interaction.

3.2 Optical Sensors and Computer Vision Technologies

Regarding the optical sensor, the processing layer must elaborate the stream of data from the camera in order to extract information from images. This information usually regards the understanding of active objects and body movements.

3.2.1 Image Analysis Techniques

Simple image analysis techniques are usually applied to the raw images extracted from a camera: a background subtraction is used to tolerate illumination variation with a running average approach that helps to understand changes in background geometry and illumination.

After a noise removal step based on a blur filtering smoothing, a blob extraction and labeling are usually done through image segmentation aimed at categorizing pixels in an image as belonging to one of many discrete regions.

Blob extraction is performed through analysis of connected components. The labeling algorithm transforms a binary image into a symbolic image in order to assign a unique label to each connected component [10].

3.2.2 Tracking Techniques

Object tracking has been a fundamental research element in the field of Computer Vision. The task of tracking consists of reliably being able to reidentify a given object for a series of video frames containing that object [11].

Countless approaches have been presented as solutions to the problem. The most common model for the tracking problem is the generative model, which is the basis of popular solutions such as the Kalman [12, 13] and particle filters [14].

In most systems, a robust background-subtraction algorithm needs to first pre-process each frame. This assures that static or background objects in the images are taken out of consideration. Since illumination changes frequently in videos, adaptive models of background, such as Gaussian mixture models, have been developed to intelligently adapt to nonuniform, dynamic backgrounds [15, 16].

Once the background has been subtracted out, all that remains are the foreground objects. These objects are often identified with their centroids, and it is these points that are tracked from frame to frame. Given an extracted centroid, the tracking algorithm predicts where that point should be located in the next frame.

3.3 Observing Human Activity

Many Computer Vision algorithms and techniques find applications in the implementation of interactive and smart environments. They can be (and are) effectively

Fig. 2 People detection via background subtraction. White blobs (*left*) represent foreground objects and can be used to extract user images in the original frame (*right*) to be used for tracking initialization

exploited not only for managing smart user interfaces, but also for detecting and tracking humans in the interface neighborhoods. This activity is mandatory in order to give the interactive environment awareness of the presence of humans and of their activities.

3.3.1 People Detection

The detection of people and their localization in the observed scene is a fundamental problem that has been studied since the very early years of researches in Computer Vision. Many algorithms and techniques have been developed over the year for this task, generating a vast amount of literature. Without getting into excessive details, it can be said that there are two kinds of approach to this task. The first aims at detecting the whole person, while the second tries to infer his presence by detecting some characteristic body part, like the face. In the first case, background subtraction is widely used to detect motion in the images so that the system can focus on a small subregion of the image (see Fig. 2). However, this requires the images to be taken from a static camera. Nowadays, pan-tilt-zoom (PTZ) cameras are getting more and more common. This new kind of cameras can be steered to frame a particular region of the whole environment, or even zoomed at a particular detail of the scene. With this kind of sensor, motion detection cannot be of any help in bounding the search area, and thus people detection must be achieved differently. For example, by employing trained classifiers, algorithms that are capable (after a proper training stage) to classify each subregion in the image stating if it contains a person or not. In this case, the whole image must be scanned (often at multiscale), and this is obviously time consuming.

3.3.2 People Tracking

People detection is often not enough. This can be used to activate smart user interfaces with the right timing or location, but in order to recognize people activity and to react to it, a visual tracking algorithm is necessary. Generally speaking, visual tracking is the activity of relating the image of an object (or person) detected on a given frame to the image of the same object on the subsequent frames. Through visual tracking, movements of a person can be followed in a video sequence, allowing a higher level of comprehension; for example, people walking toward an interactive surface can be distinguished from those walking away from it. Person's motion can also give rough information about where their attention is addressed. A person getting closer to a screen can be considered to be interested in what it shows, while a person moving away from it can be considered not interested or even looking for contents that could grab his attention. When a multicamera setup is used, the system can take great advantage from the capability of observing users from different viewpoints. This is a very common setup in the Smart Room scenario, since a single view point is usually not enough to allow a complete covering of the environment. A Smart Room is a particular case of smart environment, where the bounded extension and the known geometry of the space allow the placement of multiple sensors and smart interfaces in order to maximize the system knowledge about the user's activity, and consequently the user's experience within the smart environment.

In such a scenario, tracking information can then be exploited, for example, as a hint about what camera has the best view point of the target, in order to acquire detailed imagery of it.

3.3.3 Gaze Estimation

In order to be able to react to user's behaviors and wills, gaze estimation is very important. However, in order to reduce complexity, gaze estimation is often reduced to head pose estimation (i.e., the person is supposed to look in a fixed direction with respect to the head). For this reason, beside people tracking and localization, face detection and face pose estimation are widely applied in smart environments implementations.

It must be pointed out that pose estimation or even gaze estimation does not suffice for stating where a person is looking at, unless some prior knowledge about the particular camera setup is exploited. In other words, the position and orientation of each camera must be known, since this information is mandatory in order to translate the face pose information (which is relative the camera used to observe the target) into an absolute location within the environment. This is possible in a controlled environment such as a Smart Room.

The task of estimating the gaze direction of a person obviously requires head localization and tracking as a first step (see Fig. 3).

Once the head is correctly localized within the image frame, various techniques can be used to estimate the head pose. Most of them require fitting a rigid or elastic model of the face based on local features observed over the image. Under optimal conditions, this method may give accurate results. However, in the Smart Room typical scenario it can be difficult to effectively apply this method, since the lighting conditions can be poor (dim lights, shadows, reflections). Therefore, it can be necessary to settle for a more rough estimation. The small distances usually involved

Fig. 3 An example of face
detection and tracking in a
smart environment

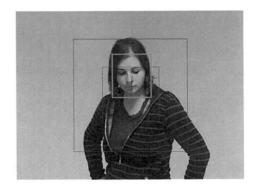

in this particular environment often allow a reasonable accuracy in the estimates,
despite the approximations.

4 State of the Art

There is a wide variety of application areas for natural Human–Computer Interaction, including information visualization, artistic installations, knowledge management software, social networking, and learning systems for disabled people. This section presents the state-of-the-art in these fields and highlights current directions for three different kinds of systems which use the natural interaction paradigm: Interactive Tabletops, Tangible user interfaces, and Smart Rooms.

4.1 Interactive Tabletop

Tabletop systems are not merely extensions of traditional desktop systems, but they refer to the interactive display surfaces that allow multiple users to interact with the digital contents on the table display, in order to support colocated concurrent activities.

Some tabletop systems consist of a projecting surface in which physical and virtual tabletop objects coexist together to implement new paradigms of interaction. An interesting example is represented by Hybrid Widgets [17], a solution based on a digital object on the display surface and a physical handle attached to it, so that users can interact with a large digital photo collection. Some solutions derive techniques from the augmented reality, like the Tablescape Plus [18], in which interactive images are projected onto vertical tabletop objects and the table surface at the same time. The IncreTable [19], a mixed reality tabletop inspired by the Incredible Machine, extends this approach to games, where players could place virtual domino blocks with digital pens or control real robots to topple over physical and virtual dominoes.

Interactive tabletop also develop new solutions for the representation of digital objects, like i-m-Top [20], a multiresolution display system, which provides a high-resolution projection image in the foveal region of the human vision by a steerable projector and a low-resolution projection image in the peripheral region by a wide-angle fixed projector. The Virtual Touch Panel Display [21] is a solution dedicated to the problem of privacy protection. It implements two diverse displays: the traditional tabletop surface and the virtual panel, an intangible and privacy-protected virtual screen created by a special optical mechanism. The EBITA framework [22] is an interesting solution to design and develop high-resolution interactive applications built on top of an Interactive Tabletop Tracking System (ITTS) using an infrared camera and a projection-based tile display, in order to create a seamless large single display.

Several applications are at last designed in the field of collaborative activities among co-located groups of people. A first example is Pictionaire [23], a tabletop system build for designers that multiple users to work with digital and physical artifacts onto an interactive high-resolution table. An interesting experiment of creative collaboration was conducted by Cao et al. [24], who used the multitouch interactive table Microsoft Surface to develop the TellTable, a new storytelling system that allows children to easily create the main elements of a story, record it, and play it back. A different approach is presented by Morris et al. [25], who focus on face-to-face collaboration and organization tasks. Their solution, called WeSearch, is a system designed to support collaborative searching and sense-making on the web for groups of four users who work at the same time around a multitouch tabletop display.

4.2 Tangible User Interface

TUIs are systems in which the user interacts with digital information via physical objects [7], used both to represent and control information.

These solutions are very popular in the field of social learning and education, like FearNot! [26], a digital storytelling environment for children, which integrates the cubic TUI called Display Cube [27] to let users to interact with the narrative of the story; or like PlayCubes [28], a dynamic tool based on the Lego-like TUI Active-Cube [29], with the objective of improving constructional ability among typically developed children; or the Music Cre8tor [30], an interactive music composition system intended for children with disabilities. The efficacy of TUIs for training were also evaluated in many situations, like for children affected by autism [31].

Tangible User Interfaces can improve quality of life; indeed, interaction paradigms like the token and constraints (TAC) [32] are used to assist cognitively impaired people for daily activities with an interactive table in a kitchen [33].

A novel approach to TUI is the Tangible Augmented Reality [34], in which the enhanced display possibilities of Augmented Reality and the intuitive manipulation of Tangible User Interfaces are combined together to develop new interfaces in the fields of music performances, collaborative games, and projected interfaces [35], in which interactive interfaces are presented on the surfaces of smart tangible objects.

Tangible technologies also take advantage of distributed environments, like for the Virtual Tug of War [36], an experimental game in which a group of children play together pulling a rope from two separate locations connected via a network connection.

At least a very interesting approach is to use a multiple-purpose framework, like the Pendaphonics [37], a tangible environment and interactive system by which it is possible to develop the design and evaluation of low-cost, flexible, and distributed tangible interaction architectures for public engagement, musical expression, and artistic performances.

4.3 Smart Room

When interaction happens inside Smart Rooms equipped with multiple audio and visual sensors, the goal is to detect, classify, and understand human activity in the space, addressing the basic questions about the "who", "where", "what", "when", and "how" of the interaction [38, 39].The goal-driven approach [40] is the most common used method to modeling the multimedia service composition which is able to reason about the users' demands and to adapt to new context situations in a nonintrusive manner. In the multimedia-enriched scenario three types of knowledge are used to support user requirements: general knowledge about life situations, such as a meeting; situation-related knowledge (e.g., the agenda of a particular meeting); live knowledge, like data gathered by sensors, external events, and user interaction [41].

Therefore, it is possible to classify the Smart Room function:

1. Annotator: a nonintrusive function, recording, and labeling events [42].
2. Assistant: semantic processing brings to adaptive actions to help the users or groups.
3. Facilitator: the environment interface is modeling to guide participants toward a goal.

It is possible to describe the enabling technologies to develop a smart meeting system based on a three-layered generic model. From physical level to semantic level, it consists of meeting capturing, meeting recognition, and semantic processing.

Regarding the meeting capturing level, audio and video sensors are used for standard capturing tasks like speech recognition, speaker identification, speech activity detector, acoustic source localization, acoustic event detection (audio), and multi-camera localization and tracking, face detection, face id, body analysis and head pose estimation, gesture recognition, object detection and analysis, text detection, and global activity detection (video). Other kind of sensors like RFID tags (Radio Frequency IDentification tags) are often used. Meeting recognition level introduces the first low-level semantic processing like gaze detection, single and group activity recognition, and id recognition. The high-level semantic processing is mainly used for activities annotation and to solve browsing issues like multidisplay mapping.

Many Computer Vision techniques are usually exploited in order to implement Smart Rooms. In fact, it is need that the environment becomes aware of the presence of people and objects moving within it, in order to interact with them.

Object tracking (which includes person tracking as a special case) has been widely studied in the last few decades, producing a wide literature. Many visual tracking techniques have been proposed over the years, each of which is usually capable of achieve good results in a particular application domain. Several classifications have been proposed, for example, in [11].

Depending on the target description, they can be grouped in points trackers (which basically make no description of the target appearance) [43, 44], shapes and contours trackers (which describe targets through their contours, thus tracking curves) [45–47], and blobs trackers (which describe targets through a pixel blob, to be characterized in some way) [48, 49].

Depending on the approach they adopt, they can be grouped in deterministic [50] and stochastic trackers [13, 14]. The former rely on the availability of a cost function whose minimum represent the object to be tracked. The latter instead try to estimate the probability density function of a random variable that describes the target position, based on iterative, noisy measures of the object position made on the image pixels.

The most recent piece of work on the topic regards stochastic, blob trackers, which make a large use of Bayesian estimation theory to give a probabilistic answer to the tracking problem. A critical problem in those trackers is the characterization of the target appearance. Despite the efforts that have been spent in the research, it still remains a hard task to find a meaningful description of an object of which often only a perspective view is known.

5 Smart Room with Tangible Natural Interaction

In this section we present a case study, a Smart Room containing different interactive systems (tabletop and walls). Such indoor environment is provided of different sensors in order to track users and analyze their behavior while they are interacting through particular kind of smart objects (TUIs).

5.1 TANGerINE Smart Room: a Case Study

Besides the interaction techniques employed to engage users in using different systems, user experience within Smart Rooms should be extended considering contextual information regarding the environment as a whole, including also the history of how the different systems are used by different users over time.

Fig. 4 A smart room divided
into Contexts and Areas

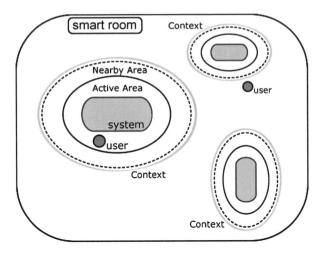

We divided the interactive environment into different contexts; each of them is conceived and defined in relation with an interactive system. Contexts are in turn physically divided into Areas (see Fig. 4):

(1) Active Area: the space where users directly interact with the system's digital contents.
(2) Nearby Area: the area right around the system, where users can still see the digital contents but cannot reach them directly.

Interactive systems like tabletops or walls engage the users in editing and arranging digital multimedia contents. It should be possible for users to move across different interactive contexts transporting with them some of these contents and other metadata regarding the user profile and his history of operations.

Instead of asking the user to explicitly authenticate every time he accesses another interactive context (going against the guidelines for natural interaction), or tracking the user actively across the space (addressing hard issues in obtaining a robust and efficient recognition, requiring a complete sensor instrumentation of the environment or forcing the users to wear some identifying device), we modeled our scenario around another entity that is the real subject of the interaction. As users interact naturally with digital elements on interactive surfaces, they are now able to transport data across different contexts just carrying with them a tangible object (TUI). In this way, tangibles involved in such systems allow intuitive manipulation of virtual objects linking them directly to those real.

In the scenario described so far, we are interested in tangibles as the embodiment of some aspects of the interaction between the user and the domain of multimedia contents handled by the application. Such tangibles can assume different roles depending on the type of workflow provided by an interactive system. If the system principally provides a "fruition" interface towards digital contents, it provides the user a presentation of choices that can be selected by using a personal smart object. Consequently, as the users move in the environment, a history of their choices is associated to the user, providing contextual information useful in the following experiences. Instead, if the system provides more production-oriented functions, in which digital contents can be arranged and manipulated, the production can be stored in the object and moved across the interactive systems in the Smart Room. In order to develop this case study, we used the TANGerINE platform. TANGerINE (TANGible Interactive Natural Environment) is a research project on tangible and natural interfaces. It was born by a collaboration between MICC—Media Integration and Communication Centre (http://www.micc.unifi.it/), University of Florence, and Micrel Lab (http://www-micrel.deis.unibo.it/), University of Bologna.

5.2 TANGerINE Smart Cube

We have designed and developed a smart-object, a physical cube-shaped object (TANGerINE SMart Cube [9]: SMCube) with accelerometer sensors on board which allows the system to understand user manipulation on it. An integrated Computer Vision module is able to track SMCubes inside an Active Area (TANGerINE tabletop) evaluating their position and rotation. SMCube is an all-round interaction tool: selector, digital object collector, manipulator, 3D avatar.

The TANGerINE SMCube (see Fig. 5) is a cube case with 6.5-cm edge. It embeds a node presented in [51], where the wireless layer includes a bluetooth transceiver and an actuation layer. The latter drives infrared LEDs placed on every face of the cube. The LEDs are arranged in order to detect the cube's coordinates on the table and its orientation and to distinguish it among different cubes [9]. The node

Fig. 5 TANGerINE SMCube electronic components

is designed for low-power operation and can run up to 12 hours with a 500-mAh battery. Each SMCube is identified by a programmable id number and can receive queries and controls to exchange bidirectional information with the context in which is placed. Its basic functionality consists in extracting tilt to derive which of the six faces is the top or the bottom face at a certain instant. The result is stored, sent, and translated in visual feedback by activating the LEDs matrix on SMCube [9].

5.2.1 Manipulation State Awareness

The accelerometer embedded in the TANGerINE SMCube provides the ability to understand if the cube is held by a person or is motionless on the tabletop. The detection is based on the tilt and has been tested taking into account noise due to furniture structural vibrations and accidental noise (keyboard typing, etc.). It is considered also the disambiguation between the "still on table" and "still in hands" cases, taking into account hands tremor and other clues.

5.2.2 Gesture Detection Algorithm

Many gesture detection algorithms are used to understand gestures and states, usually data from the three-axes accelerometer is sampled at 40 Hz into overlapped windows of 16 consecutive samples. The variance of the data within each window is used to classify the gesture performed using a C4.5 decision tree previously trained with the WEKA toolkit over a set of prestored instances. The choice of this algorithm is motivated by its easiness of implementation and the limited amount of resources needed. A valid gesture is detected when the classifier returns the same class for N ($N = 3$) consecutive windows. N defines a trade-off between robustness of classification and reactiveness.

The node can operate in one of the following mode:

- Continuous transmission: the data stream is sent to the base station.
- Periodic transmission: the active face and the gesture performed are sent periodically to the base station.
- Asynchronous transmission: the active face and the gesture performed are sent only when a change is detected.

5.2.3 Bluetooth-Based Proximity Awareness

It is possible to exploit the ability of Bluetooth protocol to discover neighbor Bluetooth devices and their identity and to exchange proximity information. In fact, by means of the inquiry procedure, the RSSI (Received Strength Signal Indicator) referred to a certain device can be read. The Bluetooth transceiver inside the TANGerINE SMCube enables the general system to use the inquiry procedure to extract its RSSI and consequently the proximity of the cube to the work area and decide to automatically associate it.

The object is therefore enabled to act as interaction device with the application. The inquiry procedure can be repeated periodically to check the proximity of other objects.

5.3 Computer Vision Applied to the TANGerINE Platform

In this section we provide the description of the Computer Vision (CV) module applied to the tabletop interface. The CV algorithm works in the tabletop Active Area (see Fig. 4), the interactive visualization surface where users interact with both physical and digital elements.

Computer Vision techniques are applied to obtain LEDs detection and tracking in order to understand TANGerINE SMCube's position on the tabletop surface. The analysis of LEDs pattern gives us the absolute orientation of the SMCube (see Fig. 6).

Infrared LEDs mounted on the cube's faces are easily detected by a monochrome camera equipped with a matching band-pass filter (see Fig. 7).

For each frame of video (captured at 60 fps at a resolution of 752×480 pixels), just simple image processing operations (noise removal, background subtraction, thresholding, and connected components analysis) are done. For every point (blob) detected, an algorithm is run in order to search for a known pattern. The matrix of LEDs pictured in Fig. 7 has been designed to provide both the two-dimensional orientation of the cube and the identification of the cube. The orientation is evaluated

Fig. 6 TANGerINE SMCube onto the TANGerINE tabletop

Fig. 7 TANGerINE SMCube
LED matrix

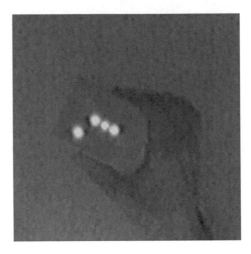

in relation to the absolute axis perpendicular to the table surface. The cube form-factor and the border size of the face provide enough space to avoid ambiguous detections, allowing cubes to be adjacent in every orientation.

5.4 Observing Human Activity in TANGerINE Smart Room

As stated in Sect. 3.2, there are many Computer Vision techniques that can be exploited in a Smart Room scenario in order to make the system aware of the users' presence. In the following, we refer to a particular Smart Room implementation with the facilitator function: smart interfaces embedded in the environment are used to guide participants toward a (common) goal (see Sect. 4.3). As stated in Sect. 5.1, the TANGerINE Smart Room can host several interactive surfaces. To ensure the maximum level of responsiveness while keeping the computational load within reasonable boundaries, users are detected and tracked since they enter the Nearby Area of each interactive surface (see Fig. 4). For this task, several cameras are used. First of all, a ceiling-mounted fish-eye camera is used to acquire an overall view of the Smart Room. In case the field of view of a single camera is too small, a ceiling-mounted camera for each surface can be employed. From this static point of view, background modeling and background subtraction can be used to detect motion in the environment and thus to detect users moving around the interactive surfaces. Images are acquired in near infrared in order to obtain better illumination conditions. Noise reduction, thresholding, and several morphological operators are employed to accurately detect and segment foreground objects as pixel "blobs." After selecting people blobs from the set of foreground blobs detected over the image, it is needed to associate each of them with the id of a user being tracked by the system. Position and size of each blob can appear to be flickering because of several factors that can lead to inaccurate segmentation of the foreground with respect to the background. These values can however be considered as noisy measures of the actual position and size of the target users. To achieve accurate persons tracking a particle filter algorithm is used to process these noisy measures. Particle filtering is a Bayesian filtering technique capable of estimating the probability density function of a state vector value which, in our case, represents each person's position and size inside the TANGerINE Smart Room. The particle filter has the ability of estimating multi-modal distribution, thus managing multiple hypothesis about the targets position.

One of the key features of the TANGerINE framework is to make the smart environment aware of the presence and of the interests of the users. To achieve this result, it is important to estimate the focus of attention of the Smart Room users. Given the particular environment and the typical use cases of the TANGerINE Smart Room, it is impossible to achieve such a result without using a rich setup of fixed and/or PTZ cameras. Since the gaze is the most relevant hint for the focus of attention esti-mation, information provided by the people tracker is used together with the known position and orientation of the cameras, to choose the most convenient point of view to acquire high-resolution images of the user's face. This way, head pose estimation becomes feasible. Usually, head pose estimation is achieved in two steps. First, the head must be accurately localized. Since the goal is to estimate the gaze direction, the problem can be reduced to face detection and thus addressed by using trained classifiers or skin detectors (which are commonly used in these cases). Then, pro-vided that a convenient portion of the face is visible, a rigid or elastic model of the face is fitted on the head image, based on the observation of some low-level fea-tures taken over the image. This method usually leads to a quite accurate estimation of the gaze but requires optimal conditions of operations that are not always avail-able. Instead, in the TANGerINE framework we exploit a more rough method that can be applied more easily. The method exploits different AdaBoost-based detec-tors, trained on different face poses, to detect the face and at the same time provide a rough estimation of the gaze, based on the classification confidence of each of them. In other words, each detector votes for its canonical pose, and the fusion of all detectors' [52] output lead to the final pose estimation. Though the information is quite rough, the small distances involved within the typical Nearby Area allow to bound a reasonable subregion of interest within each active surfaces where the users attention is addressed. Once the system has succeeded in estimating the focus of attention of a Smart Room user, appropriate methods to facilitate his interaction and provide a more meaningful experience can be activated.

References

1. Hewett, Baecker, Card, Carey, Gasen, Mantei, Perlman, Strong, Verplank: ACM SIGCHI, Curricula for Human–Computer Interaction (1997). http://old.sigchi.org/cdg/. Accessed 15 April 2010
2. Wania, C.E., Atwood, M.E., McCain, K.W.: How do design and evaluation interrelate in HCI research. In: Proceedings of the 6th Conference on Designing Interactive Systems, pp. 90–98. ACM, New York (2006)
3. Norman, D.A.: The Design of Everyday Things. MIT Press, Cambridge (1998)
4. Marsic, I., Medl, A., Flanagan, J.: Natural communication with information systems. Proc. IEEE 88(8), 1354–1366 (2000)

5. Norman, D.A.: The Invisible Computer. MIT Press, Cambridge (1999)
6. Weiser, M., Brown, J.S.: Designing calm technology. PowerGrid Journal, vol. 1.01 (1996)
7. Ishii, H., Ullmer, B.: Tangible bits: towards seamless interfaces between people, bits and atoms. In: Proc. ACM CHI on Human Factors in Computing Systems Conference (1997)
8. Fishkin, K.P.: A taxonomy for and analysis of tangible interfaces. Pers. Ubiquitous Comput. 8(5), 347–358 (2004)
9. Baraldi, S., Del Bimbo, A., Landucci, L., Torpei, N., Cafini, O., Farella, E., Pieracci, A., Benini, L.: Introducing TANGerINE: a tangible interactive natural environment. In: Proc. ACM Multimedia (2007)
10. Suzuki, K., Horiba, I., Sugie, N.: Linear-time connected-component labeling based on sequential local operations. Comput. Vis. Image Underst. (2003). doi:10.1016/S1077-3142(02)00030-9
11. Yilmaz, A., Javed, O., Shah, M.: Object tracking: a survey. ACM Comput. Surv. (2006). doi:10.1145/1177352.1177355
12. Welch, G., Bishop, G.: An introduction to the Kalman filter. Technical Report, TR 95-041, University of North Carolina at Chapel Hill (2004)
13. Wan, E.A., der Merwe, R.V.: The unscented Kalman filter for non-linear estimation. In: Proc. of Symposium 2001 on Adaptive Systems for Signal Processing, Communications and Control (2000)
14. Arulampalam, S., Maskell, S., Gordon, N., Clapp, T.: A tutorial on particle filters for on-line non-linear/non-Gaussian Bayesian tracking. IEEE Trans. Signal Process. (2002). doi:10.1234/12345678
15. Wren, C.R., Azarbayejani, A., Darrell, T., Pentland, A.: Pfinder: real-time tracking of the human body. IEEE Trans. Pattern Anal. Mach. Intell. 19(7), 780–785 (1997)
16. Stauffer, C., Grimson, W.: Adaptive background mixture models for real-time tracking. In: Proc. of CVPR, pp. 246–252 (1999)
17. Butz, A., Hilliges, O., Terrenghi, L., Baur, D.: Hybrid widgets on an interactive tabletop. In: Extended Abstracts of the Ninth International Conference on Ubiquitous Computing (2007)
18. Kakehi, Y., Naemura, T., Matsushita, M.: Tablescape plus: interactive small-sized vertical displays on a horizontal tabletop display. In: TABLETOP '07, Second Annual IEEE International Workshop on Digital Object, pp. 155–162 (2007)
19. Leitner, J., Haller, M., Yun, K., Woo, W., Sugimoto, M., Inami, M.: IncreTable, a mixed reality tabletop game experience. In: Proc. of the 2008 International Conference on Advances in Computer Entertainment Technology (2008). doi:10.1145/1501750.1501753
20. Hu, T.-T., Chia, Y.-W., Chan, L.-W., Hung, Y.-P., Hsu, J.: I-m-Top: an interactive multi-resolution tabletop system accommodating to multi-resolution human vision. In: Horizontal Interactive Human Computer Systems (2008). doi:10.1109/TABLETOP.2008.4660202
21. Chan, L.-W., Hu, T.-T., Lin, J.-Y., Hung, Y.-P., Hsu, J.: On top of tabletop: a virtual touch panel display. In: Horizontal Interactive Human Computer Systems (2008). doi:10.1109/TABLETOP.2008.4660201
22. Kim, M., Cho, Y., Park, K.S.: Design and development of a distributed tabletop system using EBITA framework. In: Ubiquitous Information Technologies & Applications (2009). doi:10.1109/ICUT.2009.5405719
23. Hartmann, B., Morris, M.R., Benko, H., Wilson, A.D.: Pictionaire: supporting collaborative design work by integrating physical and digital artifacts. In: Proc. of the 2010 ACM Conference on Computer Supported Cooperative Work (2010). doi:10.1145/1718918.1718989
24. Cao, X., Lindley, S.E., Helmes, J., Sellen, A.: Telling the whole story: anticipation, inspiration and reputation in a field deployment of TellTable. In: Proc. of the 2010 ACM Conference on Computer Supported Cooperative Work (2010). doi:10.1145/1718918.1718967
25. Morris, M.R., Lombardo, J., Wigdor, D.: WeSearch: supporting collaborative search and sensemaking on a tabletop display. In: Proc. of the 2010 ACM Conference on Computer Supported Cooperative Work (2010). doi:10.1145/1718918.1718987
26. Leichtenstern, K., Andre, E., Losch, E., Kranz, M., Holleis, P.: A tangible user interface as interaction and presentation device to a social learning software. In: Networked Sensing Systems (2007). doi:10.1109/INSS.2007.4297402

27. Kranz, M., Schmidt, D., Holleis, P., Schmidt, A.: A display cube as tangible user interface. In: Adjunct Proc. of the Seventh International Conference on Ubiquitous Computing (Demo 22) (2005)

28. Jacoby, S., Gutwillig, G., Jacoby, D., Josman, N., Weiss, P.L., Koike, M., Itoh, Y., Kawai, N., Kitamura, Y., Sharlin, E.: PlayCubes: monitoring constructional ability in children using a tangible user interface and a playful virtual environment. In: Virtual Rehabilitation International Conference, pp. 42–49 (2009)

29. Kitamura, Y., Itoh, Y., Kishino, F.: Real-time 3D interaction with ActiveCube. In: CHI '01 Extended Abstracts on Human Factors in Computing Systems (2001). doi:10.1145/634067.634277

30. Rigler, J., Seldess, Z.: The music Cre8tor: an interactive system for musical exploration and education. In: Proc. of the 7th International Conference on New Interfaces for Musical (2007). doi:10.1145/1279740.1279842

31. Sitdhisanguan, K., Chotikakamthorn, N., Dechaboon, A., Out, P.: Evaluation the efficacy of computer-based training using tangible user interface for low-function children with autism. In: Digital Games and Intelligent Toys Based Education (2008). doi:10.1109/DIGITEL.2008.28

32. Ullmer, B., Ishii, H., Jacob, R.J.: Token+constraint systems for tangible interaction with digital information. ACM Trans. Comput.-Hum. Interact (2005). doi:10.1145/1057237.1057242

33. Boussemart, B., Giroux, S.: Tangible user interfaces for cognitive assistance. In: Proc. of the 21st International Conference on Advanced Information Networking and Applications Workshops (2007). doi:10.1109/AINAW.2007.346

34. Billinghurst, M., Kato, H., Poupyrev, I.: Tangible augmented reality. In: ACM SIGGRAPH ASIA 2008 Courses (2008). doi:10.1145/1508044.1508051

35. Molyneaux, D., Gellersen, H.: Projected interfaces: enabling serendipitous interaction with smart tangible objects. In: Proc. of the 3rd International Conference on Tangible and Embedded Interaction (2009). doi:10.1145/1517664.1517741

36. Harfield, A., Jormanainen, I., Shujau, H.: First steps in distributed tangible technologies: a virtual tug of war. In: Proc. of the 8th International Conference on Interaction Design and Children (2009). doi:10.1145/1551788.1551822

37. Hansen, A.S., Overholt, D., Burleson, W., Jensen, C.N., Lahey, B., Muldner, K.: Pendaphonics: an engaging tangible pendulum-based sonic interaction experience. In: Proceedings of the 8th International Conference on Interaction Design and Children (2009). doi:10.1145/1551788.1551859

38. Potamianos, G.: Audio-visual technologies for lecture and meeting analysis inside smart rooms. In: Proc. HCSNet Workshop on the Use of Vision in Human–Computer Interaction (2006)

39. Potamianos, G., Zhang, Z.: A joint system for single-person 2D-face and 3D-head tracking in CHIL seminars. In: Stiefelhagen, R., Garofolo, J. (eds.), Lecture Notes in Computer Science, vol. 4122. Springer, Berlin (2006)

40. Hummel, K.A., et al.: Supporting meetings with a goal-driven service-oriented multimedia environment. In: 1st ACM International Workshop on Multimedia Service Composition (2005)

41. Yu, Z., Ozeki, M., Fujii, Y., Nakamura, Y.: Towards smart meeting: enabling technologies and a real-world application. In: Proc. of the 9th ACM International Conference on Multimodal Interfaces (2007). doi:10.1145/1322192.1322210

42. Chen, H., Perich, F., Chakraborty, D., Finin, T., Joshi, A.: Intelligent agents meet semantic web in a smart meeting room. In: IEEE Internet Computing, pp. 854–861 (2004)

43. Veenman, C., Reinders, M., Backer, E.: Resolving motion correspondence for densely moving points. IEEE Trans. Pattern Anal. Mach. Intell. **23**, 54–72 (2001)

44. Serby, D., Meier, E., Van Gool, L.: Probabilistic object tracking using multiple features. In: Proc. 17th International Conference on Pattern Recognition, vol. 2, pp. 184–187 (2004)

45. Isard, M., Blake, A.: CONDENSATION—conditional density propagation for visual tracking. Int. J. Comput. Vis. **29**, 5–28 (1998)

46. Comaniciu, D., Ramesh, V., Meer, P.: Kernel based object tracking. IEEE Trans. Pattern Anal. Mach. Intell. **25**, 564–575 (2003)

47. Yilmaz, A., Li, X., Shah, M.: Contour-based object tracking with occlusion handling in video acquired using mobile cameras. IEEE Trans. Pattern Anal. Mach. Intell. **26**, 1531–1536 (2004)
48. Nummiaro, K., Koller-Meier, E., Gool, L.V.: An adaptive color-based particle filter. Image Vis. Comput. **21**, 99–110 (2002)
49. Bagdanov, A.D., Dini, F., Del Bimbo, A., Nunziati, W.: Improving the robustness of particle filter-based visual trackers using online parameter adaptation. In: Proc. of IEEE International Conference on Advanced Video and Signal based Surveillance (2007)
50. Allen, J.G., Xu, R.Y.D., Jin, J.S.: Object tracking using CamShift algorithm and multiple quantized feature spaces. In: Proc. of VIP '05, Australian Computer Society, Inc. (2005)
51. Baraldi, S., Del Bimbo, A., Landucci, L., Torpei, N., Cafini, O., Farella, E., Zappi, P., Benini, L.: Tangerine SMCube: a smart device for human computer interaction. In: Proc. of 3th European Conference on Smart Sensing & Context (2008)
52. Viola, P., Jones, M.: Robust real-time object detection. Int. J. Comput. Vis. (2001). doi:10.1234/12345678

Gesture Control for Consumer Electronics

Caifeng Shan

Abstract The user interfaces of Consumer Electronics (CE) have been limited to devices such as remote control and keypad for a long time. With digital contents becoming more and more complex and interconnected, consumers are expecting more natural and powerful user interfaces. Automatic recognition of human gestures provides a promising solution for natural user interfaces. Recent years have witnessed much interest on gesture control in CE industry. In this chapter, we present a review on gesture control technologies for CE devices. We introduce different sensing technologies and then focus on camera-based gesture sensing and interpretation. Computer vision research on different steps, including face/hand detection, tracking, and gesture recognition, are discussed. We also introduce the latest developments on gesture control products and applications.

1 Introduction

The user interfaces of Consumer Electronics (CE) products (e.g., TV) have been limited to devices such as remote control and keypad for a long time. These interfaces are neither natural nor flexible for users and limit the speed of interaction. With digital contents becoming more and more complex and interconnected, consumers are expecting natural and efficient user interfaces.

Audition and vision are two important modalities for human–human interaction. The more efficient and powerful user interfaces can be achieved if the machines could "listen" and "see" as humans do. Automatic speech recognition has been well studied, and many commercial systems have been available. Voice-based interfaces have the advantage of a preestablished vocabulary (natural language). However, it may be inappropriate both for the protracted issuing of commands and for changing parameters by increments such as volume control. Moreover, in noisy environments

C. Shan (✉)
Philips Research, Eindhoven, The Netherlands
e-mail: caifeng.shan@philips.com

L. Shao et al. (eds.), *Multimedia Interaction and Intelligent User Interfaces,*
Advances in Pattern Recognition,
DOI 10.1007/978-1-84996-507-1_5, © Springer-Verlag London Limited 2010

(both indoor and outdoor), it is difficult to use voice control. On the contrary, vision-based interfaces provide a promising alternative in many cases. With the advances of sensing hardware and computing power, visual sensing and interpretation of human motion has received much interest in recent years.

Human gestures are meaningful or intentional body movements, i.e., physical movements of the fingers, hands, arms, head, face, or body, for example, hand gestures, head pose and movements, facial expressions, eye movements, and body gestures. Gestures can be used as replacement for speech words or used together with speech words. As a universal body language, the gesture is one of the most natural and effective means for humans to communicate nonverbally. The ability to recognize gestures is indispensable and important for successful interpersonal social interaction. Automatic recognition of human gestures is a key component for intelligent user interfaces. Gesture recognition has been an active research area in multiple disciplines including natural language processing, computer vision, pattern recognition, and human–computer interaction [1–3]. Recent years have witnessed much interest on gesture control in CE industry [4, 5]. Gesture control has many applications, for example, virtual remote control for a TV or other home appliances, gaming, and browsing public information terminals in museums, window shops, and other public spaces. In recent Consumer Electronics Shows (CES), many companies showed prototypes or upcoming products with gesture control.

In this chapter, we present an overview on gesture recognition technologies for CE devices. The human body can express a huge variety of gestures, and hand and arm gestures have received the most attention in research community [2]. We introduce different sensors that can be used for gesture sensing and then focus on camera-based computer vision technologies. Three main components of vision-based gesture recognition, including face/hand detection, tracking, and gesture recognition, are discussed. We also introduce the latest developments on gesture control products and applications. The chapter is organized as follows. We introduce the sensing technologies in Sect. 2. Section 3 discusses the existing research on vision-based gesture recognition. We describe the gesture-control applications and products in Sect. 4. Finally, Sect. 5 concludes the paper with discussions.

2 Sensing Technologies

Different sensing technologies can be used for gesture recognition. Instrumented gloves (including exoskeleton devices mounted on the hand and fingers) can be wear to measure the position and configuration of the hand. Similarly, in some optical systems, markers are placed on the body in order to measure body motion accurately. Two types of markers, passive, such as reflective markers, and active, such as markers flashing LED lights, can be used. Although these methods can provide reliable and precise gesture data (e.g., parameters of hand and fingers), the user has to wear the expensive and cumbersome device with reduced comfort; the calibration needed can also be difficult [2]. Therefore they are too intrusive for mainstream use in CE devices. In the following, we introduce some enabling technologies that can be considered for CE devices. These sensors can be categorized into two kinds: (1) contact-based sensors, for example, multitouch screen and accelerometer, and (2) contact-free sensors such as cameras.

Haptics   Gestures can be sensed through haptic sensors. This is one of the commonly used gesture-sensing technologies in current CE devices, for instance, touch or multitouch screens (e.g., tablet PC and Apple iPhone). It is similar to recognizing gestures from 2D input devices such as a pen or mouse. In [6], multitouch gestural interactions were recognized using Hidden Markov Models (HMM). Haptic gesture sensing and interpretation is relatively straightforward as compared with vision-based techniques. However, it requires the availability of a flat surface or screen, and the user has to touch the surface for input. This is often too constraining, and techniques that allow the user to move around and interact in more natural ways are more compelling [2].

Handhold Sensors   Another approach to gesture recognition is the use of handhold sensors. For example, in a presentation product from iMatt [7], the presenter can interact with the projector and screen using gestures, which are sensed by a handhold remote control. Similarly, Cybernet Systems [8] developed a weather map management system enabling the meteorologist to control visual effects using hand gestures that are sensed with a handhold remote control. Accelerometers and gyroscopes [9] are two types of sensors used, which measure the variation of the earth magnetic field in order to detect the motion. The Wii-mote from Nintendo uses built-in accelerometers to measure the game player's gestures. Another example is the MX Air Mouse from Logitech, which can be waved around to control programs via gestures, based on the built-in accelerometers. Since the user has to hold the sensor, this technique is often intrusive, requiring the user's cooperation.

Vision   Vision-based gesture control relies on one or several cameras to capture the gesture sequences; computer vision algorithms are used to analyze and interpret captured gestures. Although, as discussed above, some vision systems require the user to wear special markers, vision-based techniques have focused on marker-free solutions. With camera sensors becoming low-cost and pervasive in CE products, vision technologies have received increasing attention, which allow unobtrusive and passive gesture sensing. Different kinds of camera sensors have been considered. Near Infrared (IR) cameras can be used to address insufficient lighting or lighting variations [10, 11]. Stereo cameras or time-of-flight cameras can deliver the depth information, which enables more straightforward and accurate gesture recognition. Vision-based gesture recognition approaches normally consist of three components: body part detection, tracking, and gesture recognition. We will discuss these in details in Sect. 3.

Ultrasound   Ultrasonic sensors can also be used to detect and track gestures. For example, NaviSense [12] and EllipticLabs [13] developed ultrasound-based finger/hand gesture recognition systems (illustrated in Fig. 1). The iPoint system from

 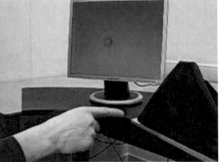

Fig. 1 Ultrasound based gesture control from NaviSense [12] (*Left*) and EllipticLabs [13] (*Right*)

NaviSense is able to track finger movements to navigate and control a cursor on the display, which can be used in mobile devices to support touchless messaging. The problems of using ultrasonic sensors were discussed in [9, 14].

Infrared Proximity Sensing   Recently Microsoft [15] has developed a gesture control interface for mobile phones based on IR proximity sensors. As shown in Fig. 2, IR signal is shone outwards from the device via a series of IR LEDs embedded along each side; reflections from nearby objects (e.g., fingers) are sensed using an array of IR photodiodes. When the device is put on a flat surface (e.g., table), the user can perform single and multitouch gestures using the space around the mobile device. In the Virtual Projection Keyboard [16], an image of the full-size keyboard is projected onto a flat surface. When the user presses a key on the projected keyboard, the IR layer is interrupted; the reflections are recognized in three dimensions (Fig. 2).

Each sensing technology has its limitations, so it is promising to combine different sensors for better gesture recognition. However, the integration of multiple sensors is complex, since each technology varies along several dimensions, including accuracy, resolution, latency, range of motion, user comfort, and cost.

3 Vision-Based Gesture Recognition

A first prototype of vision-based gesture control for CE devices can be tracked back to 1995 [17], when Freeman and Weissman developed a gesture control for TVs. As shown in Fig. 3, by exploiting the visual feedback from the TV, their system enables a user to adjust graphical controls by moving the hand. A typical interaction session is the following: (1) TV is off but searching for the trigger gesture (open hand); (2) When TV detects the trigger gesture, TV turns on, and the hand icon and graphics overlays appear; (3) The hand icon follows the user's hand movement, and a command is executed when the hand covers a control for 200 ms; (4) User closes hand to leave the control mode, and the hand icon and graphical control disappear

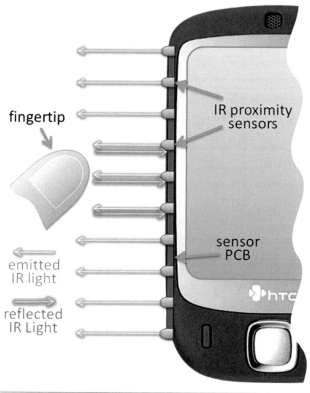

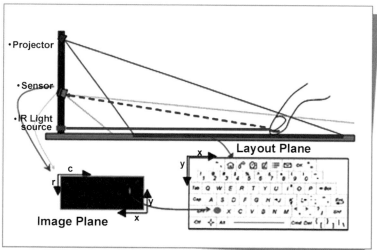

Fig. 2 IR reflection-based gesture control: (*Top*) SideSight [15]; (*Bottom*) Virtual Projection Keyboard [16]

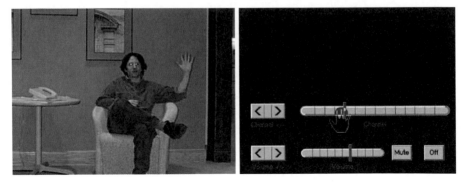

Fig. 3 Gesture control for TV [17]: the tracked hand is echoed with a hand icon on the TV

after one second. This gesture recognition system was also applied to interactive video games [18].

The general approach to vision-based gesture recognition consists of three steps: body part detection, tracking, and gesture recognition. The first step is to automatically find the body part of interest (e.g., face, hand, etc.) in the input image. Initialized by the detection, a visual tracking method is normally adopted to track the body part over time. Based on the tracked (or detected) body part, gesture recognition is thereafter performed, which can be static posture recognition in the single frame or dynamic gesture recognition in the sequence. In this section, we review research in each of these steps.

3.1 Body Part Detection

The face and hands are the major body parts involved in gesture interaction, with the ability of expressing a huge number of gestures. Most of gesture recognition systems developed so far target recognizing hand gestures and face/head gestures. In these systems, face detection and/or hand detection are required as the first step. In the following, we introduce existing work in these topics.

Face detection plays a crucial role in face-related vision applications. Due to its practical importance, face detection has attracted a great amount of interest, and numerous techniques have been investigated over the years (see [19] for a survey). In these methods, facial features, such as edge, intensity, shape, texture, and color, are extracted to locate the faces using statistical or geometric models. The face detection scheme proposed by Viola and Jones [20, 21] is arguably the most commonly employed frontal face detector, which consists of a cascade of classifiers trained by AdaBoost employing Haar-wavelet features. AdaBoost [22, 23] provides a simple yet effective approach for stagewise learning of a nonlinear classification function. Later their approach was extended with rotated Haar-like features and different boosting algorithms [24]. In [25], by incorporating Floating Search into AdaBoost, FloatBoost was proposed for improved performance on multiview face detection.

Many other machine learning techniques, such as Neural Network and Support Vector Machine (SVM), have also been introduced for face detection. In [26], the Bayes classifier was adopted with discriminating feature analysis for frontal face detection. The input image, its 1D Haar-wavelet representation, and its amplitude projections are combined to derive a discriminating feature vector. Later the features were extended and combined with an SVM-based classifier [27]. To improve the detection efficiency, Garcia and Delakis [28] designed a convolutional neural network for face detection, which performs simple convolutional and subsampling operations. More recently, the approach in [26], Viola and Jones's approach [20, 21], and the approach in [28] are modified and combined for a fast and robust face detector in [29]. Overall, face detection technique is fairly mature, and a number of reliable face detectors have been built based on existing approaches.

Compared to face detection, less work has been done on finding hands in images [30]. Most earlier attempts to hand detection make assumptions or place restrictions on the environment. For example, in the prototype developed in [17], a hand template was used for hand detection and tracking based on normalized correlation of local orientations. Their approach works with clean background and could fail in case of cluttered background. Skin color is one of the distinctive features of hands. Zhu et al. [31] presented a skin color-based hand detector. Skin color can be modeled in different color spaces using nonparametric (e.g., color histograms) or parametric (e.g., Gaussian Mixture Models) methods. Skin color-based methods may fail if skin-colored objects exist in background. Furthermore, lighting conditions (e.g., insufficient lighting) could also make them less reliable. With a skin color prior, Bretzner et al. [32] used multiscale blob detection of color features to detect an open hand with possibly some of the fingers extended. Kölsch and Turk [33] presented an approach to finding hands in grey-level images based on their appearance and texture. They studied view-specific hand detection following the Viola and Jones' method [20]. To address the high computational cost in training, a frequency analysis-based method was introduced for instantaneous estimation of class separability, without the need for training. In [34], a hand detector was built based on boosted classifiers, which achieves compelling results for view- and posture-independent hand detection.

Considering gradient features could better encode relevant hand structures, Zondag et al. [35] recently investigated Histogram of Oriented Gradients (HOG) features for real-time hand detector. Cluttered background and variable illumination were considered in their data (shown in Fig. 4). Toshiba has developed a gesture control system for displays [36, 37]. The system initially performs face detection. Once a face is detected, the user is prompted to show an open hand gesture within the area below the face (as shown in Fig. 5), which works for multiple users. The scale of the detected face is used to define the size of the interaction area, and the areas are ordered according to scale, giving easier access to users who are closer to the camera. The first detection of an open hand triggers the gesture tracking and recognition. Face recognition is also triggered by hand detection, and the content and functionality can be customized according to the user's profile.

Fig. 4 Positive and negative examples for hand detection [35]

Fig. 5 Toshiba's gesture control is initialized by face detection and hand detection [36, 37]

3.2 Gesture Tracking

After detecting the body part of interest (e.g., face or hand), a tracking method is usually needed to track the gesture over time. Visual tracking in complex environments, a challenging issue in computer vision, has been intensively studied in the last decades (see [38] for a survey). Here we review relevant work on gesture tracking, mainly hand tracking and face/head tracking.

Hand tracking, aiming to estimate continuous hand motion in image sequences, is a difficult but essential step for hand gesture recognition. A hand can be represented by contours [39, 40], fingertips [41], color [42], texture, and so on. The edge feature-based hand tracker in [17] works when the hand moves slowly but tends to be unstable when motion blur occurs. Isard and Blake [40] adopted parameterized B-spline curves to model hand contours and tracked hands by tracking the deformed curves. However, the contour-based trackers usually constrain the viewpoint [39] and assume that hands keep several predefined shapes. Oka et al. [41] exploited fingertips for hand tracking. Many color-based trackers have been utilized to track hand motion based on skin color cues [42, 43].

In order to overcome limitations of each individual feature, many approaches have considered multiple cues for hand tracking [44–48]. In [45], the contour-based hand tracker was augmented by skin-colored blob tracking. Huang and Reid [44] developed a Joint Bayes Filter for tracking and recognition of the articulated hand motion, where particle filtering [49] was adopted for color-region tracking to assist HMM in analyzing hand shape variations. Kölsch and Turk [47] presented a multicue tracker that combines color and short tracks of local features under "flocking" constraints; the color model is automatically initialized from hand detection. However, this approach struggles with rapid hand motion and skin-colored background objects. In [50], we combined particle filtering and mean shift [51, 52] for real-time hand tracking in dynamic environments, where skin color and motion were utilized for hand representation. In [36], normalized cross-correlation (NCC) was adopted for frontal fist tracking, which works for slow hand motion. In case of failure, a second tracker using color and motion (CM) was used. NCC tracker and CM tracker were switched online, and a Kalman filter was used to combine the estimates with a constant-velocity dynamic model.

Another kind of approaches to hand tracking is based on 3D model [53–57]. These methods have the ability to cope with occlusion and self-occlusion and can potentially obtain detailed and accurate gesture data. Usually, the state of a hand is estimated by projecting the prestored 3D hand model to the image plane and comparing it with image features. Lu et al. [53] presented a model-based approach to integrate multiple cues, including edges, optical flow, and shading information, for articulated hand motion tracking. In [58], the eigen-dynamics was introduced to model the dynamics of natural hand motion. Hand motion was modeled as a high-order stochastic linear dynamic system (LDS) consisting of five low-order LDSs, each of which corresponds to one eigen-dynamics. Sudderth et al. [55] adopted nonparametric belief propagation for visual tracking of a geometric hand model. 3D hand tracking can also base on 3D data obtained by stereo cameras or scanners [59]. In [60], a 3D search volume was set for efficient palm tracking using two cameras.

Face/head tracking has been widely studied in the literature because of its practical importance. Reliable head tracking is difficult due to appearance variations caused by the nonrigid structure, occlusions, and environmental changes (e.g., illumination). 3D head models have been utilized to analyze head movements. Basu et al. [61] adopted a 3D rigid ellipsoidal head model for head tracking, where the optical flow was interpreted in terms of rigid motions. Cascia et al. [62] presented a 3D cylinder head model and formulated head tracking as an image registration problem in the cylinder's texture map image. To avoid the troubles of 3D model maintenance and camera calibration, view-based 2D face models have also been proposed, such as Active Appearance Model [63] and bunch graph model of Gabor jets [64]. Tu et al. [65] investigated head pose tracking in low-resolution video by modeling facial appearance variations online with incremental weighted PCA.

We introduced in [66] a probabilistic framework for simultaneous head tracking and pose estimation. By embedding the pose variable into the motion state, head

| (a) | (b) | (c) | (d) | (e) |

Fig. 6 Simultaneous head tracking and pose estimation using particle filtering. (**a**) An input frame. (**b**) Particles are resampled and propagated in the location space. (**c**) Weighted resampling is performed with respect to the skin-color-based importance function. (**d**) Particles are weighted by the shape likelihood function, and the particles with high likelihoods are resampled (we show here 10 particles for illustration) for propagation and evaluation in the pose space. (**e**) The particles are evaluated in the pose space, and the final result is obtain by the MAP estimation

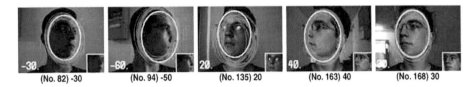

| (No. 82) -30 | (No. 94) -50 | (No. 135) 20 | (No. 163) 40 | (No. 168) 30 |

Fig. 7 Head tracking and pose estimation results in one sequence

pose tracking and recognition were formulated as a sequential maximum a posteriori (MAP) estimation problem solved by particle filtering. Faces were represented by ellipses bounding them. We adopted the partitioned sampling [67] to divide the state space into partitions, allowing efficient tracking with a small number of particles. Some intermediate results in one example frame are shown in Fig. 6. Figure 7 shows some examples of head tracking and pose estimation in one sequence. Based on our approach, a real-time head control interface for a robotic wheelchair was implemented.

Adaptation to changing appearance and scene conditions is a critical property a hand or head tracker should satisfy. Ross et al. [68] represented the target in a low-dimensional subspace which is adaptively updated using the tracking results. In [69], Grabner et al. introduced the online boosting for adaptive tracking, which allows online updating of discriminative features of the target object. Compared to the approaches using a fixed target model such as [70], these adaptive trackers are more robust to appearance changes in video sequences. One main drawback of these adaptive approaches is their susceptibility to drift, i.e., gradually adapting to nontargets, because the target model is updated according to the tracked results, which could be with errors. To address this problem, a mechanism for detecting or correcting drift should be introduced. In [71], global constraints on the overall appearance of the face were added. Grabner et al. [72] introduced an online semi-supervised boosting to alleviate the problem. They formulated the update process in a semi-supervised fashion which uses the labeled data as a prior and the data collected during tracking as unlabeled samples.

3.3 Gesture Recognition

Human gestures include static configurations and postures (e.g., hand posture, head pose, facial expression, and body posture) and dynamic gestures (e.g, hand gesture, head gestures like shaking and nodding, facial action like raising the eyebrows, and body gestures). Therefore, gesture recognition can be categorized as static posture recognition and dynamic gesture recognition. A static posture is represented by a single image, while a dynamic gesture is represented by a sequence of images.

In [17, 18, 73], Freeman et al. adopted steerable filters to derive local orientations of the input image and then used the orientation histogram to represent hand posture. The local orientation measurements are less sensitive to lighting changes. Figure 8 illustrates the orientation histograms of several hand postures. To make it work in complex background, in [74], we first derived the hand contour based on skin color and then computed the orientation histograms of hand contour for posture recognition. The process is shown in Fig. 9. In [75], Gabor Jets were adopted as local image description for hand posture recognition in complex backgrounds. Fourier descriptors were exploited in [43] to represent the segmented hand shape.

Starner et al. [10] developed a wearable hand control device for home appliances. By placing a camera on the user body, occlusion problems can be minimized. To make the system work in a variety of lighting conditions, even in the dark, the camera is ringed by near Infrared LEDs and has an infrared-pass filter mounted in the front (see Fig. 10). The prototype can recognize four hand poses (Fig. 10) and six dynamic gestures. Region-growing was used to segment hand region, and a set of eight statistics were extracted from the blob for posture description. In [76, 77], Kösch et al. presented a mobile gesture interface that allows control of wearable computer with hand postures. They used a texture-based approach to classify tracked hand regions into seven classes (six postures and "no known hand posture"). A gesture control interface for CE devices was presented in [78], in which seven hand postures were defined. In the prototype, the hand is segmented using a skin color model in the YCbCr color space, and moment invariants are extracted for posture recognition using a neural network classifier.

Dynamic gestures are characterized by the spatio-temporal motion structures in image sequences. A static posture can be regarded as a state of a dynamic gesture. Handwriting with a pen or mouse in 2D input devices is dynamic gestures that had been well studied [2]; many commercial systems of pen-based gesture recognition have been available since the 1970s. However, compared with pen-based gestural system, the visual interpretation of dynamic gestures is much more complex and difficult. Two main difficulties are: (1) temporal segmentation ambiguity, i.e., how to decide the starting and ending points of continuous gestures. The existing systems usually require a starting position in time and/or space or use static pose to segment gestures. (2) spatial-temporal variability. This is because gestures vary among individuals, which even vary from instance to instance for a given individual.

Many methods used in speech recognition can be borrowed for dynamic gesture recognition because of the similarity of the domains, for example, Dynamic Time Warping (DTW) and Hidden Markov Model [43, 79]. Other approaches, including

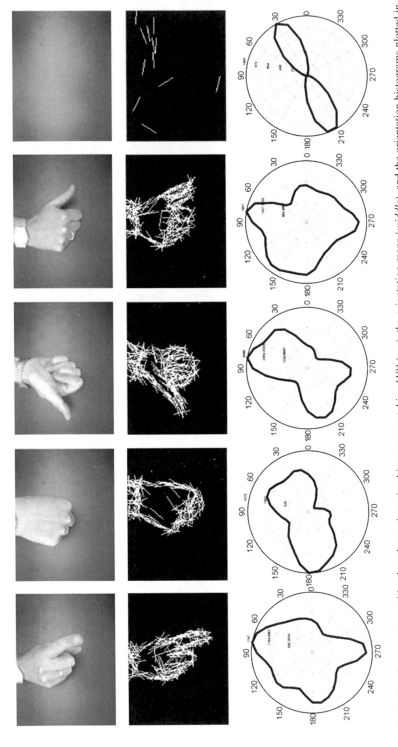

Fig. 8 Hand posture recognition based on orientation histogram matching [18] (*top*), the orientation maps (*middle*), and the orientation histograms plotted in polar coordinates

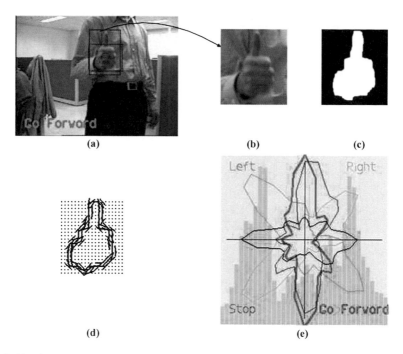

Fig. 9 Hand posture recognition using the orientation histogram of hand contour. (**a**) hand localization by tracking; (**b**) rectangle bounding hand region; (**c**) hand contour segmented based on skin color; (**d**) local orientations of hand contour; (**e**) posture recognition by matching the orientation histogram of hand contour (plotted in polar coordinates)

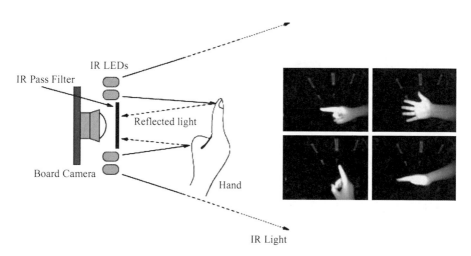

Fig. 10 The Gesture Pendant developed in [10]. (*Left*) sideview of the infrared setting; (*Right*) the four hand poses

Finite State Machines (FSM) [80], Dynamic Bayesian Networks (DBN) [81], and Time Delayed Neural Network TDNN) [82], have also been introduced to model the temporal transitions in gesture state spaces. Gesture recognition can also been addressed by trajectory matching [83–85]. The trajectory templates are first learned from training samples; in the testing phase, the input trajectory is matched with learned templates. Black et al. [83, 84] adopted a particle-filtering-based probabilistic framework for dynamic gesture recognition.

4 Gesture Control: Products and Applications

In recent years, many commercial gesture control systems or prototypes have been developed. Gesture control has been implemented in many CE devices. In this section, we present a review on current gesture control products and applications. We first introduce some gesture control products and solutions.

GestureTek [86] is one of the leading companies working on gesture recognition technologies. By converting hand or finger movements into mouse control, their product GestPoint provides a touch-free "point-to-click" control interface. Two cameras are used to capture and track hand or finger movements inside a control frame. For reliable tracking in varied lighting conditions and even with poor illumination, IR lighting is utilized. GestureTek's Illuminate series provides surface computing with a touch-free gesture control, which enables users navigate dynamic content by pointing fingers or waving hands (shown in Fig. 11). Their GestFX series allows the users to control the visual content projected on the floor, wall, or table space with their body motion; an example is shown in Fig. 11.

Toshiba has been actively working on vision-based gesture control. Their Qosmio laptops support hand gesture control. For example, forming a fist allows the user to

Fig. 11 The Illuminate series (*left*) and the GestFX system (*right*) from GestureTek [86]

Fig. 12 Gesture interaction systems from Fraunhofer [90]: (*Left*) iPoint Explorer and (*Right*) iPoint Presenter

move the cursor around the screen, and pressing the thumb down on top of the fist makes a selection. In IFA 2008, Toshiba showed gesture control for TVs. In their systems, a single webcam is used to sense the user's hand movement at the distance of 1–3 meters.

Mgestyk [87] have developed 3D gesture control solutions, using 3D cameras provided by 3DV Systems [88]. Since gesture recognition is performed directly on 3D depth data, their 3D system can capture small hand movements accurately, even depth-based gestures. Any data beyond a certain depth (such as people walking in the background) can be ignored. The system is reliable to lighting variations and even works in total darkness without using lighting sources. Softkinetic [89] has also been working on 3D gesture recognition solutions, based on a depth-sensing camera.

Fraunhofer Institute for Telecommunications HHI [90] has developed gesture interaction systems using a pair of stereo cameras. Their hand tracker can measure the 3D position of the user's fingertips at a rate of 50 Hz. They combine camera sensor with other sensors for reliable performance. For example, in the iPoint Explorer system (Fig. 12), ultrasonic sensors and two cameras are utilized for reliable sensing. In the iPoint Presenter system (Fig. 12), IR lights and cameras are adopted for detection and tracking of multiple fingers. LM3LABS [91] is also working on gesture interaction using stereo camera sensors.

Gesture control can be applied for most of CE devices including TV/displays, game consoles, mobile phones, and so on. In the following, we discuss current gesture control applications for CE devices.

TVs or Displays Many companies have recently introduced gesture control for TVs or displays. As mentioned above, Toshiba developed gesture-control interface for TV. In CES 2008, JVC showed a TV that reacts on hand claps and hand gestures.

Fig. 13 The EyeMobile
engine from GestureTek [86]
tracks three movements:
shake, rock, and roll

The user can move his/her hand as pointer; the icon in the screen is clicked by bending and extending fingers. Samsung also introduced a gesture-control TV in CES 2008, based on the WAVEscape platform using a stereo near-IR vision system. In CES 2009, Hitachi showed a gesture-controlled TV, which integrates the 3D sensors provided by Canesta [92] and gesture recognition software from GestureTek.

Gaming   Sony's PlayStation comes with Eye Toy, a set-top camera, which enables players to interact with games using full-body motion. With built-in LED lights, Eye Toy works when the room is with poor illumination. Microsoft also supports game-control games in their Xbox 360. Both Sony and Microsoft licensed GestureTek's patents on gesture control. Microsoft Xbox 360 will support more gesture interaction by using 3D cameras from 3DV Systems. Freeverse [93] developed gesture-based ToySight for Apple's iSight camera.

Mobile Phones   Many mobile phones, including Sony Ericsson, Nokia, HTC, and Apple iPhone, started to support gesture control. For example, for Sony Ericsson Z555, the user can let it go mute or snooze the alarm by waving the hand to the build-in camera. GestureTek has developed middleware for gesture control on mobile phones. Their EyeMobile engine measures movement when a user shakes, rocks, or rolls the device (shown in Fig. 13). EyeMobile can also track a person's movements in front of the device. Samsung filed patents on gesture control for mobile phones and devices, where the predefined finger motions captured by the camera are translated into on-screen control. EyeSight [94] developed vision algorithms on the mobile phone that can detect and recognize 3D hand motions in front of the camera.

Automobiles   Gesture control can be used in automotive environments for controlling applications such as CD-player and telephone, which reduces visual and mental distraction by allowing the driver to keep the eyes on the road. Many car manufacturers have developed gesture-control interfaces [95]. A prototype implemented in a BMW limousine [11] can recognize 17 hand gestures and 6 head gestures using IR lighting and camera. Head gestures are recognized to detect shaking and nodding for communicating approval or rejection, while hand gestures provide a way to skip CD-tracks or radio channels and to select shortcut functions (Fig. 14). Another system, called iGest [96], can recognize 16 dynamic and 6 static gestures. General Motors [97] has developed iWave, a gesture-based car navigation and entertainment system. In the Gesture Panel [98], as shown in Fig. 15, a camera is aimed at a grid of IR LEDs to capture gestures that are made between the camera and the grid.

Fig. 14 BMW's gesture control prototype [11]. (*Left*) skipping audio tracks by hand gestures; (*Right*) reference coordinate system for hand gestures with interaction area

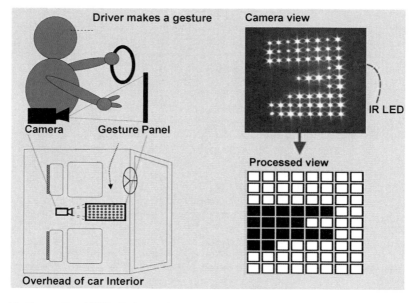

Fig. 15 Gesture Panel [98]. (*Left*) over-head and side view of the placement; (*Right*) camera view of a gesture and the corresponding binary representation

5 Conclusions

Gesture control provides a promising direction for natural user interfaces. Recent years have witnessed much interest on gesture control in CE industry. In this chapter, we present a overview on gesture control technologies. Different sensing technologies are discussed, among which vision-based gesture sensing and interpretation is more powerful, more general, and less unobtrusive. We review computer vision research on each component of vision-based gesture recognition. Latest developments on gesture control products and applications are also presented.

One trend is to use stereo or 3D depth-sensing sensors for gesture recognition. Many difficulties with normal cameras are avoided with 3D sensors, for example, background noises and lighting variations. Although currently the 3D sensors are more expensive than normal cameras, more and more low-cost 3D sensing technologies are becoming commercially available.

With advance in sensing hardware and computer vision algorithms, vision-based gesture recognition technologies will become eventually mature for industrial applications. We believe that gesture control will be in widespread use in numerous applications in near future. We also believe that future user interfaces may ultimately combine vision, voice, and other modalities as we humans do, leading to multimodal interaction.

References

1. Pavlovic, V.I., Sharma, R., Huang, T.S.: Visual interpretation of hand gestures for human–computer interaction: a review. IEEE Trans. Pattern Anal. Mach. Intell. **19**(7), 677–695 (1997)
2. Turk, M.: Gesture recognition. In: Stanney, K. (ed.) Handbook of Virtual Environment Technology. Lawrence Erlbaum Associates, Hillsdale (2001)
3. Mitra, S., Acharya, T.: Gesture recognition: a survey. IEEE Trans. Syst. Man Cybern., Part C, Appl. Rev. **37**(3), 311–324 (2007)
4. Geer, D.: Will gesture-recognition technology point the way? Computer **37**(10), 20–23 (2004)
5. McLeod, R.G.: Gesture control: new wave in ce products. PC World **8** (2008)
6. Webel, S., Keil, J., Zoellner, M.: Multi-touch gestural interaction in X3D using hidden Markov models. In: ACM Symposium on Virtual Reality Software and Technology, pp. 263–264 (2008)
7. imatt. http://www.imatte.com/
8. Cybernet. http://www.cybernet.com/
9. Ogris, G., Stiefmeier, T., Junker, H., Lukowicz, P., Troster, G.: Using ultrasonic hand tracking to augment motion analysis based recognition of manipulative gestures. In: IEEE International Symposium on Wearable Computers, pp. 152–159 (2005)
10. Starner, T., Auxier, J., Ashbrook, D., Candy, M.: The gesture pendant: a self-illuminating, wearable, infrared computer vision system for home automation control and medical monitoring. In: International Symposium on Wearable Computers, pp. 87–94 (2000)
11. Althoff, F., Lindl, R.: Walchshäusl. Robust multimodal hand- and head gesture recognition for controlling automotive infotainment systems. In: VDI-Tagung: Der Fahrer im 21. Jahrhundert (2005)
12. Navisense. http://www.navisense.com/
13. Elliptic labs. http://www.ellipticlabs.com/
14. Stiefmeier, T., Ogris, G., Junker, H., Lukowicz, P., Troster, G.: Combining motion sensors and ultrasonic hands tracking for continuous activity recognition in a maintenance scenario. In: IEEE International Symposium on Wearable Computers, pp. 97–104 (2006)
15. Butler, A., Izadi, S., Hodges, S.: Sidesight: Multi-"touch" interaction around small devices. In: ACM Symposium on User Interface Software and Technology, pp. 201–204 (2008)
16. Celluon. http://www.celluon.com/
17. Freeman, W.T., Weissman, C.: Television control by hand gestures. In: Proceedings of the IEEE International Workshop on Automated Face and Gesture Recognition (FG'95), Zurich, Switzerland, June 1995, pp. 179–183 (1995)
18. Freeman, W.T., Anderson, D., Beardsley, P., Dodge, C., Kage, H., Kyuma, K., Miyake, K., Roth, M., Tanaka, K., Weissman, C., Yerazunis, W.: Computer vision for interactive computer graphics. IEEE Comput. Graph. Appl. **18**(3), 42–53 (1998)
19. Yang, M.-H., Kriegman, D., Ahuja, N.: Detecting faces in images: a survey. IEEE Trans. Pattern Anal. Mach. Intell. **24**(1), 34–58 (2002)

20. Viola, P., Jones, M.: Rapid object detection using a boosted cascade of simple features. In: IEEE Conference on Computer Vision and Pattern Recognition (CVPR), pp. 511–518 (2001)
21. Viola, P., Jones, M.: Robust real-time face detection. Int. J. Comput. Vis. **57**(2), 137–154 (2004)
22. Freund, Y., Schapire, R.E.: A decision-theoretic generalization of on-line learning and an application to boosting. J. Comput. Syst. Sci. **55**(1), 119–139 (1997)
23. Schapire, R.E., Singer, Y.: Improved boosting algorithms using confidence-rated predictions. Mach. Learn. **37**(3), 297–336 (1999)
24. Lienhart, R., Kuranov, D., Pisarevsky, V.: Empirical analysis of detection cascades of boosted classifiers for rapid object detection. In: DAGM 25th Pattern Recognition Symposium, Madgeburg, Germany, September 2003, pp. 297–304 (2003)
25. Li, S.Z., Zhang, Z.: Floatboost learning and statistical face detection. IEEE Trans. Pattern Anal. Mach. Intell. **26**(9), 1–12 (2004)
26. Liu, C.: A Bayesian discriminating features method for face detection. IEEE Trans. Pattern Anal. Mach. Intell. **25**(6), 725–740 (2003)
27. Shih, P., Liu, C.: Face detection using discriminating feature analysis and support vector machine. Pattern Recognit. **39**(2), 260–276 (2006)
28. Garcia, C., Delakis, M.: Convolutional face finder: a neural architecture for fast and robust face detection. IEEE Trans. Pattern Anal. Mach. Intell. **26**(11), 1408–1423 (2004)
29. Chen, Y.-N., Han, C.-C., Wang, C.-T., Jeng, B.-S., Fan, K.-C.: A CNN-based face detector with a simple feature map and a coarse-to-fine classifier. IEEE Trans. Pattern Anal. Mach. Intell. (2010)
30. Wu, Y., Huang, T.S.: View-independent recognition of hand postures. In: IEEE Conference on Computer Vision and Pattern Recognition (CVPR), pp. 88–94 (2000)
31. Zhu, X., Yang, J., Waibel, A.: Segmenting hands of arbitrary color. In: IEEE International Conference on Automatic Face & Gesture Recognition (FG), pp. 446–453 (2000)
32. Bretzner, L., Laptev, I., Lindeberg, T.: Hand gesture recognition using multi-scale colour features, hierarchical models and particle filtering. In: Proceedings of the IEEE International Conference on Automated Face and Gesture Recognition (FG'02), pp. 405–410 (2002)
33. Kölsch, M., Turk, M.: Robust hand detection. In: IEEE International Conference on Automatic Face & Gesture Recognition (FG), pp. 614–619 (2004)
34. Ong, E.J., Bowden, R.: A boosted classifier tree for hand shape detection. In: IEEE International Conference on Automatic Face & Gesture Recognition (FG), pp. 889–894 (2004)
35. Zondag, J.A., Gritti, T., Jeanne, V.: Practical study on real-time hand detection. In: IEEE International Workshop on Social Signal Processing (2009)
36. Stenger, B., Woodley, T., Kim, T.-K., Hernandez, C., Cipolla, R.: AIDIA—adaptive interface for display interaction. In: British Machine Vision Conference (BMVC), vol. 2, pp. 785–794 (2008)
37. Stenger, B., Woodley, T., Kim, T.-K., Cipolla, R.: A vision-based system for display interaction. In: British Computer Society Conference on Human–Computer Interaction, pp. 163–168 (2009)
38. Yilmaz, A., Javed, O., Shah, M.: Object tracking: a survey. ACM Comput. Surv. **38**(4), 13 (2006)
39. McAllister, G., McKenna, S.J., Ricketts, I.W.: Hand tracking for behaviour understanding. Image Vis. Comput. **20**(12), 827–840 (2002)
40. Isard, M., Blake, A.: Condensation—conditional density propagation for visual tracking. Int. J. Comput. Vis. **29**(1), 5–28 (1998)
41. Oka, K., Sato, Y., Koike, H.: Real-time tracking of multiple fingertips and gesture recognition for augmented desk interface systems. In: Proceedings of the IEEE International Conference on Automated Face and Gesture Recognition (FG'02), pp. 411–416 (2002)
42. Laptev, I., Lindeberg, T.: Tracking of multi-state hand models using particle filtering and a hierarchy of multi-scale image features. In: Proceedings of the IEEE Workshop on Scale-Space and Morphology (2001)
43. Ng, C.W., Ranganath, S.: Real-time gesture recognition system and application. Image Vis. Comput. **20**(13–14), 993–1007 (2002)

44. Huang, F., Reid, I.: Probabilistic tracking and recognition of non-rigid hand motion. In: Proceedings of the IEEE International Workshop on Analysis and Modeling of Faces and Gestures (AMFG'03), pp. 60–67 (2003)
45. Isard, M., Blake, A.: ICONDENSATION: unifying low-level tracking in a stochastic framework. In: Proceedings of the European Conference on Computer Vision (ECCV'98), Freiburg, Germany, January 1998. vol. 1, pp. 893–908 (1998)
46. Yang, M.H., Ahuja, N., Tabb, M.: Extraction of 2d motion trajectories and its application to hand gesture recognition. IEEE Trans. Pattern Anal. Mach. Intell. **24**(8), 1061–1074 (2002)
47. Kölsch, M., Turk, M.: Fast 2d hand tracking with flocks of features and multi-cue integration. In: IEEE Conference on Computer Vision and Pattern Recognition Workshop (2004)
48. Yuan, Q., Sclaroff, S., Athitsos, V.: Automatic 2d hand tracking in video sequences. In: Proceedings of the IEEE Workshop on Applications of Computer Vision (WACV'05) (2005)
49. Arulampalam, M., Maskell, S., Gordon, N., Clapp, T.: A tutorial on particle filters for on-line nonlinear/non-Gaussian Bayesian tracking. IEEE Trans. Signal Process. **50**(2), 174–189 (2002)
50. Shan, C., Tan, T., Wei, Y.: Real-time hand tracking using a mean shift embedded particle filter. Pattern Recognit. **40**(7), 1958–1970 (2007)
51. Bradski, G.R.: Computer vision face tracking for use in a perceptual user interface. Intel Technol. J. Q. **2** (1998)
52. Comaniciu, D., Ramesh, V., Meer, P.: Real-time tracking of non-rigid objects using mean shift. In: IEEE Conference on Computer Vision and Pattern Recognition (CVPR), pp. 142–149 (2000)
53. Lu, S., Metaxas, D., Samaras, D., Oliensis, J.: Using multiple cues for hand tracking and model refinement. In: Proceedings of the IEEE Conference on Computer Vision and Pattern Recognition (CVPR'03), pp. II: 443–450 (2003)
54. Bray, M., Koller-Meier, E., Van Gool, L.: Smart particle filtering for 3d hand tracking. In: Proceedings of the IEEE International Conference on Automated Face and Gesture Recognition (FG'04), pp. 675–680 (2004)
55. Sudderth, E.B., Mandel, M.I., Freeman, W.T., Willsky, A.S.: Visual hand tracking using nonparametric belief propagation. In: Proceedings of the IEEE Conference on Computer Vision and Pattern Recognition Workshop (CVPRW'04) (2004)
56. Chang, W.Y., Chen, C.S., Hung, Y.P.: Appearance-guided particle filtering for articulated hand tracking. In: Proceedings of the IEEE Conference on Computer Vision and Pattern Recognition (CVPR'05) (2005)
57. Stenger, B., Thayananthan, A., Torr, P.H.S., Cipolla, R.: Model-based hand tracking using a hierarchical Bayesian filter. IEEE Trans. Pattern Anal. Mach. Intell. **28**(9), 1372–1384 (2006)
58. Zhou, H., Huang, T.S.: Tracking articulated hand motion with eigen dynamics analysis. In: Proceedings of the IEEE International Conference on Computer Vision (ICCV'03), pp. 1102–1109 (2003)
59. Tsap, L.V.: Gesture-tracking in real time with dynamic regional range computation. Real-Time Imaging **8**(2), 115–126 (2002)
60. Inaguma, T., Saji, H., Nakatani, H.: Hand motion tracking based on a constraint of three-dimensional continuity. J. Electron. Imaging **14**(1), 013021 (2005)
61. Basu, S., Essa, I., Pentland, A.: Motion regularization for model-based head tracking. In: Proceedings of the IEEE Conference on Pattern Recognition (ICPR'96), Vienna, Austria, pp. 611–616 (1996)
62. Cascia, M.L., Sclaroff, S., Athitsos, V.: Fast, reliable head tracking under varying illumination: an approach based on registration of texture-mapped 3d models. IEEE Trans. Pattern Anal. Mach. Intell. **22**(4), 322–336 (2000)
63. Cootes, T.F., Walker, K., Taylor, C.J.: View-based active appearance models. In: Proceedings of the IEEE International Conference on Automated Face and Gesture Recognition (FG'00), Grenoble, France, March 2000, pp. 227–233 (2000)
64. Kruger, N., Potzsch, M., von der Malsburg, C.: Determination of faces position and pose with a learned representation based on labeled graphs. Image Vis. Comput. **15**(8), 665–673 (1997)

65. Tu, J., Huang, T.S., Tao, H.: Accurate head pose tracking in low resolution video. In: Proceedings of the IEEE International Conference on Automatic Face and Gesture Recognition (FG'06), Southampton, UK, May 2006

66. Wei, Y., Shan, C., Tan, T.: An efficient probabilistic framework for simultaneous head pose tracking and recognition in video sequences. Technical report, National laboratory of Pattern Recognition, Chinese Academy of Sciences (2004)

67. MacCormick, J., Blake, A.: A probabilistic exclusion principle for tracking multiple objects. Int. J. Comput. Vis. **39**(1), 57–71 (2000)

68. Ross, D., Lim, J., Lin, R.-S., Yang, M.-H.: Incremental learning for robust visual tracking. Int. J. Comput. Vis. **77**(1–3), 125–141 (2008)

69. Grabner, H., Grabner, M., Bischof, H.: Real-time tracking via on-line boosting. In: British Machine Vision Conference (BMVC), pp. 47–56 (2006)

70. Avidan, S.: Support vector tracking. IEEE Trans. Pattern Anal. Mach. Intell. **26**(8), 1064–1072 (2004)

71. Kim, M., Kumar, S., Pavlovic, V., Rowley, H.: Face tracking and recognition with visual constraints in real-world videos. In: IEEE Conference on Computer Vision and Pattern Recognition (CVPR), pp. 1–8 (2008)

72. Grabner, H., Leistner, C., Bischof, H.: Semi-supervised on-line boosting for robust tracking. In: European Conference on Computer Vision (ECCV), pp. 234–247 (2008)

73. Freeman, W.T., Roth, M.: Orientation histograms for hand gesture recognition. In: Proceedings of the IEEE International Workshop on Automated Face and Gesture Recognition (FG'95), Zurich, Switzerland, June 1995, pp. 296–301 (1995)

74. Shan, C.: Vision-based hand gesture recognition for human–computer interaction. Master's thesis, National laboratory of Pattern Recognition, Chinese Academy of Sciences (2004)

75. Triesch, J., von der Malsburg, C.: A system for person-independent hand posture recognition against complex backgrounds. IEEE Trans. Pattern Anal. Mach. Intell. **23**(12), 1449–1453 (2001)

76. Kölsch, M., Turk, M., Höllerer, T., Chainey, J.: Vision-based interfaces for mobility. Technical Report TR 2004-04, University of California at Santa Barbara (2004)

77. Kölsch, M.: Vision Based Hand Gesture Interfaces for Wearable Computing and Virtual Environments. PhD thesis, University of California, Santa Barbara (2004)

78. Premaratne, P., Nguyen, Q.: Consumer electronics control system based on hand gesture moment invariants. IET Comput. Vis. **1**(1), 35–41 (2007)

79. Ren, H., Xu, G.: Human action recognition with primitive-based coupled-HMM. In: Proceedings of the IEEE Conference on Pattern Recognition (ICPR'02), vol. II, pp. 494–498 (2002)

80. Hong, P., Turk, M., Huang, T.S.: Gesture modeling and recognition using finite state machines. In: Proceedings of the IEEE International Conference on Automated Face and Gesture Recognition (FG'00), pp. 410–415 (2000)

81. Pavlovic, V.: Dynamic Bayesian Networks for Information Fusion with Applications to Human–Computer Interfaces. PhD thesis, University of Illinois at Urbana-Champaign (1999)

82. Yang, M.H., Ahuja, N.: Recognizing hand gesture using motion trajectories. In: Proceedings of the IEEE Conference on Computer Vision and Pattern Recognition (CVPR'99), January 1999, vol. I, pp. 466–472 (1999)

83. Black, M.J., Jepson, A.D.: Recognition temporal trajectories using the CONDENSATION algorithm. In: Proceedings of the IEEE International Conference on Automated Face and Gesture Recognition (FG'98), Japan, pp. 16–21 (1998)

84. Black, M.J., Jepson, A.D.: A probabilistic framework for matching temporal trajectories: CONDENSATION-based recognition of gestures and expressions. In: Proceedings of the European Conference on Computer Vision (ECCV'98) (1998)

85. Psarrou, A., Gong, S., Walter, M.: Recognition of human gestures and behaviour based on motion trajectories. Image Vis. Comput. **20**(5–6), 349–358 (2002)

86. Gesturetek. http://www.gesturetek.com/

87. Mgestyk. http://www.mgestyk.com/

88. 3dv systems. http://www.3dvsystems.com/

89. Softkinetic. http://www.softkinetic.net/
90. fraunhofer hhi. http://www.hhi.fraunhofer.de
91. Lm3labs. http://www.lm3labs.com/
92. Canesta. http://www.canesta.com/
93. Freeverse. http://www.freeverse.com/
94. eyesight. http://www.eyesight-tech.com/
95. Pickering, C.: Gesture recognition could improve automotive safety. Asia-Pacific Engineer—Automotive-Design (2006)
96. Canzler, S., Akyol, U.: GeKomm – Gestenbasierte Mensch–Maschine Kommunikation im Fahrzeug. PhD thesis, Rheinisch-Westfälische Technische Hochschule Aachen (2000)
97. Gm-cmu. http://gm.web.cmu.edu/demos/
98. Westeyn, T., Brashear, H., Atrash, A., Starner, T.: Georgia tech gesture toolkit: supporting experiments in gesture recognition. In: International Conference on Multimodal Interfaces (ICMI), pp. 85–92 (2003)

Empirical Study of a Complete System for Real-Time Face Pose Estimation

Tommaso Gritti

Abstract In this paper we focus on the task of fully automatic real-time face 3D pose estimation, both person independent and calibration free. We developed a complete system, which is capable of self initializing, estimates the pose robustly and detects failure of tracking. As a first contribution, we describe the initialization step, which does not rely on any user interaction. As a second contribution we detail a robust tracking methodology, capable of dealing with fast user motion and varying lighting conditions. This includes improvements on both the matching error metric and the search algorithms. We show how the choice of the texture representation can strongly influence the stability of the pose estimation. We finally extensively evaluate the performance of the system on realistic videos. The results show that the proposed method is both adaptable to different users and robust to lighting changes.

1 Introduction

Head pose estimation has a very large potential in many different fields. In the signage business, there is a natural trend toward automatic gathering of statistical information from faces of the audience passing by. In the medical domain, face registration starts to appear as a welcome possibility to reduce invasiveness in operations while maintaining, or improving, the required accuracy. In consumer applications, the need of being closer and closer to customers needs, pushes for new, and often unexpected, ways of interaction. In surveillance and border control, the automatic search and verification of identity is always a priority, and solutions working in unconstrained environments are still lacking.

The estimation of the head pose carries by itself much information with regards to body language and interest in the surrounding environment of a person. Face pose estimation can also be seen as a much needed preprocessing, which is used

T. Gritti (✉)
Philips Research Laboratories, Eindhoven, The Netherlands
e-mail: tommaso.gritti@philips.com

L. Shao et al. (eds.), *Multimedia Interaction and Intelligent User Interfaces,*
Advances in Pattern Recognition,
DOI 10.1007/978-1-84996-507-1_6, © Springer-Verlag London Limited 2010

to improve information extraction from faces. The information available on faces is rich and diverse: gender, age, expression, gaze. All these characteristics can be extracted automatically, and most methods can benefit from a good face registration. An example is given in our recent work [11], where we showed that face registration errors have a large influence on the estimation of facial expression.

A very large amount of research has been devoted to the task of head pose estimation. Refer to [5] for a recent survey on the topic. Estimation of face pose can be roughly categorized in two main classes of approaches, single-image-based and iterative/video-based. In the first class we find representation of nearly all regression and dimensionality reduction methods available. Nonlinear Regression methods [4, 20, 22, 24], manifold embedding based on linear subspaces [25, 27], and nonlinear ones [15, 23]. Image retrieval methods have also been applied to the problem [12]. A common property of this first class of methods is not to explicitly incorporate the knowledge of temporal continuity available in tracking systems. While very useful in many applications which require the estimation on a single image, we are interested in systems which exploit tracking to improve performance.

These algorithms belong to the second class. 3D deformable models are a common methodology, even though often far from real-time [2]. Other methods are based on sparse features instead of a mesh: [9, 33] exploit Ransac estimation, while [17] adopts online feature selection. Initially only modeling 2D deformations [6], more recently extensions of Active Appearance Models started to cope with the 3D pose estimation problem [19]. In [8], a system is proposed in which the optimal pose is obtained without the use of a gradient descent estimation, which is typically both the slowest component and the most susceptive to local minima. Our system can be seen as an improvement of the approach described in [8].

While some of the available methods show relatively high accuracy on test databases, very few focus on real-world applications. The difference between performing well on one or more databases and being able to deliver face pose estimation robustly in any environment can be surprisingly large. There is a need for algorithms which can be deployed and tested in every day situation.

In this paper we aim at improving current state-of-the-art in automatic face pose estimation for systems which require real-time execution and adaptability to different people and to unconstrained environments. We describe a complete system which allows one to automatically estimate the 3D face pose of a user standing in front of a camera. First, we elaborate on a possible initialization step which does not assume any user input. We investigate the influence of different texture representations on the stability of the pose estimation. We then focus on the design of an improved matching criterion, which is at the core of the search for an optimal pose. We describe different search methodologies, to be used in combination with the matching error. We also adopt a 2D feature tracker and verify whether it can improve the estimation. To obtain quantitative error measurement, we propose a new semiautomatic annotation methodology. We finally run an extensive set of experiments to evaluate the performance of the proposed system.

The remainder of this paper is structured as follows: Sect. 2 describes a general concept of 3D pose estimation, together with the selected pose estimation algorithm,

3D mesh, and texture extraction methodology. Section 3 discusses the automatic initialization of the pose. Section 4 details the tracking algorithm. In Sect. 5 experimental results are shown, in which the influence on the parameters and the benefits of each proposed contribution are discussed. Section 6 presents our conclusions.

2 Problem Definition

2.1 Problem Statement

Given a 3D nondeformable body, free to move in 3D space, the total number of degrees of freedom are 6, three rotational and three translational. We can then define the pose of an object with the vector

$$\mathbf{b} = [t_x, t_y, t_z, \theta_x, \theta_y, \theta_z]^T. \tag{1}$$

Notice that, in the case in which the focal length of the camera is not known, the distance of the object from the camera, t_z, can be substituted by a scaling factor α.

The pose estimation problem can be formalized as follows. We are given:

- An image of a certain known object
- A set of n distinguishable points on such image (n 2D coordinates), $\mathbf{c}^i$
- A 3D model of an object
- A set of n distinguishable vertexes on such object (n 3D coordinates), $\mathbf{w}^i$, which correspond to the set of points selected on the image

The goal is then to estimate the 3D rigid transformation $\mathbf{T}$ which must be applied to the reference 3D object in order for its perspective projection to match the given image. More formally, defining $\mathbf{c}^i$ as the homogeneous coordinates of the image points, and $\mathbf{w}^i$ as the homogeneous coordinates of the 3D points,

$$s\mathbf{c}^i = \begin{pmatrix} s \cdot c_u^i \\ s \cdot c_v^i \\ s \end{pmatrix} = \mathbf{K}\left(\begin{pmatrix} \mathbf{R} & \mathbf{t} \\ \mathbf{0}^T & 1 \end{pmatrix} \right) \begin{pmatrix} w_X^i \\ w_Y^i \\ w_Z^i \\ 1 \end{pmatrix} = \mathbf{K}\mathbf{T}\mathbf{w}^i \tag{2}$$

where $\mathbf{K}$ contains the intrinsic camera parameters, and $\mathbf{T}$ is the extrinsic parameters matrix, containing a rotation matrix $\mathbf{R}$ and a translation vector $\mathbf{t}$.

We can formulate the problem in the specific case of head pose estimation as follows: the reference object is a generic or person specific 3D mesh, the target image contains the face of a subject whose head pose must be estimated, and the problem can be seen as the ability to infer the orientation of a person's head relative to the view of a camera [5]. Please refer to Fig. 1 for a visual representation of the problem.

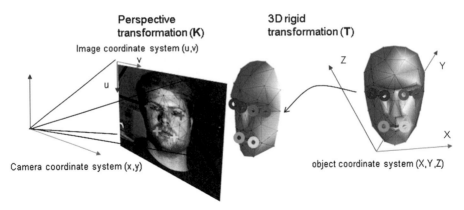

Fig. 1 Overview of pose estimation process: a 3D mesh (*on top right*) undergoing the needed rigid transformation so that the perspective projection of its 3D feature points (*circles*) match the corresponding 2D feature points on the image (*crosses*)

2.2 Pose Estimation Algorithm

The transformation in (2) expresses the most general relationship between a set of 3D points and the corresponding set of 2D points. Matrix **K** contains all the parameters which must be specified to achieve an accurate projection. Depending on the level of detail with which the optical system is modeled, the number of parameters in **K** can vary from one (i.e., focal length) to more than ten, when correction for lens distortions is required. Typically, they are estimated during a camera calibration procedure [30].

One of the assumptions of the method we propose, is the possibility of running the algorithm without any calibration or manual initialization phase. To this aim, we ignore lens distortions (i.e., assume a pin-hole camera) and adopt a weak perspective model, which assumes that the depth of the observed object is small compared to the distance from which it is observed. The number of intrinsic parameters is then effectively reduced to the camera focal length and the sensor center. If the center of the sensor is assumed, in first approximation, to be aligned with the optical axis of the lens, the only remaining parameter is the camera focal length. Please refer to [14] for an analysis of the effects of different approximations to perspective.

Pose estimation from a set of 2D to 3D point correspondences has been solved with a large variety of methods [13]. Among the many available ones, we selected Posit [7], a fast and robust pose estimation algorithm, which exploits the simplifications of weak perspective to solve the pose estimation problem with as few as five 2D to 3D point correspondences.

2.3 3D Mesh

A key ingredient in the pose estimation problem is the underlying 3D model. While it is clear that the more faithfully the model resembles the object whose pose is to be estimated, the more accurately the estimation will be, it is also evident that the complete system must be taken into account. Given the approximations which are made in the pose estimation step, the maximum achievable accuracy is already hampered. For this reason, we adopt a very generic 3D model, CANDIDE-3 [1], which sacrifices accuracy in favor of generalization.

Note that, even though a simplified set of deformations is available for the CANDIDE-3 mesh, we opt for a fully rigid mesh. In our experience, most facial deformations can be effectively taken care of by a smart matching error applied to a rigid mesh. The first image in Fig. 6 shows a front view of the CANDIDE-3 mesh.

2.4 Texture Extraction

Given a 3D mesh of known geometry and a defined pose **b** such that every mesh vertex can be projected onto the image plane (through (2)), it is possible to extract a geometrically normalized texture. We follow the notation introduced in [8]. We define **x** as the geometrically normalized facial image, obtained by orthogonal projection of the CANDIDE-3 mesh onto an image plane. The transformation between the perspective projection of the mesh, fitted with a pose **b** on a given input image **y**, and the normalized facial image, is an affine piecewise transform, W:

$$\mathbf{x}(\mathbf{b}) = W(\mathbf{y}, \mathbf{b}). \tag{3}$$

Once a size for the target normalized facial image **x** is chosen, the computation of the normalized texture can be implemented extremely efficiently, through the use of precomputed lookup tables [21]. See Fig. 6 for an example of a normalized face image.

3 Automatic Initialization

In this section we will describe the steps involved in achieving a fast and fully automated mesh initialization. This component of the system, while relatively straight forward, is often overlooked by iterative methods, even if they typically require an initial pose close enough to the ground truth to be effective.

3.1 Face and Feature Detection

After the introduction of a fast and robust face detection by Viola and Jones [32] and the optimized implementation of such method available in open source libraries

[16], it is trivial to adopt a face detector as a first, rough indication of the position of the desired target.

The Viola and Jones face detector cannot guarantee, by itself, an accurate enough fit to a face, in order to be directly used as initialization for our method. There are three main causes of this inaccuracy. The first one is related to the fact that, in order to detect faces of different sizes, the desired image must be scanned at multiple scales. The ratio between two consecutive scales is tightly connected to the maximum achievable speed of detection: the closer to 1.0 the ratio is, the larger the amount of scales which must be scanned, and the slower the detector speed. In order to achieve a real-time detector, the number of scales used in the detector must be limited. In a similar fashion, the density of horizontal and vertical scan affects the accuracy with which a face can be localized. The third main cause of inaccuracy comes from the amount of variation in facial appearance: even if the detector is capable of recognizing a face, the exact position on which the detector will have a positive response depends on the appearance. While the first two limitations can be overcome by adopting faster hardware and choosing a very dense scan, the third reason cannot be compensated for. See leftmost image in Fig. 2 for an example of accuracy of face detection.

In order to improve the accuracy of the initialization, we trained separate eyes and mouth detectors using cascaded AdaBoost and Haar-wavelets. As a positive training set, we used 2115 face images from the FERET and BioID Databases, from which we extracted eyes and mouth patches. The negative training set is constituted by all remaining patches within the face regions. We run these detectors respectively in the upper half and lower half of the detected face region. For each detector, the left and right sides of the rectangular area (i.e., eyes and mouth corners) are chosen as feature points and refined by searching for corners in the neighborhood. The obtained points, $\mathbf{fp}^{det}$, are the inputs for the next step of the initialization phase. See second and third images in Fig. 2.

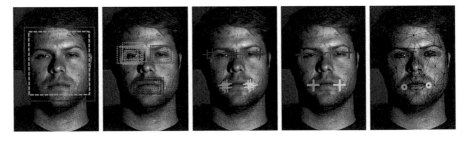

Fig. 2 *From left to right*: face detection result for a dense scan (*green dotted rectangle*) and coarser scan (*red solid rectangle*). Facial feature detections. Respective detected corners, $\mathbf{fp}^{det}$. Vector median of each group of points, $\mathbf{fp}^{vm}$. Mesh obtained after initialization

3.2 Mesh Initialization

We now deal with the task of placing the mesh as closely as possible to the optimal position given the available detections of eyes and mouth. In order to estimate the 3D pose of the face, exploiting the Posit algorithm (Sect. 2.2), as few as five point correspondences are necessary. We noticed that a small variation in the estimation of the features can lead to quite a large error in the estimated mesh 3D pose. This is caused by the mismatch between the CANDIDE-3 mesh and the true geometry of the face under analysis. Given the importance of the initialization phase for the performance of the complete system, we opt for robustness over accuracy.

We exploits the knowledge of the fact that current face detection algorithms are effective mainly for fully frontal faces, i.e., with a yaw angle (left–right rotation) smaller than 30 degrees and pitch (up–down rotation) to smaller than 20 degrees. We assume that the face, during this initialization phase, is undergoing only an in-plane rotation, i.e., with a yaw and pitch angles of 0 degrees. Thanks to this assumption, we need to estimate only a 2D transformation (i.e., 2D rotation, scaling, and translation). This initialization method is less accurate than a full 3D estimation but more robust to the inaccuracies of the 2D feature detections.

We proceed then with few simple steps, described in Algorithm 1, where $\mathbf{fp}^{det}$ is the set of detected feature points, as described in Sect. 3.1, $\hat{\mathbf{fp}}_0^{3D}$ is the set of 2D feature points obtained back-projecting the corresponding mesh 3D points onto the image plane, and $\mathbf{b}_0$ is the estimated initial mesh pose. Step 2 is achieved by computing a scaling factor as ratio of the distance between the 2D feature points and the corresponding distance between the respective 3D points on the mesh. This is possible since we assume an in-plane rotation of the mesh. Once the mesh size is estimated, in Step 3, a simple in plane rotation and 2D translation is estimated.

Algorithm 1: INITIALIZATION($\mathbf{fp}^{det}$)

---

1 – Compute vector median for each set of the 6 feature
    points: left eye corners, right eye.
    corners and mouth corners: $\mathbf{fp}^{vm}$
2 – Find mesh size given 6 corresponding feature
    points $\mathbf{fp}^{vm}$.
3 – Compute in plane rotation and 2D translation for
    mesh of estimated size, using $\mathbf{fp}^{vm}$.
if *isValidPose*(see Sect. 4.5)
    4a – re-project on image mesh 3D points: $\hat{\mathbf{fp}}_0^{3D}$.
    5a – start 2D feature tracker point tracker for
        each of them: $\mathbf{fp}_0^{LK} = \hat{\mathbf{fp}}_0^{3D}$.
  return $\mathbf{b}_0$
  else
    4b – re-initialize mesh position.

It is important to understand the motivation of Step 4a. There are two factors affecting the mismatch between the original feature points $\mathbf{fp}^{vm}$ and the back-projected set $\hat{\mathbf{fp}}^{3D}$: the weak perspective approximation (to a lesser degree) and the difference between the mesh shape and the real 3D geometry of the tracked face. These two approximations affect the accuracy of the tracking. The back-projection step is needed to avoid drifting during tracking.

Please refer to two rightmost images in Fig. 2 for an example of $\mathbf{fp}^{vm}$ and the computed initial mesh.

4 Tracking

The approach described in the previous section proved, in our experience, to be fast and robust enough to avoid initializations too far from the optimal position. As already mentioned, the aim of such initialization is to automatically place the mesh close enough to the optimal position, so that the adaptive tracking component is able to converge to the optimal estimation. We now need to tackle the task of improving the initial estimate while copying with subject movements.

4.1 Overview of Method

The adopted adaptive tracking is summarized in Algorithm 2, where $\tilde{\mathbf{b}}_t$ is the estimated mesh pose, and $\mathbf{fp}_t^{LK}$ is the current set of 2D feature points, obtained from feature point tracker, as described in Sect. 4.2. Pose estimation is described in Sect. 2.2,

---

Algorithm 2: TRACKING($\mathbf{fp}_t^{LK}$)

---

1 – Get updated 2D feature points position from tracker $\mathbf{fp}_t^{LK}$.
2 – Run Posit algorithm to estimate 3D mesh pose, and set it as initial pose, $\mathbf{b}_t$.
3 – Run mesh pose adaptation, starting from $\mathbf{b}_t$, and obtain updated pose, $\tilde{\mathbf{b}}_t$.
if *isValidPose* (see Sect. 4.5)
    4a – reproject on image mesh 3D points: $\hat{\mathbf{fp}}_t^{3D}$ given mesh pose $\tilde{\mathbf{b}}_t$
    5a – start a Lucas-Kanade feature point tracker for each of them: $\tilde{\mathbf{fp}}_t^{LK} = \hat{\mathbf{fp}}_t^{3D}$
  return $\tilde{\mathbf{b}}_t$
else
    4b – stop tracking and start initialization.

---

the adaptation step in Sect. 4.3, and the definition of whether a pose is valid in Sect. 4.5.

4.2 2D Feature Tracking

In order to allow for fast movements of the user, we adopt the Lucas–Kanade feature tracker [26]. More specifically, we opted for the pyramidal implementation [3], available in OpenCV [16]. Each of the six reprojected mesh points, $\hat{\mathbf{fp}}_t^{3D}$, is used to initialize a feature point tracker. It is important here to keep in mind that the most relevant condition for a point to be a "good feature" to track is that both Eigen values of the structure tensor are larger than the noise level, i.e., that it possesses gradients on both directions [26]. This is often satisfied for the selected facial feature points, eyes and mouth corners.

As an optional step, it is possible to search, in the neighborhood of each facial feature point, for a feature point which is respecting the Eigen value criterion (i.e., an "even better feature"). This step would once again favor robustness over accuracy, since it would move a detected feature to a close enough point, more likely to be robustly tracked.

4.3 Adaptation Step

Thanks to the use of the 2D feature point tracker, the pose estimated at each frame can be considered to be in the neighborhood of the optimal solution.

The aim of the adaptation step is twofold: refining the estimated pose, and cope with variations introduced by the possible drifting in the tracking of facial features. Since we adopt a nondeformable mesh, the degrees of freedom which can be varied in the search of the best fit are six, as in the case of any rigid body.

Together with the definition of the matching criterion of Sect. 4.4, the adaptation step can be seen as a search for a local minimum. As such, different search strategies can be exploited. We will investigate the performance of three different methods:

- *Recursive Search (RS)*: each dimension is scanned, one after the other. After each search in one dimension, the pose of the mesh is updated with the parameter which achieves the lowest matching error, and the search proceeds in the next dimension.
- *Hierarchical Search (HS)*: it proceeds as for the *Recursive search*, but after each iteration (i.e., a round of search along all dimensions), the search step along each dimension is halved.
- *Locally Exhaustive and Directed Search (LEDS)*: this method first searches locally in each direction for the best parameter. Each search is independent of the other. After the best parameter is found for each direction, a refinement step is computed. See [8] for further details.

An example of such search strategies, applied to the simplified case of two dimensions, is shown in Fig. 3. The parameters we adopted for each approach are listed in Table 1. From these values we can see how the total amount of positions searched for along each dimension is roughly the same for all methods: 15 in the case of RS and LEDS, and 12 for HS. Since the amount of steps searched for during an iteration is directly related to the total computation time, we opted for a similar computational complexity for all search strategies. This fact will be clear by analyzing the average computation time presented in Table 2 and discussed in Sect. 5.2.4.

4.4 Matching Criterion

As for any optimization problem, a function to be minimized must be defined. Two quantities are used jointly to define the goodness of the current pose:

- *Number of detections on mesh texture*: we assume that a mesh whose estimated pose is close enough to the ground truth will be characterized by a texture which closely resembles a frontal face. Facial feature detectors should then be able to locate the features for which they have been trained.
- *Reconstruction error of mesh texture*: we adopt the distance of the mesh texture to its projection onto an Eigen face space as a further confidence value.

The matching error is defined as follows:

$$ME = \left(\sum_i^i ME_i^{dn} + ME^{re} \right) \Big/ 4, \quad i = \text{face, eye, mouth} \tag{4}$$

where ME_i^{dn} and ME^{re} are defined in (5) and (8), respectively.

Many additional terms could be explored. A simple refinement would include a term which favors a smoother estimation, i.e., penalizing large angle variations. Another possible extension would include computation of a skin probability map and exploit it in order to stop the tracking in the case in which the total probability on the extracted mesh texture would remain very low for some consecutive frames. Additionally, for the case of a static camera and relatively stable background, the foreground probability could be computed for every pixel and adopted in a similar way as the skin probability map. The type of application scenario in which the system should be deployed would determine whether these extensions could be applied. For the case of skin color, for example, the addition would not be feasible for systems working in low light conditions, in which a gray-scale camera and possibly active InfraRed illumination would be exploited; for the case of background modeling, scenarios in locations with a fast changing background, such as a shopping mall, would not benefit, or possibly even deteriorate from this component. In our implementation, we opted for the two above-mentioned terms to keep the system as widely applicable as possible.

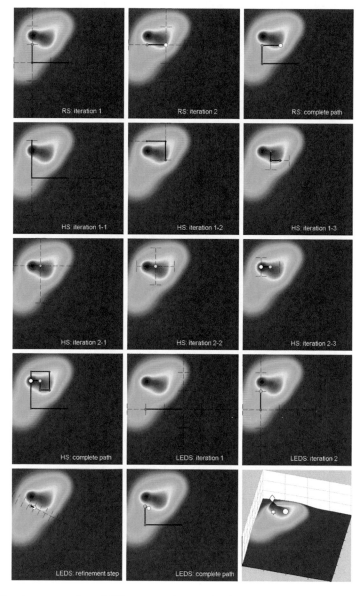

Fig. 3 Visual representation of different search strategies for the simplified case of a two-dimensional search. Images are ordered *from left to right, top to bottom*. *Images 1–3*: Recursive Search. *Images 4–10*: Hierarchical Search (two iterations, each constituted by three decreasing step size searches). *Images 11–14*: Local Exhaustive and Directed Search. The starting position coincides with the center of the plane. Thin *dotted lines* represent the searched positions at each iteration. *Thick lines* show the selected move. The *bottom right image* shows the final position reached by RS (*circle*), HS (*diamond*), and LEDS (*star*). Please note that, to limit total number of images, we show in this example three decreasing size steps for the case of Hierarchical Search, while in our system, four steps are adopted, as listed in Table 1

Table 1 Parameters adopted for the search with different algorithms. In the case of all search strategies, given an odd number of steps, n, for each iteration, $(n-1)/2$ steps are searched around the initial value in each dimension. For the case of Recursive Search, for example, we search up to $\pm 7 \cdot 0.857°$ around the initial value for yaw, pitch, and roll. In the case of Hierarchical Search, only one step at each side of the initial yaw, pitch, and roll value is tested, with a distance of $\pm 3.2°$, and then the search is repeated with a smaller step size, for higher accuracy. For all algorithms, the values given in the table indicate the search corresponding to one iteration

Algorithms		Yaw/Pitch/Roll	Scale	ShiftX/Y
RS	steps number	15	15	15
	steps size	0.8571°	0.006 S_{Mesh}	0.0023 S_{Mesh}
HS	steps number	3 (repeated 4 times)	3 (repeated 4 times)	3 (repeated 4 times)
	steps size at each round	3.2°	0.0224 S_{Mesh}	0.0086 S_{Mesh}
		1.6°	0.0112 S_{Mesh}	0.0043 S_{Mesh}
		0.8°	0.0056 S_{Mesh}	0.0021 S_{Mesh}
		0.4°	0.0028 S_{Mesh}	0.0011 S_{Mesh}
LEDS	steps number	15	15	15
	steps size	0.8571°	0.006 S_{Mesh}	0.0023 S_{Mesh}
	refinement step	10 steps of 0.15 each of the distance between original point and end point (in 6-dimensional space).		

4.4.1 Detection on Mesh Texture

For the first term of the matching criterion, we first compute the normalized face image, $\mathbf{x}(\mathbf{b})$, as described in Sect. 2.4. We then run face, eye, and mouth detectors on it. We fix a maximum number of detections for each detector: N_{face}^{max}, N_{eye}^{max}, and N_{mouth}^{max} for face, eye, and mouth detectors, respectively (3, 50, and 50 in our setup). For the case of face detection, the detector is run on the complete texture image at N_{face}^{max} different scales. In the case of eye and mouth detection, each detector is run solely in the appropriate facial region, at multiple scales, and only the first N_{eyes}^{max} and N_{mouth}^{max} are kept. The match error given by the detections is computed as follows:

$$\text{ME}_i^{dn} = \left(1 - N_i/N_i^{max}\right), \quad i = \text{face, eye, mouth.} \qquad (5)$$

This term clearly favors a mesh whose position allows for good detections on the registered image. Refer to last row of Fig. 4 for examples of detections.

4.4.2 Reconstruction Error of Mesh Texture

For the second contribution, we again extract the mesh texture, as described in Sect. 2.4, and then compare it to its projection onto an Eigen face space [31]. More specifically, if we are given a database of N registered images, $\mathbf{I}_{h,w}^i$, they are first vectorized into $\mathbf{x}_{n,1}^i$, as shown in Fig. 5. We can then apply Principal Component Analysis (PCA) on them and obtain a mean texture, $\bar{\mathbf{x}}$, and a set of Eigen vectors,

Table 2 Accuracy of different search methods on annotated test video sequences. One or two (1)/(2) iterations of: Hierarchical search (HS), Recursive search (RS) and Local exhaustive directed search (LEDS). Addition of Lucas–Kanade 2D feature tracker (LK). Average result of the three methods (Avg). Columns 1–3: angular distance is computed as absolute distance between ground truth and estimated values, in degrees. Column 4: MSE is computed from all estimated mesh coordinates when compared to ground truth, in pixels. Column 5: percentage of frames in which an estimate for the pose is obtained. Column 6: execution time in milliseconds. Both angular and MSE distances are computed only on frames in which a pose was successfully detected. Values corresponding to best performance for each column are highlighted in bold characters. All results are obtained with texture size of 40 × 40 pixels, 35 Eigen vectors, and gamma correction followed by Ggauss as texture preprocessing

Algorithms	Errors on test videos				Percentage of frames with estimated pose	Execution speed
	Yaw	Pitch	Roll	MSE		
LEDS(1) + LK	6.3 ± 2.3	8.2 ± 3.0	2.7 ± 0.7	6.0 ± 1.8	0.89 ± 0.09%	87.7 ± 7.9 ms
LEDS(2) + LK	6.4 ± 2.6	8.5 ± 3.2	2.6 ± 0.8	6.5 ± 2.8	0.90 ± 0.10%	92.5 ± 8.5 ms
LEDS(1)	12.6 ± 4.2	9.8 ± 3.3	7.3 ± 4.5	26.4 ± 22.5	0.69 ± 0.19%	81.7 ± 7.0 ms
LEDS(2)	12.8 ± 4.1	9.8 ± 3.7	7.9 ± 6.4	26.0 ± 22.1	0.72 ± 0.20%	85.2 ± 6.3 ms
HS(1) + LK	**5.5 ± 1.9**	**7.5 ± 3.4**	**2.2 ± 0.5**	**5.5 ± 1.4**	0.90 ± 0.09%	83.0 ± 8.3 ms
HS(2) + LK	5.9 ± 2.5	7.8 ± 3.0	2.5 ± 0.9	5.6 ± 1.6	0.90 ± 0.09%	109.1 ± 11.7 ms
HS(1)	10.8 ± 4.0	8.7 ± 2.9	4.8 ± 2.7	17.5 ± 18.9	0.73 ± 0.21%	77.3 ± 5.4 ms
HS(2)	10.3 ± 4.0	8.7 ± 3.1	4.9 ± 3.6	17.3 ± 18.3	0.75 ± 0.20%	105.0 ± 12.5 ms
RS(1) + LK	7.7 ± 3.0	8.5 ± 3.4	2.9 ± 1.3	6.5 ± 1.9	0.89 ± 0.09%	87.5 ± 7.9 ms
RS(2) + LK	7.3 ± 2.5	8.8 ± 3.3	2.8 ± 0.8	6.5 ± 2.0	0.90 ± 0.09%	118.8 ± 11.4 ms
RS(1)	11.7 ± 4.1	9.2 ± 3.0	5.7 ± 4.2	20.2 ± 18.5	0.72 ± 0.21%	82.0 ± 5.6 ms
RS(2)	11.2 ± 3.6	9.3 ± 3.3	5.0 ± 3.1	18.1 ± 20.1	0.75 ± 0.19%	114.5 ± 10.1 ms
LK	9.3 ± 3.8	8.8 ± 3.1	4.6 ± 2.7	14.0 ± 4.2	0.88 ± 0.13%	**62.6 ± 7.0 ms**
Avg(1) + LK	6.5 ± 2.0	8.1 ± 3.2	2.6 ± 0.7	6.0 ± 1.6	0.89 ± 0.09%	86.1 ± 8.0 ms
Avg(2) + LK	6.7 ± 2.5	8.3 ± 3.1	2.7 ± 0.9	6.1 ± 2.0	0.90 ± 0.09%	115.8 ± 11.4 ms
Avg(1)	11.7 ± 3.0	9.2 ± 2.9	5.9 ± 3.3	21.4 ± 19.6	0.71 ± 0.20%	80.3 ± 5.8 ms
Avg(2)	11.1 ± 3.0	9.4 ± 3.0	5.5 ± 3.3	19.3 ± 19.6	0.74 ± 0.19%	110.6 ± 9.3 ms

Fig. 4 Examples of reconstruction error for different mesh positions. *From top to bottom*: mesh pose, normalized face image $\mathbf{x}(b_t)$ of 300×300 pixels, reconstructed image $\hat{\mathbf{x}}(b_t)$, using 30 Eigen vectors, error image $|\mathbf{x}(b_t) - \hat{\mathbf{x}}(b_t)|$ (in which red pixels represent higher reconstruction error), and eyes/mouth detections on warped image. Eye detectors are run only in the upper half of the texture, while mouth only in the bottom half

arranged into a matrix $\mathbf{X}_{n,N}$, also known as Eigen faces. A desired number, $K \leq N$, of Eigen vectors is kept, producing matrix $\mathbf{X}_{n,K}$. A texture image, $\mathbf{I}(b_t)$, registered at current frame with pose $\mathbf{b}_t$, is vectorized into $\mathbf{x}(b_t)$ and then projected onto the Eigen face space:

$$\hat{\mathbf{x}}(b_t) = \bar{\mathbf{x}} + \mathbf{X}_{n,K} \mathbf{X}_{n,K}^{T} \left(\mathbf{x}(b_t) - \bar{\mathbf{x}} \right). \tag{6}$$

From this formula the effect of the value of K should be clear: K represents effectively the number of dimensions onto which the registered texture is projected. The lower K, the fewer the dimensions, and the larger the distance between the input texture and its projection. For the limit case of $K = N$, the number of dimensions

Fig. 5 Example of image vectorization. An input image $\mathbf{I}_{h,w}$, of height h and width w, is rearranged, row after row, into a column vector $\mathbf{x}_{n,1}$, where $n = h \cdot w$

equals the number of training images, and the projection is exactly the same as the input image. This choice would be in contrast with the motivation behind the projection onto the Eigen space, which is to reduce the dimensionality of the input data, in a way in which only samples lying close to the training data are barely changed, and samples far away are strongly affected. The distance between the original vector and its projection can also be interpreted as texture reconstruction error and can be computed as

$$e(\mathbf{x}) = \left\| \mathbf{x}(b_t) - \hat{\mathbf{x}}(b_t) \right\|^2. \tag{7}$$

An example of texture reconstruction error is shown in the fourth row of Fig. 4. We express the contribution of the texture reconstruction error to the matching criterion as

$$\mathrm{ME}^{\mathrm{re}} = \min\big(e(\mathbf{x})/(\bar{e} + 3\sigma_{\bar{e}}), 1\big) \tag{8}$$

where $\bar{e}$ is the average error of reconstruction obtained on the database of registered images not used to build the Eigen face space, and $\sigma_{\bar{e}}$ is its standard deviation. Any texture for which $e(\mathbf{x})$ is larger than $(\bar{e} + 3\sigma_{\bar{e}})$ will receive a contribution of 1. This clipping implies that, outside a realistic range of errors, the importance of $\mathrm{ME}^{\mathrm{re}}$ will decrease (i.e., all tested mesh poses will receive the same penalty equal to 1), and the detection terms, $\mathrm{ME}^{\mathrm{dn}}_i$, will be more relevant in the choice.

To construct the Eigen face space, we used the FERET and BioID Databases for a total of 2115 images. To be effective in different conditions, methods based on appearance typically require the training databases to contain variations in facial appearance, ethnicity, age, gender, expression, and illumination. The amount of required variation can be reduced by adopting alternative texture representations. We also noticed that, with a standard appearance model, especially lighting conditions have a strong influence on the convergence of the algorithm. For these reasons, we apply a preprocessing to the normalized face image. The aim of the preprocessing is twofold: to reduce the amount of samples needed in the training and to obtain a representation which is less dependent on the lighting conditions. In Sects. 5.1 and 5.2.6 we will show the influence of the following preprocessing applied to the normalized face images:

- *Ggauss*: Gaussian smoothing applied to gradient image [18].
- *gamma + Ggauss*: gamma correction followed by Gaussian smoothing applied to gradient image.

Fig. 6 Normalized face images. *From left to right*: CANDIDE-3 mesh; normalized face image; gamma corrected image. Ggauss applied to image; Ggauss applied to gamma-corrected image; Illumination normalization applied to image. For better visibility, textures are extracted at 300×300 pixels and adjusted for better contrast

• *Illumination normalization*: method introduced in [29] as a simple preprocessing chain to improve identity recognition under strong illumination changes.

To compute Gauss filter, we presmooth the image with a Gaussian kernel size of 3 pixels, followed by a Sobel filter along both directions, and a final Gaussian smoothing on the gradient intensity image with a Gaussian kernel of 12 pixels. As gamma correction, we adopt a low power, with $\gamma = 0.2$, as proposed in [29]. Refer to Fig. 6 for an example of the effect of such preprocessing on a normalized face image. It is visible that, given a face with strong side illumination, applying Ggauss produces an image with lack of features on the darker side of the face. On the same image, by simply applying gamma correction before Ggauss, the obtained image shows a more even distribution of details between the two sides. The same can be noticed in the image processed with Illumination Normalization.

4.5 Detection of Failed Tracking

Notwithstanding the large amount of variation that the combination of the 2D feature tracking and the adaptation step can cope with, the eventuality of a failure during tracking must be taken into account. Different criteria are used jointly to detect the event of lost tracking. We first verify if the estimated pose is outside the allowed range. This is a natural choice, since the chosen mesh models only the front part of the head, it cannot cope with angles of yaw and pitch respectively beyond 45 and 35 degrees. We then consider how large the matching error has been in the last 5–10 frames. Once this value is above a certain threshold, the tracking is stopped, and the initialization is started. The selected threshold obviously plays an important role: in our system it is automatically estimated, once a user is first detected, by running multiple mesh initializations (without starting the tracking) and observing the matching error. From this set of values a safe range is computed. The only assumption in this process is that the user, once in front of the system, maintains a relatively frontal pose in the first few frames. As mentioned in Sect. 4.4 for the case of additional terms in the design of the matching criterion, the same extra terms could be exploited for the detection of tracking failure.

5 Results

In this section we will thoroughly analyze the performance of the proposed methodology. Section 5.1 will investigate the robustness of the texture reconstruction error against strong illumination changes, for the case of static images. In Sect. 5.2 an analysis of the accuracy of the complete system on several videos is discussed in depth, to reveal the influence of the various parameter choices.

5.1 Stability Analysis for Static Images

As a first experiment, we study the stability of given pose against perturbations for the case of static images with different illuminations and subjects. In particular, we focus on the effect of different texture representations on the stability of the original pose. To this aim, we need to establish the influence of the texture preprocessing, texture size, and number of Eigen vectors on the reconstruction error, as defined in Sect. 4.4.2.

The principle is simple: in an ideal case, a mesh with a perfect pose will have the lowest reconstruction error, and all the surrounding poses will have a higher one (i.e., the optimal pose is a local minimum in the reconstruction error).

To verify whether this hypothesis holds, we manually annotate 50 images from the Yale Face Database B [10]. We also added a mirrored (left–right) version of each input image, to reduce influence of the particular background behind the subjects. Each annotated image constitutes a ground truth pose. See Fig. 7 for a few samples of the images in the database. We then displace the mesh pose, starting from the ground truth, in the six-dimensional space (see (1)) and compute the reconstruction error, e(**x**), following (7). Given the difficulty of visualizing results for the six-dimensional space, we reduce the problem to a two-dimensional space. To this aim, for each Δt_x, Δt_y position, we compute the minimum value of e(**x**) reached in the remaining four-dimensional space (yaw, pitch, roll, scale). More formally,

$$e(\mathbf{x})_{\Delta t_x, \Delta t_y} = \min\left(e\left(\mathbf{x}(\mathbf{b}_{\Delta t_x, \Delta t_y} + \Delta \mathbf{p})\right)\right), \tag{9}$$

Fig. 7 Sample images from Yale Face Database B used to compute the influence of the texture representation on the stability of the pose

$$\mathbf{b}_{\Delta t_x, \Delta t_y} = \mathbf{b} + [\Delta t_x, \Delta t_y, 0, 0, 0, 0], \tag{10}$$

$$\Delta \mathbf{p} = [0, 0, k_1 \Delta \alpha_z, k_2 \Delta \theta_x, k_2 \Delta \theta_y, k_2 \Delta \theta_z] \tag{11}$$

while, for each $\Delta t_x, \Delta t_y$, we test all poses with the parameter set belonging to

$$\Delta \alpha_z = 0.2 \alpha_z^0, \tag{12}$$

$$\Delta \theta_x, \Delta \theta_y, \Delta \theta_z = 4°, \tag{13}$$

$$k_1 = \{-4, \ldots, +4\}, \tag{14}$$

$$k_2 = \{-2, \ldots, +2\} \tag{15}$$

where α_z^0 is the mesh scale at the annotated ground truth. We evaluate $\Delta t_x, \Delta t_y$ on a matrix defined by

$$\Delta t_x, \Delta t_y = k_3 \sigma \quad k_3 = \{-4, \ldots, +4\}, \tag{16}$$

$$\sigma = 0.05 S_{\text{Mesh}} \tag{17}$$

where S_{Mesh} is the size of the mesh, in pixels, at the annotated ground truth. While the problem visualized in this two-dimensional space is not fully matching the original stability problem in six dimensions, it does nonetheless indicate how deep is the local minimum around the optimal pose, compared to its neighborhood.

Some examples of ground truth and perturbed poses are displayed in Fig. 4. Also shown are the extracted texture and its difference, for each pixel, with respect to the reconstructed texture.

Figure 8 shows the average $e(\mathbf{x})_{\Delta t_x, \Delta t_y}$ for different preprocessing applied to the texture, obtained over the 100 annotated images. Without preprocessing, no clear

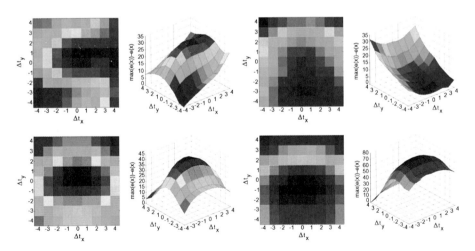

Fig. 8 Average error surface (over 100 images), $\max(e(\mathbf{x})) - e(\mathbf{x})_{\Delta t_x, \Delta t_y}$, obtained for different preprocessing applied to the normalized faces. *Top left*: no preprocessing. *Top right* Ggauss preprocessing. *Bottom left*: gamma correction followed by Ggauss. *Bottom right*: Illumination Normalization. Texture size of 40×40 pixels and 30 Eigen vectors used

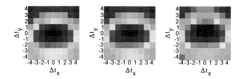

Fig. 9 Average error surface (over 100 images), $\max(e(\mathbf{x})) - e(\mathbf{x})_{\Delta t_x, \Delta t_y}$, obtained for different texture sizes. *Left*: 25×25 pixels. *Middle*: 25×39 pixels. *Right*: 40×40 pixels. In all three cases, we apply, as preprocessing, gamma correction followed by Ggauss, and we use 30 Eigen vectors for the reconstruction

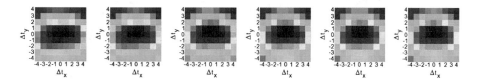

Fig. 10 Average error surface (over 100 images), $\max(e(\mathbf{x})) - e(\mathbf{x})_{\Delta t_x, \Delta t_y}$, obtained for different number of Eigen vectors used in the reconstruction. *From left to right*: 10, 15, 20, 25, 30, 35 Eigen vectors, respectively. For all rows, we apply, as preprocessing, gamma correction followed by Ggauss, and we use a texture size of 40×40 pixels

local maximum is obtained, while with gamma correction followed by Ggauss, a nearly perfect local maximum is visible. The advantage of applying gamma correction is clear when comparing the second and third images. The Illumination Normalization method [29] is less effective, most likely because of the absence of blurring, which allows for a larger basin of attraction.

Figure 9 shows $e(\mathbf{x})_{\Delta t_x, \Delta t_y}$ for different texture sizes. The influence on the error surface is limited. Even less marked is the influence of the number of Eigen vectors, i.e., the K value in (6), used in the texture reconstruction step, as visible in Fig. 10. This implies that the choice among these parameters can be based upon efficiently of execution, i.e., smaller texture size and fewer Eigen vectors.

5.2 Accuracy on Videos

The results of the previous section demonstrated the advantage of selecting the optimal texture preprocessing, in order to be robust to light changes. Let us now proceed to evaluate the performance of the complete system on a large set of representative videos. Figure 11 shows examples of estimated mesh pose on few frames of the videos used to benchmark the system.

5.2.1 Semi-Automatic Annotation

While it is fairly simple to obtain a qualitative evaluation, a quantitative analysis requires ground truth annotation, which is typically a very laborious task. In [28] an

Fig. 11 Examples of estimated mesh pose on few frames of the videos used to benchmark the system. All results are obtained with method HS(1)+LK, as shown in Table 2, with texture size of 40×40 pixels, 35 Eigen vectors, and gamma correction followed by Ggauss as texture preprocessing

automatic method is proposed, which consists of rendering a texture mapped mesh, with known pose, and use the generated video as a test sequence. While adopted also in [8], the generated sequence is typically far from realistic. We opt thus for a different method.

To speed up the procedure, we adopt a semiautomatic annotation approach. To this aim, the user is asked to annotate the first frame of the test video (i.e., manually position the mesh on the image). Our algorithm is then run and suggests a pose for the next frame. The estimated mesh is rendered on the test video, and the user is asked to refine the pose. The refined pose is then again used as input to the algorithm to estimate the next frame. During this procedure, the real-time constraint is not strictly mandatory, and we can thus select any parameter choice to get the best fitting during the annotation.

Following this procedure, we annotated 22 short videos for a total length of 8293 frames. We compared the estimated pose against the ground truth, both in terms of angular distance (i.e., Yaw, Pitch, Roll) and in terms of average Mean Square Error (MSE) of the distance of all mesh points from the ground truth.

To test the effectiveness of the combination of the 2D feature tracker together with the adaptation step, each of the search methods described in Sect. 4.3 was run four times. With and without Lucas–Kanade 2D feature tracker and with one or two iterations of the adaptation step. The results are reported in Table 2.

5.2.2 Performance of Different Search Strategies: Angular Error

The angular error is computed as the distance between the annotated angular pose and the estimated one, and it gives an indication of the accuracy in the estimation of the 3D rotation of the head. We adopt the notation from the aerospace industry, in which yaw indicates a left/right out-of-plane rotation, pitch an up/down out-of-plane rotation, and roll a clockwise/counterclockwise in-plane rotation. Let us compare the performance of the different search strategies by observing Table 2. Hierarchical search produces consistently the highest accuracy, with and without Lucas–Kanade tracker and with one or two iterations. The advantage of the use of the 2D feature tracker is evident. All search methods benefit from the use of the feature tracker, which allows for a faster and more accurate convergence. There seems to be no benefit in employing more than one iteration in combination with the 2D feature tracker. This might be motivated by the fact that the 2D feature tracker allows one to position the mesh close enough to the optimal pose, so that no more than one iteration is needed to reach the best pose. From the results it is also evident that the estimation of the pitch angle is the most challenging, as also visible from the results reported in [8, 17]. Not only the error with respect to the pitch angle is the largest, but also variation in accuracy of the estimation for pitch angle among all methods is the smallest, if compared to all other criteria (yaw, roll, and MSE). The difficulty associated with the estimation of the pitch was also mentioned in [8], even though no hypothesis on the cause of the problem was mentioned. It seems likely that the lower accuracy is related to the amount of distortion of the normalized face image when a face undergoes rotations of the pitch angle. The matching criterion designed in Sect. 4.4 seems to favor poses with a smaller pitch angle, effectively constantly estimating a mesh pitch angle smaller than the ground truth, as visible by observing the second graph in Fig. 15. Notwithstanding the similar error in pitch angle obtained with the different methods, when the overall accuracy is considered, it is clear that a much higher error in the estimation of both the yaw, roll angles, and MSE is generated for all methods which do not adopt the 2D feature tracker.

5.2.3 Performance of Different Search Strategies: MSE

While the angular distance is important for applications which directly require the knowledge of the pose (e.g., as in the case of attention estimation), the MSE is relevant in the case of applications requiring a good face registration (e.g., facial expression recognition). In fact, the MSE is a measure of how well the position of each facial feature point is estimated on the image plane. From the values of the MSE, shown in Table 2, it is again clear how the combination of hierarchical search with 2D feature tracker guarantees the highest accuracy. Given an average error of 5 pixels, it can be reliably adopted as a face registration method. By observing the relation between the values of angular error and MSE, another remark can be made: a low angular error does not necessarily mean that a good mesh fit is obtained. This is the case of results obtained with Lucas–Kanade, which show a relatively low angular error, but a high MSE. What can be deducted from these values is that the Lucas–Kanade 2D feature tracker allows one to follow the movements of the head, but not to generate a tight fit of the mesh. It is thus important to evaluate jointly angular error and MSE.

5.2.4 Performance of Different Search Strategies: Computation Time

The computation time as shown in Table 2 is to be considered as a relative measure of performance, since the code has not been optimized. The system was run in real-time on a Pentium D 2.8 GHz with 2 Gbytes of RAM. All search strategies have run approximatively at the same speed. On the other hand, the difference of execution speed shows the advantage of using Lucas–Kanade feature tracker in combination with each of the search methods, since it allows one to achieve good accuracy with a single iteration. Naturally running the 2D feature tracker alone produces the faster execution, but the accuracy is much lower, as is clear from Table 2. As already noticed, opting for two iterations does not improve accuracy, while it affects computation time. An important consideration must be made with regards to execution time: if an algorithm is tested on a recorded video, regardless of the computation time required for each frame, the accuracy is not affected. In a real-time test though, the performance can be greatly affected by the larger motion of the subject between two successive frames, caused by the longer computation time. While we do not quantitatively present results to support this statement, in our experience faster algorithms often perform better in real time.

5.2.5 Influence of Texture Representation

In this section we investigate the effect of the different parameters which affect the texture representation. While in Sect. 5.1 we studied the variation of the texture reconstruction error as a mesh is moved away from the optimal pose, here we exploit the annotation on videos to examine the variation in accuracy as different choices are made with respect to the texture. The advantage of applying an optimal preprocessing on the texture is evident in Table 3. Gamma correction followed by Ggauss produces almost double accuracy, both with respect to angular error and MSE. Furthermore, the percentage of frames which obtain an estimate of the pose is substantially increased. The computation cost is increased, though not enough to affect performance.

Tables 4 and 5 list the same analysis with respect to, respectively, the size of the texture and the number of Eigen vectors, i.e., the K value in (6). In both cases, the results are in agreement with the stability surfaces of Figs. 9 and 10. The performance increases when opting for a texture size larger than 25×39 pixels, then remains practically constant for all larger texture sizes. The computation time, on the other hand, is strongly affected by the increase in texture size. For this reason, we selected a texture size of 40×40 pixels in our setup.

With regards to the number of Eigen vectors exploited in the texture reconstruction, the performance are marginally improved when an increasing number of Eigen vectors are used, up to 35. Above this value, performance does not increase any further. Since execution time increases linearly with the number of Eigen vectors, we adopt 35 as the value of K in our system.

5.2.6 Influence of Training Size

As mentioned in Sect. 4.4.2, the number and type of images used to derive the Eigen face space are a critical factor to derive a robust error metric. This section examines the influence of such factor.

To establish the influence of the number of images employed in the training of the Eigen faces, we proceed as follows. Given the complete set of images, a series of image subsets, each with an increasing number of images compared to the preceding one, is generated. The subsets are such that all images of the smallest set are included in the second smallest, and so forth, till the largest set, which contains all images of previous sets, together with other images. This removes the difference in performance which would be obtained in the case of random subsets, i.e., the fact that a lucky choice of few good images in the smallest set could be better than the unlucky choice of more images in a larger set. The same subsets of images are used to train Eigen faces with gamma correction followed by Ggauss and with standard textures, i.e., no preprocessing. The results are shown in Fig. 12. Observing the graphs, we can make two conclusions: in the first place, the selected texture preprocessing (gamma correction followed by Ggauss) is effective at all training sizes,

Table 3 Influence of texture preprocessing on accuracy of pose estimation. Both results are obtained with 1 iteration of Hierarchical Search, with Lucas–Kanade tracker, texture size of 40 × 40 pixels and 35 Eigen vectors, and gamma correction followed by Ggauss as texture preprocessing

Texture preprocessing	Errors on test videos				Percentage of frames with estimated pose	Execution speed
	Yaw	Pitch	Roll	MSE		
gamma + Ggauss	**5.5** ± 1.9	**7.5** ± 3.4	**2.2** ± 0.5	**5.5** ± 1.4	**0.90** ± 0.1%	83.0 ± 8.3 ms
No preprocessing	12.8 ± 7.0	9.0 ± 4.2	6.4 ± 5.6	11.8 ± 7.0	0.77 ± 0.18%	**65.5** ± 5.4 ms

Table 4 Influence of texture size on accuracy of pose estimation. All results are obtained with 1 iteration of Hierarchical Search, with Lucas–Kanade tracker, and 35 Eigen vectors, and gamma correction followed by Ggauss as texture preprocessing

Texture size	Errors on test videos				Percentage of frames with estimated pose	Execution speed
	Yaw	Pitch	Roll	MSE		
25 × 39	7.2 ± 2.5	7.8 ± 2.8	2.6 ± 0.9	8.0 ± 2.2	0.52 ± 0.13%	**40.7** ± 6.4 ms
40 × 40	5.5 ± 1.9	**7.5** ± 3.4	**2.2** ± 0.5	**5.5** ± 1.4	0.90 ± 0.09%	83.0 ± 8.3 ms
50 × 50	**5.4** ± 2.0	7.6 ± 3.2	2.4 ± 1.0	5.7 ± 1.8	**0.91** ± 0.1%	157.8 ± 11.8 ms
60 × 60	5.4 ± 2.0	7.6 ± 3.4	2.4 ± 1.3	5.8 ± 1.9	0.90 ± 0.09%	289.5 ± 15.1 ms

Table 5 Influence of number of Eigen vectors on accuracy of pose estimation. All results are obtained with one iteration of Hierarchical Search, with Lucas–Kanade tracker, texture of size 40 × 40 pixels, and gamma correction followed by Ggauss as texture preprocessing

Number of Eigen vectors	Errors on test videos				Percentage of frames with estimated pose	Execution speed
	Yaw	Pitch	Roll	MSE		
5	8.1 ± 3.8	8.1 ± 3.3	3.8 ± 1.9	8.4 ± 4.3	$0.86 \pm 0.09\%$	**69.0** ± 8.8 ms
10	6.6 ± 2.9	8.2 ± 3.6	2.9 ± 1.1	6.8 ± 2.1	$0.88 \pm 0.09\%$	71.4 ± 8.6 ms
15	7.0 ± 2.9	7.7 ± 2.6	3.6 ± 2.3	7.2 ± 2.8	$0.86 \pm 0.10\%$	74.4 ± 7.0 ms
20	7.4 ± 2.8	7.7 ± 3.2	3.4 ± 1.7	7.5 ± 2.7	$0.88 \pm 0.09\%$	75.6 ± 8.5 ms
25	7.3 ± 2.8	8.0 ± 3.1	3.2 ± 1.4	7.1 ± 2.3	$0.89 \pm 0.09\%$	76.8 ± 8.2 ms
30	6.0 ± 2.4	7.9 ± 2.9	2.6 ± 1.7	6.2 ± 2.6	$0.88 \pm 0.11\%$	80.7 ± 8.0 ms
35	**5.5** ± 1.9	7.5 ± 3.4	**2.2** ± 0.5	**5.5** ± 1.4	$0.90 \pm 0.09\%$	83.0 ± 8.3 ms
40	5.7 ± 2.3	**7.4** ± 3.1	2.2 ± 0.7	5.6 ± 1.5	**0.91** $\pm 0.06\%$	87.8 ± 10.2 ms

producing consistently better performance compared to the standard texture representation. Secondly, the adoption of the texture preprocessing results in accuracy which increases monotonically with the increase in the number of training images, which is not the case for the standard texture representation. This is a very substantial improvement, because it allows one to increase performance of the system for any enlargement of the training set, without the concern of a search for an optimal number.

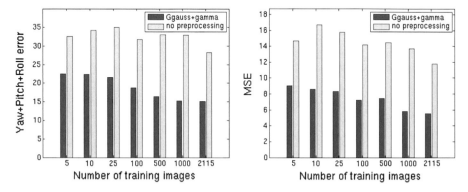

Fig. 12 Influence of training size on accuracy of estimated pose for the case of standard texture and gamma correction followed by Ggauss as texture preprocessing. *Left image*: angular error, computed as the sum of the errors in the estimation of yaw, pitch, and roll (columns 1, 2, and 3 of Table 2). *Right image*: MSE, computed as described in Sect. 5.2. Results are obtained by training an Eigen face set from an increasing number of images: 5, 10, 25, 100, 500, 1000, and 2115 (the complete set used in the system)

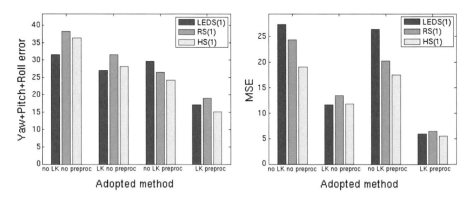

Fig. 13 Influence of different system components on accuracy of estimated pose. For all results, texture size is 40 × 40 pixels and 35 Eigen vectors are used. When indicated, texture preprocessing is gamma correction followed by Ggauss. *Left image*: angular error, computed as the sum of the errors in the estimation of yaw, pitch, and roll (columns 1, 2, and 3 of Table 2). *Right image*: MSE, computed as described in Sect. 5.2

5.2.7 Benefits of the Proposed System

To highlight at a glance the benefits of the major contributions of the proposed system, we evaluate the performance on the videos for different search strategies, while applying texture preprocessing or no preprocessing and employing or not the Lucas–Kanade 2D feature tracker. The results are collected in the two graphs of Fig. 13, for angular accuracy and MSE. For all search strategies, applying texture preprocessing improves accuracy. The same holds for the use of the 2D feature tracker. The combination of the two components proves extremely effective: angular error is halved, and MSE is reduced by nearly a factor 4. Among the search strategies,

Fig. 14 Estimated mesh on frames (*from left to right, top to bottom*): 20, 21, 22, 23,169, 214, 226, 264, 303, 339, 402, 423, 484, 511, 518, and 527. The complete pose trajectory for the video is shown in Fig. 15

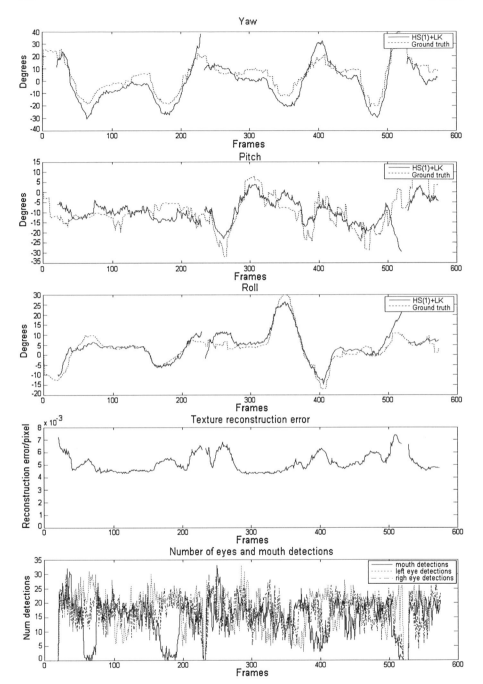

Fig. 15 *From top to bottom*: angular trajectory of the estimated pose compared to the annotated ground truth (yaw, pitch, and roll), texture reconstruction error, and eyes and mouth detections, for the input video some frames of which are shown in Fig. 14. Missing points in the estimated curves represent frames during which the system undergoes automatic initialization

hierarchical search is the most consistent and generates best results for the case of texture preprocessing and 2D feature tracker.

5.3 Analysis of Typical Results

To give an idea of the type of accuracy of the estimated mesh pose, we take a closer look to two videos. Images of the estimated mesh, superimposed to the input video, are shown in Figs. 14 and 16, for the method "HS(1) + LK", as shown in Table 2. The estimated angular pose compared to the ground truth is shown in Figs. 15 and 17, respectively. In the case of the video shown in Fig. 14, a visual inspection reveals that the estimated position of the mesh is, for most frames, quite accurate, even though the accuracy in the estimation of the angles is not as regular in time, by observing the graphs in Fig. 15. This is to be expected, given the low values of MSE obtained in the evaluation on the set of movies. The first row shows the convergence of the mesh after the initialization. In the last three images of Fig. 14, a tracking failure and consequent reinitialization is shown: this demonstrates the speed of response of the system, which is capable to detect failed tracking and automatically restart the tracking. The two bottom graphs in Fig. 15 show respectively the texture reconstruction error and the number of eyes and mouth detections on the mesh texture. By observing these two graphs we can get an idea of the underlying behavior of the matching criterion described in Sect. 4.4. In the video, there are two occurrences in which the tracking is automatically stopped: around frame 230 and frame

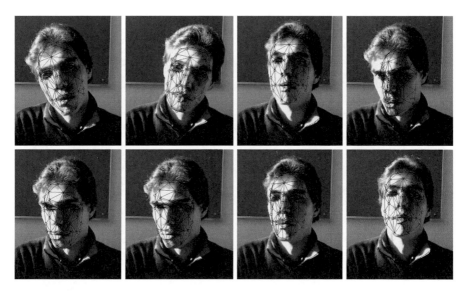

Fig. 16 Estimated mesh on frames (*from left to right, top to bottom*): 36, 75, 110, 149, 152, 153, 219, and 233. The complete pose trajectory for the video is shown in Fig. 17

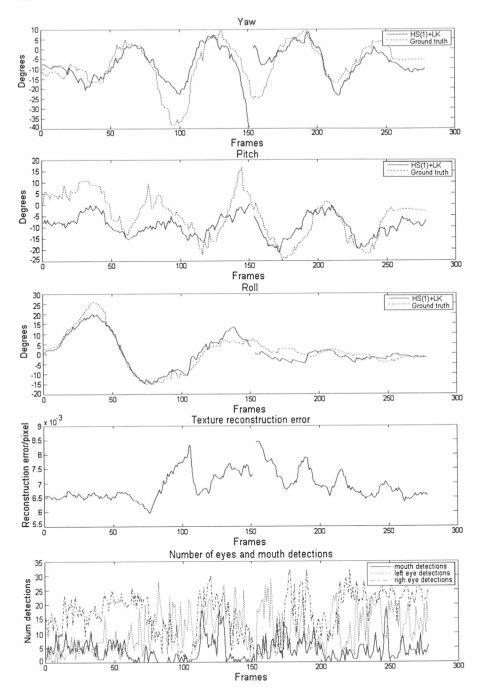

Fig. 17 *From top to bottom*: angular trajectory of the estimated pose compared to the annotated ground truth (yaw, pitch, and roll), texture reconstruction error, and eyes and mouth detections, for the input video of which some frames are shown in Fig. 16. Missing points in the estimated curves represent frames during which the system undergoes automatic initialization

520. In both situations, the texture reconstruction error is high, and no facial feature is detected for few frames.

In the second video, shown in Fig. 16, the accuracy is lower, due to the presence of strong side lighting, but the same remarks can be made by observing the graphs in Fig. 17.

5.4 Examples of Tracking Failure

In this section we briefly discuss same typical situations which are likely to negatively affect the performance of the system. Some examples of frames in which the pose estimate is largely off are shown in Fig. 18. In the first image, the problem is given by the wrong initialization: the face detection and subsequent facial feature detections fail, resulting in a much smaller face. The adaptation step does not manage to recover, and the tracking fails for the next few frames. In the second image, the user rapidly moves the head out of plane immediately after the initialization phase. The 2D feature tracker fails, and the adaptation step finds a local minimum which does not match the optimal pose, i.e., we fall outside of the zone with a single local minimum shown in Fig. 8. The error shown in the third image might be related to a combination of fast user movement and the presence of hair on the forehead: we noticed that such condition can hamper the accuracy of the system. A solution for this problem would involve either the addition of more training images of subjects with different hair styles or the exclusion of the mesh triangles related to the fore-

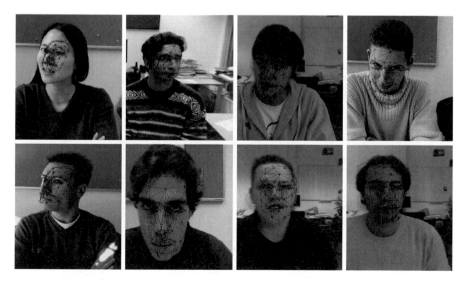

Fig. 18 Examples of bad estimation of mesh pose on the videos used to benchmark the system. All results are obtained with method HS(1)+LK, as shown in Table 2, with texture size of 40×40 pixels, 35 Eigen vectors, and gamma correction followed by Ggauss as texture preprocessing

head. The fourth image shows a typical example of error which takes place when large angles of pitch are present.

As discussed in Sect. 5.2.2, estimation of pitch is the most difficult of the three angles. The fifth image shows a similar problem with respect to the yaw angle. A similar error, possibly affected by the strong side illumination, is shown in the top right image of Fig. 16. In the case of the sixth image, a smaller pitch angle, in combination with a user very close to the camera, gives problems: as described in Sect. 2.2, we adopt a weak perspective model. Such approximation holds well for relatively large distances from the camera compared to the mesh size, i.e., the subject should not be closer to the camera than 50–60 cm. The last two images show another problem: if the system moves too quickly, motion blur causes the 2D feature tracker to fail, and the adaptation step falls outside the optimal search range. A possible solution to this problem would estimate the amount of motion blur and user movement and adapt the range of the adaptation step, either by increasing the number of iterations or by increasing the step side for each iteration.

6 Conclusions

We have described a complete system, which allows automatic 3D face pose estimation in unconstrained environments. First, we have shown a simple yet effective initialization step, which does not assume any user input and allows one to start the estimation as soon as a user appears in front of the camera. We have demonstrated how an optimal texture representation can greatly improve the estimation stability. We have designed a new matching criterion, based on both texture reconstruction error and facial feature detection on the normalized face image. This matching error is used in combination with different search algorithms to allow for a robust pose estimation. Various search strategies have been evaluated, and the benefits of the combination of a 2D feature tracker have been shown. In order to obtain quantitative error measurement, we have proposed a new semiautomatic annotation methodology. The extensive set of experiments show that the proposed method, based on hierarchical search, Lucas–Kanade 2D feature tracker, and gamma correction followed by Ggauss as texture preprocessing, produces consistently better performance than other search methods, with an accuracy of 5, 7, and 2 degrees for yaw, pitch, and roll, respectively.

References

1. Ahlberg, J.: Candide-3-un updated parameterised face. Report No. LiTH-ISY-R-2326 (2001)
2. Blanz, V., Vetter, T.: A morphable model for the synthesis of 3d faces. In: Computer Graphics, Annual Conference Series (SIGGRAPH), pp. 187–194 (1999)
3. Bouguet, J.Y.: Pyramidal implementation of the Lucas Kanade feature tracker description of the algorithm (2000)

4. Chutorian, E., Doshi, A., Trivedi, M.: Head pose estimation for driver assistance systems: a robust algorithm and experimental evaluation. In: IEEE Conference on Intelligent Transportation Systems, pp. 709–714 (2007)
5. Chutorian, E., Trivedi, M.: Head pose estimation in computer vision: a survey. IEEE Trans. Pattern Anal. Mach. Intell. **31**(4), 607–626 (2009)
6. Cootes, T., Edwards, G., Taylor, C.: Active appearance models. IEEE Trans. Pattern Anal. Mach. Intell. **23**(6), 681–685 (2001)
7. Davis, L., DeMenthon, D.: Model-based object pose in 25 lines of code. Int. J. Comput. Vis. **15**, 123–141 (1995)
8. Dornaika, F., Ahlberg, J.: Fitting 3d face models for tracking and active appearance model training. Image Vis. Comput. **24**(9), 1010–1024 (2006)
9. Gee, A., Cipolla, R.: Fast visual tracking by temporal consensus. Image Vis. Comput. **14**, 105–114 (1996)
10. Georghiades, A., Belhumeur, P., Kriegman, D.: From few to many: illumination cone models for face recognition under variable lighting and pose. IEEE Trans. Pattern Anal. Mach. Intell. **23**(6), 643–660 (2001)
11. Gritti, T., Shan, C., Jeanne, V., Braspenning, R.: Local features based facial expression recognition with face registration errors. In: 8th IEEE International Conference on Automatic Face and Gesture Recognition (2008)
12. Grujic, N., Ilic, S., Lepetit, V., Fua, P.: 3d facial pose estimation by image retrieval. In: 8th IEEE International Conference on Automatic Face and Gesture Recognition (2008)
13. Haralick, R., Lee, C., Zhuang, X., Vaidya, V., Kim, M.: Pose estimation from corresponding point data. In: IEEE Workshop on Computer Vision, Representation and Control, pp. 258–263 (1987)
14. Horaud, R., Dornaika, F., Lamiroy, B., Christy, S.: Object pose: the link between weak perspective, paraperspective, and full perspective. Int. J. Comput. Vis. **22**(2), 173–189 (1997)
15. Hu, N., Huang, W., Ranganath, S.: Head pose estimation by non-linear embedding and mapping. In: International Conference on Image Processing, pp. 342–345 (2005)
16. Intel: Opensource computer vision library
17. Jang, J., Kanade, T.: Robust 3d head tracking by online feature registration. In: 8th IEEE International Conference on Automatic Face and Gesture Recognition (2008)
18. Kittipanya Ngam, P., Cootes, T.: The effect of texture representations on aam performance. In: International Conference on Pattern Recognition, vol. II, pp. 328–331 (2006)
19. Koterba, S., Baker, S., Matthews, I., Hu, C., Xiao, J., Cohn, J., Kanade, T.: Multi-view AAM fitting and camera calibration. In: International Conference on Computer Vision, vol. I, pp. 511–518 (2005)
20. Li, Y., Gong, S., Sherrah, J., Liddell, H.: Support vector machine based multi-view face detection and recognition. Image Vis. Comput. **22**(5), 413–427 (2004)
21. Matthews, I., Baker, S.: Active appearance models revisited. Int. J. Comput. Vis. **60**(2), 135–164 (2004)
22. Moon, H., Miller, M.: Estimating facial pose from a sparse representation. In: International Conference on Image Processing, vol. I, pp. 75–78 (2004)
23. Raytchev, B., Yoda, I., Sakaue, K.: Head pose estimation by nonlinear manifold learning. In: International Conference on Pattern Recognition, vol. IV, pp. 462–466 (2004)
24. Seemann, E., Nickel, K., Stiefelhagen, R.: Head pose estimation using stereo vision for human–robot interaction. In: 6th IEEE International Conference on Automatic Face and Gesture Recognition, pp. 626–631 (2004)
25. Sherrah, J., Gong, S., Ong, E.: Face distributions in similarity space under varying head pose. Image Vis. Comput. **19**(12), 807–819 (2001)
26. Shi, J., Tomasi, C.: Good features to track. In: Proceedings of the IEEE Conference on Computer Vision and Pattern Recognition, pp. 593–600 (1994)
27. Srinivasan, S., Boyer, K.: Head pose estimation using view based eigenspaces. In: 16th International Conference on Pattern Recognition, vol. IV, pp. 302–305 (2002)
28. Strom, J.: Model-based head tracking and coding. PhD thesis, no. 733, Linkoping University, Sweden (2002)

29. Tan, X., Triggs, B.: Enhanced local texture feature sets for face recognition under difficult lighting conditions. In: IEEE International Workshop on Analysis and Modeling of Faces and Gestures, pp. 168–182 (2007)
30. Tsai, R.: An efficient and accurate camera calibration technique for 3d machine vision. In: Proceedings of the IEEE Conference on Computer Vision and Pattern Recognition, vol. 86, pp. 364–374 (1986)
31. Turk, M., Pentland, A.: Eigenfaces for recognition. J. Cogn. Neurosci. 3(1), 71–96 (1991)
32. Viola, P., Jones, M.: Rapid object detection using a boosted cascade of simple features. In: Proceedings of the IEEE Conference on Computer Vision and Pattern Recognition, pp. 511–518 (2001)
33. Zhao, G., Chen, L., Song, J., Chen, G.: Large head movement tracking using sift-based registration. In: MULTIMEDIA '07: Proceedings of the 15th International Conference on Multimedia, pp. 807–810. ACM (2007)

Evolution-based Virtual Content Insertion with Visually Virtual Interactions in Videos

Chia-Hu Chang and Ja-Ling Wu

Abstract With the development of content-based multimedia analysis, virtual content insertion has been widely used and studied for video enrichment and multimedia advertising. However, how to automatically insert a user-selected virtual content into personal videos in a less-intrusive manner, with an attractive representation, is a challenging problem. In this chapter, we present an evolution-based virtual content insertion system which can insert virtual contents into videos with evolved animations according to predefined behaviors emulating the characteristics of evolutionary biology. The videos are considered not only as carriers of message conveyed by the virtual content but also as the environment in which the lifelike virtual contents live. Thus, the inserted virtual content will be affected by the videos to trigger a series of artificial evolutions and evolve its appearances and behaviors while interacting with video contents. By inserting virtual contents into videos through the system, users can easily create entertaining storylines and turn their personal videos into visually appealing ones. In addition, it would bring a new opportunity to increase the advertising revenue for video assets of the media industry and online video-sharing websites.

1 Introduction

With the technical advances in video coding and the rapid development of broadband network delivery, online video services are dramatically boosted. There are more and more users uploading various videos of their own with the uniqueness, creativity, and interest to the popular video-sharing websites, such as YouTube [1], to broadcast themselves and share the life experience with online audience in the Internet. The characteristics of easy to create and share personal videos have led to a huge amount of video content distribution and have created phenomenal opportunities for advertisers and content owners seeking to monetize and personalize their

C.-H. Chang (✉) · J.-L. Wu
Graduate Institute of Networking and Multimedia, National Taiwan University, Taipei, Taiwan
e-mail: chchang@cmlab.csie.ntu.edu.tw

L. Shao et al. (eds.), *Multimedia Interaction and Intelligent User Interfaces,*
Advances in Pattern Recognition,
DOI 10.1007/978-1-84996-507-1_7, © Springer-Verlag London Limited 2010

video assets. Therefore, how to attract more online video audience and create significant amounts of additional revenue from the existing online video inventory is an emerging problem.

A few existing online video services start to develop video analyzing and editing tools for users to organize their videos and enrich or enhance the message conveyed in videos by inserting additional contents. For example, the YouTube analytic tool "*Hot Spots*" compares each video to other videos of similar length on YouTube to determine which points in a video are "*hot.*" Thus, users can know which part of the uploaded videos is interesting and attractive to audience by using the analytic tool. On the other hand, YouTube also provides video annotation tool for users to add speech bubbles, notes, and spotlight overlays on videos. In addition, Google developed a new type of video-based advertising, which is called "*InVideo ad,*" and had launched to try to get economic benefits from its video property. Generally, all the above-mentioned additional contents which are inserted into the videos virtually can be considered as the virtual content compared to the original content. According to different purposes, such as advertising, entertainment, and information enhancement, the inserted virtual contents could be the brand, commercial logos, interesting images, informative windows, or whatever messages which content owners desired to deliver to audiences. Since the more attractive a video is the more advertising revenue it can generate, the virtual content insertion has received tremendous attention from both academia and industry sides.

By using the virtual content insertion techniques, some existing online companies, such as Overlay.TV [2] and INNOVID [3], provided whole new advertising services to increase the additional revenue with regard to the virtual product placement for online video-sharing services. In addition to the industry, efficient methods [4] and automatic systems [5–7] for virtual content insertion have been studied in the past years. With the techniques of content-based video analysis, the geometrical relationships of the scene in videos and the surface of the flat area can be estimated for projecting the virtual content onto the scene [4]. Based on the visual attention model, a virtual content insertion system was proposed in [7] to support various types of videos by identifying suitable insertion regions and using two types of insertion methods for different situations. In [8], the ViSA system was proposed to provide the virtual spotlighted advertising for tennis videos by taking psychology, computational aesthetics, and advertising theory into account. The representation of the inserted virtual content induces an ingenious interaction between the inserted virtual content and the moving player. In the existing work, static representation is widely selected for inserting virtual contents into videos to reduce the induced intrusiveness. As a result, only limited insertion time and place are available for inserting the virtual content into videos.

Motivated by the above observations, an interesting system [9, 10] was proposed to try to break the limitations. The system can vividly evolve the inserted virtual contents in videos along an incremental and interactive evolution process and provide users a creative way to enrich and monetize their personal videos. Similar to other virtual content insertion systems, the virtual contents could be the advertisements, trademarks, commercial logos, or any other images that users indented to insert into videos. Nevertheless, the virtual content would have distinct yet dependent phases, in which different evolutional appearances and/or behaviors according to various interactions, on the basis of predefined evolutionary mechanisms provided by the system. The evolution would be triggered to develop the virtual content from an organic cell to an intelligent being with the incremental stimuli induced from interactions. As a result, with different source videos or insertion points, the interactions between the virtual content and the source video will be completely different and produce an entertaining storyline accordingly.

The benefits of the induced evolutionary pathway provided by the system are twofold. First, the partial features of the inserted virtual content revealed in each phase will arouse audiences' curiosity and make them wonder about what the virtual content finally is. Second, it provides users various points of view to observe the virtual content and imperceptibly makes itself stick to viewers' minds with enhanced impression.

Through the interaction-induced evolution, the virtual content changes its appearances and behaviors dramatically and improves the audience's viewing experience to the original video. In addition, by creating interactions between the virtual content and the source video to construct visually relevant connections will make the augmented videos visually appealing and increase its acceptability and attractiveness because such insertion is comparatively less intrusive.

2 System Overview

In this section, we describe the essential ideas for designing the presented system and then give an overview of the system architecture.

2.1 Essential Ideas

Undoubtedly, plain styles of static presentation for the virtual content would make the induced storyline likely dull and boring. Therefore, it could not make the augmented videos more entertaining and engaging. Furthermore, the inserted virtual content will be easily ignored or bring visual intrusiveness. Some researchers [11, 12] indicated that a virtual content which is semantically relevant to the videos would reduce the induced intrusiveness while inserting it into videos. Therefore, if the virtual content is selected by the users, the only thing that the system can do is to construct a visually relevant link between the virtual content and the source video content. Based on the observation and inspired by the evolutionary biology, we can create a new representation for the inserted virtual content to establish a contextual relevance in terms of visual perception. Specifically, we can assign lifelike characteristics to the virtual content and animate it by interacting with the video contents in a vivid way. The above mentioned idea is conceptually illustrated in Fig. 1.

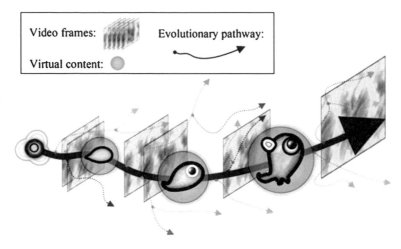

Fig. 1 The basic idea of the presented system. The videos are considered not only as carriers of message conveyed by the virtual content but also as the environment in which the lifelike virtual contents live

In the system, we break up the evolution of the inserted virtual content into three distinct yet dependent phases, that is, the *cell phase*, the *microbe phase*, and the *creature phase*. Arising from the external stimuli perceived in each phase, the appearance and behaviors of the virtual content will change in an evolutionary way and reveal more and more colors and textures. Eventually, the virtual content becomes an intelligent creature and interacts with a specific character of the source video contents, such as salient regions or attractive roles in videos.

2.2 System Overview

Figure 2 illustrates the overview of the presented system which consists of three stages: the virtual content analysis stage, the video content analysis stage, and the virtual content insertion stage. After selecting a video for inserting virtual content, both the visual and aural analyses are conducted in the video content analysis stage. For visual analysis, the frame profiling is applied to each frame of the input video for estimating the motion information and discriminating regions according to the analyzed visual features. On the other hand, the ROI estimation module localizes the region of interest in each video frame by combining various visual features. In addition to visual analysis, aural saliency analysis is performed to characterize the sound which accompanies the video. Finally, by combining the result of each module in the video content analysis stage, a multilayer feature space for the input video is automatically constructed.

In the virtual content analysis stage, the characterization module is used to analyze the appearance of the virtual content for visually evolving in terms of shapes, colors, and textures. With the output information of the characterization module, the

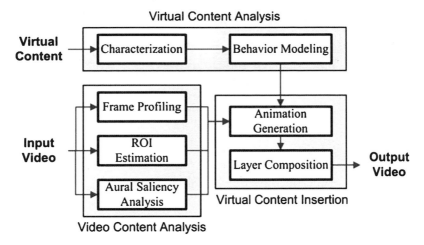

Fig. 2 The architecture of the presented system which consists of three stages: the virtual content analysis stage, the video content analysis stage, and the virtual content insertion stage

virtual content is assigned the various sensors and effectors for generating behaviors with evolutions in the behavior modeling module.

Then, in the virtual content insertion stage, the animation generation module acts on the effectors and sensors of the inserted virtual content. Therefore, according to the features perceived by the sensors of the virtual content, the effectors automatically generate the corresponding reactions. In the layer composition module, the virtual layer, in which the virtual content is animated on, is integrated with the video layer. Eventually, the augmented video with virtual content overlay is produced. The detailed processes of each module in the presented system are described in the following sections.

3 Video Content Analysis

In the video content analysis stage, the input video is analyzed, and various audio-visual features are extracted.

3.1 Frame Profiling

For the purpose of simulating the input video as the living environment that the virtual content moves and behaves in, the motion activity is defined as the source of background influence that could affect the movement of the virtual content. Then, the regions in each video frame are discriminated according to the colors and textures.

Fig. 3 An example for showing a video frame with embedded motion vectors

3.1.1 Motion Estimation

Many sophisticated motion estimation algorithms have been developed in the literature, for example, the optical flow in [13] and the feature tracking in [14]. However,
they often have high computational complexity because the operations are executed
in the pixel domain and the estimated motions are accurate.

Fortunately, in our works, an accurate motion estimation is not needed, we can
directly extract the motion information from the motion vectors of a compressed
video. Since the process is done directly in the compression domain, the induced
complexity is very low. Therefore, the motions in each video frame can be efficiently
obtained, as shown in Fig. 3. The extracted motion vectors at the coordinate of
macroblocks (x, y) in the nth video frame are denoted by $\mathbf{MV}^n(x, y)$.

3.1.2 Region Segmentation

In order to discriminate the influence induced from regions in the video frame, we
use an unsupervised image segmentation algorithm, which is called JSEG [15],
to segment each motion-vector-embedded video frame into several disjoint color-
texture regions. Note that the motion vectors which are illustrated on the video
frame can be considered as some kind of texture information for image segmentation. Therefore, in addition to color and texture, the motion vectors are also cleverly
used to segment regions in the video frame. In this way, the segmentation map for
each video frame can be constructed. The segmentation map of the nth frame is
denoted by S^n and can be defined as

$$S^n = \bigcup_j s_j^n, \quad \text{where } s_j^n \cap s_{j'}^n = \phi \text{ if } j \neq j', \tag{1}$$

where s_j^n represents the jth disjoint color-texture region in the nth frame. Note that
the number of segmentation regions may be different in each video frame. Figure 4
shows two examples of motion-vector-embedded video frame segmentation. Each
segmentation region is considered as an independent background with different influence to the virtual content, and the region boundary would restrict or affect the
movement of virtual contents according to the user-defined behavior modeling.

With the frame profiling module, the *background (BG) feature map*, which describes the motion vectors and the segmented regions for each video frame, is constructed.

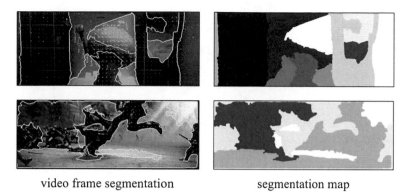

video frame segmentation   segmentation map

Fig. 4 Two examples of motion-vector-embedded video frame segmentation. The Left column shows video frame segmentation, and the right column shows the corresponding segmentation maps

3.2 ROI Estimation

Based on different combinations of visual feature models, several approaches [16, 17] have been proposed to construct a saliency map by computing the attentive strength for each pixel or image block. On the basis of the saliency map, the region-of-interest (ROI) can be easily derived by evaluating the center of gravity and the ranging variance. In the presented system, four types of video-oriented visual features, selected from low level to high level, including *contrast-based intensity*, *contrast-based color*, *motion*, and *human skin color*, are adopted to construct corresponding feature maps independently. Therefore, using different weights to linearly combine the constructed feature maps can produce various saliency maps with different meanings. In the implementation, we construct two types of saliency maps, i.e., HROI and LROI, which are defined by emphasizing the human skin color and the contrast-based color, respectively, to distinguish the attractive salient regions perceived by the virtual content in different phases. Figure 5 shows the combination methods and the corresponding feature maps.

3.3 Aural Saliency Analysis

Based on the same idea proposed in [18], we define the aural saliency response, $AR(T_h, T)$, at a time unit T and within a duration T_h, to quantify the salient strength of the sound. That is,

$$AR(T_h, T) = \frac{E_{\mathrm{avr}}(T)}{\hat{E}_{\mathrm{avr}}(T_h)} \cdot \frac{E_{\mathrm{peak}}(T)}{\hat{E}_{\mathrm{peak}}(T_h)}, \tag{2}$$

where $E_{\mathrm{avr}}(T)$ and $E_{\mathrm{peak}}(T)$ are the *average sound energy* and the *sound energy peak* in the period T, respectively. In addition, we denote by $\hat{E}_{\mathrm{avr}}(T_h)$ and $\hat{E}_{\mathrm{peak}}(T_h)$

Fig. 5 An example for
showing LROI map (*top-left*)
and HROI map (*top-right*) in
which high-intensity parts
indicate more attentive
regions

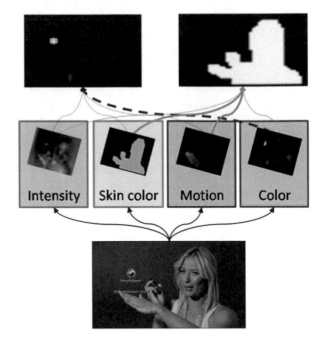

the *maximum average sound energy* and the *maximum sound energy peak* within
duration T_h. In order to suppress the noises from low frequencies, the sound energy
is defined as the weighted sum over the spectrum power of an audio signal at a given
time as follows:

$$E \triangleq \int_0^{f_s} W(f) \cdot 10 \log \left(|SF(f)|^2 + \varsigma \right) df, \qquad (3)$$

where $SF(f)$ is the *short-time Fourier transform* of the frequency component f,
and f_s denotes the sampling frequency. Figure 6 shows the weighted sound energy
for an input audio. In addition, $W(f)$ is the corresponding weighting function (cf.
Fig. 7) defined by

$$W(f) = \frac{1}{1 + e^{-f_1(f - f_2)}}, \qquad (4)$$

where f_1 and f_2 are control parameters.

After analyzing the aural saliency of an audio, we construct an *AR feature se-*
quence which describes the aural saliency response at each time unit T in the video,
as shown in Fig. 8.

4 Virtual Content Analysis

In the virtual content analysis stage, we analyze the visual features of the virtual
content for developing the appearance evolving mechanism and defining several
motion styles to synthesize the lifelike behaviors.

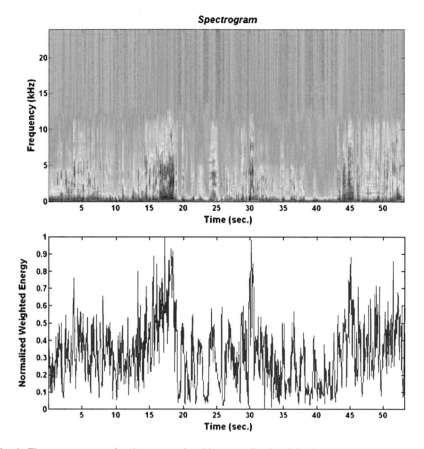

Fig. 6   The spectrogram of an input sound and its normalized weighted energy

Fig. 7   The weighting function defined by (4) with $f_1 = 3.2$ (kHz) and $f_2 = 6.4$ (kHz)

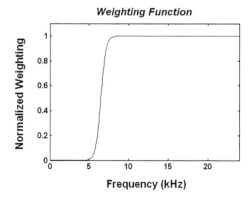

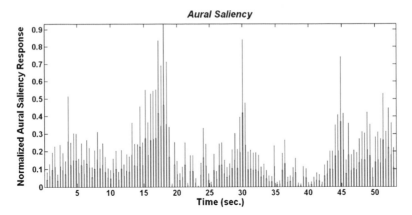

Fig. 8 The normalized aural saliency response of the audio segment given in Fig. 6

Fig. 9 Sample results of the segmentations. (**a**) Virtual content, (**b**) virtual content segmentation, and (**c**) segmentation map

(a)   (b)   (c)

4.1 Virtual Content Characterization

In order to evolve the virtual content in terms of the appearance, we analyze its visual features, such as colors and textures. Similarly, we use the prescribed color-texture segmentation algorithm JSEG to segment the virtual content image into several disjoint color-texture regions. Each region is defined as a *cell* of the virtual content. The segmentation map H for the virtual content is defined as

$$H = \bigcup_{i=1}^{N} h_i, \quad \text{where } h_i \cap h_{i'} = \phi \text{ if } i \neq i', \tag{5}$$

where h_i is the ith disjoint region in the segmentation map and N is the total numbers of regions. Figure 9 shows an example of the virtual content segmentation and the associated segmentation map.

In order to let the virtual content drop into the videos in a less-intrusive manner, the cells of the virtual content should be presented in a sequence according to a suitable order. In this work, a region with the smallest area in the segmentation map is set as the initial cell to be presented and the next one should be the smallest one in its neighbors, which directly connect to the previous selected region, to avoid discontinuity.

With the determined order, we can evolve the shape of the virtual content by controlling the opacity of each region to simulate the effect of growing up, as shown in Fig. 10.

Fig. 10 An example for showing the effect of growing up of the virtual content

Next, we define the mass of the virtual content M_{vc} as

$$M_{\text{vc}} = \lambda \cdot \sum_i \alpha_i \cdot Area(r_i),$$ (6)

where λ is a scaling factor, α_i is the opacity of the ith segmentation region, and $Area(r_i)$ is the area of the region r_i. It means that the mass of the virtual content is proportional to the area of presented cells of the virtual content.

4.2 Behavior Modeling

In the behavior modeling module, we assign various *sensors* and *effectors* for the virtual content to let it interact with the video contents and trigger evolutions. For capturing the different feature maps which are mentioned in Sect. 3, there are four types of sensors are defined, i.e., *BG sensor*, *LROI sensor*, *HROI sensor*, and *AS sensor*. Furthermore, there are two effectors defined to react with the sensor data and synthesize the behaviors, i.e., *TL effector* which controls the translation and *RS effector* which controls the rotation and scaling. In the implementation, BG sensor, LROI sensor, and HROI sensor are connected to TL effector, whereas AS sensor is connected to RS effector. In addition, we define *CT sensor* to detect the predefined events for evolving and *EV effector* to control the colors and the opacity of the virtual content *layer* to simulate evolutions. In order to make motions as physically plausible as possible, the movement of the virtual content obeys *Newton's law*. There are three types of forces defined in this system:

1. *The external force* of the region R, where the virtual content is emplaced, is defined as the resultant force exerted on the region R by the surrounding regions B and is denoted by $\mathbf{F_e}(B, R)$. The surrounding regions are given by

$$B = \{s_j \in S | s_j \cup R\}.$$

2. *The internal force* of the region Q is defined as the resultant force contributed in the region Q and is denoted by $\mathbf{F_o}(Q)$.

3. *The spontaneous force* is defined as the inherent force of the virtual content for moving actively and is denoted by F_s.

Accordingly, *TL effector* estimates the resultant force of the virtual content $\mathbf{F_{vc}}$ and calculates the displacements for the translations based on *Newton's second law* and the *law of reflection* while colliding with the boundary. In order to simulate the development of the intelligence, the behaviors of the virtual content will become complex and rich with the change of the evolution phase. An alternative evolutionary pathway for the inserted virtual content is stated in the following paragraphs.

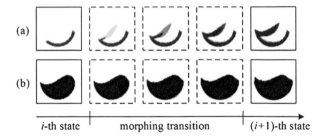

i-th state | morphing transition | (i+1)-th state

Fig. 11 Two examples for showing the morphing transition between two consecutive states. The contours in (**b**) are darkened, while (**a**) are not. The source (*left column*) and the destination (*right column*) are warped and cross-dissolved throughout the metamorphosis

4.2.1 The Cell Phase

Initially, BG sensor is activated to simulate the sense of touch, and thereby the received surrounding force is the only factor that affects the movement of the virtual content. With the sensor data, TL effector updates the resultant force of the virtual content $\mathbf{F_{vc}}$ to $\mathbf{F_e}$. The regions for the virtual content moving around are restricted to its initial inserted segmentation regions.

The event for evolving is defined as that the change of direction of $\mathbf{F_{vc}}$ is larger than a predefined threshold. Once the event is detected by CT sensor, EV effector will control the opacity to present the cell of the virtual content; otherwise, the cell will be presented piece by piece in a predefined speed.

In order to reduce the visual intrusiveness, EV effector harmonizes the virtual content with its background (the video frame) based on the idea of [8], by using the method proposed in [19]. The harmonized colors of presented cells in each state are simplified to a single color by averaging. Then, the contour of the presented cell is darkened to enhance the shape information of the virtual content. Moreover, the technique of morphing [20] is used to generate realistic transitions between two consecutive states, to further improve the effect of shape evolving, as illustrated in Fig. 11.

Once all the cells of the virtual content are presented, the virtual content would advance to the next phase.

4.2.2 The Microbe Phase

In this phase, LROI sensor is additionally activated to simulate the sense of sight, and an LROI region is detected. In order to let the virtual content be attracted by LROI region and move toward it, TL effector updates the resultant force of the virtual content as follows:

$$\begin{cases} \mathbf{F_{vc}} = \mathbf{F_e}(\overline{Q_L}, R) + \mathbf{F_s}, \\ \angle(\mathbf{F_s}) = \tan^{-1} \frac{\|y_{Q_L} - y_R\|}{\|x_{Q_L} - x_R\|}, \end{cases} \tag{7}$$

where (x_R, y_R) and (x_{Q_L}, y_{Q_L}) denote the centers of R and Q_L respectively, and $\overline{Q_L}$ represents the non-LROI region. Note that the resultant force of the virtual con-

Fig. 12 An example for showing the relations between the opacity map and the presented cell. The opacity in (**b**) is weighted, and (**a**) is not

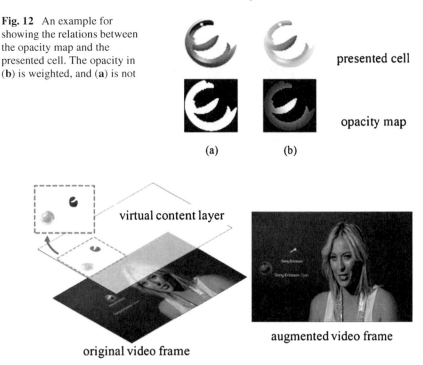

presented cell

opacity map

(a)   (b)

virtual content layer

augmented video frame

original video frame

Fig. 13 An example for showing the way to produce the effect of absorbability

tent F_{vc} would not be updated until an LROI region is detected. The virtual content is restricted to move within the $\overline{Q_L}$ region to avoid masking the salient region.

The event, in this phase, for triggering the evolving process is the collision between the virtual content and the LROI region. Each time the virtual content touches the boundary of an LROI region, the original colors of cell would be presented with the fading-in effect, and the opacity would be modulated by a Gaussian function, as shown in Fig. 12. At the same time, one of the segmentation regions in the LROI region would be visually erased by using the techniques of inpainting [21] to produce a background color overlay on it, as shown in Fig. 13. In this way, the virtual content is simulated to get the colors and textures, by absorbing the energy of the salient object, in the LROI region.

Once the original colors of the virtual content are all presented, the virtual content would evolve to the final phase.

4.2.3 The Creature Phase

In the final phase, both AS and HROI sensors are additionally activated to simulate the sense of hearing and develop a more penetrative sight. In other words, the virtual content is simulated to have the ability to dance with the perceived aural stimuli and interacts with the moving salient object in an intelligent manner.

Fig. 14 An example for
showing the transitions for
producing the jiggling effect

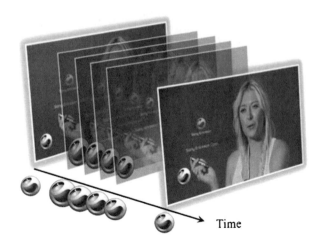

Fig. 15 An example for
showing the transitions for
simulating the astonished
expression

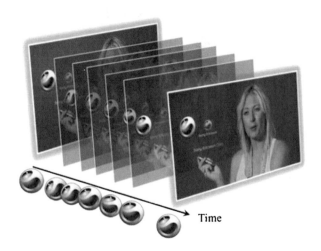

For AS sensor data, we define two thresholds, say TH_L^A and TH_H^A, for RS effector
to separately control the rotation and the scaling. If AS sensor value is larger than
TH_L^A but smaller than TH_H^A, RS effector computes a set of degrees of rotations to
generate the jiggling effect, as shown in Fig. 14. On the other hand, if AS sensor
data is larger than TH_H^A, RS effector computes the parameters of scaling to generate
the effect of astonished expression, as shown in Fig. 15.

For HROI sensor data, the virtual content is simulated to start interacting with
moving salient regions, and TL effector updates the resultant force of the virtual
content as follows:

$$\begin{cases} \mathbf{F_{vc}} = \mathbf{F_e}(\overline{Q_H}, R) + \mathbf{F_s}, \\ \angle(\mathbf{F_s}) = \tan^{-1} \frac{\|y_{Q_H} - y_R\|}{\|x_{Q_H} - x_R\|}, & \text{if } \mathbf{F_o}(Q_H) > TH^F, \\ \mathbf{F_{vc}} = \mathbf{F_e}(\overline{Q_H}, R) + \mathbf{F_o}(Q_H), & \text{otherwise,} \end{cases} \quad (8)$$

where $\overline{Q_H}$ is the non-HROI region, TH^F is a threshold, and (x_{Q_H}, y_{Q_H}) is the center of HROI region Q_H. The virtual content is restricted to movie within the $\overline{Q_H}$ region to avoid masking the moving salient region. In this way, the salient region with different levels of motions would cause TL effector producing different reactions. Specifically, if the motion of salient object is smaller than the threshold TH^F, the virtual content tends to imitate the behavior of the moving salient object. On the other hand, if the moving salient region behaves exaggeratedly, the virtual content would move to touch it.

In summary, the sensors and effectors described in this section can be considered as the *genotype* of the virtual content, and different arrangements or parameter settings of sensors and effectors can generate different evolutions and interactions.

5 Virtual Content Insertion

In the last stage, the system automatically generates impressive animations with evolutions on a virtual layer according to the extracted features and the virtual content behavior settings. Finally, the virtual layer is overlaid onto the input video to produce an augmented video with separated layers.

5.1 Animation Generation

After determining the insertion position for an input video, the animation generation module acts on the effectors and sensors of the inserted virtual content. The effectors begin to react to the features perceived by the sensors and automatically animate the inserted virtual content for each video frame, according to the prescribed behavior settings. The received motion vectors are mapped to the forces, as described in Sect. 4, to quantify the influence induced from the videos. Specifically, the external force is computed as the weighted vector sum of motion vectors in the surrounding region of the nth video frame, that is,

$$\mathbf{F}\left(B^n, R^n\right) = \sum_{(x,y) \in B^n} G(x, y, x_{R^n}, y_{R^n}) \cdot \widehat{\mathbf{MV}}^n(x, y) \cdot I_{R^n}(x, y),$$

$$\text{where } G(x, y, x_{R^n}, y_{R^n}) = e^{\left(-\frac{(x-x_{R^n})^2 + (y-y_{R^n})^2}{2\sigma^2}\right)},$$

$$\text{and } I_{R^n}(x, y) = \begin{cases} 0, & (x, y) \in R^n, \\ 1, & \text{otherwise.} \end{cases} \tag{9}$$

Note that (x_{R^n}, y_{R^n}) in (9) denotes the central macroblock in the region R of the nth video frame, and I_{R^n} is used to indicate whether the macroblock is in the region R of the nth video frame. In addition, $\widehat{\mathbf{MV}}^n(x, y)$ denotes that its direction is opposite to $\mathbf{MV}^n(x, y)$. Similarly, the internal force is computed as

$$\mathbf{F_o}\left(Q^n\right) = \sum_{(x,y) \in Q^n} G(x, y, x_{Q^n}, y_{Q^n}) \cdot \widehat{\mathbf{MV}}^n(x, y). \tag{10}$$

Accordingly, the displacement of the virtual content in the $(n+d)$th frame $\mathbf{P}^n(d)$ can be calculated by

$$\mathbf{V}^n(d) = \mathbf{V}^n + \frac{\mathbf{F}_{vc}^n}{M_{vc}^n} \cdot d, \tag{11}$$

$$\mathbf{P}^n(d) = \mathbf{V}^n \cdot d + \frac{\mathbf{F}_{vc}^n}{2 \cdot M_{vc}^n} \cdot d^2, \tag{12}$$

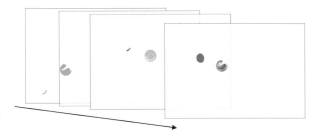

Fig. 16 Sample results of the constructed virtual layer

Fig. 17 Snapshots of the augmented video showing the evolution of the cell phase for the inserted virtual content. (**a**) The virtual content is dropped into the video and begins to evolve its shape. (**b**) The contour of the inserted virtual content (i.e., a *circle*) will appear in the end of the cell phase after a series of shape evolving

(a)   (b)

where $\mathbf{V}^n(d)$ is the simulated velocity of the virtual content in the $(n + d)$th frame, $\mathbf{F}_{vc}^n$ and M_{vc}^n respectively represent the resultant force and the mass of virtual content in the nth frame, and d is the duration of the nth frame.

Note that the animations of virtual content are constructed on a virtual layer in the animation generation module, as shown in Fig. 16. Thus, the original video frame will not be modified by the presented system.

5.2 Layer Composition

The final task of the virtual content insertion stage is to produce the augmented video by integrating the virtual layer with the input video layer. The two-layer augmented videos are implemented by using the techniques of *Flash*. Therefore, the inserted virtual content can be hidden if viewers want to see the original video. In addition, users can easily choose interesting virtual contents with different behaviors to overlay on the same source video for targeting the online audiences based on their demographic information or cultures.

Fig. 18 Snapshots of the augmented video showing the evolution of the microbe phase for the inserted virtual content. (**a**) The inserted virtual content moves toward to the discovered logo (i.e., Sony Ericsson), which is originally placed in the background, and touches the logo to absorb its colors and textures. (**b**) The original logo in the background will disappear, and the inserted virtual content will obtain the complete colors and textures in the end of the microbe phase

(a)   (b)

6 Experimental Results

This section presents the experimental results of the presented system. A source video was randomly selected from YouTube, and a commercial logo which is contextually relevant to the selected video was used as the input to the system. The snapshots of the augmented video are shown in Figs. 17, 18, and 19.

In order to make the insertion less intrusive, the virtual content should be dropped into videos with a simplified appearance and fundamental behaviors in the beginning. Since the virtual content behaves like a single-celled organism in this phase, we call the phase as the *cell phase*. Through the cell phase, the cell-like virtual content is subject to the background influence and acts passively. We assign the artificial sense of touch to the virtual content as its initial sensor in the cell phase. With the sense of touch, the shape of the virtual content would be evolved according to the level of perceived stimuli. In other words, it would grow strong to accommodate itself to the background. Generally, if the directions or amplitudes of extracted motion vectors change rapidly and are disordered in some region on consecutive video frames, such region will be looked like cluttered and even unrecognizable. Consequently, it will be less striking and will not distract audiences' attention if

Fig. 19 Snapshots of the augmented video showing the evolution of the creature phase for the inserted virtual content. (**a**) The inserted virtual content is rubbed by the character's hand and shrinks to express astonishment at the salient sound. (**b**) The inserted virtual content finally moves to the location where the logo is originally placed in the background

(a)   (b)

the shape of the virtual content changes quickly in such cluttered region. Therefore, with strange disorder fluid force induced from the background, the evolving speed will be faster. Note that the visual information of the virtual content that viewer can confirm is only its contour in the end of the cell phase, as shown in Fig. 17. In this way, the inserted virtual content will arouse audience's curiosity and tickle their imaginations.

Besides the sense of touch, the virtual content is assigned the artificial sense of sight in the end of the cell phase. Therefore, the virtual content in the microbe phase will begin to discover and actively move close to the salient object, with colorful appearance, and develop the synonymous ability to enhance its own colors and textures. Each time the virtual content touches the colorful object, it will absorb the object's colors and textures and finally reveal its complete visual information, as shown in Fig. 18. The evolution process in the phrase would make viewers wonder about what the virtual content truly is.

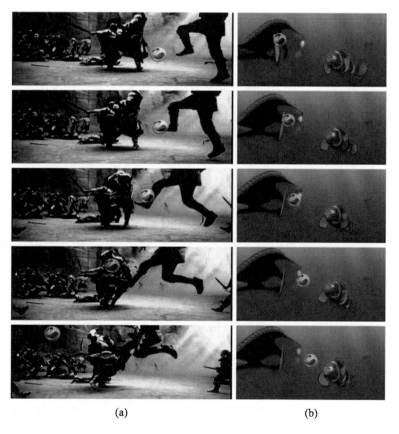

(a)   (b)

Fig. 20 Snapshots of sample results showing interesting interactions between the inserted logo (i.e., Sony Ericsson) and the roles of the films, (**a**) "*300*" and (**b**) "*Finding Nemo.*" The inserted logo is kicked away like a ball by a solder in (**a**) and is flipped by the blue fish in (**b**)

In the creature phase, we assign the artificial sense of hearing to the virtual content, so that it will dance with the perceived aural stimuli and interact with the moving salient object in an intelligent manner, as shown in Fig. 19.

In this way, a visually strong connection between the virtual content and the
source video could be constructed, and the entertaining storyline with uncertainty
could be produced automatically.

In addition to the advertising videos, several movies were selected to be fed into
the presented system for the purposes of testification and entertainment. Several
interesting interactions between the inserted virtual content and the role in the source
video are automatically generated by the presented system, as shown in Figs. 20
and 21. Note that the entertaining events occurred in the videos are not planned
by users in advance. In other words, the events occurred in videos depend only on
the properties of videos and the predefined genotype of the inserted virtual content.
Therefore, a new storyline, which is induced by a series of interaction events, can
be generated automatically in the augmented video.

We recorded a personal video, which contained only a person doing some actions. With the virtual content embedded by the presented system, the person can
interactively play with the virtual content through the webcam, as shown in Fig. 22.

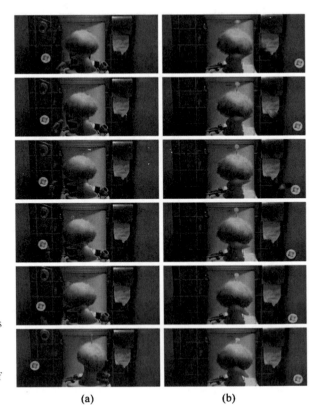

Fig. 21 An example for
showing the interesting events
in the film "*CJ7*." The
inserted logo (i.e., Micorsoft)
is hit by the objects, which
are thrown by the character of
the film, wherever the logo
moves in (**a**) and (**b**)

(**a**)   (**b**)

Fig. 22 Snapshots of the recorded personal video "*Plays*". The sequence shows the inserted logo (i.e., Sony Ericsson) which moves toward the person in (**a**) and is hit after rebounding off the wall in (**b**)

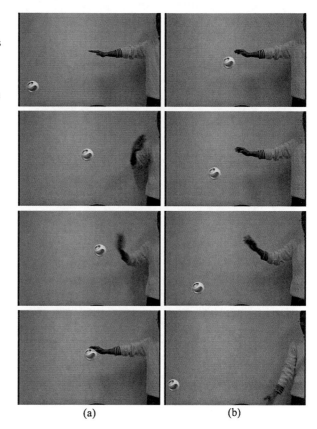

(a)   (b)

7 Summary

We have presented a novel system which provides lifelike animations for inserting virtual content into personal videos, in a vivid way, to enhance the impression and acceptability of the inserted virtual content. The experimental results show that the augmented videos produced by the presented system improve the audience's viewing experience on the original video content and fascinate viewers with interesting interactions and induced entertaining storyline.

The presented system can be used for several application scenarios. For example, users can pick an arbitrary image as a virtual content for friends to interact with via the webcam and guess what it is, just like playing an interactive game. In addition, users can create and visualize a script of interesting stories for the inserted virtual content in videos and generate a unique personal video with originality for personal branding. For educational purposes, the inserted virtual content could enrich the lecture videos and provide a new type of adaptive video learning [22]. Furthermore, it could also be treated as a whole new advertising-oriented tool for users to monetize their video assets on the online video-sharing websites.

References

1. YouTube: http://www.youtube.com
2. Overy.TV: http://www.overlay.tv
3. INNOVID: http://www.innovid.com
4. Yu, X., Jiang, N., Cheong, L., Leong, H., Yan, X.: Automatic camera calibration of broadcast tennis video with applications to 3D virtual content insertion and ball detection and tracking. Comput. Vis. Image Underst. **113**(5), 643–652 (2009)
5. Wan, K., Yan, X.: Advertising insertion in sports webcasts. IEEE Trans. Multimed. **14**(2), 78-8-2-8 (2007)
6. Lai, J.-H., Chien, S.-Y.: Tennis video enrichment with content layer separation and real-time rendering in sprite plane. In: Proc. 10th IEEE Workshop on Multimedia Signal Processing (MMSP'08), pp. 672–675 (2008)
7. Liu, H., Jiang, S., Huang, Q., Xu, C.: A generic virtual content insertion system based on visual attention analysis. In: Proc. 16th ACM Int. Conf. Multimedia (MM'08), pp. 379–388 (2008)
8. Chang, C.-H., Hsieh, K.-Y., Chung, M.-C., Wu, J.-L.: ViSA: virtual spotlighted advertising. In: Proc. 16th ACM Int. Conf. Multimedia (MM'08), pp. 837–840 (2008)
9. Chang, C.-H., Chiang, M.-C., Wu, J.-L.: Evolving virtual contents with interactions in videos. In: Proc. 1st ACM Int. Workshop on Interactive Multimedia for Consumer Electronics (IMCE'09), pp. 97–104 (2009)
10. Chiang, M.-C., Chang, C.-H., Wu, J.-L.: Evolution-based virtual content insertion. In: Proc. 17th ACM Int. Conf. Multimedia (MM'09), pp. 995–996 (2009)
11. Mccoy, S., Everard, A., Polak, P., Galletta, D.F.: The effects of online advertising. Commun. ACM **50**(3), 84–88 (2007)
12. Li, H., Edwards, S., Lee, J.: Measuring the intrusiveness of advertisements: scale development and validation. J. Advert. **31**(2), 37–47 (2002)
13. Beauchemin, S.S., Barron, J.L.: The computation of optical flow. ACM Comput. Surv. **27**(3), 433–466 (1995)
14. Shi, J., Tomasi, C.: Good features to track. In: Proc. Computer Vision and Pattern Recognition, pp. 539–600 (1994)
15. Deng, Y., Manjunath, B.S.: Unsupervised segmentation of color-texture regions in images and video. IEEE Trans. Pattern Anal. Mach. Intell. **23**(8), 800–810 (2001)
16. Cheng, W.-H., Wang, C.-W., Wu, J.-L.: Video adaptation for small display based on content recomposition. IEEE Trans. Circuits Syst. Video Technol. **17**(1), 43–58 (2007)
17. Walther, D., Koch, C.: Modeling attention to salient proto-objects. Neural Netw. **19**, 1395–1407 (2006)
18. Ma, Y., Hua, X., Lu, L., Zhang, H.: A generic framework of user attention model and its application in video summarization. IEEE Trans. Multimed. **7**(5), 907–919 (2005)
19. Cohen-Or, D., Sorkine, O., Gal, R., Leyvand, T., Xu, Y.: Color harmonization. ACM Trans. Graph. **25**(3), 624–630 (2006)
20. Wolberg, G.: Image morphing: a survey. Computer **14**, 360–372 (1998)
21. Patwardhan, K.A., Sapiro, G., Bertalmio, M.: Video inpainting under constrained camera motion. IEEE Trans. Image Process. **16**(2), 545–553 (2007)
22. Chang, C.-H., Lin, Y.-T., Wu, J.-L.: Adaptive video learning by the interactive e-partner. In: Proc. 3rd International Conference on Digital Game and Intelligent Toy Enhanced Learning (DIGITEL'10), pp. 207–209 (2010)

Physical Activity Recognition with Mobile Phones: Challenges, Methods, and Applications

Jun Yang, Hong Lu, Zhigang Liu, and Péter Pál Boda

Abstract   In this book chapter, we present a novel system that recognizes and records the physical activity of a person using a mobile phone. The sensor data is collected by built-in accelerometer sensor that measures the motion intensity of the device. The system recognizes five everyday activities in real-time, i.e., stationary, walking, running, bicycling, and in vehicle. We first introduce the sensor's data format, sensor calibration, signal projection, feature extraction, and selection methods. Then we have a detailed discussion and comparison of different choices of feature sets and classifiers. The design and implementation of one prototype system is presented along with resource and performance benchmark on Nokia N95 platform. Results show high recognition accuracies for distinguishing the five activities. The last part of the chapter introduces one demo application built on top of our system, physical activity diary, and a selection of potential applications in mobile wellness, mobile social sharing and contextual user interface domains.

J. Yang (✉) · Z. Liu · P.P. Boda
Nokia Research Center, 955 Page Mill Road, Palo Alto, CA 94304, USA
e-mail: jun.8.yang@nokia.com

Z. Liu
e-mail: zhigang.c.liu@nokia.com

P.P. Boda
e-mail: peter.boda@nokia.com

H. Lu
Dartmouth College, 6211 Sudkioff Lab, Hanover, NH 03755, USA
e-mail: hong.lu@dartmouth.edu

L. Shao et al. (eds.), *Multimedia Interaction and Intelligent User Interfaces,*
Advances in Pattern Recognition,
DOI 10.1007/978-1-84996-507-1_8, © Springer-Verlag London Limited 2010

1 Introduction

1.1 Background of Physical Activity Recognition

User context awareness is one of the emerging mobile applications and services in the area of ubiquitous computing. In general, user context means user's activity, location, preference, situation, emotion, etc. With increasingly powerful mobile phones, most of user context includes a variety of sensing components embedded in mobile phones, such as accelerometer, GPS, microphone, Bluetooth, camera, etc. Mobile phones can create continuous sensing systems that are able to collect sensor data important to a user's daily life, namely, what is the user doing, where is the user, and whom is the user staying with? In this book chapter, we investigate the methods of recognizing users' daily physical activity by accelerometer sensors with mobile phones. The machine learning method can be extended to other domains as well, such as location awareness and proximity detection. Some motion enabled applications will be discussed at the end.

Why can accelerometer data be used to infer human's physical activity? Let us take a look at the mean and standard deviation of magnitudes of accelerometer samples collected by one person for one week. They are simply clustered into six clusters by k-means method. The results of six cluster centroids and percentages are listed in Table 1. After carefully studying the centroid values in Table 1, it is not hard to find the similarities between the six clusters and our everyday motions {sitting, standing, walking, running, driving, bicycling, etc.}. Cluster 1 occupies 80% of all data with the smallest standard deviation, so it is probably related to stationary activity. Cluster 2 has a little smaller mean than that of Cluster 1, so Cluster 2 is highly related to quasi-static activity. Cluster 5 has a little larger mean and standard deviation than those of both Clusters 1 and 2 and occupies 10%, so it is probably related to driving (or relatively still). Clusters 3, 4, and 6 have higher standard deviations than Cluster 5, so they must be intensive physical activities. Cluster 3 is related to walking (or medium moving), and Cluster 4 is related to running (or intensive moving). Cluster 6 occupies 4% of all data, and it is probably related to some transitional activities (such as from sitting to standing, from standing to walking, or taking phone out of pocket, etc.), which has almost the same mean as stationary data but slightly larger standard deviation. Based on the visualization of the colored clusters depicted in Fig. 1, it indicates that useful features extracted from accelerometer data can infer human physical activities.

Several existing works have explored user activity inferencing methods with accelerometer sensors [7, 18, 27]. They can be divided into two major approaches: sensor-worn lab experiment approach and sensor-enabled mobile phone approach. In a well-cited work, Bao and Intille [7] first used multiple accelerometer sensors worn on different parts of the human body to detect common activities such as sitting, standing, walking, or running. Lester et al. [18] developed a small low-power sensor board to be mounted on a single location on the body. Then a hybrid approach was presented to recognize activities, which combines the boosting algorithm to discriminatively select useful features and HMMs (Hidden Markov Models) to capture

Table 1 K-means clustering results

Cluster No.	Centroid (meanM, stdM)	Percentage
1	(58.8689, 0.2871)	80%
2	(56.8244, 1.1331)	4%
3	(60.4005, 13.7888)	1%
4	(64.3576, 22.9281)	1%
5	(60.2872, 1.5234)	10%
6	(58.8354, 6.2127)	4%

Fig. 1 Map of clustered magnitude features

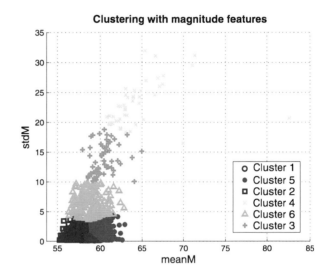

the temporal regularities and smoothness of the activities. Furthermore, Lester et al. extended their work to a practical personal activity recognition system in another paper [17]. However, the assumption made from lab experiment is usually not suitable for practical applications in regular mobile environment. In [23], a phone-centric sensing system CenceMe is introduced, and it is assumed that the mobile phone's position on the human body is fixed (e.g., in a pocket, clipped to a belt or on a lanyard), and an inference model can be trained according to a handful of body positions.

There are also previous works considering the phone's orientation problem. In [16], a method is described to derive the body part location of an accelerometer sensor where the user is walking. Also, in [13], an adaptive context inference scheme can automatically detect the sensor position on the user's body and select the most relevant inference method dynamically. However, it is not practical to divide all kinds of phone orientations into a handful of categories and make an inference model according to each of them.

In [24], Mizell has shown that the accelerometer signal averages over a reasonable time period can produce a good estimate of the gravity-related component. In a previous work [14], it has shown that many activities are determined by vertical orientation and changes thereof. In a most recent paper [15] dealing with sensor displacement in motion-based onbody activity recognition systems, the authors have discussed that if only accelerometer is available, the best we can do is to identify the segments of the signal dominated by the gravity component and make recognition based on the information about vertical orientation. Inspired by these results, we use orientation-independent features, such as vertical and horizontal components in acceleration, to recognize daily motion activities. Our methods uses a single built-in accelerometer. With a set of carefully designed features extracted from the accelerometer data, our deployed system is able to recognize five common activities (i.e., stationary, walking, running, cycling, and in-vehicle) without the GPS sensor. As far as we now, this is the first work to explore the feasibility of orientation-independent features for physical activity recognition. We further discuss how to reduce the complexity of feature computation for mobile devices with less computing power while maintaining good recognition performance. The work can be generalized to a large scale of context awareness applications using phone-based physical activity recognition.

1.2 Practical Challenges on Mobile Devices

Mobile phone-based physical activity recognition has its unique challenges. Usually it requires that all the processing is done on the phone in realtime. Although the computing capacity of mobile phones has grown in recent years, the computation and energy resource is still limited in most of the mobile devices. It is very important that our mobile activity recognition system only uses moderate CPU and memory, less battery budget, and not to jeopardize the user's experience of normal mobile phone operations. Other challenges are related to the uncertainty of how phone users carry and use the device. The developer has no control over these aspects, so the system should be robust to various practical conditions. We highlight three challenges that arise from practical usage of the mobile phone-based activity recognition as follows:

- *Data calibration.* Different accelerometer sensors have different offsets and scaling factors. Normalization is needed to ensure sensor data quality. To obtain correct offsets and scaling parameters for the normalization process, the sensor needs to be calibrated before using. We introduce a simple technique for users to calibrate the phone's accelerometer. The scheme is similar to the one presented in [21]; however, our method does not assume any prior knowledge about the hardware and avoids high cost of recursive processing.
- *Efficiency.* The tradeoff between resource and accuracy is a main consideration, when we design the mobile phone-based activity recognition system. The computation in the activity recognition system should be lightweight. Differing from an offline activity recognition system whose main metric is the recognition accuracy, a realtime online activity recognition usually has to find a balance between recognition accuracy and efficiency. The choice of signal processing module, feature set, and classifier is the key problem here. The system designer has

to shape the processing pipeline based on the requirement of the application. The most precious algorithms often cost more, so the developers have to choose low-computation alternatives or adopt duty cycles to reduce the system load.

- *Robustness.* The phone users carry their phone in many different ways (e.g., in pants pocket, in hand, in a backpack, on the belt, etc.). Phone orientation greatly affects the accelerometer sensor readings. We use vector projection to decompose the acceleration and make the extracted features orientation independent [32]. Our methods makes no assumption about the phone's orientation. This allows the user to carry the phone as usual, and our method is able to intelligently adapt itself to different usage scenarios.

2 Accelerometer Based Physical Activity Recognition Methods

In this part, we first briefly introduce the data format of accelerometer sensors in Sect. 2.1. In Sect. 2.2, we present the calibration method required to estimate parameters for accelerometer data normalization. In Sect. 2.3, the 3-D calibrated signals are filtered and projected onto 2-D signals to get orientation-independent vertical and horizontal acceleration components. Some useful features in both time and frequency domain are discussed for the 2-D components in Sect. 2.5. Several classifiers are discussed, and their performances are compared to each other in Sect. 2.6. Finally, we simply discuss the smoothing techniques in Sect. 2.7.

2.1 Data Format

We use Nokia N95 phones to collect accelerometer data. The N95 phone is equipped with a built-in accelerometer that is a triaxial MEMS motion sensor (LIS302DL) made by STMicro [2]. It has dynamically user selectable full scales of $\pm 2g/\pm 8g$ (where g is the gravitational acceleration, $g = 9.81$ m/s^2), and it is capable of measuring accelerations with an output data rate of 100 Hz or 400 Hz [6]. The digital output has 8-bit representation with each bit equaling to 18 mg. The configuration of sensor device on N95 phones is set to $\pm 2g$. The sampling frequency of N95 accelerometer sensor is reduced to a dynamic range from 32 Hz to 38 Hz by calling the Nokia Python S60 sensor API over Symbian platform. The N95 accelerometer sensor was originally only used for video stabilization and photo orientation, in order to keep landscape or portrait shots oriented as taken. Nokia Research Center has developed an application interface directly accessing the accelerometer, allowing a software to use the data from it.

Each reading of accelerometer sensor consists 3-D accelerations along X-axis, Y-axis, and Z-axis according to *local* coordinate system of *current* phone orientation. What does this local mean? In Fig. 2, a global coordinate system is shown as (X, Y, Z), and the local coordinate system based on phone's current orientation is shown as (X', Y', Z'). There is a rotation (ϕ, ρ, θ) between these two coordinate

Fig. 2 Global and local
coordinate system of 3-D
accelerometer readings

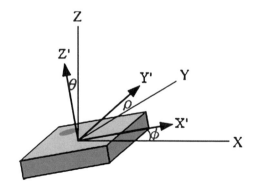

Fig. 3 Accelerometer
readings from a static phone

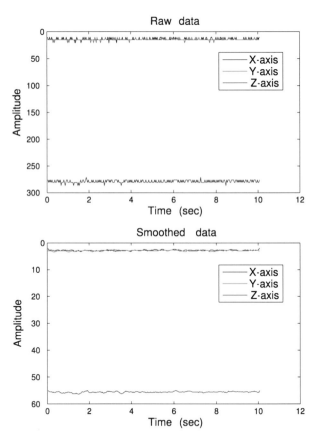

systems. Unfortunately, it is very hard to know this rotation if there is no fixed reference points. Otherwise, we can easily transform the accelerometer data points back
into the points in the global coordinate system.

To observe the raw data, a few seconds of samples of (x, y, z) readings from a
phone sitting on a table are plotted in Fig. 3. It can be seen that both x and y are
around -15 while z is around -280. Theoretically, x and y should be zero since

there is no acceleration at all, and z should be measured as $-g$. So there exists sensor offsets that affect data quality. As shown in the top subplot of Fig. 3, there is a ± 5 jittering noise present in accelerometer data when phone is fully static on the table. We can reduce the effect of jittering noise by scaling down (x, y, z) readings by a factor M and rounding, followed by a smoothing technique using a moving-average filter of span L.

After selecting $M = 5$ and $L = 5$, a new series of readings are generated and shown in the bottom subplot of Fig. 3. Statistics of raw accelerometer readings, such as mean and standard deviation, are

$$(m_x, m_y, m_z) = (-13.97, -14.53, -279.01)$$

and

$$(\sigma_x, \sigma_y, \sigma_z) = (2.23, 2.23, 2.85),$$

while mean and standard deviation of smoothed accelerometer readings are

$$(m_{x'}, m_{y'}, m_{z'}) = (-2.78, -2.89, -55.59)$$

and

$$(\sigma_{x'}, \sigma_{y'}, \sigma_{z'}) = (0.18, 0.20, 0.24).$$

It can be seen that proposed smoothing technique greatly removes jittering noise and smooths out data by more significant standard deviation reduction than mean reduction. The effect of proposed smoothing effect on accelerometer readings from a moving phone is shown in Fig. 4. When calibration process is applied to accelerometer data, the scaling procedure is not required since the data will be calibrated to gravity level. But smoothing can still help to reduce the noise present in the data.

2.2 Accelerometer Sensor Calibration

Biaxial or triaxial accelerometer sensors commonly used in mobile phones have a drift of sensitivity and offset on every axis, as shown in the last section. The accelerometer calibration procedure is to accurately determine the scaling factor (i.e., sensitivity) and offset parameters of the three independent, orthogonal axes. In most mobile applications, calibration for accelerometer is needed to assure sensor data quality and get accurate readings in terms of g-force. Noncalibrated accelerometer data will result in unknown sensitivity, i.e., Analog to Digital Converter (ADC) scaling factor, and offset that increases its maintenance cost and limits its enabled mobile applications. However, parameters of accelerometer sensor, such as sensitivity and offset, are seldom discussed in real mobile systems which assume preknowledge of the parameters, although the estimation of calibration parameters is a key step before any application can be launched from a practical point of view.

Traditional calibration of triaxial accelerometers can be carried out as a calibration of sensitivity and offset of three independent, orthogonal axes. We do

Fig. 4 Accelerometer readings from a moving phone

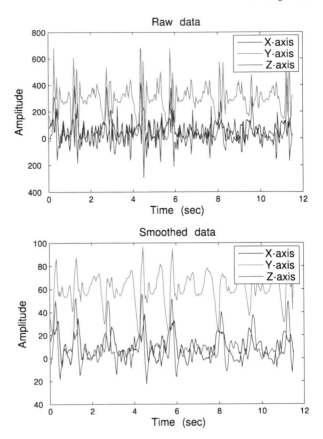

not consider cross-axis sensitivities here, as traditional calibration of accelerometers is already good enough for most applications. Under this assumption, let $\mathbf{a} = (a_x, a_y, a_z)$ be a vector of raw triaxial accelerometer reading from mobile devices, and $\mathbf{g} = (g_x, g_y, g_z)$ a calibrated vector measured in g ($g = 9.81$ m/s^2). Obviously, if the device is still, the sensor only subjects to g, whose value is known. Therefore, the user just has to get the g samples along the positive and negative direction for each of the three axes. To do this, the user has to hold the accelerometer sensor in six different orientations and make the corresponding axis strictly point to g direction. Once the positive and negative g samples of all the axis are obtained, we can calculate the parameter as follows. For example, let (a_1, a_2, a_3) and (a'_1, a'_2, a'_3) as the positive and negative g readings along X-axis,

$$offset_x = \frac{a_1 + a'_1}{2}, \qquad scale_x = \frac{|a_1 - a'_1|}{2}.$$

We only use a_1 and a'_1 here, since we only care about X-axis for now. If the user performs the procedure exactly, Y- and Z-axes should not subject to gravity, and thus a_2, a_3, a'_2, a'_3 should be all zero. However in practice, it is impossible to hold the sensor strictly along the g direction, so the reading along Y- and Z-axes will still be a small value close to zero. Repeating the same procedure, we can get the parameters for Y- and Z-axes. However, we can see that this procedure is error prone. It is difficult for the end user to determine the exact direction of the gravity and hold the sensor accordingly. Usually, the procedure needs to be carefully performed several times and use the average values.

To address the inconvenience in the traditional method, we can adopt a more complicated solution, which involves more computation but is easier to get right. Since calibration is an one-time operation, computation is not a big concern here. Let K_x, K_y, K_z and b_x, b_y, b_z be respective sensitivity gains and offsets of triaxial accelerometer to be estimated; we have

$$g_{\text{axis}} = K_{\text{axis}} \cdot a_{\text{axis}} + b_{\text{axis}}, \quad \text{where axis} = x, y, z.$$

According to reference [21], if the accelerometer sensor is in a static status, then the modulus of calibrated accelerations $\sqrt{g_x^2 + g_y^2 + g_z^2}$ is equal to $1g$. We define a target function

$$f(K_x, K_y, K_z, b_x, b_y, b_z) \triangleq \sqrt{(K_x \cdot a_x + b_x)^2 + (K_y \cdot a_y + b_y)^2 + (K_z \cdot a_z + b_z)^2}$$

and then have $f(K_x, K_y, K_z, b_x, b_y, b_z) = 1$.

A general solution to the above parameter estimation problem is a linear least square estimator based on linear approximation of the function $f(\cdot)$[21]. Without the loss of generality, we use the initial estimation of parameters $(K_0, K_0, K_0, 0, 0, 0)$, where K_0 is an unknown scaling factor. This assumption is reasonable for most commercial accelerometers since by design the sensitivity for all axes should be approximately the same and the offsets should be close to zero. After applying Taylor expansion of $f(\cdot)$ around the point $(K_0, K_0, K_0, 0, 0, 0)$, we obtain the overdetermined system of linear equations

$$f(K_x, K_y, K_z, b_x, b_y, b_z)$$
$$\approx \frac{a_x^2}{\|\mathbf{a}\|} \cdot K_x + \frac{a_y^2}{\|\mathbf{a}\|} \cdot K_y + \frac{a_z^2}{\|\mathbf{a}\|} \cdot K_z + \frac{a_x}{\|\mathbf{a}\|} \cdot b_x + \frac{a_y}{\|\mathbf{a}\|} \cdot b_y + \frac{a_z}{\|\mathbf{a}\|} \cdot b_z = 1.$$

It can be seen that the above formula does not depend on the initial value of K_0. *This allows us to design a novel calibration method that requires no precalibration knowledge (device-independent) and significantly less computation.* Once a few raw accelerometer readings under quasi-static conditions are obtained, the parameters of sensitivity and offset can be estimated directly without recursion. Let $\mathbf{a}_i = (a_{x,i}, a_{y,i}, a_{z,i})$ be the ith quasi-static accelerometer reading ($i = 1, 2, \ldots, N$, $N \geq 6$). Let the ith row vector of matrix A be

$$\left[\frac{a_{x,i}^2}{\|\mathbf{a}_i\|}, \frac{a_{y,i}^2}{\|\mathbf{a}_i\|}, \frac{a_{z,i}^2}{\|\mathbf{a}_i\|}, \frac{a_{x,i}}{\|\mathbf{a}_i\|}, \frac{a_{y,i}}{\|\mathbf{a}_i\|}, \frac{a_{z,i}}{\|\mathbf{a}_i\|} \right]. \tag{1}$$

The linear least square estimator is

$$[\hat{K}_x \ \hat{K}_y \ \hat{K}_z \ \hat{b}_x \ \hat{b}_y \ \hat{b}_z] = [1\,1\,1\ldots1] \cdot A \cdot (A^T A)^{-1}, \tag{2}$$

where $[1\,1\,1\ \ldots\ 1]$ is all-one row vector of length N.

Table 2 Parameter
estimation of two calibration
methods

	$\frac{1}{K_x}$	$\frac{1}{K_y}$	$\frac{1}{K_z}$	$\frac{\hat{b}_x}{K_x}$	$\frac{\hat{b}_y}{K_y}$	$\frac{\hat{b}_z}{K_z}$
lab [21]	305.10	299.60	296.42	2.06	13.63	24.50
user manual	303.88	297.90	295.48	2.70	14.47	25.54

Designing a quasi-static moment detector in time domain is necessary for the calibration procedure to obtain quasi-static accelerometer samples. For each M-second sliding window of the accelerometer samples, the mean and standard deviation are calculated along x, y, z axes, respectively. If for all x-, y-, z-axes, the standard deviation falls below a threshold σ, we assume that the standard deviation is only contributed by noise and the device itself is quasi-static. The mean of the frame (m_x, m_y, m_z) becomes one input candidate. The frame length M and standard deviation σ control the quality of the input candidate. However, there are minor chances that it is not, e.g., the device is in free fall, or the user of phone is in an evenly accelerating vehicle. We can filter out this kind of problematic candidates by using longer frame length and checking the signal magnitude range.

Based on the above analysis, a user-friendly manual calibration procedure can be listed as follows:

1. Phone has six surfaces as a cubic object. Put each surface of phone roughly perpendicular to g-force stationary for a couple of seconds and take the mean of those frames qualified by above quasi-static moment detector as inputs;
2. Form matrix A as in (1) to all input quasi-static accelerometer readings;
3. Use formula (2) to estimate sensitivity and offset of the device.

The whole procedure usually takes no more than one minute and can be implemented in a user-friendly way, such as voice announcement.

The performance of two different accelerometer calibration methods is shown in Table 2. The first three columns are the scaling factors and the rest are the offsets for axes X, Y, and Z, respectively. The first row contains the calibration parameters obtained carefully in a controlled lab experiment using the traditional method. The second row contains the calibration results from the proposed user manual calibration method. We use 2-second frames and set the threshold $\sigma = 2\%$. The user is requested to generate 12 different samples of different orientations. The parameters estimated from user manual calibration is very close to lab-based calibration.

To quantify the calibration error, we test the manual calibration method over a 80-sample test set containing static readings of the gravity only when the phone is tilted in different angles. Each test point is the average of accelerometer readings over 2-second frame to smooth out hardware measurement noise. The result is shown in Fig. 5. The calibration error is up to 1.1% for user manual calibration. On average, the calibration error of user manual calibration can achieve 0.55%.

Fig. 5 Calibration errors

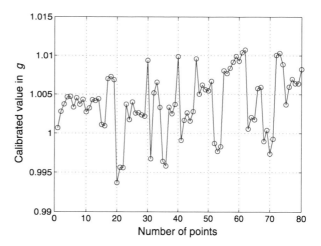

2.3 Signal Projection

For a triaxial accelerometer, the raw readings are measured according to the local coordinate system which is determined by the current sensor orientation. Some activity recognition research works fix the specialized accelerometers to a subject's body and simply use the local 3-D readings [7]. However, we have no control over how users carry their mobile phones. The tilt of the device will change the orientation of the coordinate system. One easy way to avoid the effect of accelerometer orientation is to use features that are not affected by changes in orientation, such as magnitude-based features [17]. However, this approach can lead to significant information loss.

We use orientation-independent signal projection that translates the local coordinate system to the global vertical and horizontal plane. The first step in this process is to estimate the gravity direction in the local coordinate system. In [24], Mizell shows that the mean of accelerometer readings along each axis over a long period of time can produce a good estimate of the gravity direction. The same approach is used here to estimate the gravity over a sliding time window (usually several seconds) of accelerometer readings, denoted by (x, y, z). A longer window is more precise but has a longer delay and vise versa. The gravity vector, $\mathbf{v} = (m_x, m_y, m_z)$, where m_x, m_y, and m_z are the means of respective axes, is calculated for the projection.

Let $\mathbf{a}_i = (x_i, y_i, z_i), i = 1, 2, \ldots, N$, be the acceleration vectors at given time points in the sliding window, where N is the length of the window. In our system, N is set to 128, around 4 seconds of accelerometer data length. The projection of $\mathbf{a}_i$ onto the vertical axis $\mathbf{v}_{\text{norm}}$ can be computed as the vertical component of $\mathbf{a}_i$. Let p_i^{in} be the inner product, and $\mathbf{p}_i$ be the projection vector, i.e.,

$$p_i^{\text{in}} = \langle \mathbf{a}_i, \mathbf{v}_{\text{norm}} \rangle, \qquad \mathbf{p}_i = p_i^{\text{in}} \cdot \mathbf{v}_{\text{norm}},$$

Fig. 6 Original 3-D
accelerometer signal

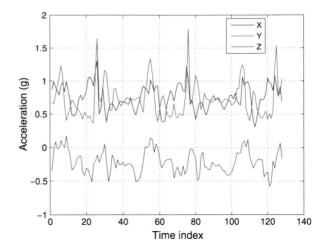

where $\mathbf{v}_{\text{norm}}$ is the normalized unit vector of $\mathbf{v}$. Then the horizontal component $\mathbf{h}_i$ of the acceleration vector $\mathbf{a}_i$ can be computed by vector subtraction, i.e.,

$$\mathbf{h}_i = \mathbf{a}_i - \mathbf{p}_i.$$

Clearly, by using the accelerometer alone, it is impossible to know the direction of $\mathbf{h}_i$ relative to the horizontal axis in global triaxial coordinate system. We only know that $\mathbf{h}_i$ lies on the horizontal plane which is orthogonal to the estimated gravity vector $\mathbf{v}$. So we simply take the magnitude of $\mathbf{h}_i$, denoted by $\|\mathbf{h}_i\|$, as a measure of horizontal movement. Finally, we get $\{(p_i^{\text{in}}, \|\mathbf{h}_i\|), i = 1, 2, \ldots, N\}$, in which both components are independent of the phone's current orientation.

For example, the original 3-D calibrated accelerometer data of 4-second windows is plotted in Fig. 6. After our signal projection, the vertical and horizontal components are shown in Fig. 7. The periodic up-and-down pattern of consistent walking from 3-D signal is still kept in orientation-independent 2-D signal, although the signal is projected onto a lower-dimensional space.

2.4 Data Collection

Similar to general pattern recognition methods, physical activity recognition needs data collection for training and generating classification models. Data of five activities, such as stationary, walking, running, cycling, and in-vehicle, are recorded to cover common everyday human movements. The most naturalistic data should be acquired from people who perform their normal everyday activities when they carry mobile phones. Unfortunately, obtaining such data requires strict supervision by researchers to record ground truth for algorithm training and testing. To work around this, we use user-controlled collection process that can allow more flexibility and variability in user behavior.

Fig. 7 Projected 2-D accelerometer signal

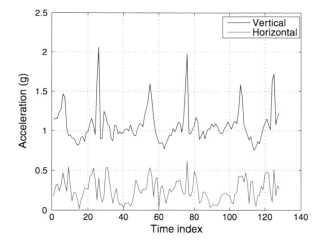

Table 3 Data set of physical activities

Index	Label	Number of samples
1	Stationary	15769
2	Walking	12424
3	Cycling	6700
4	Running	4212
5	In-vehicle	13046

During data collection, each participant carried multiple phones in different body positions and used a separate phone as a remote control to annotate the beginning and end of each activity via Bluetooth. Before the participant performs each activity, he was required to input his name, phone's body position, and activity class name as labels for training and testing purpose. Each activity should last at least 20 minutes. The data set should be collected from people varying in age, gender, height, and weight to include all kinds of varieties. Based on this principle, we collected a data set from eight people, six females and two females. The data set's structure is shown in Table 3. In total there are 52151 qualified samples, each around 4-second continuous accelerometer readings. The data set can be easily separated into a training set and a test set.

2.5 Feature Extraction and Selection

The raw accelerometer data set has a large number of attributes, which includes irrelevant information and confusing noise. Usually, it is hard to build an effective classification model directly on the raw data set. Feature extraction can compute useful information hidden in the data set and eliminate noise as well. It can also lead to a more understandable model because of fewer attributes and allow the data to be more visualized. The most important thing is that the amount of time and memory required by classification system is reduced with feature extraction. It is beneficial for realtime phone-based activity recognition.

Previous works have explored some useful features from raw accelerometer signals. In [7], mean, energy, spectral entropy, and correlation features are extracted from the sliding window signals for activity recognition. More FFT frequency features, such as cepstral coefficients and band-pass filtered coefficients, are introduced in [18] later. Time domain only features are extensively studied in [22], like root mean square, standard deviation, cumulative histogram, nth percentile, and zero crossing rates. To recognize the different daily activities, we summarize several commonly used motion features as follows:

1. *Mean.* The mean value of acceleration data over a window is the DC component of the motion signal.
2. *Variance.* The variance shows how dynamic is the activity. Low dynamic activity, such as stationary, will have a low value. Vigorous activity, such as running, will have a higher value.
3. *Standard deviation.* It basically captures the same thing as variance and is used in some previous works.
4. *Energy.* The energy feature is to capture the intensity of the motion. It is effective to tell the difference between stationary, walking, and running.
5. *Root mean square.* RMS is similar to energy to measure the intensity of the activity.
6. *Correlation between axes.* Correlation is useful for distinguish activities that involve motion in a single one dimension and multiple dimensions.
7. *ZCR and MCR.* ZCR means zero crossing rate, and MCR denotes to mean crossing rate. They capture the cyclic pattern of the activity. It can be seen as an approximation of the frequency. The advantage of it is that computation is conducted in time domain and no FFT computation is involved.
8. *Spectral peak.* It shows the dominant frequency of the activity.
9. *Spectral entropy.* It shows whether the energy is evenly distributed in different frequency. For stationary activity like sitting, the spectral entropy will be high. For activities like walking or running, the spectrums are usually peaky, and the spectral entropy is usually low.
10. *Spectral sub-band energy.* It captures how energy distributed in different frequency bands. Human daily activities, such as walking and running, usually fall in low-frequency band (i.e., <3 Hz), whereas in-vehicle activity will have more energy in high-energy band.
11. *Spectral sub-band energy ratio.* It utilizes the sub-band energy. But instead of directly use the sub-band energy, which might be a long vector and make the classification cost high, it summarizes energy distributed in different frequency bands with ratios between selected bands. The ratio between low-energy band and high-energy band is a good indicator of in-vehicle activity, as vehicle vibration can be captured in high-frequency components of signals.

These numerical features can be extracted from individual 3-D axis or from the two projected components. As mentioned before, we want the feature to be orientation independent, so we just calculate the features from the projected components of accelerometer data. Therefore, all features are computed in pairs, one for the vertical component and the other for the horizontal component. Feature extraction is usually a highly computational process. Not all the features are necessary to compute; which features to use depends on the characteristic of the target activities. In order to save computational power on the phone, we select distinctive features from the feature set using the correlation-based feature selection (CFS) method in WEKA toolkit [30]. The new feature subset should contain highly correlated features within the particular class but are uncorrelated with each other. We add one more rule that less frequency features should be used as possible as we can, since FFT transformation involves more computing power than pure computation in time domain. Based on the data set we have collected, it shows that the following subclass of features are less correlated:

- Means of vertical and horizontal components
- Variance of vertical component
- MCR of vertical and horizontal components
- Spectral energies, spectral peaks
- Spectral energy ratios

2.6 Classification Algorithms

For classification problems, a classifier is a systematic approach to building classification models from an input data set. The training set is used by each classifier to build a classification model, which is applied to the test set consisting of data with unknown class labels. Confusion matrix can be used to measure the performance of a classifier. One performance metric such as accuracy, is used to summarize the overall performance in a single number.

We evaluate and compare several classifiers provided by WEKA, namely C4.5 Decision Trees (DT), Naive Bayes (NB), k-Nearest Neighbor (kNN), and the Support Vector Machine (LibSVM) [11]. Decision tree classifier is a simple but widely used classification technique, which partitions the feature space according to a tree structure. Naive Bayes classifier assumes that each feature is conditionally independent given the class label and estimates the class-conditional probability. k-Nearest Neighbor classifier is a kind of lazy classifier which does not require model building but uses a simple distance rule to classify a test example. SVM works well with high-dimensional data and searches for a hyperplane with the largest margin. We also build a multivariate-Gaussian (MG) maximum likelihood classifier based on mean vector and covariance matrix estimated from each class and then forming a multivariate Gaussian model respectively. It can be also viewed as a Gaussian Mixture Model (GMM) classifier with a single component. The following Table 4 shows training and testing complexity of these classifiers as well as their decision outputs.

Table 4 Properties of classifiers

	DT	NB	kNN	SVM	MG
Training complexity	Low	Low	None	High	Moderate
Testing complexity	Low	Low	High	Moderate	Moderate
Decision output	Hard	Soft or Hard	Hard	Hard or Soft	Soft or Hard

Table 5 Classifier accuracy performances

Feature Set	DT	NB	kNN	SVM	MG
All (24)	92.8%	87.7%	90.4%	90.1%	89.7%
TD (6)	90.3%	81.8%	89.7%	84.1%	85.1%
FD (18)	92.6%	87.9%	88.1%	86.0%	88.5%
Vertical (12)	91.3%	83.0%	87.6%	84.6%	85.6%
Horizontal (12)	87.3%	73.4%	86.6%	80.3%	82.4%

In Table 5, different feature subsets are listed along with number of features, and their classification accuracies are compared by 10-fold cross-validation testing. TD features means time-domain features, and FD means frequency-domain features. From the accuracy results we find that vertical features contain more motion information than horizonal features. For most of the classifiers, frequency-domain features are more important than time-domain features. The DT classifier is found to achieve the best recognition accuracy with low computational complexity. kNN, SVM, and MG classifiers have very close performance. The MG classifier has better performance than naive Bayes classifier as it can capture the correlation among features.

For the same activity, the pattern of accelerometer data can vary dramatically across different body positions. To address the issue, one technique we use is further dividing user activities as needed during the training phase into separate activity subclasses according to body positions. At run time, the system performs inference based on the subclass models and merges the subclass labels back to original semantic labels in the end. Although the classifier is body dependent, the final result is not sensitive to body position. The split-and-merge process increases the average accuracy from 92.8% to 94.1% for the DT classifier. If we use selected 18 features discussed in Sect. 2.5 and apply the split-merger process, the accuracy can be increased from 90.1% to 94.5% for the SVM classifier and from 89.7% to 94.3% for the MG classifier. We noticed that, when using the SVM classifier, the features need to be normalized to the same unit level first, i.e., $[-1, 1]$. But for MG classifier, the normalization is no longer needed since it uses a probability model to infer the motion states. Our method uses only the phone accelerometer sensor (no GPS as in [28]) and makes no assumption about the device orientation or body position.

Confusion matrices are listed in Table 6 for the DT classifier and in Table 7 for the MG classifier. It shows that the accuracy for stationary, walking, and running

Table 6 Confusion matrix of DT classifier

Ground truth\classified	Stationary	Walking	Running	Cycling	In-vehicle
Stationary	0.9716	0	0	0.0124	0.0160
Walking	0.0042	0.9693	0.0105	0.0157	0.0002
Running	0.0084	0.0039	0.9792	0.0078	0.0006
Cycling	0.0430	0.0133	0.0012	0.9107	0.0318
In-vehicle	0.0250	0.0021	0	0.0855	0.8873

Table 7 Confusion matrix of MG classifier

Ground truth\classified	Stationary	Walking	Running	Cycling	In-vehicle
Stationary	0.9833	0.0017	0	0.0058	0.0092
Walking	0.0046	0.9686	0.0033	0.0194	0.0040
Running	0.0114	0.0164	0.9674	0.0031	0.0017
Cycling	0.0410	0.0338	0.0003	0.8841	0.0407
In-vehicle	0.0234	0.0088	0	0.0666	0.9012

is quite high, but for cycling and in-vehicle, it is relatively lower. This is because low-speed driving is easy to be confused with cycling, and vice visa.

2.7 Smoothing Algorithms

The outputs from the above static classifiers are not smooth in the sense of sequence detection as correlation between adjacent activities is not considered. Usually a second-level smoothing technique is used to capture the temporal correlation on top of the static classifier, like the HMM model used in [18]. To build a high-level smoothing classifier, we propose to use the following three algorithms:

1. Activity sequence is smoothed by a majority voting scheme with a sliding window of certain memory length.
2. Use a hard-input and hard-output HMM model to smooth the output from the DT classifier. The smoothing matrix (or emission matrix), defined as $E\{s_i' = m | s_i = n\}$ for $m, n \in \mathcal{A}$, can be estimated according to confusion matrix in Table 6. The state transition matrix can be either learned by EM algorithm from a history of classified motion sequence or estimated from collected ground truth data, which is denoted as $P\{s_{i+1} = m | s_i = n\}$, where $m, n \in \mathcal{A} = \{$stationary, walking, running, cycling, in-vehicle$\}$.
3. Use a soft-input and hard-output HMM model to smooth the output from the MG classifier. The emission matrix can be the likelihood of MG model for each class (hidden state). The state transition matrix can be either learned by EM algorithm from a history of observed likelihoods or estimated from collected ground truth data.

The performance of smoothing algorithms will be shown in the next section when physical activity diary is generated.

3 System Design and Implementation

The overall accelerometer-based activity recognition system is shown in Fig. 8. The preprocessing consists of: *normalization* that converts the raw reading into gravitational units (i.e., G); *calibration* is a one-time process, which provides the parameters for normalization; *admission control* that filters out unrelated movement; and *projection* that translates the 3-axis accelerometer data to an orientation-independent global coordinate system. Then we extract a set of carefully designed features that are used to classify five common physical activities: stationary, walking, cycling, running, and in-vehicle as discussed in Sect. 2.5. DT classifier—which outputs direct hard decisions—is used for its efficiency and ease of implementation. We also implemented the MG classifier to output soft decisions.

We validated the system architecture and algorithms through prototype implementations on the Nokia N95. The core signal processing and classification algorithms are written in C. The kissFFT [10] library is used for FFT calculation. Other tasks (e.g., GUI, access sensing hardware) is done by Symbian C++ [26]. The whole system is implemented as a background service (process) on the Nokia N95.

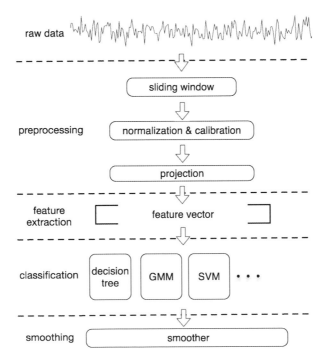

Fig. 8 Accelerometer-based activity recognition system

Table 8 Runtime benchmark

Stage	Time (ms)
normalization	0.16
admission control	0.08
projection	0.65
feature extraction	4.21
classification	<0.01

Using the native APIs from Symbian, we collect continuous accelerometer data with approximately 32-Hz sample rate. The sensing thread collects raw data from the accelerometer sensor hardware and feeds it to the processing thread, which in turn processes the raw data through normalization, feature extraction, and classification. The multithread approach is necessary to avoid missing any accelerometer data while the classification is performed on data already received. Circular buffers and associated semaphores are implemented between the sensing and processing threads to ensure continuous and asynchronous operation. On the Nokia N95, the processing threads are implemented with standard Symbian threads, whereas the sensing threads are actually implemented as Active Objects running inside the main Symbian thread. Active Objects are lightweight compared to threads (meaning no cost of context switching) and suitable for simple operations like reading of raw sensor data.

Since the entire activity recognition system is run on a mobile phone, we spent much effort to make the software implementation efficient and robust. The prototype is optimized for CPU usage, and we exchange additional memory usage for lower CPU load. All possible computation is precalculated offline beforehand. For example, the MG classifier actually uses directly the inverse and determinant of covariance matrix as the parameter. Rather than using Σ, we precompute Σ^{-1} and $|\Sigma|$ offline and use them directly in the system. To reduce memory operations, memory blocks are preallocated and initialized as much as possible when the application is loaded. We also use passing of pointers instead of memory copy whenever it is allowed. Table 8 shows the runtime benchmark.

Another critical factor of the system is its power consumption. Fortunately, accelerometer sensor hardware itself consumes little energy to operate. The majority of the power budget is spent on processing of the accelerometer data after they are acquired. We performed some benchmark testing on the Nokia N95, and the results show an average of about 40-mW power consumption for our activity recognition system. For comparison, a Nokia N95 typically consumes about 100 mW when it is in idle state and with screen off. In our tests, the Nokia N95 can run the activity recognition process continuously for 1.5–2 days before it runs out of battery. This meets the basic requirement on batter life for many applications, such as diary or wellness, that could be built on top of our physical activity recognition system. We believe that there are still room to improve further on power consumption with tighter optimization of the code and better understanding of the application requirements.

Last but not the least, usability is also very important for any activity recognition system. In particular, accelerometer calibration posts a challenge as different phones may have different accelerometer hardware. That means that the scaling factor and offset may vary between phone manufacturers, different phone models from the same manufacturer (e.g., Nokia N95 vs N97), or even from phone to phone for the same model. As discussed before, our solution for calibration does not assume any preknowledge about the accelerometer hardware. In addition, the accelerometer calibration is done on demand, usually during the first time the system is launched, and it can be a quick voice guided manual calibration process as discussed in Sect. 2.2.

4 Applications and Use Cases

The goal of physical activity recognition system is potentially threefold: (i) to provide information to individuals about their life motion patterns that can be used to generate derivative healthcare and wellness measurements; (ii) to provide more texture to social communication by motion presence; and (iii) to enable contextual, cognitive, and adaptive user interfaces by real-time motion monitoring. In the following, we describe a number of applications that can be built on our system architecture.

4.1 Physical Activity Diary

One immediate demo application of physical activity recognition is to use continuous accelerometer sensing and inferencing on the phone to generate a user's physical activity diary. The motion sequences can be produced by the aforementioned decision tree classifier and followed by a majority vote smoothing of window size 15 (representing one minute). The motion pattern can be visualized by summarizing the statistics of each motion. Figure 9 shows the distribution of motion states of one user in a typical weekday, and Fig. 10 shows the distribution of motion states of the same user in a typical weekend. Obviously, the most dominant activity is stationary during the weekday, while the walking and driving activity increases significantly during weekends. Actually, the users did not cycle during the data collection period. However, we observe some cycling events that are due to the misclassification of walking and vehicle activity.

By continuous accelerometer sensing and physical activity recognition running in the background, we produce a time series log of classified activities geo-tagged with GPS coordinates. The diary is stored in the phone and can be uploaded, processed, and visualized in a dynamic way, such as a timestamp view or a map view. As shown in Fig. 11, one day diary of user's motions are plotted with different colors representing different motions. As also shown in Fig. 12 of Google map, the places where the user stays for a long time are annotated with tags. The color of the

Fig. 9 Typical physical
activities in a weekday

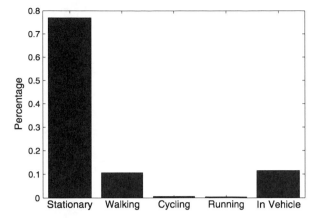

Fig. 10 Typical physical
activities in a weekend

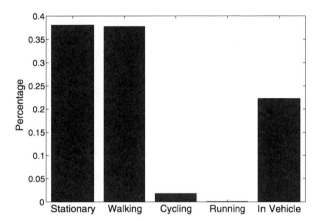

Fig. 11 Physical activity
diary

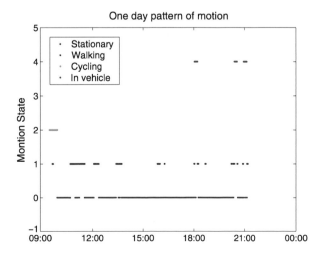

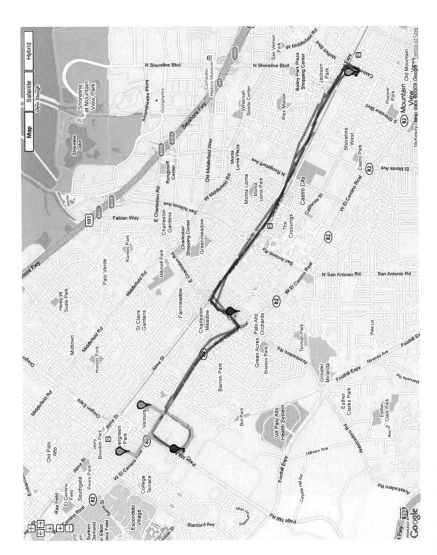

Fig. 12 Physical activity log on Google map

tag indicates the duration of the stay, red for long stay, green for short visit. The location trajectory is also color coded by the motion states, green for walking, red for cycling/running, blue for vehicle, and stationary is omitted, so that the transportation methods between places can be clearly identified. Other than just recording the user's daily life, the diary can be used in many ways. For example, the location trace can be used for personalized point of interest recommendations. We view this usage more like an enabling element that blends physical activities with virtual presentation than an end mobile application.

4.2 Mobile Healthcare and Wellness

One important application for physical activity recognition is in the domain of human health and wellness, like activity-aware computing for healthcare introduced in [29] that enables users to move from activity-based interaction toward activity-aware engagement. For example, monitored activities can help hospital staff better understand patients' motion status and provide specialized care in a timely manner.

For example, CardioTrainer [1] is a next-generation mobile fitness application that can be your virtual training partner for running, biking, hiking, skiing, or just about any outdoor activities. The Sleep Cycle alarm clock [5] is a bio-alarm clock that analyzes your sleep patterns and wakes you when you are in the lightest sleep phase. Nokia Research Center has released a step counter application [4] to count steps and calculate the distance when user is walking. Another Nokia-created application related to healthcare is Nokia Sports Tracker [3] that is based on GPS tracking. However these mobile wellness applications require users first to select and create the workout they are going to perform and then start to operate. With the help of proposed physical activity recognition system, we can automatically achieve the same functions without users' manual input while they perform daily activities as usual. In [19], a system for automatic monitoring of calories expended using a single body-worn accelerometer sensor is presented based on physical activity recognition.

The application can work as follows. The activity recognition system is running in the background while classifying a user's motion from each accelerometer data frame. If the user's motion is stationary or in-vehicle, only the resting metabolic calorie expenditure is calculated. If the user's motion is walking or running, step rate is estimated, which is then used to derive average speed by combining the user's height and weight. From the speed estimation, we can use a couple of sports medicine formulas to calculate horizontal movement calorie expenditure in addition to the resting metabolic calorie expenditure. The calculated calorie can be expressed to the user in an interactive way, on a daily, weekly or monthly basis. From the history of calorie expenditure the user can have a clear picture of his recent activity status and exercise more if there is a need.

4.3 Human-Centric Sensing and Sharing in Mobile Social Networks

From social interaction point of view, sharing became a dominant activity as recent rise of social networking sites indicate. To take it to the extremes, sharing can be implemented in an entirely automatic way, meaning that all sensor and contextual data available for an individual user can be aggregated to a sharing platform (not specifying here where to do higher level classification, inference, etc.). Depending on privacy settings, one might share exact location, mood, activity, etc. type of contextual information with family, closer or wider set of friends, colleagues, a community, or the entire web. The main challenge is the presentation and the visual rendering, in the right larger context, of any user-related sensor or context information. Focusing on the physical activity dimension only, potential usage of this type of information can be appended to different applications, like status or mood indicator in messaging, physical diary as a log of daily activities, presence information, etc. One obvious use of the activity information is related to the Contact or Phonebook application, as demonstrated in our earlier work WebCall [20].

The other possible application is related to human-centric sensing and sharing in mobile social networks. In such a sensing system, humans are the sensing focus, and the visualization of sensor-based information is for the benefit of common people and their friends and community. Additionally, it is human's mobility that enables both sensing coverage of large public spaces over time and allows an individual to collect very targeted information about his or her daily life patterns and interactions.

There are related works in this area. As introduced in [23], the CenceMe application combines the inference of the presence of individuals using off-the-shelf, sensor-enabled mobile phones with sharing this information through social networking applications such as Facebook and MySpace. Micro-Blog, a participatory sensing presented in [12], uses smart phone equipped sensors to record contents and share them in a real-time web-based interactive way. PEIR [25], the Personal Environmental Impact Report, is a participatory sensing application that uses location data sampled from everyday mobile phones to calculate personalized estimates of environmental impact and exposure. Physical activity recognition results can be used as social sensing and sharing for mobile social networks.

4.4 User Interfaces

Beyond sharing, physical activity information provides a higher-level context input to any UI implementation. Context-aware user interfaces are another important category of applications that can be enabled by physical activity recognition. Unlike a desktop PC or even a laptop, mobile phones are to be carried by people almost all the time. That means that the use of mobile phones is subject to quite different conditions caused by various user activities. It would be desirable to adapt mobile devices' operations according to users' current physical activity to better serve the users' needs. As we all have different usage patterns of our mobile devices, dependent on personal preferences, location, day of time, or activity, it is intuitive to use physical activity information to trigger the UI operation. Following are three examples for different levels of device and application UI:

– *Usage Scenario 1:* Physical activity-based input and output rendering of the UI.

For instance, a user may need to read the device screen while he or she is walking or running. Powered by physical activity recognition, the device can detect such condition and improve its UI by simple actions such as increasing the size of the fonts or buttons so that they are easy to read and manipulate. The device can also increase the ring volume so that the user will not miss phone calls given that the noise level will likely be higher under those motion conditions.

– *Usage Scenario 2:* Application operation changes based on the physical activity information.

One particular example we want to discuss here is the "car mode." Operating mobile phones while driving is becoming one of the major causes for car accidents. Some states in the US, such as California, have already banned the use of mobile phones for making or receiving phone calls while the user is driving, unless the call handing is done hands free (e.g., through headphone). Although more and more people start to use headphones, there are still many users who either do not have a headphone or simply do not use it due to the hassle of setting it on. That means in practice that many users still make or receive phone calls with hands while driving. Some people choose a better compromise and take phone calls with the speaker on. Even if people do wear headphones, operating all the menus and buttons on phone still distracts the drivers and creates safety risks.

One potential solution would be that the phone automatically detects that a person is in a vehicle and switches to car mode. While in car mode, a phone can change the overall UI to the specific form that minimizes the distraction. This, for example, can include reducing the number of buttons and menu options, increasing font and button size, using voice command and announcement (e.g., caller's name), or automatically switching on the speaker if the headphone is not connected to the phone. In addition to UI adaptation, the device can also automatically perform other actions that would be useful for the user. For instance, it can send automatic SMS message to an important caller indicating that the callee is driving and will return the call later. Similarly, the phone can detect a meeting event in calendar and send an SMS message to the meeting organizer if it calculates that the driver is likely to be late. For family members and close friends, the phone can also offer a realtime presence service so that people remotely can see a car icon displayed on their phone book indicating that the user is driving. That allows them to make informed decision on whether it is a good time to call. The automatic presence service can also be integrated with social networking services. Going to the extremes, the phone can even lock applications and only leave essential ones accessible to the driver. Again, the goal is to reduce the distractions caused by the device.

While the idea of car mode is intuitive, care must be taken in its implementation. First, our current activity recognition engine cannot distinguish a driver from a passenger. In practice, this may not be a big issue as most drivers in countries like US do drive alone most of the time. In case the user is indeed in the passenger's seat, the application can always allow a user to cancel car mode. Second, the implementation must have a good handling of false alarms, which happens when the phone detects that a user is in a vehicle while actually he is not. It would be inconvenient and embarrassing for a user's phone to switch into speakerphone mode while he is in a public place, not in his car. Besides various techniques— such as temporal smoothing—to reduce the false alarm rate, the adaptation itself should be designed carefully so that the damage is minimal in case a false alarm does happen. It is worth emphasizing that this is a general but critical principle for any UI adaptation according to contextual information. The activity recognition can never be 100% accurate and any "smart" UI feature must take that into account.

– *Usage Scenario 3:* The set of applications that are offered by the device dependent on the combination of the physical activity and location information.

   The car mode is a prime example of how a reduced set of applications and limited functionalities (e.g., not allowing any application beyond accepting a call) can be offered based on the recognized driving activity. Taking this further, significant location [31] and physical activity together can trigger the application selection for, e.g., being at the work place (top three applications being Calendar, Contacts for colleagues, and Mail), being on a business trip (Calendar with travel itinerary, Maps, and a dedicated call button to the travel secretary), etc. All these examples are imaginative ones, nevertheless, they intend to highlight how contextual information can eventually trigger primary application offerings.

Focusing on the user interaction itself, recent UI implementations are gradually supporting more and more multimodal type of access modes, a combination of touch, gesture, keyboard and speech inputs, and more. On the output side, visual, audio, haptic feedbacks, and their combinations are common. Multimodal user interface research goes back to several decades. Especially the speech and language technology research community has been active in reaching out to other modalities by integrating them with spoken dialogue capabilities. While individual input and output modality technologies are available for a long time and provide in stand-alone mode of operation highly accurate performance, the challenges with the integration of multiple modalities still remain in the focus of the research community. One of the challenges is how to combine in an efficient and accurate manner different input modalities and derive a single semantic interpretation of the user input. Adding contextual and sensor information to the multimodal user input integration eventually aims to determine the user intention in a given context [8, 9].

5 Conclusion and Future Work

In this book chapter, we investigated physical motion recognition using mobile phones with built-in accelerometer sensors. We took a different approach from the prior art that involved rigid training data collection under supervision with wearable external sensors. Data processing and smoothing techniques were discussed first to reduce the noise present in accelerometer data and improve its quality. A device-independent calibration process was introduced to estimate the scaling factor and offset existing in the sensor and normalize the accelerometer signal to gravity. Since phone's position on a human body is varying from person to person, its orientation cannot be partially or relatively fixed. We explored orientation-independent features extracted from magnitudes and from vertical and horizontal components in acceleration for five common physical activities, such as stationary, walking, running, cycling, and in-vehicle. We found that decision tree achieves the best performance among several static classifiers, while vertical/horizontal features are significant enough to provide robust performance. Furthermore, a well-designed light-weight activity recognition system was able to provide a usable platform for generating a demonstration application, physical activity diary. Finally, we discussed some potential applications and UI adaption in different domains related to physical activity recognition.

Although several important aspects of physical activity recognition and interaction with mobile phones have been studied, such as phone-orientation-independent features, light-weight system design for mobile CPU, and general static classifiers for common human motions, there are still some open research problems worth further consideration.

- *Dynamic classifiers.* Static classifiers like decision tree and GMM are mainly used. HMM model is only used for smoothing the classified activity sequence. If HMM model or similar Markov model is built directly on a sequence of extracted features, the overall classification accuracy can be improved since more temporal correlation is captured in the model.
- *Natural activity model.* Taking the approach known in speech and language technology as modeling a grammar or language model, we can develop a higher-level dependency network for sequences of physical activities. Triggered by location and/or date and time, having a sort of "activity grammar," one can, for instance, predict the next most likely activity knowing previous activity states. This phase of the research requires more data collection; however, it can be implemented as part of an ongoing trial and provide improved performance while running previous versions of the system. This might also provide better performance for in-vehicle detection, as it must be always proceeded by walking. For the physical diary application, an overall template can be created for weekdays and weekends having prior knowledge of the most likely sequences of daily activities.
- *Model adaption.* Accelerometer data was only collected from eight people, and a classification model was generated on top of this limited data set. How to generate an adaptive model based on more training data from new users is an interesting research problem. The solution can scale the whole system to a larger population and build more useful and interesting applications.

References

1. Cardio trainer. Website http://www.worksmartlabs.com/cardiotrainer/about.php
2. Nokia sensor APIs. Website http://wiki.forum.nokia.com/index.php/Nokia_Sensor_APIs
3. Nokia sports tracker. Website https://sportstracker.nokia.com/nts/main/index.do
4. Nokia step counter. Website http://betalabs.nokia.com/betas/view/nokia-step-counter
5. Sleep cycle alarm clock. Website http://www.lexwarelabs.com/sleepcycle/
6. Stmicroelectronics analog and digital accelerometers. Website http://www.st.com/stonline/products/families/sensors/accelerometers.htm
7. Bao, L., Intille, S.S.: Activity recognition from user-annotated acceleration data. In: Pervasive, pp. 1–17 (2004)
8. Boda, P.P.: A maximum entropy based approach for multimodal integration. In: ICMI '04: Proceedings of the 6th International Conference on Multimodal Interfaces, pp. 37–338. ACM, New York (2004)
9. Boda, P.P.: A contextual multimodal integrator. In: ICMI '06: Proceedings of the 8th International Conference on Multimodal Interfaces, pp. 129–130. ACM, New York (2006)
10. Borgerding, M.: Kiss fft. (2008). Website http://sourceforge.net/projects/kissfft/
11. EL-Manzalawy, Y., Honavar, V.: WLSVM: Integrating LibSVM into Weka Environment (2005). Software available at http://www.cs.iastate.edu/~yasser/wlsvm
12. Gaonkar, S., Li, J., Choudhury, R.R., Cox, L., Schmidt, A.: Micro-blog: sharing and querying content through mobile phones and social participation. In: MobiSys '08: Proceeding of the 6th International Conference on Mobile Systems, Applications, and Services, pp. 174–186. ACM, New York (2008)
13. Kawahara, Y., Kurasawa, H., Morikawa, H.: Recognizing user context using mobile handsets with acceleration sensors. In: PORTABLE '07: IEEE International Conference on Portable Information Devices, Orlando, FL, pp. 1–5 (2007)
14. Kern, N., Schiele, B., Junker, H., Lukowicz, P., Troster, G.: Wearable sensing to annotate meeting recordings. In: Proceedings of the Sixth International Symposium on Wearable Computers ISWC, pp. 186–193 (2002)
15. Kunze, K., Lukowicz, P.: Dealing with sensor displacement in motion-based onbody activity recognition systems. In: UbiComp '08: Proceedings of the 10th International Conference on Ubiquitous Computing, New York, NY, USA, pp. 20–29 (2008)
16. Kunze, K., Lukowicz, P., Junker, H., Tröster, G.: Where am I: recognizing on-body positions of wearable sensors. In: LOCA'04: International Workshop on Locationand Context-Awareness, pp. 264–275. Springer, Berlin (2005)
17. Lester, J., Choudhury, T., Borriello, G.: A practical approach to recognizing physical activities. In: Pervasive Computing. Lecture Notes in Computer Science, pp. 1–16. Springer, Berlin (2006)
18. Lester, J., Choudhury, T., Kern, N., Borriello, G., Hannaford, B.: A hybrid discriminative/generative approach for modeling human activities. In: Proceedings of the International Joint Conference on Artificial Intelligence (IJCAI), pp. 766–772 (2005)
19. Lester, J., Hartung, C., Pina, L., Libby, R., Borriello, G., Duncan, G.: Validated caloric expenditure estimation using a single body-worn sensor. In: Ubicomp '09: Proceedings of the 11th International Conference on Ubiquitous Computing, pp. 225–234. ACM, New York (2009)
20. Liu, Z., Pang, H.-Y., Yang, J., Yang, G., Boda, P.: Webcall—a rich context mobile research framework. In: MobiCASE 2009: The 1st Annual International Conference on Mobile Computing, Applications, and Services, San Diego, CA, USA (2009)
21. Lotters, J., Schipper, J., Veltink, P., Olthuis, W., Bergveld, P.: Procedure for in-use calibration of triaxial accelerometers in medical applications. Sens. Actuators A, Phys. **68**(1–3), 221–228 (1998)
22. Maurer, U., Smailagic, A., Siewiorek, D.P., Deisher, M.: Activity recognition and monitoring using multiple sensors on different body positions. In: BSN '06: Proceedings of the International Workshop on Wearable and Implantable Body Sensor Networks, pp. 113–116. IEEE Computer Society, Washington (2006)

23. Miluzzo, E., Lane, N., Fodor, K., Peterson, R., Lu, H., Musolesi, M., Eisenman, S., Zheng, X., Campbell, A.: Sensing meets mobile social networks: the design, implementation and evaluation of the CenceMe application. In: Proceedings of the 6th ACM Conference on Embedded Network Sensor Systems, pp. 337–350. ACM, New York (2008)
24. Mizell, D.: Using gravity to estimate accelerometer orientation. In: ISWC '03: Proceedings of the 7th IEEE International Symposium on Wearable Computers, p. 252. IEEE Computer Society, Washington (2003)
25. Mun, M., Reddy, S., Shilton, K., Yau, N., Burke, J., Estrin, D., Hansen, M., Howard, E., West, R., Boda, P.: Peir, the personal environmental impact report, as a platform for participatory sensing systems research. In: MobiSys '09: Proceedings of the 7th International Conference on Mobile Systems, Applications, and Services, pp. 55–68. ACM, New York (2009)
26. Nokia. Symbian c (2009). Website http://www.forum.nokia.com/Technology_Topics/ Development_Platforms/Symbian_C
27. Ravi, N., Dandekar, N., Mysore, P., Littman, M.L.: Activity recognition from accelerometer data. IAAI-05: American Association for Artificial Intelligence (2005)
28. Reddy, S., Burke, J., Estrin, D., Hansen, M., Srivastava, M.: Determining transportation mode on mobile phones. In: Proceedings of the 12th IEEE International Symposium on Wearable Computers (2008)
29. Tentori, M., Favela, J.: Activity-aware computing for healthcare. IEEE Pervasive Comput. **7**(2), 51–57 (2008)
30. Witten, I.: Weka: practical machine learning tools and techniques with Java implementations. Dept. of Computer Science, University of Waikato (1999)
31. Yang, G.: Discovering significant places from mobile phones—a mass market solution. In: MELT '09: The 2nd International Workshop on Mobile Entity Localization and Tracking in GPS-less Environments, Orlando, FL, USA (2009)
32. Yang, J.: Toward physical activity diary: motion recognition using simple acceleration features with mobile phones. In: IMCE '09: Proceedings of the 1st International Workshop on Interactive Multimedia for Consumer Electronics, Beijing, China, pp. 1–10 (2009)

Gestures in an Intelligent User Interface

Wim Fikkert, Paul van der Vet, and Anton Nijholt

Abstract In this chapter we investigated which hand gestures are intuitive to control a large display multimedia interface from a user's perspective. Over the course of two sequential user evaluations, we defined a simple gesture set that allows users to fully control a large display multimedia interface, intuitively. First, we evaluated numerous gesture possibilities for a set of commands that can be issued to the interface. These gestures were selected from literature, science fiction movies, and a previous exploratory study. Second, we implemented a working prototype with which the users could interact with both hands and the preferred hand gestures with 2D and 3D visualizations of biochemical structures. We found that the gestures are influenced to significant extent by the fast paced developments in multimedia interfaces such as the Apple iPhone and the Nintendo Wii and to no lesser degree by decades of experience with the more traditional WIMP-based interfaces.

1 Two Sides of the Same Coin

Intelligence and intuitiveness are two sides of the same coin in multimedia interfaces. Computational intelligence is required to analyze human behavior. When the behavior comes natural to the user, it makes the interface self-explanatory for the users. These multimedia interfaces are found in ambient intelligent environments. The inhabitants of these environments are surrounded by a wide variety of sensors that look at these people [9, Chap. 2]. The combined sensor data is analyzed by com-

W. Fikkert (✉) · P. van der Vet · A. Nijholt
University of Twente, Enschede, The Netherlands
e-mail: f.w.fikkert@ewi.utwente.nl

P. van der Vet
e-mail: p.e.vandervet@ewi.utwente.nl

A. Nijholt
e-mail: a.nijholt@ewi.utwente.nl

L. Shao et al. (eds.), *Multimedia Interaction and Intelligent User Interfaces,*
Advances in Pattern Recognition,
DOI 10.1007/978-1-84996-507-1_9, © Springer-Verlag London Limited 2010

puterized algorithms that try to interpret the behavior of these inhabitants in order to formulate a meaningful response [36].

The nature of the interaction is of great influence to the type of behavior that lies at the basis of the interaction. On the one hand, there are proactive interactions in which the system actively provides the user with information based on indirect requests [43]. Examples of such systems are virtual guides [21], showing or hiding context based on the distance to a screen in a shopping centre [46] and interactive art expositions [15]. The type of interaction on which we focus in this chapter is direct and explicit interaction: the user gives commands explicitly to the interface [4]. System responses should be transparent, logical, and self-explanatory [12].

Gesture interfaces can be applied in various display-rich environments. The work described here focuses on very large displays in these environments that span entire walls. As display technology is getting cheaper, the availability of such displays increases rapidly [38]. Currently, research into interactive large displays focuses primarily on touch-sensitive screens [11]. However, it is not always possible nor desirable to touch the screen in order to interact with it. First, hygiene of surfaces that are being touched during interactions is an issue [49], especially in sterile environments such as operating rooms [48]. Second, when standing at arm's length from a wall-sized display, it is impossible to get an overview of its contents [39]. The gesture interfaces on which we focus in this chapter are large, and they cannot be touched. The resulting gesture-based interaction takes place at a distance between arm's length and a couple of meters away where the overview of the display can be attained [14].

The intuitiveness of two-way interactions between user and system can be described by the mismatch between the user's internal goals, on the one hand, and, on the other hand, the expectations and the availability of information that specifies the state of the technological environment or artifact and how it might be changed [34]. Norman [33] names this the "gulf of execution." It describes the gap between the psychological language (or mental model) of the user's goals and the physical action-oriented language of the device controls via which it is operated. Likewise, the "gulf of evaluation" is the difficulty of assessing the state of the system and how well the artifact supports the discovery and interpretation of that state. The goal of the work described in this chapter is to formulate "intuitive gestures." These are gestures that minimize the mismatch in Norman's "gulf of execution." We take a human perspective on the way that these gestures should take form. The hands form the effectors that perform actions to control the system. The input devices or sensors that the system should employ to look at the user are based on the way that the effectors/hands gesture, not the other way around.

The remainder of this chapter is structured as follows. Section 2 gives an overview of gesture-based interfaces and how they are intuitive or not. Section 3 then describes an experiment in which we have investigated which gestures are preferred by potential users of these gesture-based interfaces. The results of this first experiment feed a second, see Sect. 4, in which we investigated the user experience of a large display gesture interface. We conclude this chapter in Sect. 5 with a discussion based on our findings and an outlook in future work in this field.

2 Related Work

Cohen [5] formulated requirements for selecting the gestures in a gesture interface: he argues that the gestures should fit a useful environment, that the system can recognize nonperfect gestures, that the system can interpret both a gesture's static and dynamic information components, and that the gesture is recognized as quickly as possible, even before the full gesture is completed. More user-centered requirements have also been specified [32]: gestures should be easy to perform and remember, intuitive, metaphorically and iconically logical toward functionality and ergonomic, and not physically stressing when used often. However, in most (experimental) gesture interfaces, an idiosyncratic gesture set is defined for a limited set of tasks [26, 47]. Moreover, the gesture that is selected is often more technology driven than user driven. The sensor in the interface determines the "best" gesture for a task; for example, the BumpTop system requires users to learn the shape of complex cursor trajectories [1]. The limitations of the technologies that are used are often directly translated to the gestures that can be detected. We now give a brief overview of gesture sets that have been proposed in both literature and commercial products for explicit command giving.

By addressing purely gesture-based input we come across the problem of how to select or manipulate objects in the absence of other modalities that can "click." A popular solution is to use dwell time thresholds that activate a select command whenever the user points to a target for some time, with a hand-held device [24], extended index finger [46], or eye-tracker for gaze location estimation [51]. Even though this solution is a simple one, it introduces a fixed, constant lag insofar that the interactions can suffer from the "Midas touch effect" [19]. With only the hand, we also need to consider that depressing a physical button or tapping a display surface produces a kinaesthetic feedback that confirms the click action. When beyond arm's length, there is no such surface to touch which will degrade the performance significantly when manipulating virtual objects [50]. Vogel and Balakrishnan [47] argue that the hand itself can serve as a source of kinaesthetic feedback that confirms gesture actions through some tension in the hand. Grossman et al. [17] designed a gesture for clicking named *ThumbTrigger* in which the hand is shaped like a pistol: the thumb and index finger are extended while the rest of the hand is closed in a fist. With *ThumbTrigger*, clicking was done by pressing the thumb on the (bent) middle finger as if pressing an invisible button. A click or clutch action should be designed to minimize hand movement side effects that will influence pointing precision [47].

2.1 A Human's Perspective

When a gesture set is designed from the human perspective, the gestures are categorized by terms such as intuitiveness, naturalness, and ease of use. A responsive workbench has demonstrated that natural manipulation of virtual 3D models with both hands is feasible [6]. Their tabletop system rear-projected the 3D models while two PINCH datagloves were used to detect one-handed and two-handed gesturing. Three types of gesture-task combinations were defined: unimanual, bimanual symmetric, and bimanual asymmetric. Guiard [18] was the main inspiration for manipulating objects bimanually by dividing tasks between the two hands. Users have been observed to combine two otherwise independent one-handed tools in a synergistic fashion [6]. State transitions between interface tasks mainly occurred by picking up physical tools, for example, a magnifying glass, to switch the system's state to "zooming." These physical tools made the interface states explicit for the user: users made 3D curves with two hands by pressing buttons on hand-held spatial position sensors [16]. By combining the movements from two hands, detailed curves could be produced that were impossible to create with one hand. Nielsen et al. [32] found iconic gestures such as drawing a square to represent objects (e.g., a card), and, for selecting, they found pointing with an index finger to the object or by waving the hand in the general direction of that object. Other tasks such as move or select all required an explicit state-transition gesture that resulted in rather obscure gestures such as stopping an action with a "halt" emblem [46]. These signal gestures are explicit and potentially intuitive for the users. However, they are complex, which makes it hard to learn so that the gap in the gulf of execution might actually widen rather than close. A Wizard of Oz setting was used in the SmartKom system to discover a gesture set for controlling it [3]. Users pointed with one or more fingers and with one or two hands. Selecting was done by circling around an object or region while new forms of interactions such as "no" or "go back" were realized by a kind of waving of the hands. Our results from a similar approach [13] showed that users tend to come up with gestures that look a lot like those made by other users. In addition, users stick to these gestures no matter how inconvenient it was to gesture like that.

2.2 A System's Perspective

Formulating a gesture set from a system's perspective puts the focus heavily on sensors and how they can detect features from the hands. This perspective typically does not accommodate the user with intuitive gestures. Kavakli et al. [23] identify 32 gestures due to the limitation of their sensor set-up—in which finger flexure values vary between fully flexed ($<10\%$) and closed ($>90\%$)—and the physical restrictions if of the human hand. They further explored these gestures in a working prototype. Their free-hand sketching application, DesIRe, was used to construct 3D drawings by directly observing and reacting to both hands. The DesIRe system included 29 gestures that transition between states and manipulate the 3D mesh. Gesture recognition was hard coded: bending a finger past a threshold value changed the appropriate phalanx-sensor from 0 to 1. The lack of any visual representation of the gesture set, in combination with seemingly random gesture-task combinations, makes this idiosyncratic gesture set hard to learn for end-users. A similarly hard to learn gesture interface is described by [41], who defined several hand shapes to represent tasks such as pointing or clutching. These hand shapes could be detected by an elaborate multicamera system by virtue of one or two fingers protruding in the left, top, or bottom sides of the detected hand shape. Tse et al. [45] built a gesture interface on top of the existing strategy game Warcraft 3. Using a DiamondTouch tabletop [7], users were required to mark bounding boxes with two hands and issue commands to the selection by speech. Other gestures could not be implemented because of the lack of support from the DiamondTouch for disambiguation of two or more touches. The SixthSense prototype is a mobile gesture interface that uses a projector instead of a display to visualize information on any surface [28]. The gestures in Sixth-Sense are based on popular multitouch systems and the Apple iPhone. The gesture set focuses on WIMP-like interfaces through pointing by ray-casting and selecting through button-up and button-down hand shapes with the thumb protruding from or enclosed in the hand, respectively.

3 Experiment 1: Intuitive Gesturing

In a previous Wizard of Oz experiment we found that uninstructed users make gestures of their own accord that are very alike [12]. After formulating a set of commands that form the basis of a gesture interface, we evaluated the gestures observed in the Wizard of Oz experiment and other gestures from literature and science fiction movies with an online questionnaire. We found that for each command, one or two gestures are preferred. The method used to gain access to a large user group, an online questionnaire, might have been influenced by participants not fully understanding, appreciating, and imagining what it would be like to issue commands in that way. It is hard to imagine and fully appreciate the workings of an interface without having experienced it. For one thing, it is difficult to imagine the lack of tactile feedback in an interaction with bare hands. This lack of feedback might even hamper those tasks where precision and feedback are crucial, for which applications that exploit multitouch surfaces are prime examples [8]. In addition, any tactile feedback that is offered should be matched to other feedback, for example, visual feedback that the interface provides [35]. It is also hard to imagine what it would be like to perform a certain gesture repeatedly in an interface. Gestures might be strenuous for the hands and arms involved [47] or simply impossible to perform for certain users [32]. This experiment validates the findings of our online questionnaire by requiring subjects to perform gestures repeatedly, giving them the chance to experience rather than imagine the complete interaction. In doing so, we gain more insight into our findings so far. The interactions should last long enough for the user to fully appreciate the gesture and to comment on it. This section describes the method (Sect. 3.1), the results (Sect. 3.2), and the conclusions of this experiment (Sect. 3.3).

3.1 Method

To prevent biases from a different experiment setup, we reused the setup from the online questionnaire with some additions that we will describe in this section. We define four states in the system that the user can interact with: out-of-range, tracking, selected, manipulating. By gesturing or, in other words, giving a command to the system, the user can switch between these system states. We chose to include zooming as an implementation of the manipulation state because most literature on gesture-based interfaces focuses on manipulating images, often with a demonstrator application to resize, position, and orient photos. For each of the resulting four commands, we selected a number of frequently occurring gestures from literature, see Sect. 2, science fiction movies, and our previous experiments [12]. The commands were ordered in a predefined sequence because users would need to make up their mind first, for example, about how they would point before they could select. The commands that we presented to the user are, in this order: point, select, deselect, and resize. The various gestures were completely randomized per command. In total, we selected 16 gestures for the 4 commands mentioned above. The commands were ordered in a predefined sequence because users would need to make up their mind first, for example, about how they would point before they could select. The gestures, then, were completely randomized per command.

Some examples of the gestures that we selected follow. For pointing (3 gestures), we included *Ray-casting* [4] in addition to two more indirect approaches. For select (5 gestures), *AirTap* [47] and *ThumbTrigger* [17] were selected. Deselect had 4 gestures including *Select other*, where another object is selected to deselect the current one (from MS Windows). For resize (4 gestures), we introduced moving two fingers apart as with the Apple iPhone. Also, *Referenced PullPush* from the movie Minority Report showed the dominant hand serving as a reference for resizing with the distance to the other hand defining the amount, see Fig. 2.

3.1.1 Setup

Gestures were introduced in a video clip showing both hand movements and the response of the interface. The video clips, see Figs. 1 and 2, were shot in a mocked-up setting. The interface in the video clips was an abstracted system that responded solely through visual feedback. For each gesture, after viewing its video clip, we asked subjects to stand at a marked distance of two meters in front of a large display (52-inch diameter). This setting was the same as where we videotaped the video clips. There, they performed the gesture at least three times while the abstract application reacted to their hand(s) gesturing. Gesturing took place in a so-called gesture space that was directly in front of the participant, reaching to arm's length [27, p. 89]. The application was partially controlled by an operator who switched between the three application's states. The operator was introduced at the beginning of the investigation, and the participants were allowed to talk out loud to the operator. In order to get the participants to appreciate the gesture fully, the operator would ask them questions that addressed comfort and ease of use while they were gesturing. These questions aimed at engaging in a discussion on the gesture, not on judgment of it.

Subjects wore a simple glove, see Fig. 4(a), that was made up from elastic bands to which an IR LED and AA battery were sewn. The experiment's setup is depicted in Fig. 3. A Nintendo Wiimote[1] was mounted on top of the 52″ large display, see Fig. 4(b). Its camera was used to detect the IR LED on the subject's index finger tip so that the cursor could be controlled through ray casting with an extended index finger [25]. The system was calibrated so that pointing, for example, to the top-left corner of the display placed the cursor there as well.

Participants were asked to score the gestures (on 7-point Likert-style scales) for intuitiveness ("1: very difficult"–"7: very intuitive"), physical effort ("1: little effort"–"7: much effort") required, and if they would gesture in this way ("1: no way"–"7: for certain"). In addition to these questions, we asked our participants to

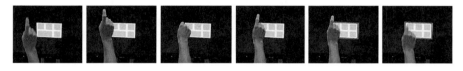

Fig. 1 *AirTap* [47]

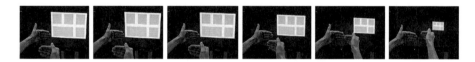

Fig. 2 *Referenced PullPush* from the movie Minority Report

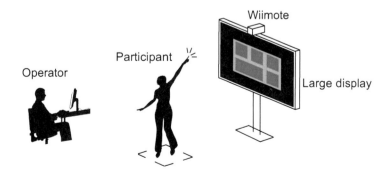

Fig. 3 Experiment setup for validating the findings of our online questionnaire: a schematic overview with the position of operator, participant, and the large display

---

[1]http://www.nintendo.com/wii, 25 March 2010.

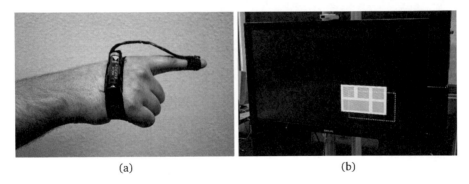

(a)   (b)

Fig. 4 (**a**) The "glove" that our participants wore with an infrared LED mounted on the tip of the index finger and (**b**) the large display with a Wiimote mounted on top, facing the user

formulate a top-three of gestures for each task upon having performed all gestures. Participants were asked, after filling out all questions for a task, to comment on their preferences. They were also asked to provide gestures that they considered to be good alternative gestures.

Two experiment conditions can be distinguished. First, we randomly selected ten percent of the participants in our online questionnaire based on availability. By comparing the ratings from this group with the ratings from the remaining 99 participants in the online questionnaire [12], we can assert whether the results from the questionnaire are a good representation. In other words, we can assert whether our participants could understand, appreciate, and imagine how the gesture would work in an interface. Second, we asked a similarly sized group of volunteers with similar experience and who had *not* filled out the online questionnaire to participate in the same investigation. With this condition we investigate the potential bias that results from having filled out the online questionnaire and thus having seen the gestures before in the online videoclips. Although six months had passed between filling out the online questionnaire and the validation condition, we could not be sure that this would not influence our findings. The experiment conditions are identified either with condition Qx, in which users had already filled out the questionnaire entirely, or with condition Xp with only novice participants.

3.2 Results

3.2.1 Condition Qx

A total of ten subjects participated in this investigation; each one had filled out the online questionnaire at an earlier moment, roughly six months before. We selected the participants randomly and on their availability. Participants were 28 years old on average (ranging 24–36 years, $\sigma = 3$ years). The investigation took on average 53 minutes ($\sigma = 11$ minutes, ranging from 40 minutes to 70 minutes). All participants completed the investigation. One participant was female, the others were male. In our sample, one subject held a BSc's degree, seven held a Master's degree, one held a PhD degree, and one was an undergraduate student. All participants were right-handed. The participants were familiar with the Apple iPhone ($\mu = 4.0$, $\sigma = 1.6$), with PDAs and smartphones ($\mu = 5.3$, $\sigma = 1.7$), and with online videoclips ($\mu = 5.3$, $\sigma = 1.6$). In addition, they rated their familiarity with other gesture interfaces highly ($\mu = 4.9$, $\sigma = 2.1$). Examples of gesture interfaces that they meant by this are the Nintendo Wii and its Wiimote controller, prototypes developed at the university, touch-sensitive tables, and other surfaces, data gloves and public ticket machines. A D'Agostino–Pearson K^2 analysis showed that there are normal distributions for the familiarity ratings with the iPhone, PDA, smart phones, etc. The trials data in condition Qx do not follow normal distributions: intuitiveness scored $K^2 = 17.545$ ($p < -0.01$), physical effort $K^2 = 6.786$ ($p = 0.03$), and "would use" scored $K^2 = 7.683$ ($p = 0.02$). The trials data are mostly deformed as a result of low values for kurtosis.

3.2.2 Condition Xp

Ten subjects participated in this investigation, none of whom had previously filled out the online questionnaire. The participants were 25 years old on average (ranging 22–29 years, $\sigma = 2$ years), and they needed 61 minutes to complete the investigation on average ($\sigma = 9$ minutes). All participants completed this condition of the experiment. Two participants were female, the others were male. In this group, three subjects held a BSc's degree, while the other seven held a Master's degree. One participant was left-handed, the other nine were right-handed. The participants were familiar with the Apple iPhone ($\mu = 5.3$, $\sigma = 1.4$) but not so much with PDAs and smartphones ($\mu = 3.4$, $\sigma = 1.4$). In addition, they were familiar with online videoclips ($\mu = 5.0$, $\sigma = 1.8$), and they rated their familiarity with other gesture interfaces highly ($\mu = 4.5$, $\sigma = 1.8$). The examples of such gesture interfaces that were mentioned were the Nintendo Wii and mouse gestures in the Opera browser. A D'Agostino–Pearson K^2 analysis shows that there is a normal distribution for participants personal answers regarding the familiarity with, for example, the Apple iPhone. The data collected in condition Xp do not follow normal distributions: intuitiveness scored $K^2 = 18.600$ ($p < 0.01$), physical effort $K^2 = 11.039$ ($p < 0.01$), and "would use" scored $K^2 = 11.549$ ($p < 0.01$). The trials data are mainly deformed as a result of low values for kurtosis and skewness.

3.2.3 Sample Summary

Comparing the three samples, we observed a significantly higher rating ($p = 0.02$) for the subject's familiarity with PDAs and smartphones in condition Qx when compared to Xp. Due to the nonnormal distributions of our count-based data, from conditions Qx and Xp we used a Kruskal–Wallis H analysis to discover differences between the ratings for the gestures per task. After finding significant differences, we then examine those findings in more detail with pair-wise Mann–Whitney U analysis.

3.2.4 Commands: Pointing

In a comparison between the two conditions we found no significant differences between them on intuitiveness ($\chi^2 = 0.845$, $p = 0.66$), physical effort ($\chi^2 = 2.252$, $p = 0.32$), and "would use" ($\chi^2 = 2.718$, $p = 0.26$). The analysis per gesture can be found in Table 1.

In the trials data from condition Qx we found a significant difference between gestures for intuitiveness and whether the participant would use this gesture, but we did not observe a significant difference for physical effort. A significant difference was found in the trials data from condition Xp for all three questions. Compared to the results in condition Qx, these differences are similar. The top-three rankings for pointing gestures showed a clear preference (9 subjects) for *Ray-casting* over its alternatives.

In conditions Qx and Xp, our participants wondered whether fine movements for *Ray-casting* would not suffer from jitter. For *Repetitive taps*, our subjects argued that it would be viable for small distances where precision is required but that it is very unsuitable for long distances, mainly due to fatigue. The same comments were made concerning the time spent in interaction: longer tasks would fatigue the user too much. One participant mentioned his preference for pointing with the whole hand instead of only the index finger. With respect to both tapping gestures, some subjects argued that it would work better when using both hands: when moving the cursor to the right, the left hand would be better suited, whereas the right hand is best for moving the cursor left. For *Tap once* our users found it hard to time when to stop the cursor movement. As an alternative pointing gesture, it was proposed to use some gesture, for example, *AirTap*, to switch the cursor between objects on the screen. In both conditions, participants mentioned their preference to combine these pointing gestures. For example, *Ray-casting* provides an easy means to cross large

Table 1 Differences between conditions Qx and Xp for the *point* gestures. Kruskal–Wallis H analysis results with mean ranks are reported ($N = 10$)

	Condition	Qx	Xp	χ^2	p
Ray-casting	Intuitiveness	78.35	56.40	3.454	0.18
	Physical effort	75.40	55.20	2.229	0.33
	Would use it	48.25	58.60	1.552	0.46
Repetitive taps	Intuitiveness	70.35	65.95	1.468	0.48
	Physical effort	62.85	54.85	0.316	0.85
	Would use it	72.20	52.25	1.894	0.39
Tap once	Intuitiveness	53.75	49.00	1.659	0.44
	Physical effort	69.80	55.55	1.039	0.60
	Would use it	42.25	43.80	6.097	<0.05

distances, and fine tuning can be accomplished with *Repetitive taps*. We observed in all three gestures that most users will bend their preferred hand in awkward poses so that they can keep pointing with their index finger.

Alternatively, *Tap once* could also be implemented with a deceleration measure so that the cursor could be "thrown" across the surface until it would stop automatically. The distance traveled is then based on the intensity of the gesture as has been implemented by the BumpTop interface [1]. In BumpTop, icons are represented as physical objects that behave in a believable manner due to a physics simulation. Another alternative gesture that was mentioned was *Ray-casting* with just finger movements while the hand and arm are left in rest, for example, alongside the body. This gesture would depend to large extent on the visual feedback on the display.

3.2.5 Commands: Selecting

Comparing the ratings for the select gestures in the two conditions, we found no significant differences for intuitiveness ($\chi^2 = 2.912$, $p = 0.23$), physical effort ($\chi^2 = 4.104$, $p = 0.13$), and "would use" ($\chi^2 = 4.572$, $p = 0.10$). The analysis per gesture can be found in Table 2.

The results from condition Qx show a significant difference between the gestures for intuitiveness, physical effort, and whether the participant would use this gesture. The preference for a specific gesture is less pronounced due to the smaller user group in condition Qx. Participants rated *AirTap*, *ThumbTrigger*, *Encircling*, and *FistGrab* similarly with respect to intuitiveness. *AirTap* also scored similarly to *ThumbTrigger* and *FistGrab* based on physical effort, but both *Dwelling* and *Encircling* scored significantly higher. *ThumbTrigger* did score higher in conditions Qx

Table 2 Differences between conditions Qx and Xp for the *select* gestures. Kruskal–Wallis H analysis results with mean ranks are reported ($N = 10$)

	Condition	Qx	Xp	χ^2	p
AirTap	Intuitiveness	40.25	61.35	4.029	0.13
	Physical effort	62.25	49.55	1.093	0.58
	Would use it	37.80	67.45	5.280	0.07
ThumbTrigger	Intuitiveness	90.50	94.75	22.455	<0.01
	Physical effort	39.85	44.65	6.796	<0.05
	Would use it	83.75	92.00	16.417	<0.01
Dwelling	Intuitiveness	49.35	47.35	2.921	0.23
	Physical effort	81.60	54.65	4.569	0.10
	Would use it	54.25	53.95	0.725	0.70
Encircling	Intuitiveness	68.35	56.55	0.733	0.69
	Physical effort	66.70	47.90	1.691	0.43
	Would use it	56.55	61.30	0.122	0.94
FistGrab	Intuitiveness	70.15	70.60	2.272	0.32
	Physical effort	68.90	52.70	1.178	0.56
	Would use it	59.75	72.75	1.552	0.46

and Xp with respect to intuitiveness than *Dwelling*, *Encircling*, and *FistGrab*. In addition, *ThumbTrigger* scored significantly lower in conditions Qx and Xp on physical effort, except when compared to *AirTap*. Participants would use either *AirTap*, *ThumbTrigger*, or *FistGrab* to issue a select command where the difference between *AirTap* and *ThumbTrigger* with the other three gestures was the most pronounced. For the select gestures in condition Xp, a difference was revealed for intuitiveness and for physical effort but not for whether the participant would use this gesture. In total, six subjects from condition Qx rated *ThumbTrigger* as the best gesture, closely followed by *AirTap*, which was placed as second best by five subjects. In condition Xp, there was a draw of four subjects, each preferring one of the gestures, and five subjects placing *AirTap* or *ThumbTrigger* as second best. Third best in both conditions was *FistGrab*.

In comments in conditions Qx and Xp our subjects felt that *AirTap* was very familiar to the mouse-paradigm but that it would be preferred if you could tap toward the screen ("as if pressing a button in a lift") instead of having to press your finger down. In doing so, the cursor would also remain more stationary. *ThumbTrigger* also mimicked the mouse-paradigm, while some participants compared it to a pistol-shaped hand. Our subjects liked the fact that *ThumbTrigger* allows selecting while pointing, but they argued to relax the hand somewhat instead of keeping the middle, ring, and pinkie fingers bent. In addition, some subjects mentioned that it is nice to separate the act of pointing from the act of selecting. *Dwelling* was considered to be inaccurate with possibilities for accidental selection events in addition to taking too long to select an object. *Encircling* took too much effort and time but was considered to be suitable for multiple-object selection. *FistGrab* was familiar from everyday life but was linked more to picking up and moving objects (dragging) than for selecting them. Some participants commented that both *FistGrab* and *ThumbTrigger* would move the index finger when changing the hand tension which reduced pointing accuracy. Others mentioned that they preferred to use *ThumbTrigger* when pinching the tips of the middle finger and the thumb together to relieve tension in the hand.

3.2.6 Commands: Deselecting

There were no significant differences between the two conditions for the ratings of the deselect gestures intuitiveness ($\chi^2 = 3.386$, $p = 0.18$), physical effort ($\chi^2 = 0.862$, $p = 0.65$), and "would use" ($\chi^2 = 2.942$, $p = 0.23$). This is also illustrated in Table 3, where the analysis results are given per gesture. In condition Qx, we did not find a significant difference between gestures for intuitiveness and whether the participant would use this gesture. The difference for physical effort was significant however ($\chi^2 = 6.092$, $p < 0.05$). Contrary to these findings for the trials data from condition Qx, the data from condition Xp revealed a difference on intuitiveness ($\chi^2 = 13.850$, $p < 0.01$) and whether the participant would use this gesture ($\chi^2 = 14.995$, $p < 0.01$) but not for physical effort. The results from conditions Qx and Xp are largely the same; however, there is a significant difference

Table 3 Differences between conditions Qx and Xp for the *deselect* gestures. Kruskal–Wallis H analysis results with mean ranks are reported ($N = 10$)

Condition		Qx	Xp	χ^2	p
DropIt	Intuitiveness	69.00	62.50	0.888	0.64
	Physical effort	55.20	55.25	0.492	0.78
	Would use it	66.45	72.30	1.985	0.37
Jerky retract	Intuitiveness	66.90	63.00	0.583	0.75
	Physical effort	69.75	52.00	1.390	0.50
	Would use it	52.30	68.20	1.098	0.58
Retract to rest	Intuitiveness	64.25	55.20	0.359	0.84
	Physical effort	67.45	65.05	0.834	0.66
	Would use it	67.95	57.10	0.649	0.72
Select other	Intuitiveness	70.15	80.65	5.605	0.06
	Physical effort	54.55	50.30	1.314	0.52
	Would use it	78.00	70.60	4.606	0.10

between preference for *Select other* over *DropIt* with respect to intuitiveness. Subjects in conditions Qx and Xp placed *Select other* on top in their rankings closely followed by *DropIt* and *Jerky retract*.

Our subjects commented that *Select other* was very familiar from computer operating systems such as Windows and Mac OS X. They argued that deselect of individual targets should be possible when having selected multiple objects in a row. In addition, although we showed *AirTap* for selecting something other than the on-screen object, most subjects spontaneously used their preferred select-gesture; in most cases, *ThumbTrigger*. *DropIt* looked similar to the hand shape when *Raycasting*, and our subjects wondered how this gesture is started when, for example, *AirTap* was used to select an object. In addition, the difference between the relaxed hand shape and *DropIt* was thought to be too subtle. On the other hand, some participants did mention that *DropIt* is the opposite of *FistGrab* and that these two gestures might be suitable for dragging an object instead of for (de)selecting. For *Retract to rest*, our subjects commented that the arm movements were too large when having to move back and forth between rest and the gesture space. In that respect, *Jerky retract* was better because it leaves the arm in the gesture space. However, the jerky movement strained the arm which was disliked.

3.2.7 Commands: Resizing

Comparing the two conditions on the gestures for resizing, we found no significant differences in intuitiveness ($\chi^2 = 3.936$, $p = 0.14$), physical effort ($\chi^2 = 2.726$, $p = 0.26$), and "would use" ($\chi^2 = 0.398$, $p = 0.82$). We did find some differences when analysing the ratings of the two conditions per gesture, see Table 4. Although there was no difference in whether the participants would use it, *Referenced Pull-Push* scored significantly higher on intuitiveness and lower on the physical effort required to perform the gesture in conditions Qx and Xp.

Table 4 Differences between conditions Qx and Xp for the *resize* gestures. Kruskal–Wallis H analysis results with mean ranks are reported ($N = 10$)

	Condition	Qx	Xp	χ^2	p
Fingers apart	Intuitiveness	60.80	45.75	1.982	0.37
	Physical effort	59.80	72.30	1.522	0.47
	Would use it	43.20	40.45	6.951	<0.05
Hands apart	Intuitiveness	76.28	74.55	5.337	0.07
	Physical effort	44.67	38.85	6.573	<0.05
	Would use it	79.89	81.25	9.060	0.01
PullPush	Intuitiveness	65.30	59.75	0.272	0.87
	Physical effort	63.50	67.30	0.676	0.71
	Would use it	57.35	56.05	0.236	0.89
Referenced PullPush	Intuitiveness	80.20	76.80	7.240	<0.05
	Physical effort	54.25	30.50	8.978	0.01
	Would use it	67.10	78.85	4.104	0.13

Looking at the results from condition Qx, we found no significant differences between the resize gestures for each of the three questions: intuitiveness, physical effort, and "would use." We found that *Hands apart* scored better than the other three gestures, although the difference with *Fingers apart* was barely significant. Condition Xp did show a significant difference between the four resize gestures on intuitiveness ($\chi^2 = 11.322$, $p = 0.01$) and whether the participant would use this gesture ($\chi^2 = 11.801$, $p < 0.01$). Comparing the findings of conditions Qx and Xp, we see largely the same results, although the physical effort required to perform *Referenced PullPush* is not different from that of *Fingers apart*. In addition, *Hands apart* scored significantly better than *Fingers apart* on both intuitiveness and whether the participant would use the gesture. The subjects in both conditions ranked *Hands apart* as the best gesture for resizing. In condition Qx, *Fingers apart* was ranked second, while *PullPush* was ranked second in condition Xp. For both conditions, *Referenced PullPush* was ranked third best.

For *Fingers apart*, our subjects argued that for minor changes in size, this gesture would work as adequately as it would for small displays. However, for larger changes, the fingers would have to repeatedly gesture from start to stop, which made the gesture physically taxing. Also, the starting-posture was a bit difficult to determine. Some subjects mentioned that they felt that this gesture is only suited for smaller displays due to the match in their physical sizes. Quek [37] described this repeated form of gesturing as beats or strokes [27, pp. 15–16]. The *Hands apart* gesture was more precise in that respect, although one subject would have preferred it if the distance between the hands had matched the object's size from the user perspective. For *PullPush*, it was also hard to determine the starting posture, and the limited arm's length introduced a problem for larger zoom ranges. *Referenced PullPush* was very novel, and our subjects liked the reference to the starting position, although one subject said that it could be more explicit by adding a "click" sound when placing both hands together. However, having to use both hands was more tiring. Three subjects, all from condition Xp, tried to spontaneously move both hands in *Referenced*

PullPush, while the others had to be told explicitly. By moving the reference hand, the zoom range could be extended. For *Fingers apart*, one subject proposed the use of the hand's distance to the body as a means to accelerate or decelerate the resize speed. For both *Fingers apart* and *PullPush*, our subjects had difficulty traversing larger resize ranges. They mentioned to "have to pick up the mouse" and to "need to regesture," by which they meant that the same gesture had to performed repeatedly while moving the hand from and to the gesture space in between repetitions.

3.3 Conclusion

There were some differences between the gesture ratings in the two conditions. However, we will show below that these differences are minimal and that they can easily be explained and rationalized. Some preferences were less pronounced in conditions Qx and Xp than they were in the online questionnaire. In most of those cases, the preference did exist, but it was not significant due to the limited number of subjects that took part in conditions Qx and Xp. For pointing, we found no significant differences: in both conditions the *Ray-casting* gesture was preferred to point at locations on the screen. However, the subjects from condition Qx did find *Ray-casting* more fatiguing than the participants in condition Xp: having to keep one's arm outstretched for pointing is fatiguing for prolonged interactions. Fine tuning the act of pointing was demonstrated by using *Tap once* after initial coarse pointing with *Ray-casting*. There was a difference with our previous findings concerning the selecting gestures. *AirTap* was liked overwhelmingly in the online questionnaire, but in both validation conditions *ThumbTrigger* scored similarly. Our subjects liked the physical feedback that *ThumbTrigger* offered upon "clicking," although they did not miss this form of feedback in *AirTap*. Previously we had found that *DropIt* and *Select other* were both preferred for deselecting, but now we found a significant preference for only *Select other*. Especially the fact that this gesture is familiar from existing WIMP interfaces led to this choice, hinting that our subjects prefer predictable and recognizable interactions. In addition, the users in conditions Qx and Xp commented that when using *DropIt*, it requires them to first make a fist before they can perform the deselect-gesture *DropIt*. This requires an additional step that broadens the gap in the "gulf of execution" [33]. To resize objects, our subjects preferred *Hands apart* significantly. The difference in physical effort involved between the two conditions did not differ. Our subjects mentioned that when they had to resize more, the amount that the hands could indicate enabled much more precise resizing.

In general, our subjects found it better to use just one hand for gesturing because that was already fatiguing for prolonged interaction sessions. However, two hands offer an explicit means to indicate distances. Resizing is a prime example, but for pointing with *Repetitive taps*, it was proposed to indicate the start of the movement with one hand and to use the other to stop. We found that subjects found it hard to imagine why we included the activate and deactivate task: it was unclear what this task was supposed to do in existing interfaces they are familiar with. We consider it important that all subjects felt that they were in actual control during both conditions Qx and Xp. This ensures that our findings are based on experience with a working interface. A main contributor was the fact that pointing through *Ray-casting* actually worked and that the gesture could be detected robustly by the operator. Although some participants mentioned that they did hear the operator pressing buttons during the investigation, they did not feel hindered or influenced by it.

4 Experiment 2: Gesturing in the Interface

The main thing that was lacking from the previous experiment is an interface that is fully controlled by the user. The partial control of the interface was influenced, at times, by a mismatch between the intended interaction and the user's intentions. In this section we correct this shortcoming by evaluating an interface that the user can fully control. As a starting point, we use the gestures we evaluated previously, among others, *ThumbTrigger* and *Hands apart*. The work presented here does not include building a system for unobtrusive gesture recognition. We rather employ existing technologies and techniques for looking at users gesturing as much as possible in our evaluation of a gesture interface for command-giving to large displays beyond arm's length. This section describes the method (Sect. 4.1), the results (Sect. 4.2), and the conclusions of this experiment (Sect. 4.3).

4.1 Method

For this experiment, we asked the participants to perform selected gestures repeatedly. In this way, they could experience what it will be like to interact with a gesture-based interface for a limited period, roughly 20 minutes, and imagine what it would be like to do so for a prolonged period. This gives us qualitative insight into gesture-based interaction and, more precisely, the users' perception of employing gestures in this interaction.

We employed a qualitative analysis of the interaction through questionnaires before—concerning previous experience and personal background—and after—concerning the experience during the interactions—each trial. Our participants performed four randomized pattern-matching tasks on a high-resolution large display of 400×125 cm. Each task consisted of finding a goal-state that was a certain orientation and zoom-level of a 3D mesh. We provided an image of the desired goal-state to the participant. This image could be referred to at any moment. As a starting point, we offered the participant four different 3D meshes to choose from. These meshes are biochemical structures that are used by, for example, biochemists, to discover function from the form of the structure. The participants were not required to have any knowledge of the biochemical structures or of its visualization standards. We thus reduced the task to a more simple pattern-matching task.

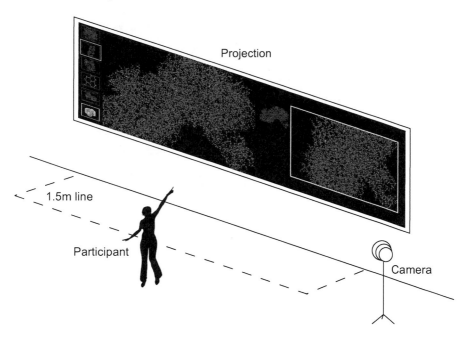

Fig. 5 The setup used in this prototype. The camera stood at the back of the room, to the right of the participant, who could see the whole display. Users could walk around but not stand closer than 1.5 meters to the display

Users were allowed to walk freely in front of the display: the projectors that were used to create the display were hung from the ceiling so that the user could not cast shadows. Users were not allowed to come within 1.5 meters of the screen. This limitation meant that the user could not be at arm's length, or closer, of the screen, see Fig. 5 [10].

The graphical user interface that we used in this experiment consisted of three borderless panels which were, from left to right, an options menu, a 3D mesh, and a collection of 2D screenshots. The menu contains six options: loading a specific mesh, toggling a bounding box, and creating a screenshot of the current 3D mesh. The menu was visible continuously. By selecting a biochemical structure from the menu, the 3D representation of that structure would be loaded in the middle panel with a set starting orientation and zoom-level. These settings were identical for all four structures. The structure could be rotated and zoomed in and out. To enable the user to switch easily between previously visited locations, we facilitated the use of screenshots that could be ordered as the participant saw fit. To ensure that all available commands were indeed repeatedly given by each participant, we requested the creation of at least two and deletion of at least one screenshot per goal that was offered. Screenshots were presented in the right-most panel. Each screenshot could also be loaded so that the 3D mesh that was its origin was again displayed.

The best-scoring gestures from our previous experiments are the basis for this experiment. Each of the following commands was evaluated with a questionnaire in which we asked how easy it is to learn and remember the gesture ("1: easy to learn"—"7: difficult to learn"), comfort for the hands while gesturing ("1: cramped"—"7: comfortable"). We placed a small wireless device on each hand: each contained a red laser and two buttons that could be placed freely on the hand. The buttons were placed on the same location at the beginning of each trial, and users were encouraged to try out their best fit after a brief training session.

4.1.1 Out-of-Range and Tracking

Ray-casting is used to detect whether a participant was in the out-of-range or in the tracking state. We placed a laser on each hand, and, using a camera, we could detect when the user was pointing on the screen and with which hand. We distinguished the participant pointing at each of the three panels with one or two hands.

4.1.2 Select and Deselect

Both *ThumbTrigger* and *Pinch* were evaluated in this experiment. It was possible to select and deselect in the menu and screenshot panels; however, the meaning of this was different for each panel. In the menu panel, each of the six options could only be selected. In the screenshot panel, the user could select a screenshot to restore it to the 3D panel. Selecting screenshots or menu options could be undone by selecting another option or screenshot. For deselecting, *Select other* was opted given the positive feedback that we had received on it.

4.1.3 Rotate

A special selection case is rotating in a 3D visualization. The participant performed *ThumbTrigger* with one hand on the 3D panel to rotate the biochemical structure to the desired orientation. It was possible to rotate around the x and y axes. It was possible to rotate around the viewing axis (the z axis) using *PinkieTrigger* with one hand. This approach to rotating, which is known as ArcBall [20], is typical for the rotation schemes that are used in 3D design and drawing applications such as Autodesk AutoCAD®.

4.1.4 Resizing

The prevailing gestures for the resize command were *Hands apart* and *Fingers apart*. Given the scale of the large display and the comments we noted in the previous evaluations, we chose to focus on *Hands apart*. Participants performed *Thumb-Trigger* with both hands to signal the beginning and ending of their resize gesture. The users pressed both of their thumbs down for the duration of this gesture. Resizing was possible on both the 3D panel and on the screenshot panel. For both panels, the participants moved both hands on the target, structure, or screenshot that they wished to resize. By performing *ThumbTrigger* and moving the hands apart for enlarging and toward each other for shrinking, the participant could resize the target to the desired size.

4.1.5 Restore and Remove

Restoring a screenshot could be done with *PinkieTrigger*. By performing this gesture, the structure with the orientation and size depicted in the screenshot would be restored in the 3D panel so that the participant could continue manipulating it from there. Lastly, screenshots could be removed by performing a *PinkieTrigger* gesture with both hands on them. The participant pointed at the target that they wished to be removed. After performing *PinkieTrigger*, the screenshot was removed from the screenshot panel. It was not possible to undo this action.

4.2 Results

A total of twenty-three subjects participated in this within-subjects design. All participants studied at or worked for our university. Participants were 29 years old on average (ranging 24–47 years, $\sigma = 5$ years). All participants completed the experiment. Five participants were female, and eighteen were male. Eight subjects held a Bachelor's degree, thirteen subjects held a Master's degree, and two a PhD degree. All participants were right-handed. One subject was familiar with the structure of ice but had not seen the other three structures before taking part. All other participants were unfamiliar with the four structures that were used in the prototype.

Table 5 shows the results of the ratings of our participants' knowledge related to gesture interfaces. Participants were moderately familiar with pen-based devices such as a PDA and tablet PC, and they also mentioned the Nintendo DS, cellphones, and the Apple iPhone in this category. The participants were not familiar with the

Table 5 Experience of our subjects before taking part in the investigation; all scores on scale 1–7 except values of "avg. hours at PC" ($N = 23$)

	mean	std. dev.	variance	kurtosis	skewness	K^2	p
avg. hours at PC	7.9	2.3	5.2	−0.4	−0.7	2.3	0.31
pen-based devices	4.3	2.2	4.9	−1.8	0.2	3.0	0.22
iPhone	2.9	2.3	5.5	−0.4	1.1	5.6	0.06
other multitouch	3.4	1.8	3.1	−0.4	0.7	2.6	0.27
Wii (mote)	3.8	1.6	2.6	−0.8	0.3	1.4	0.49
other gesture int.	2.5	1.7	2.9	1.4	1.5	9.9	<0.01
video clips	3.5	1.5	2.3	−1.1	0.3	1.9	0.39

Apple iPhone but more so with other multitouch systems. They mentioned the touch tables at our research group [11], the Apple iPhone itself, the Apple Touchpad, and the trackpad on their notebook. Our participants were moderately familiar with the Nintendo Wii and its Wiimote controllers but less so with other gesture interfaces for which they mentioned the Playstation EyeToy, data gloves, photoplay, the Personal Space Station [31], and Firefox mouse gestures. Our participants were not so familiar with video clips of gesture interfaces. "Minority Report" was mentioned explicitly nine times, while other sources were "The Island" (2), "Paycheck," "Star Trek" (2), "Iron Man," and also Oblong's G-Stalt[2] and Microsoft's Surface multitouch table. Other gesture interfaces that were named included: "camera-based interfaces," "gesture detection in large rooms such as waving and pointing," "endoscopic operation robot in surgery," "EMG-based guitars," "Microsoft Natal," and, again, "Firefox mouse gestures." A D'Agostino–Pearson K^2 analysis showed that there are normal distributions for these ratings, except for experience with other gesture interfaces ($K^2 = 9.860$, $p < 0.01$), see Table 5. This deformation is a result of high values for skewness and for kurtosis.

4.2.1 Questionnaire

A D'Agostino–Pearson K^2 analysis showed that the ratings for the whole interaction do not follow a normal distribution. Tables 6 and 7 present these results. We can see that the overall experience was positive. Our participants understood how the lasers were used for pointing; the pointing accuracy, operation speed, and comfort while interacting were high, and there was limited fatigue in the hands and arms while interacting. The rating for the "fun-factor" was high as well. The smoothness of the interaction scored somewhat lower.

There was only one participant who explicitly commented that the interaction could have been smoother. Three participants mentioned that "Getting used to [it] is

Table 6 Overall interaction ratings of the experience during the experiment. Scoring was adjusted so that 1: negative score (worst), 7: positive score (best) ($N = 23$)

	mean	std. dev.	variance	kurtosis	skewness	K^2	p
how lasers worked	6.4	0.8	0.6	2.9	−1.6	13.7	<0.01
pointing accuracy	5.0	1.1	1.1	1.9	−1.3	9.6	<0.01
interaction smoothness	3.9	1.2	1.5	−0.3	0.1	0.4	0.82
operation speed	4.6	1.2	1.4	−0.1	−0.2	0.3	0.86
interaction comfort	5.1	1.1	1.1	3.0	−1.3	11.3	<0.01
fatigue in hands	6.0	1.3	1.7	2.7	−1.6	12.9	<0.01
fatigue in arms	5.6	1.2	1.5	2.6	−1.4	11.5	<0.01
fun or boring?	6.1	1.0	1.1	1.9	−1.3	9.0	0.01

[2]http://oblong.com, 25 March 2010.

Table 7 Detailed interaction ratings, per command that could be given. Scoring was adjusted so that 1: negative score (worst), 7: positive score (best). ($N = 23$)

command	question	mean	std. dev.	variance	kurtosis	skewness	K^2	p
rotate 3D	learn gestures	5.9	1.4	1.8	2.2	−1.6	11.8	<0.01
	gesture comfort	5.7	1.2	1.4	3.8	−1.9	17.9	<0.01
zoom 3D	learn gestures	6.0	0.8	0.7	0.2	−0.6	1.9	0.38
	gesture comfort	5.7	1.0	1.1	1.0	−1.1	6.4	0.04
move 2D	learn gestures	6.7	0.5	0.2	−1.29	−0.9	5.4	0.1
	gesture comfort	6.0	0.8	0.6	2.2	−1.2	8.9	0.7
zoom 2D	learn gestures	6.4	0.6	0.3	−0.7	−0.3	1.2	0.55
	gesture comfort	5.9	1.0	1.0	2.4	−1.3	10.5	<0.01
restore	learn gestures	5.4	1.3	1.6	−0.7	−0.5	2.1	0.35
	gesture comfort	5.7	1.1	1.2	0.6	−1.0	4.9	0.09
options	learn gestures	6.8	0.4	0.2	0.2	−1.5	7.9	0.01
	gesture comfort	6.3	0.9	0.7	2.5	−1.5	12.0	<0.01
delete	learn gestures	5.5	1.2	1.4	−0.8	−0.3	1.5	0.46
	gesture comfort	5.9	0.9	0.8	0.9	−1.1	5.7	0.06

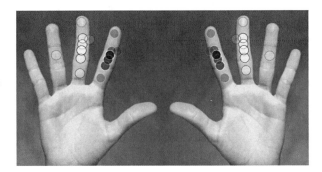

Fig. 6 Button placement on the hands. The *black dots* represent the A button, while the *white dots* represent the B buttons. The more intense the dot, the more participants placed a button there

difficult because the lasers have the same color," by which they meant that they at times had difficulties in determining which laser dot originated from where. On that respect, it was also mentioned that "Inaccuracy was not so much a bother because you get visual feedback from the interface *and* the lasers."

Figure 6 shows where the buttons were placed on the participants' hands. Although we placed the buttons in the middle of the index and middle fingers at the beginning of each trial, after the practice session, we asked each participant if the buttons were placed comfortably and, if not, how they would prefer to place them. Only three participants decided to change the buttons when so asked. Others did so of their own accord, mostly because the rings were either too wide or too narrow. This was especially true for the five female participants, due to their slender fingers: they slid the rings down as far as needed to keep them from falling off entirely.

4.2.2 Observations

The most prevalent posture for our participants to stand in was with their upper arms along their body and both their lower arms pointing towards the screen, even when they were only actively using one or even neither of the hands. When asked why they did not stretch their arms for pointing, they commented that it was the most comfortable way for them to stand. It was rare for participants to walk around in front of the display, although we did explicitly explain to them that it was allowed as long as they did not cross the 1.5-meter line. We did notice that all participants were switching the leg on which they were standing to stand more comfortably. When performing the pattern matching tasks, most participants first loaded each of the four molecules to discover what they were looking at. After this exploration stage, they started manipulating the structure to fit the requested goal. Almost none of the participants noticed that they switched hands for pointing, between their left and right hands. When asked why they did so, they were at first surprised to find out that this was the case after which they mentioned that it was the most comfortable way for them to point. One participant commented that she was "very right-handed" when performing the tasks, although we observed that she too was switching her left and right hands for pointing. We did not observe any participant always using the left hand to point to the left side of the display, or vice versa. All participants mentioned, when asked, that they liked the visual feedback that the laser dots provided to them. They also argued that it was clear that when they did not press a button, the interface would not respond. One participant preferred to have the laser attached to his fingertip, but the other participants frequently mentioned that they liked pointing with their whole hand: they argued that it was more comfortable to keep their fingers relaxed. One participant had significant difficulties in perceiving depth in the Jmol panel, while two other participants suggested that perception of the 3D structure could be improved by using 3D goggles [42]. One participant mentioned that she felt that the response time of the interface was high but that she accepted it because it was a new type of interface. Were this to happen on her PC, it would be totally unacceptable.

4.3 Conclusion

The gestures that were preferred in our previous experiment were evaluated. We built a working prototype with two wireless, glove-like devices that enabled our participants to interact beyond arm's length with a large display through gestures such as *ThumbTrigger*, *PinkieTrigger*, and *Hands apart*. Our subjects experienced this interaction for twenty minutes after a practice session of five minutes. By giving our subjects a chance to interact for this amount of time, we obtained qualitative feedback on the interactions. A set of four pattern matching tasks was given to our subjects. These tasks were designed in such a way that they required the subjects to repeatedly give commands to the interface to achieve the required goal. An image

Fig. 7 One of the 23 users participating in our experiment. Note the small wireless devices placed on each hand and the placement of their buttons

of a complex 3D mesh (a biochemical structure) was presented that the subjects had to reproduce by rotating and resizing a 3D mesh. In addition, the user could manipulate that image, and other images that could be made in the process of finding the requested target state, by moving and resizing them.

We found that all participants enjoyed giving commands through gesturing in our interface. They experienced gesturing as accurate, fast, and comfortable. There was no fatigue in the hands and arms to speak of even though our participants tended to keep their arms tensed for the entire duration of the trial. The smoothness of the interaction could have been better which manifested itself mainly in rotating and zooming the 3D mesh. This was caused by the 3D rendering software we used which was not fully customizable to our needs. Our participants preferred to shape the *ThumbTrigger* and *PinkieTrigger* gestures to fit their own comfort, placing the buttons that we used to detect the thumb pressing against another finger so that it was most comfortable for them. This mostly meant that the subject had to minimally bend his finger so that he could give a command with minimal effort. Women could not always place the buttons as they desired because the rings did not fit tightly enough on their more slender fingers. However, this was of no influence on our findings for comfort, accuracy, smoothness, and fatigue. The combinations of gesture for giving a specific command were easy to learn and remember for the duration of our trials.

We can conclude that the gestures that we evaluated in our earlier experiments are fun (see Fig. 7), comfortable, and efficient for giving commands to a large display beyond arm's length. A wearable device was used in this experiment to robustly detect the gestures. None of our participants mentioned they felt uncomfortable to wear such a device even though it had to be tightly strapped to the subject's hands and arms. We suspect that a smaller device, which would still be attached to the back of the hand, might be more comfortable still. It has been argued in HCI literature [22] that unobtrusive gesture recognition is a desirable way to interact through gesturing with an intelligent environment. However, we argue that by giving the user an explicit means to interact, for example, through buttons on a small wearable device, the interface will be more transparent for the user. In addition, holding or wearing a control device is an explicit signal to each user as to who is in control of the display [29]. This is, however, a topic for further research.

5 Conclusion and Discussion

Gesture interfaces that are operated at a distance can be applied in display-rich environments. We mention just some examples of these environments that are packed with displays that are on the walls, floor, and embedded in the furniture. In smart meeting rooms, scientists analyze and interpret complex data structures such as they occur in life science research projects [40]. In shopping areas, display windows try to catch the eye of passers-by through interactive product information [30, 47]. The surgeon's hands must remain sterile for the duration of the surgery in operating rooms of the future that facilitate easy access to a patient's information [48, 49]. The aim of this work is to explore, from a perspective of human behavior, which gestures are suited to control large display surfaces at a distance; why that is so; and, equally important, how such an interface can be made a reality.

Our first experiment was a validation of our earlier findings because the users had previously merely imagined what it would be like to gesture as proposed. The gestures selected through a previous online questionnaire were validated with a prototype interface in which the user could point through ray-casting but where the start and end of a gesture were detected by an operator. Users with a similar background evaluated the suitability of each gesture to give a specific command by experiencing it. We found only minimal differences between the evaluations of the gesture from the online setting and after repeatedly experiencing it. These differences were mostly caused by users preferring to rest their hands as much as possible to increase the comfort while interacting. The users found it, above all, *fun* to interact through gestures in a seemingly working gesture interface. We also learned that participants consider it important that switching between resting and interacting is both easy and fast to do. The preferred gestures again show that there is a strong preference for gestures that mimic the pressing of a button. This evidence also supports evaluating gesture interactions through video prototypes as has been argued for by Tognazzini [44] and Bardram et al. [2]. Video prototypes offer a relatively fast means to evaluate the workings of a mature interface without having to build it.

To consolidate our previous findings we designed, built, and evaluated a gesture interface with which the user can interact with 3D and 2D visualizations on a wall-sized display. This second experiment also provided us with experience in building and working with an operational gesture interface. Interactions consisted of the gestures for issuing commands that were preferred in our previous experiments. Again, we found that our participants preferred to interact with the least amount of effort and with the highest comfort possible. There was little variation between users in the shape of the gestures that they preferred: tapping the thumb on one of the other fingers, known as *ThumbTrigger* [17], was the prevalent gesture. The prevalent gestures that we found in our studies: *Ray-casting* for pointing, *ThumbTrigger* was preferred for selecting objects and menu items, *Fingers apart* combined with

ThumbTrigger for resizing, dragging with the thumb pressed down in *ThumbTrigger* for rotating in 3D and dragging in 2D, and *PinkieTrigger* for alternate selection commands.

The experience that our users had at the beginning of both experiments influenced our findings. We do not know the exact extent of this influence, but it is notable to find that gestures such as *Fingers apart* that have become popular from the Apple iPhone have been accepted so easily and significantly in the gestures that are suited for controlling large displays at a distance. In addition, the standard WIMP paradigm has, over the past decades, indoctrinated high-tech citizens who form the potential users of the systems for which we are designing gesture-based interfaces. The WIMP paradigm is intensely familiar for these users. We demonstrate with our findings that the appeal of these existing and new interfaces provides undeniably strong reasons for preferring gestures that mimic already existing interactions. Interactions such as pressing mouse buttons and the drag-and-drop paradigm are the cause for this appeal. It is plausible to assume that these paradigms are, in turn, based on easy to learn and remember metaphors from everyday life where we manipulate the objects around us with our hands all the time. We argue here that the strive in HCI to define natural interactions that are, supposedly, best suited for novice users and long-term usage alike, should not deny the strong influence of existing interfaces. When they encounter a gesture interface, users expect it to work in ways they are familiar with, however limited.

References

1. Agarawala, A., Balakrishnan, R.: Keepin' it real: pushing the desktop metaphor with physics, piles and the pen. In: Proceedings of the SIGCHI Conference on Human Factors in Computing Systems (CHI '06), pp. 1283–1292. ACM, New York (2006)
2. Bardram, J., Bossen, C., Lykke-Olesen, A., Nielsen, R., Madsen, K.H.: Virtual video prototyping of pervasive healthcare systems. In: Proceedings of the 4th Conference on Designing Interactive Systems (DIS '02), pp. 167–177. ACM, New York (2002)
3. Beringer, N.: Evoking gestures in SmartKom—design of the graphical user interface. In: Gesture-Based Communication in Human–Computer Interaction. Lecture Notes in Computer Science, vol. 2915, pp. 409–420. Springer, Berlin (2002)
4. Bolt, R.: "Put-that-there": Voice and gesture at the graphics interface. SIGGRAPH Comput. Graph. **14**(3), 262–270 (1980)
5. Cohen, C.: A brief overview of gesture recognition. Online (1999)
6. Cutler, L., Froehlich, B., Hanrahan, P.: Two-handed direct manipulation on the responsive workbench. In: Proceedings of the 1997 Symposium on Interactive 3D Graphics (SI3D '97), pp. 107–114. ACM, New York (1997)
7. Dietz, P., Leigh, D.: Diamondtouch: a multi-user touch technology. In: Proceedings of the 14th Annual ACM Symposium on User Interface Software and Technology (UIST '01), pp. 219–226. ACM, New York (2001)
8. Fiebrink, R., Morris, D., Morris, M.: Dynamic mapping of physical controls for tabletop groupware. In: Proceedings of the 27th International Conference on Human Factors in Computing Systems (CHI '09), pp. 471–480. ACM, New York (2009)
9. Fikkert, W.: Gesture interaction at a distance. PhD thesis, University of Twente (2010)
10. Fikkert, W., D'Ambros, M., Bierz, T., Jankun-Kelly, T.: Interacting with visualizations. In: Kerren, A., Ebert, A., Meyer, J. (eds.) Human-Centered Visualization Environments. Lecture Notes in Computer Science, vol. 4417, pp. 77–162. Springer, Berlin (2007)

11. Fikkert, W., Hakvoort, M., van der Vet, P., Nijholt, A.: Experiences with interactive multi-touch tables. In: The 3rd International Conference on Intelligent Technologies for Interactive Entertainment (INTETAIN '09). Lecture Notes of the Institute for Computer Sciences, Social Informatics and Telecommunications Engineering, vol. 9, pp. 193–200. Springer, Berlin (2009)

12. Fikkert, W., van der Vet, P., Nijholt, A.: Gestures for large display control. In: Gesture in Embodied Communication and Human-Computer Interaction. Lecture Notes in Computer Science, vol. 5934, p. 12. Springer, Berlin (2009)

13. Fikkert, W., van der Vet, P., Rauwerda, H., Breit, T., Nijholt, A.: A natural gesture repertoire for cooperative large display interaction. In: Advances in Gesture-Based Human–Computer Interaction and Simulation. Lecture Notes on Computer Science, vol. 5085, pp. 199–204. Springer, Berlin (2009)

14. Gill, S., Borchers, J.: Knowledge in co-action: social intelligence in collaborative design activity. AI Soc. **17**(3), 322–339 (2003)

15. Gonzales, A., Finley, T., Duncan, S.: (perceived) interactivity: does interactivity increase enjoyment and creative identity in artistic spaces? In: Proceedings of the 27th International Conference on Human Factors in Computing Systems (CHI '09), pp. 415–418. ACM, New York (2009)

16. Grossman, T., Balakrishnan, R., Kurtenbach, G., Fitzmaurice, G., Khan, A., Buxton, W.: Creating principal 3d curves with digital tape drawing. In: Proceedings of the SIGCHI Conference on Human Factors in Computing Systems (CHI '02), pp. 121–128. ACM, New York (2002)

17. Grossman, T., Wigdor, D., Balakrishnan, R.: Multi-finger gestural interaction with 3d volumetric displays. In: Proceedings of the 17th Annual ACM Symposium on User Interface Software and Technology (UIST '04), pp. 61–70. ACM, New York (2004)

18. Guiard, Y.: Asymmetric division of labor in human skilled bimanual action: The kinematic chain as a model. J. Mot. Behav. **19**(4), 486–517 (1987); slightly edited version of an article originally published

19. Hansen, D.: Committing eye tracking. PhD thesis, IT University of Copenhagen (2003)

20. Hinckley, K., Tullio, J., Pausch, R., Proffitt, D., Kassell, N.: Usability analysis of 3d rotation techniques. In: Proceedings of the 10th Annual ACM Symposium on User Interface Software and Technology (UIST '97), pp. 1–10. ACM, New York (1997)

21. Hofs, D., Theune, M., op den Akker, R.: Natural interaction with a virtual guide in a virtual environment: a multimodal dialogue system. J. Multimodal User Interfaces **3**(1–2), 141–153 (2010)

22. Jaimes, A., Sebe, N.: Multimodal human computer interaction: a survey. Comput. Vis. Image Underst. **108**(1–2), 116–134 (2007)

23. Kavakli, M., Taylor, M., Trapeznikov, A.: Designing in virtual reality (desire): a gesture-based interface. In: Proceedings of the 2nd International Conference on Digital Interactive Media in Entertainment and Arts (DIMEA '07), pp. 131–136. ACM, New York (2007)

24. König, W., Bieg, H.J., Reiterer, H.: Laserpointer – Interaktion für große, hochauflösende displays. In: Mensch und Computer 2007: Interaktion im Plural, 7. Konferenz für interaktive und kooperative Medien, pp. 69–78. Oldenbourg, Munich (2007)

25. Lee, J.C.: Hacking the Nintendo Wii remote. IEEE Pervasive Comput. **7**(3), 39–45 (2008)

26. Malik, S., Ranjan, A., Balakrishnan, R.: Interacting with large displays from a distance with vision-tracked multi-finger gestural input. In: Proceedings of the 18th Annual ACM Symposium on User Interface Software and Technology (UIST '05), pp. 43–52. ACM, New York (2005)

27. McNeill, D.: Hand and Mind: What Gestures Reveal About Thought. University of Chicago Press, Chicago (1992)

28. Mistry, P., Maes, P., Chang, L.: Wuw – wear Ur world: a wearable gestural interface. In: Proceedings (Extended Abstracts) of the 27th International Conference on Human Factors in Computing Systems (CHI EA '09), pp. 4111–4116. ACM, New York (2009)

29. Morris, M., Huang, A., Paepcke, A., Winograd, T.: Cooperative gestures: multi-user gestural interactions for co-located groupware. In: Proceedings of the SIGCHI Conference on Human Factors in Computing Systems (CHI '06), pp. 1201–1210. ACM, New York (2006)

30. Mubin, O., Lashina, T., van Loenen, E.: How not to become a buffoon in front of a shop window: a solution allowing natural head movement for interaction with a public display. In: Human–Computer Interaction (INTERACT '09). Lecture Notes in Computer Science, vol. 5727, pp. 250–263. Springer, Berlin (2009)
31. Mulder, J., van Liere, R.: The personal space station: Bringing interaction within reach. In: Proceedings of the 4th Virtual Reality International Conference (VRIC '02), pp. 73–81. IEEE, New York (2002)
32. Nielsen, M., Störring, M., Moeslund, T., Granum, E.: A procedure for developing intuitive and ergonomic gesture interfaces for hci. In: Gesture-Based Communication in Human–Computer Interaction. Lecture Notes in Computer Science, vol. 2915, pp. 409–420. Springer, Berlin (2004)
33. Norman, D.: The Design of Everyday Things. Doubleday, New York (1988)
34. Norman, D.: Cognitive artifacts. In: Carroll, J. (ed.) Designing Interaction: Psychology at the Human–Computer Interface, pp. 17–38. Cambridge University Press, Cambridge, UK (1991)
35. Ott, R., Thalmann, D., Vexo, F.: Haptic feedback in mixed-reality environments. The Vis. Comput., Int. J. Comput. Graph. **23**(9), 843–849 (2007)
36. Pantic, M., Pentland, A., Nijholt, A., Huang, T.: Human computing and machine understanding of human behavior: a survey. In: Proceedings of the 8th International Conference on Multimodal Interfaces (ICMI '06), vol. 8, pp. 239–248. ACM, New York (2006)
37. Quek, F.: Unencumbered gestural interaction. IEEE Trans. Multimed. **3**(4), 36–47 (1996)
38. Rauwerda, H., Roos, M., Hertzberger, B., Breit, T.: The promise of a virtual lab in drug discovery. Drug Discov. Today **11**, 228–236 (2006)
39. Rauwerda, H., de Leeuw, W., Adriaanse, J., Bouwhuis, M., van der Vet, P., Breit, T.: The role of e-BioLabs in a life sciences collaborative working environment. In: Proceedings of the eChallenges (2007)
40. Rauwerda, H., van der Vet, P., Kulyk, O., Wassink, I., Fikkert, W., de Leeuw, W., Adriaanse, J., van Dijk, B., van der Veer, G., Bouwhuis, M., Breit, T., Nijholt, A.: E-science support for OMICS experimentation. In: Benelux Bioinformatics Conference (2007)
41. Schlattman, M., Klein, R.: Simultaneous 4 gestures 6 DOF real-time two-hand tracking without any markers. In: Proceedings of the 2007 ACM Symposium on Virtual Reality Software and Technology (VRST '07), pp. 39–42. ACM, New York (2007)
42. van Schooten, B., van Dijk, B., Zudilova-Seinstra, E., de Koning, P., Reiber, H.: Evaluating visualisation and navigation techniques for interpretation of mra data. In: International Joint Conference on Computer Vision, Imaging and Computer Graphics Theory and Applications (VISIGRAPP '09), pp. 405–408. INSTICC Press, Portugal (2009)
43. Streitz, N., Nixon, P.: The disappearing computer. Commun. ACM **48**(3), 32–35 (2005)
44. Tognazzini, B.: The "Starfire" video prototype project: a case history. In: Proceedings of the SIGCHI Conference on Human Factors in Computing Systems (CHI '94), pp. 99–105. ACM, New York (1994)
45. Tse, E., Shen, C., Greenberg, S., Forlines, C.: Enabling interaction with single user applications through speech and gestures on a multi-user tabletop. In: Proceedings of the Working Conference on Advanced Visual Interfaces (AVI '06), pp. 336–343. ACM, New York (2006)
46. Vogel, D., Balakrishnan, R.: Interactive public ambient displays: transitioning from implicit to explicit, public to personal, interaction with multiple users. In: Proceedings of the 17th Annual ACM Symposium on User Interface Software and Technology (UIST '04), pp. 137–146. ACM, New York (2004)
47. Vogel, D., Balakrishnan, R.: Distant freehand pointing and clicking on very large, high resolution displays. In: Proceedings of the 18th Annual ACM Symposium on User Interface Software and Technology (UIST '05), pp. 33–42. ACM, New York (2005)
48. Wachs, J., Stern, H., Edan, Y., Gillam, M., Feied, C., Smith, M., Handler, J.: Gestix: a doctor-computer sterile gesture interface for dynamic environments. In: Soft Computing in Industrial Applications. Advances in Soft Computing, vol. 39, pp. 30–39. Springer, Berlin (2007)
49. Wachs, J., Stern, H., Edan, Y., Gillam, M., Handler, J., Feied, C., Smith, M.: A gesture-based tool for sterile browsing of radiology images. J. Am. Med. Inform. Assoc. **15**(3), 321–323 (2008)

50. Wang, Y., MacKenzie, C.: The role of contextual haptic and visual constraints on object manipulation in virtual environments. In: Proceedings of the SIGCHI Conference on Human Factors in Computing Systems (CHI '00), pp. 532–539. ACM, New York (2000)
51. Zhang, X., MacKenzie, S.: Evaluating eye tracking with ISO 9241, part 9. In: Human–Computer Interaction. HCI Intelligent Multimodal Interaction Environments. Lecture Notes in Computer Science, vol. 4552, pp. 779–788. Springer, Berlin (2007)

Video Summary Quality Evaluation Based on 4C Assessment and User Interaction

Tongwei Ren, Yan Liu, and Gangshan Wu

Abstract As video summarization techniques have attracted increasing attention for efficient multimedia data management, quality evaluation of video summary is required. To address the lack of automatic evaluation techniques, this chapter proposes a novel full-reference evaluation framework to assess the quality of the video summary according to various user requirements. First, the reference video summary and the candidate video summary are decomposed into two sequences of Summary Units (SUs), and the SUs in these two sequences are matched by frame alignment. Then, a similarity-based assessment algorithm is proposed to automatically provide comprehensive human-like evaluation results of the candidate video summary quality from the perspective of Coverage, Conciseness, Coherence, and Context (4C), respectively. Considering the evaluation, criteria of video summary quality are usually application-dependent, the incremental user interaction is utilized to gather the user requirements of video summary quality, and the required evaluation results are transformed from the 4C assessment scores. The proposed framework is experimented on a standard dataset of TRECVID 2007 and shows a good performance in automatic video summary evaluation.

1 Introduction

The exponential growth of multimedia data and the wide application of multimedia technology have led to the significant need for efficient multimedia data man-

T. Ren (✉) · G. Wu
State Key Laboratory for Novel Software Technology, Nanjing University, Nanjing, China
e-mail: rentw@graphics.nju.edu.cn

G. Wu
e-mail: gswu@nju.edu.cn

Y. Liu
Department of Computing, The Hong Kong Polytechnic University, Hong Kong, Hong Kong
e-mail: csyliu@comp.polyu.nju.hk

L. Shao et al. (eds.), *Multimedia Interaction and Intelligent User Interfaces,*
Advances in Pattern Recognition,
DOI 10.1007/978-1-84996-507-1_10, © Springer-Verlag London Limited 2010

agement [19]. Video summarization provides a means to manage video collections more efficiently by generating a concise statement, called a summary, in such a way that the user can understand the content of the video file(s) by merely viewing the summary [12]. A good video summary epitomizes the essentials of the original video in the form of storyboard (a collection of still images) [30] or video skim (a much shorter video clip) [17]. An informative and concise video summary enables efficient access to the voluminous, redundant, and unstructured video collections [5].

Although video summarization has received more and more attention, a systematic evaluation framework for video summarization is still unavailable [29]. Currently, the quality of the video summary is mainly assessed by human individuals [1, 14, 28], which is seriously influenced by human factors. Moreover, this kind of manual evaluation has high labor cost and time cost [23]. The missing of the automatic evaluation in video summarization also results in the problem that each work on video summarization may demonstrate its performance using its own evaluation method and often be short of the performance comparison with different techniques [29].

Due to the limitation of manual evaluation for video summary, automatic evaluation techniques providing the human-like assessment are highly demanded [15]. Some work has been done to evaluate the quality of the video summary by automatically calculating the inclusion and redundancy based on predefined ground truth [4, 8, 27, 32]. However, the uniform framework with comprehensive consideration for automatic evaluation is still missing. For example, the correct order of the content is very important for a good video summary, but this criterion and its interaction with other criteria have not been fully explored by current work. Moreover, the existing automatic evaluation techniques only provide the evaluation results according to their defined criteria respectively. They cannot satisfy the various user requirements of video summary quality in different applications.

To address the problem of current work on automatic evaluation for video summary, we propose a uniform framework providing automatic video summary quality evaluation according to various user requirements. The framework focuses on full-reference quality evaluation for video summary, meaning that the candidate video summary is evaluated based on the comparison with a predefined reference video summary. Full-reference quality evaluation is initially defined by Wang et al. to evaluate the quality loss of the image after some processing via comparing with a complete perfect reference [31]. Relatively, there exist nonreference quality evaluation [25] and reduced-reference quality evaluation [10] when the reference is not or only partially available. Considering the users may have more ambiguous perception of the perfect video summaries than in other applications, e.g., image compression, we utilize one or several defined reference video summaries to represent the perfect summaries and eliminate the inconsistence in evaluation. Furthermore, to satisfy various user requirements of video summary quality in different applications, we divide the whole evaluation procedure into two steps. We first generate a requirement-independent intermediate evaluation results by assessing the video summary quality according to a general criteria and then transform the intermediate evaluation results to the final ones to satisfy the user requirements. In this chapter, we utilize the 4C criteria in [6] as the intermediate evaluation criteria. It provides a comprehensive description of video summary quality, including the aspects of information representation, such as coverage and conciseness, and the aspects of user perception, such as coherence and context. The existing human-like evaluation criteria can be mainly derived from the criterion or combinations of the criteria in these four aspects. In the evaluation framework, we propose several novel methods to calculate the scores on these criteria automatically. With the 4C assessment results, we use the incremental user interaction to gather the necessary information of user requirements and generate the required evaluation results by automatically transforming the 4C assessment scores.

The chapter is organized as follows. Section 2 introduces current quality evaluation methods for video summary. Section 3 proposes a novel framework of video summary quality evaluation and some initial processing algorithms, such as summary unit generation and matching. Section 4 provides the automatic 4C assessment algorithm for providing comprehensive intermediate evaluation results. Section 5 presents the transformation between the 4C assessment scores and the required evaluation results using user-interaction-based automatic transformation. Section 6 shows the performance of the proposed framework and techniques by experimenting on the standard datasets. The chapter is closed with conclusion and further work.

2 Related Work

Referencing the classification of text summarization assessment [2], quality evaluation of video summary can be classified into two categories, intrinsic evaluation and extrinsic evaluation. The former tests the summaries by themselves, while the latter tests the summaries based on how they interact with the completion of some other tasks. In this chapter, we use intrinsic evaluation to assess the video summary quality.

Based on the difference of human's interaction, current quality evaluation methods for video summary can be further categorized to manual evaluation and automatic evaluation [29]. Manual evaluation mainly involves independent users judging the quality of the generated video summaries and calculates the cognitive value based on psychological metrics [8]. The direct and the most widely used manual evaluation is asking the different persons to grade the summary individually and calculate the mean opinion score (MOS) as the quality score of the summary [9]. But only using the overall score is too rough in evaluation. So different evaluation criteria are proposed to define the desirable characters for a good summary. A typical set of evaluation criteria was proposed by He et al. [6], who provided the 4C criteria for an ideal video summary:

- *Coverage*: the set of segments selected for the summary should cover all the "key" points.
- *Conciseness*: any segment selected for the summary should contain only necessary information.

– *Coherence*: the flow between the segments in the summary should be natural and fluid.
– *Context*: the segments selected and their sequencing should be such that prior segments establish appropriate context.

Existing work of manual evaluation can be mainly recapitulated by the criteria or combinations of the criteria under these 4C criteria. For example, in the task of rushes summarization for TRECVID 2007 [22], the criterion of ground-truth inclusion actually can be considered as one way to measure the coverage of the summary.

Although manual evaluation is probably the most useful and realistic form of video summary evaluation [29], it suffers from several problems. First, manual evaluation is seriously affected by human factors [22]. Illustrated using TRECVID 2007 rushes summarization task, one evaluator is asked to evaluate four hundred and thirty-two video clips from eighteen rushes files. Moreover, for each rushes file, the evaluator should assess twenty-four very similar summaries. Consequently, it is so difficult to guarantee that the evaluator can keep the consistent scoring criterion throughout the evaluation, although he may intend to [22]. The human factors of manual evaluation can be removed or partially removed by some statistical techniques based on large dataset experiments. Unfortunately, it leads to high labor cost and huge time consumption [29]. For these reasons, the large user-set study is not widely employed [8]. Even for the TRECVID 2007, each video summary is only evaluated by three persons, which is far from what is required by statistical sufficiency. In addition, the invested labor and time in the user study for evaluating one algorithm is not reusable for another algorithm; all the effort has to be repeated each time when an algorithm has been changed or a new algorithm has been developed [7].

Due to the limitation of manual evaluation, the automatic evaluation techniques for video summary are highly demanded. Currently, automatic evaluation techniques can be classified into two categories. One category focuses on assessing the objective criteria, such as the length of the summary [22], while another category works on providing the human-like assessment by quantitative analysis of multimedia content. To map human's judgment, most automatic evaluation methods manually define a set of ground-truth or/and keyframes. Silva et al. [27] and Yahiaoui et al. [32] calculate the coverage of video summary by using the total keyframe number in summary or keyframe number in average keyframe set in place of the ground truth inclusion. Huang et al. [8] calculate precision, recall, and redundancy rate by matching the predefined ground truths in order to evaluate the content coverage and redundancy of video summary. Dumont et al. [4] use machine learning methods to train the automatic assessors on the manually generated ground truth and evaluate the ground truth inclusion of video summary by the assessors. Unfortunately, these methods only provide the evaluation of video summary quality in one or several aspects. Some important factors influencing video summary quality, such as the order of video content, are ignored in current work. Moreover, the existing automatic methods can only provide the evaluation results according to their defined criteria. The users cannot obtain the quality evaluation of video summary according to the requirements outside these criteria. Till now, a uniform framework with comprehensive considerations of automatic evaluation for video summary is unavailable yet.

3 Uniform Framework for Video Summary Quality Evaluation

Figure 1 shows the framework of full-reference quality evaluation system for video summary. The reference video summary is assumed to be the only perfect abstraction of the original video file, which can be automatically or manually generated by any approaches or tools. This means that a candidate video summary will obtain a full mark in any criterion of evaluation if and only if the candidate video summary is the same with the reference one in this criterion. If there exist more than one reference summary, the evaluation is carried out on each reference video, and the best evaluation result is chosen as the final result. In this way, full-reference video summary quality evaluation is formalized to the problem of pair-wise video sequence comparison for evaluation purpose.

Although many techniques have been proposed to compare the similarity of the video sequences [13, 26], none of them have been successfully applied to video summary quality evaluation because of the different targets of the tasks. Most existing works of video sequence comparison are designed for video retrieval and classification [19], so they focus on providing qualitative results, for example, relevance or irrelevance for video retrieval. In other words, the target of these algorithms is to capture the main content while keeping insensitive to the details. But for video summary evaluation, the main content of the candidate summaries are almost identical. The difference of certain kinds of details often represents the difference of the quality. Therefore, these existing video sequence comparison techniques are not directly applicable to video summary evaluation. In this chapter, we address the problem by aligning the video summaries and compare the video summaries based on the alignment result. Considering that the video content may be represented with incorrect order in the candidate summary, we first decompose the reference summary and the candidate summary into a set of Summary Units (SUs) respectively and then apply frame alignment algorithm in matching the SUs from the two summaries.

Based on the SU matching result, we compare the reference summary and the candidate summary for quality evaluation. To provide a flexible evaluation mecha-

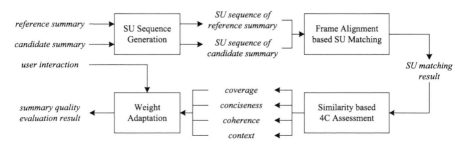

Fig. 1 Uniform framework for quality evaluation of video summary

nism satisfying various user requirements, we divide the following evaluation into two steps that generate the requirement-independent intermediate evaluation results and transform the intermediate evaluation results to the final results satisfying user requirements respectively. We first calculate the quality scores of the candidate summary individually in four aspects: coverage, conciseness, coherence, and context, which are derived from the 4C criteria in [6] and treated as the intermediate evaluation results. Then, we utilize the incremental user interaction to gather user requirements of video summary quality. The users are asked to manually evaluate some training data according to their required criteria. Based on the user interaction, the transformation model from the 4C assessment scores to the required evaluation results is generated. For the different candidate summaries evaluated by the same criteria, only once user interaction and transformation model generation are needed. Finally, the evaluation results of the candidate summary quality are generated by automatic transformation.

3.1 Summary Unit Sequence Generation

Simply speaking, summary unit is defined as the component to compose a video summary. It can be a video scene, shot, subshot, and even a frame for different video files and different summarization targets. Definitely, if the spatial separability is permitted, SU can be a special region of the frame or an object, and if the spatial-temporal separability is permitted, SU can be defined as a trajectory. Moreover, SU also can be a data package of synchronized or unsynchronized video, audio, and close caption. Due to the page limitation, we only consider the temporal separability of the video file for video summary quality evaluation, e.g., subshot is used as SU in this chapter. Thus a video summary can be described as an SU sequence with the appropriate order.

Considering a video summary S with N SUs, it can be represented using the SU sequence $S = \{SU_1, SU_2, \ldots\}_N$. Hence, the reference summary and the candidate summary can be represented as follows:

$$
\begin{aligned}
RS &= \{SU_{R_1}, SU_{R_2}, \ldots\}_{N_R}, \\
CS &= \{SU_{C_1}, SU_{C_2}, \ldots\}_{N_C},
\end{aligned}
\tag{1}
$$

where RS and CS denote the reference summary and the candidate summary, and N_R and N_C are the SU numbers of RS and CS, respectively. The following evaluation is based on the comparison of these two SU sequences. In this chapter, we generate the SU sequences using the twin-comparison algorithm in [33].

3.2 Frame Alignment-Based Summary Unit Matching

After SU sequence generation, we build the comparison between the reference summary and the candidate summary on the basis of SU matching. This means that we check each SU in the candidate summary by looking for the most similar SU in the reference summary and compare the reference summary and the candidate summary based on the SU matching result. Various algorithms are available for subshots matching [4, 20]. Considering the requirement of matching accuracy, we treat SU as a time-order frame sequence and match SUs by aligning the corresponding frame sequences with the Needleman–Wunsch algorithm [21]. The frame alignment-based SU matching method can provide more accurate matching result than clustering-based methods for it can distinguish the detail differences between two adjacent SUs with similar content.

We represent SU_{R_i} in the reference summary as a frame sequence $\{f_1^{R_i}, f_2^{R_i},$ $\ldots\}_{m_i}$ and SU_{C_j} in the candidate summary as a frame sequence $\{f_1^{C_j}, f_2^{C_j}, \ldots\}_{n_j}$, where m and n are the frame numbers of SU_{R_i} and SU_{C_j}, respectively. Then, we use the Needleman–Wunsch algorithm to achieve the optimal matching of SU_{R_i} and SU_{C_j}. The Needleman–Wunsch algorithm utilizes dynamic programming in alignment, and the objective function is defined as follows:

$$
\begin{aligned}
s_{p1} &= \chi\left(f_p^{R_i}, f_1^{C_j}\right), \\
s_{1q} &= \chi\left(f_1^{R_i}, f_q^{C_j}\right), \\
s_{pq} &= \max\left(s_{p(q-1)}, s_{(p-1)q}, s_{(p-1)(q-1)} + \chi\left(f_p^{R_i}, f_q^{C_j}\right)\right),
\end{aligned}
\tag{2}
$$

where $\chi(f_p^{R_i}, f_q^{C_j})$ is a function to denote whether $f_p^{R_i}$ and $f_q^{C_j}$ can be matched.

In our previous work [24], we utilize the similarity on local HSV color histogram to judge whether two frames can be matched. Though local HSV color histogram has good performance in video content similarity measurement, it cannot effectively distinguish the video frames with similar content but different details. It may lead to the inaccuracy in SU matching and influence the further quality evaluation. Therefore, we use Scale-Invariant Feature Transform (SIFT) [16] instead of local HSV color histogram in this chapter, which is effective in distinguishing different visual content and widely used in near-duplicate video detection [3, 11]. For each frame $f_p^{R_i}$ in SU_{R_i} and each frame $f_q^{C_j}$ in SU_{C_j}, we detect the keypoints in them with Hessian Affine detector and match the keypoints in the two frames by calculating their local gradient histogram distance. If the local gradient histogram distance of two keypoints is smaller than a predefined threshold (usually 0.3), the two keypoints are matched; otherwise, they are not matched. Note here that in order the matched frames in alignment to be highly similar, each keypoint kp_x in $f_p^{R_i}$ (or kp_y in $f_q^{C_j}$) is only required to look for its matched keypoint within the 16×16 neighboring region around the corresponding position in $f_q^{C_j}$ (or $f_p^{R_i}$). This constraint can well reduce the computational cost and avoid the keypoint mismatching. If no such keypoint exists, the contribution of keypoint kp_x (or kp_y) in frame matching is set to 0; otherwise, the contribution of the two keypoints is both set to 1. Each keypoint is only allowed matching one keypoint, and the match value of $f_p^{R_i}$ and $f_q^{C_j}$ is calculated

Fig. 2 Aligned frame sequences of two SUs in the reference summary and the candidate summary

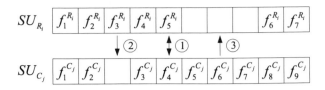

as follows:

$$Mat\left(f_p^{R_i}, f_q^{C_j}\right) = \frac{1}{N_p^{R_i}} \sum_{kp_x \in f_p^{R_i}} \varphi(kp_x) + \frac{1}{N_q^{C_j}} \sum_{kp_y \in f_q^{C_j}} \varphi(kp_y), \qquad (3)$$

where $N_p^{R_i}$ and $N_q^{C_j}$ are the numbers of keypoints in frames $f_p^{R_i}$ and $f_q^{C_j}$, respectively, $\varphi(kp_x)$ and $\varphi(kp_y)$ denote the contributions of keypoints kp_x and kp_y in frame matching, respectively, and $Mat(f_p^{R_i}, f_q^{C_j})$ denotes the matching value of $f_p^{R_i}$ and $f_q^{C_j}$. If the matching value of $f_p^{R_i}$ and $f_q^{C_j}$ is larger than a predefined threshold thr_{fm} ($thr_{fm} = 0.6$ in our experiments), we consider the two frames as matched, i.e., $\chi(f_p^{R_i}, f_q^{C_j}) = 1$; otherwise, $\chi(f_p^{R_i}, f_q^{C_j}) = 0$.

As shown above, we obtain the frame alignment result between two SUs in the reference summary and the candidate summary. Figure 2 shows an example of the result of frame alignment. If a frame in SU_{R_i} (or SU_{C_j}) matches the corresponding frame in SU_{C_j} (or SU_{R_i}), such as $f_5^{R_i}$ and $f_4^{C_j}$, we call it "matched frame"; otherwise, such as $f_3^{R_i}$ and $f_6^{C_j}$, we call it "unmatched frame."

To judge whether SU_{C_j} matches SU_{R_i}, the alignment score of frame alignment is calculated as

$$Align(SU_{R_i}, SU_{C_j}) = s_{m_i n_j}. \qquad (4)$$

Considering that SU_{R_i} and SU_{C_j} may partly match, that is, that SU_{C_j} may lose some frames of SU_{R_i} or contain some redundant frames, we calculate the final alignment score as follows:

$$Align(SU_{R_i}, SU_{C_j}) = \frac{1}{\min(m_i, n_j)} s_{m_i n_j}. \qquad (5)$$

If the maximal alignment score for SU_{C_j}, according to some SU_{R_i} in all the SUs in the reference summary, is higher than the predefined threshold thr_{SU} ($thr_{SU} = 0.8$ in our experiments), SU_{C_j} is considered to match SU_{R_i}; otherwise, SU_{C_j} is considered as a noise SU. The summary unit matching algorithm is provided in Table 1.

After SU matching, each SU_{C_j} in the candidate summary matches an SU_{R_i} in the reference summary or is considered as a noise SU.

Table 1 Frame alignment-based SU matching between the reference summary and the candidate summary

---

Algorithm: Summary unit matching

Input: $SU_{C_j} = \{f_1^{C_j}, f_2^{C_j}, \ldots\}_{n_j} \in CS$

$SU_{R_k} = \{f_1^{R_k}, f_2^{R_k}, \ldots\}_{m_k} \in RS, \forall k, k \in \{1, 2, \ldots, N_R\}$

Output: SU_{R_i} or NULL

---

1. for each $SU_{R_k} = \{f_1^{R_k}, f_2^{R_k}, \ldots\}_{m_k} \in RS$,

   calculate the matching value of each frame pair ($f_p^{R_k}$ and $f_q^{C_j}$),

   match SU_{R_k} and SU_{C_j} using frame alignment:

   $$score_{R_k} = Align(SU_{R_k}, SU_{C_j}).$$

2. select $SU_{R_i} \in RS$ with the maximal score:

   $$i = \arg \max_{1 \leq k \leq N_R} (score_{R_k}).$$

3. if $score_{R_i} > thr_{SU}$, return $score_{R_i}$;

   else, return NULL.

Here

   RS: the reference summary

   CS: the candidate summary

   SU_{R_k}: any SU in the reference summary

   SU_{C_j}: an SU in the candidate summary

   $f_p^{R_k}$: any frame in SU_{R_k}

   $f_q^{C_j}$: any frame in SU_{C_j}

---

4 Similarity-Based Automatic 4C Assessment

The assessment with 4C criteria provides a comprehensive human-like evaluation of video summary quality. It is used to generate the requirement-independent intermediate results as the basis of the further evaluation in our framework. In 4C assessment, we assess the 4C scores of the candidate summary by comparing with the reference summary based on the SU matching result. In the following, we discuss the assessment of coverage, conciseness, coherence, and context, respectively.

4.1 Coverage Assessment

Coverage of the candidate summary represents how much content of the reference summary is covered by the candidate summary.

We define the coverage of the candidate summary as the sum of the coverages of all the SUs in the reference summary:

$$Cov(CS) = \frac{1}{N_R} \sum_{i=1}^{N_R} Cov(SU_{R_i}). \tag{6}$$

For each SU_{R_i} in the reference summary, the coverage of SU_{R_i} is calculated as follows: if none of the SUs in the candidate summary matches SU_{R_i}, $Cov(SU_{R_i})$ is 0; if there only one SU_{C_j} matches SU_{R_i}, $Cov(SU_{R_i})$ is the content of SU_{R_i} covered by SU_{C_j}; if there exist many SUs in the candidate summary that match SU_{R_i}, we choose the SU_{C_j} with the highest alignment score to SU_{R_i} to calculate.

The covered content of SU_{R_i} can be calculated as the sum of the covered content of the frames in SU_{R_i} based on the result of frame alignment in SU matching. As shown in Fig. 2, for a matched frame, such as $f_5^{R_i}$, its covered content can be calculated as the similarity between it and its corresponding frame in alignment. For an unmatched frame, such as $f_3^{R_i}$, its content may be partly covered by the corresponding frames of its nearest matched frame, since the adjacent frames in a video file are usually interrelated in content which calls "temporal redundancy" of video characteristics.

To clearly explain the covered content calculation of SU_{R_i}, we define the concept "related frame." For a matched frame, its related frame is the corresponding frame which matches it. For an unmatched frame, look for the nearest matched frame(s) before or/and after it. If only one matched frame is found, we define the related frame of the found matched frame as the related frame of current unmatched frame; if two matched frames are found, we choose the more similar corresponding frame to current unmatched frame as its related frame. For example, in Fig. 2, $f_5^{R_i}$ matches $f_4^{C_j}$, and the related frame of $f_5^{R_i}$ is $f_4^{C_j}$. $f_3^{R_i}$ does not match any frame in SU_{C_j}, so we look for the nearest matched frame(s) of $f_3^{R_i}$ in SU_{R_i} ($f_2^{R_i}$ and $f_4^{R_i}$) and select the more similar corresponding frame from $f_2^{C_j}$ and $f_3^{C_j}$ as the related frame of $f_3^{R_i}$. In this way, the coverage of SU_{R_i} can be represented as the sum of the similarity between its frames and their related frames. It is calculated as follows:

$$Cov(SU_{R_i}) = \begin{cases} \max_j \left(\frac{1}{m_i} \sum_{p=1}^{m_i} Sim(f_p^{R_i}, RF(f_p^{R_i})) \right) & \text{if } SU_{C_j} \text{ matches } SU_{R_i}, \\ 0 & \text{if no SU matches } SU_{R_i}, \end{cases} \tag{7}$$

where $RF(f_p^{R_i})$ is the related frame of $f_p^{R_i}$ in SU_{C_j}, and $Sim(\cdot, \cdot)$ is the similarity between two frames. In frame similarity measurement, we divide the frames into 4×4 regions with same size and shapes. For each region, 16-bins color histogram on HSV color space is extracted according to MPEG-7 [18]. Each frame is represented by a 256-bins feature vector, and the similarity between two frames is calculated according to Euclidean distance of their feature vectors.

4.2 Conciseness Assessment

Conciseness of the candidate summary represents how much redundant content is contained in the candidate summary.

We define the conciseness of the candidate summary as the sum of the conciseness of all the SUs in the candidate summary:

$$Coc(CS) = \frac{1}{N_C} \sum_{j=1}^{N_C} Coc(SU_{C_j}). \tag{8}$$

For each SU_{C_j} in the candidate summary, the conciseness of SU_{C_j} is calculated as follows: if SU_{C_j} is a noise SU, $Coc(SU_{C_j})$ is 0; if only SU_{C_j} but no other SU in the candidate summary matches a SU_{R_i} in the reference summary, $Coc(SU_{C_j})$ is the useful content of SU_{C_j} which is also contained by SU_{R_i}; if there exist many SUs in the candidate summary which match the same SU_{R_i} in the reference summary, we select the SU_{C_j} with the highest alignment score to SU_{R_i} to calculate and consider that the concisenesses of the other unselected SUs are 0.

Similar to coverage assessment, conciseness of SU_{C_j} is calculated as the sum of the contained useful content in frames of SU_{C_j}. Based on the result of frame alignment in SU matching, the useful content contained in a frame of SU_{C_j} is calculated as the similarity between it and its related frame in SU_{R_i}, and the conciseness of SU_{C_j} is calculated as follows:

$$Coc(SU_{C_j}) = \begin{cases} \frac{1}{n_j} \sum_{q=1}^{n_j} Sim(f_q^{C_j}, RF(f_q^{C_j})) \\ \quad \text{if } SU_{C_j} \text{ is the selected SU matching } SU_{R_i}, \\ 0 \quad \text{if } SU_{C_j} \text{ is a noise or unselected SU,} \end{cases} \tag{9}$$

where $RF(f_q^{C_j})$ is the related frame of $f_q^{C_j}$ in SU_{R_i}, and $Sim(\cdot, \cdot)$ is defined as in (7).

4.3 Coherence Assessment

Coherence of the candidate summary represents how coherent is the candidate summary in representation.

We consider the coherence of the candidate summary in two aspects: inter SU coherence and inner SU coherence. Inter SU coherence means the coherence between SUs, and inner SU coherence means the coherence within each SU. The coherence of the candidate summary is defined as follows:

$$Coh(CS) = \omega_1 \cdot Coh_{\text{inner}}(CS) + \omega_2 \cdot Coh_{\text{inter}}(CS), \tag{10}$$

where ω_1 and ω_2 are positive weight coefficients, and $\omega_1 = \omega_2 = 0.5$ in our experiments.

We first assess the inter SU coherence by comparing the mean values of the distances between two adjacent SUs in the reference summary and the candidate summary. The distance between two adjacent SUs in a video summary S is calculated as the distance between the last frame of the former SU and the first frame of the latter SU:

$$Dis_{inter}(SU_{S_k}, SU_{S_{k+1}}) = \mathcal{D}(f_{n_k}^{S_k}, f_1^{S_{k+1}}), \tag{11}$$

where SU_{S_k} and $SU_{S_{k+1}}$ are two adjacent SUs in video summary S; $f_{n_k}^{S_k}$ and $f_1^{S_{k+1}}$ are the last frame of SU_{S_k} and the first frame of $SU_{S_{k+1}}$, respectively; and $\mathcal{D}(\cdot, \cdot)$ denotes the distance between two frames, which is calculated by Euclidean distance of their local HSV color histogram feature vectors.

The inter SU coherence is calculated as follows:

$$Coh_{inter}(CS) = 1 - \max\left(0, \frac{1}{N_C - 1} \sum_{j=1}^{N_C - 1} Dis_{inter}(SU_{C_j}, SU_{C_{j+1}})\right.$$

$$\left. - \frac{1}{N_R - 1} \sum_{i=1}^{N_R - 1} Dis_{inter}(SU_{R_i}, SU_{R_{i+1}})\right). \tag{12}$$

Next, we define the inner SU coherence of the candidate summary as the sum of the inner coherences of all SUs:

$$Coh_{inner}(CS) = \frac{1}{N_C} \sum_{j=1}^{N_C} Coh_{inner}(SU_{C_j}). \tag{13}$$

The inner coherence of SU_{C_j} is calculated by comparing to its matching SU_{R_i} in the reference summary. To calculate the inner coherence of each SU, we define the "average distance" between two frames f_p and f_q as follows:

$$\widetilde{\mathcal{D}}(f_p, f_q) = \begin{cases} \frac{1}{q-p} \sum_{k=p}^{q-1} \mathcal{D}(f_k, f_{k+1}), & p < q, \\ 0, & p \geq q, \end{cases} \tag{14}$$

where $\widetilde{\mathcal{D}}(,)$ denotes the average distance between two frames.

Then, we evaluate the inner SU coherence by comparing the distance between each frame and its successive frame with the average distance between their related frames:

$$Coh_{inner}(SU_{C_j}) = 1 - \frac{1}{n_j - 1} \sum_{k=1}^{n_j - 1} \max\left(0, \mathcal{D}(f_k^{C_j}, f_{k+1}^{C_j})\right.$$

$$\left. - \widetilde{\mathcal{D}}(RF(f_k^{C_j}), RF(f_{k+1}^{C_j}))\right), \tag{15}$$

where $RF(f_k^{C_j})$ is the related frame of $f_k^{C_j}$ in SU_{R_i}.

Note here that a noise SU in the candidate summary does not have a matching SU in the reference summary and its frames do not have their related frames. Hence, we replace the average distance between the related frames in (15) with the mean value of the distances between each frame and its successive frame in all the SUs of the reference summary. The inner coherence of a noise SU is calculated as

$$Coh_{\text{inner}}(SU_{C_j}) = 1 - \frac{1}{n_j - 1} \sum_{k=1}^{n_j-1} \max\left(0, \mathcal{D}\left(f_k^{C_j}, f_{k+1}^{C_j}\right)\right.$$

$$\left. - \frac{1}{N_R} \sum_{i=1}^{N_R} \widetilde{\mathcal{D}}\left(f_1^{R_i}, f_{m_i}^{R_i}\right)\right), \tag{16}$$

where $f_1^{R_i}$ and $f_{m_i}^{R_i}$ are the first and the last frames of SU_{R_i}.

4.4 Context Assessment

Context of the candidate summary represents how ordered the SUs of the candidate summary are.

Since the noise SUs and the missing SUs do not influence the order of the other SUs in the candidate summary, we ignore them in context assessment. For the repeated SUs in the candidate summary, that is, when more than one SU matches the same SU in the reference summary, we retain one of the SUs in the candidate summary each time and compute the mean value of its contexts in all situations. So the context of the candidate summary is defined as follows:

$$Cot(CS) = \frac{1}{N_S} \sum_{k=1}^{N_s} Cot_k(CS), \tag{17}$$

$$N_S = \prod_{i=1}^{N_R} \max(1, N_i), \tag{18}$$

where N_i is the number of SUs in the candidates summary that match SU_{R_i} in SU matching, and N_S is the number of all possible situations.

To calculate the context of the candidate summary, we define the order of SUs. If SU_{S_i} and SU_{S_j} are two SUs in a video summary S, then the order of SU_{S_i} and SU_{S_j} is

$$O_S(SU_{S_i}, SU_{S_j}) = \begin{cases} 1 & \text{if } SU_{S_i} \text{ appears in front of } SU_{S_j} \text{ in } S, \\ 0 & \text{otherwise.} \end{cases} \tag{19}$$

For SU_{C_j} and SU_{C_q} in the candidate summary, we define the "inversion" as follows:

$$Inv(SU_{C_j}, SU_{C_q}) = \begin{cases} 1, & O_{CS}(SU_{C_j}, SU_{C_q}) \neq O_{RS}(SU_{R_i}, SU_{R_p}), \\ 0, & O_{CS}(SU_{C_j}, SU_{C_q}) = O_{RS}(SU_{R_i}, SU_{R_p}), \end{cases} \tag{20}$$

where SU_{C_j} and SU_{C_q} match SU_{R_i} and SU_{R_p} in SU matching, respectively.

We define the context of the candidate summary as follows:

$$Cot_k(CS) = 1 - \frac{\sum_{j \neq q} \mathcal{E}(SU_{C_j}, SU_{C_q}) \cdot Inv(SU_{C_j}, SU_{C_q})}{\sum_{j \neq q} \mathcal{E}(SU_{C_j}, SU_{C_q})}, \tag{21}$$

where $\mathcal{E}(SU_{C_j}, SU_{C_q})$ is the effect of SU_{C_j} to the understanding of SU_{C_q}.

In this chapter, we assume that the viewer will not trace back and only consider the effect of the prior SUs to the understanding of the following SUs. We consider the effect of SU_{C_j} to the understanding of SU_{C_q} to be determined by the distance between their matched SUs in the reference summary and calculated as follows:

$$\mathcal{E}(SU_{C_j}, SU_{C_q}) = \begin{cases} F(|p - i|), & O_{RS}(SU_{R_i}, SU_{R_p}) = 1, \\ 0, & \text{otherwise,} \end{cases} \tag{22}$$

where F is a decreasing function, e.g., $F(x) = 1/x$.

According to the above methods, we can obtain the scores of the candidate summary on 4C criteria. But these scores may not exactly match the manual evaluation results though they are highly related to user perception. So, we fit the scores to generate the final 4C automatic assessment results.

We utilize linear regression to fit the score on each criterion:

$$\begin{pmatrix} s_{Cov} \\ s_{Coc} \\ s_{Coh} \\ s_{Cot} \end{pmatrix} = \begin{pmatrix} \alpha_{Cov} \\ \alpha_{Coc} \\ \alpha_{Coh} \\ \alpha_{Cot} \end{pmatrix} + \text{diag}(\beta_{Cov}, \beta_{Coc}, \beta_{Coh}, \beta_{Cot}) \begin{pmatrix} Cov(CS) \\ Coc(CS) \\ Coh(CS) \\ Cot(CS) \end{pmatrix}, \tag{23}$$

where $s_{Cov}, s_{Coc}, s_{Coh}, s_{Cot}$ are the final 4C assessment scores, and $\alpha_{Cov}, \alpha_{Coc}, \alpha_{Coh}, \alpha_{Cot}, \beta_{Cov}, \beta_{Coc}, \beta_{Coh}, \beta_{Cot}$ are the weight coefficients.

These weight coefficients can be calculated by the least squares method:

$$(\alpha_\#, \beta_\#) = \arg\min \sum \left(s'_\# - \alpha_\# - \beta_\# \cdot \#(CS)\right)^2, \tag{24}$$

where $\#$ is a criterion in 4C criteria, including Cov, Coc, Coh, and Cot; $s'_\#$ is the manual evaluation result on the criterion; $\#(CS)$ is the automatic assessment score on the criterion before fitting.

5 User Interaction Based Individual Evaluation

Though 4C criteria can provide comprehensive description of video summary quality, the viewpoint and perspective of video summary quality are usually application-dependent [29]. This means that the users may require individual evaluation results with various criteria in different applications. For example, the rushes summarization task in TRECVID 2007 requires evaluating video summary quality in "INclusion of ground truth" (IN), "EAse of understanding" (EA), and "lack of redundancy"

(RE) [22]. Designing the automatic assessment methods for each required evaluation criterion as above will lead to high labor cost of experts, and the existing automatic assessment methods cannot be well reused when new criteria are required. In our framework, we propose an effective approach to transform the automatic 4C assessment results to the evaluation results satisfying user requirements. For any required criteria, the approach can build the transformation model between 4C criteria and the required criteria with some user interaction, and automatically transform the 4C assessment scores to the required evaluation results.

5.1 User Interaction Based Requirement Gathering

In the procedure of building the transformation model, we first gather the user requirements of video summary quality by means of user interaction. The training data with limited size is generated, and the automatic 4C assessment scores and the manual evaluation results with the required criteria on the training data are used to build the transformation model.

To gather the user requirements, we ask the users to evaluate the training data with their criteria. In the user interaction, each user watches a reference summary for three times to make the video content familiar and evaluates the corresponding candidate summaries in a random order. To eliminate the influence of evaluation order, the first evaluated candidate summary for each video file will be evaluated again. When evaluating a candidate summary, the users are allowed to watch the reference summary again but forbidden any operation in the candidate summary playing. Figure 3 shows the interface used in user interaction. The reference summary and the candidate summary are displayed in the top of the interface. When evaluating a candidate summary, the user can choose to watch the reference summary first (press the left button with the text "play RS") or directly watch the candidate summary (press the right button with the text "play CS"). If the user chooses to watch the reference summary first, the candidate summary will be automatically played following the reference summary. After watching the candidate summary, the users are asked to input the quality scores according to his/her required criteria, from 1 to M representing the quality from the worst to the best in the corresponding criterion. The textboxes for inputting evaluation results are in the bottom of the interface. Since the number of the required criteria may be variable in different evaluations, the required criteria are shown available (in white color) and marked with the corresponding criteria labels (such as "IN", "EA", "RE").

5.2 Transformation of 4C Assessment Scores

When obtaining the user interaction results, we build the transformation model for adapting the 4C assessment scores to the required individual evaluation results. We

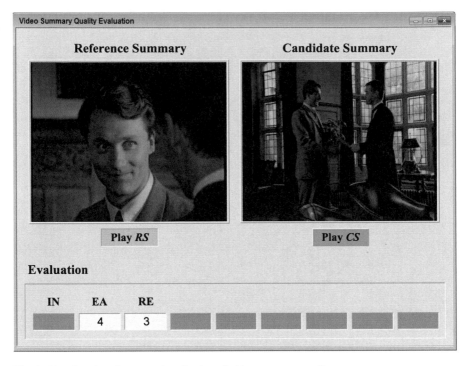

Fig. 3 User interface for manual evaluation of video summary quality

use the weighted-sum model in this chapter, and more complex transformation models are left for the future work.

We represent the scores of the required evaluation criteria as

$$\mathbf{G} = (g_1, g_2, \dots, g_N)^T, \tag{25}$$

where N is the number of aspects in the required evaluation criteria.

Then we calculate the elements of $\mathbf{G}$ by the weighted sums of the 4C assessment scores. Each g_j in $\mathbf{G}$ can be represented as

$$g_j = 1 + (M - 1) \cdot (\lambda_{j0} + \lambda_{j1} s_{Cov} + \lambda_{j2} s_{Coc} + \lambda_{j3} s_{Coh} + \lambda_{j4} s_{Cot}), \tag{26}$$

where $\lambda_{j0}, \lambda_{j1}, \dots, \lambda_{j4}$ are the weight coefficients for evaluation result transformation. We constrain the value of λ_{j0} in the range of $[-1,1]$ and the values of the other coefficients in the range of $[0, 1]$, and $\lambda_{j1} + \lambda_{j2} + \lambda_{j3} + \lambda_{j4} = 1$. The constants 1 and $(M - 1)$ are used to ensure g_j in the range of $[1, M]$.

To simplify representation, let $\mathbf{X} = (x_0, x_1, x_2, x_3, x_4)^T$ and $\mathbf{Y} = (y_1, y_2, \dots, y_N)^T$, where $x_0 = 1$, x_1 to x_4 denote $s_{Cov}, s_{Coc}, s_{Coh}, s_{Cot}$ in that order, and $y_j = (g_j - 1)/(M - 1)$. Since the 4C assessment scores are in the range of $[0,1]$ and the evaluation scores with the required criteria are from 1 to M, each element

Table 2 Transformation model from the 4C assessment scores to the individual evaluation results

Algorithm: Transforming 4C assessment scores to the required evaluation results

Input: 4C assessment scores on the training data

 manual evaluation results with the required criteria on the training data

Output: weight coefficient matrix Λ

1. Generate the observation matrix $\widehat{\mathbf{X}}$ from 4C assessment scores

$$\widehat{\mathbf{X}} = \begin{bmatrix} x_{01} & x_{02} & \cdots & x_{0r} \\ x_{11} & x_{12} & \cdots & x_{1r} \\ \vdots & \vdots & & \vdots \\ x_{41} & x_{42} & \cdots & x_{4r} \end{bmatrix}.$$

2. Generate the observation matrix $\widehat{\mathbf{Y}}$ from the manual evaluation results with the required criteria

$$\widehat{\mathbf{Y}} = \begin{bmatrix} y_{11} & y_{12} & \cdots & y_{1r} \\ y_{21} & y_{22} & \cdots & y_{2r} \\ \vdots & \vdots & & \vdots \\ y_{N1} & y_{N2} & \cdots & y_{Nr} \end{bmatrix}.$$

3. Calculate the weight coefficient matrix Λ by multivariate linear regression

$$\lambda_{\mathbf{j}} = (\lambda_{j0}, \lambda_{j1}, \ldots, \lambda_{j4}) = \arg\min \sum_{k=1}^{r} (y_{jk} - \lambda_{j0}x_{0k} - \lambda_{j1}x_{1k} - \cdots - \lambda_{j4}x_{4k})^2,$$

$$\Lambda = (\lambda_{\mathbf{1}}; \lambda_{\mathbf{2}}; \ldots; \lambda_{\mathbf{N}}).$$

in $\mathbf{X}$ and $\mathbf{Y}$ is in the range of $[0, 1]$. Then, (26) can be represented as

$$y_j = \lambda_{\mathbf{j}}\mathbf{X} = \lambda_{j0}x_0 + \lambda_{j1}x_1 + \cdots + \lambda_{j4}x_4. \tag{27}$$

Considering each variable y_j in $\mathbf{Y}$ separately, we calculate the transformation between $\mathbf{X}$ and $\mathbf{Y}$ by multivariate linear regression. Assuming that there are r independent observations of y_j, the best weight coefficient vector λ_j for y_j can calculated by the least squares method:

$$(\lambda_{j0}, \lambda_{j1}, \ldots, \lambda_{j4}) = \arg\min \sum_{k=1}^{r} (y_{jk} - \lambda_{j0}x_{0k} - \lambda_{j1}x_{1k} - \cdots - \lambda_{j4}x_{4k})^2, \tag{28}$$

where $(x_{0k}, \ldots, x_{4k}, y_{jk})$ denotes the kth observation of y_j.

Table 2 shows the procedure of calculating the weight coefficient matrix for transforming the 4C assessment scores to the required evaluation results.

With multivariate linear regression, an $N \times 5$ weight coefficient matrix Λ will be generated. In matrix Λ, the coefficients in each row represent the weights of the 4C assessment scores in calculating the result of the corresponding required criterion, and the sum of the coefficients in each column represents the weight of the corresponding 4C criterion in the required evaluation criteria. The evaluation results according to user requirements can be transformed from 4C assessment results as follows:

$$G = 1 + (M - 1) \cdot \Lambda \mathbf{X}. \tag{29}$$

5.3 Incremental User Interaction

The complexity of correlations between the 4C assessment scores and the different required criteria are usually different. For example, the IN and RE criteria used in TRECVID 2007 have direct correlation to the coverage and conciseness criteria, respectively, but the EA criterion has more complex correlation to 4C criteria. For these required criteria, the sizes of training data to build their transformation models may be different.

In order to reduce the labor cost in user interaction, we carry out the user inter-action in an incremental way. Initially, a subset of the training data is selected by random sampling in the 4C assessment score space. After the evaluators evaluate the subset and the corresponding weight coefficient matrix is generated, we calcu-late the mean absolute error (MAE) in each criterion on the subset. Since the subset is selected by random sampling, we consider that the weight coefficients can well transform the 4C assessment scores to the required evaluation results if the MAE in some criterion is smaller than a predefined threshold,\ and stop the evaluators to further evaluate in this criterion by setting the corresponding textbox to unavailable, such as the IN criterion in Fig. 3. For the remaining criteria, we incrementally pro-vide more candidate summaries by randomly sampling in the training data till the MAEs in all criteria are smaller than the predefined threshold or all the candidate summaries in the training data are evaluated.

6 Experiments

We validate the performance of the proposed full-reference evaluation techniques for video summary on the standard dataset from TRECVID 2007 rushes summa-rization task. There are three reasons to select this dataset for our experiment. First, as a global competition in video summarization, TRECVID rushes summarization task provides an accepted dataset and the corresponding video summaries generated by different participants for each original video, which can be used to generate the reference summaries and the candidate summaries. Second, the rushes videos are the unedited raw footages with several repeats of each shot, so the summaries generated from rushes usually have more problems in redundancy and context than the sum-maries generated from other videos. It can more efficiently validate the performance of 4C assessment algorithm. Third, TRECVID provides the criteria to evaluate the generated video summaries that can be used to validate the user interaction-based individual evaluation method.

While building the dataset in our experiments, we select ten rushes from 42 files that have different source files, durations, retake times, and movie tones. The selected rushes are: MRS025913, MRS042543, MRS042548, MRS043400, MRS044500, MRS048779, MRS145918, MRS157445, MRS157475, MS210470. Each video file used in our experiments is generated from one selected rush, and it includes one typical shot with multiple retakes. The reference summary of each video file is generated by manually assembling the extracted frames. We also select ten participants from total twenty-four participants, whose provided summaries include the corresponding parts of our selected video shot files and have different performances in the competition. The ten selected participants are: attlabs, cityu, cmu, cost292, hkpu, kddietal, ntu, thu-icrc, ucal, umadrid. Each participant provides one candidate summary for each video file in the experiments, so totally there are one hundred candidate summaries. We randomly select fifty candidate summaries to build the training data and treat the rest fifty candidate summaries as the test data. To provide the manual evaluation results, we invite ten volunteers as the evaluators in our user studies. They are in age of 20 to 40, including undergraduate and graduate students, officers, and company employees. To our knowledge, they have no idea about our work before the user studies. To eliminate the personal evaluation preference, the mean value of the evaluation results from all evaluators to the same candidate summary in each criterion is treated as the final manual evaluation result of the candidate summary in this criterion.

In this section, the first experiment provides the validation of the 4C assessment algorithm, the second experiment presents the feasibility of the incremental user interaction, and the third experiment shows how to effectively transform the 4C assessment scores to the evaluation results with the required criteria.

6.1 Validation of 4C Assessment Algorithm

We first demonstrate the 4C assessment algorithm on shot 103 in rushes file MRS044500, which has been chosen as the demo video in the TRECVID 2007 for rushes summarization task.

The reference summary is generated manually, and eight candidate summaries are described in Table 3. We decompose the reference summary and the candidate summaries to a set of SUs as shown in Fig. 4 and calculate the scores of candidate summaries' quality by 4C assessment.

Table 4 shows the 4C assessment results of the candidate summaries. Candidate summary 1 obtains full scores in all four criteria because it is totally same with the reference summary. Candidate summaries 2 to 5 are four artificially generated summaries with the obvious problems in coverage, conciseness, coherence, and context, respectively. Candidate summary 2 misses the last two SUs of reference summary,

Fig. 4 Video summaries for the rushes file of shot 103 in MRS044500. Here, the SUs in the reference summary (*RS*) are represented with $SU_1, \ldots, SU_8$. The SUs in the candidate summaries are represented according the SUs in the references summary: SU_i denotes a same SU to the SU_i in *RS*; $RDSU_i$ denotes a reduced SU of the SU_i in *RS*; $RTSU_i$ denotes a retake of the SU_i in *RS*; $NRSU_i$ denotes a near SU of the SU_i in *RS*, which can be a retake, a reduced one, or any other similar one; SU_{noise} denotes a noise SU

Table 3 Different candidate video summaries for the rushes file of shot 103 in MRS044500

CS No.	Description of the candidate summary
CS 1	same with the reference summar
CS 2	remove the last two SUs from the reference summary
CS 3	add two noise SUs in the head and end of the reference summary
CS 4	drop the first 20% and the last 20% frames of each SU in the reference summary
CS 5	invert the orders of the SUs in the reference summary
CS 6	a retake of the reference summary
CS 7	baseline summary (select 1 second in each 25 seconds of the original video)
CS 8	a summary from one participant in TRECVID 2007

Table 4 4C assessment scores on shot 103 in MRS044500

CS No.	s_{Cov}	s_{Coc}	s_{Coh}	s_{Cot}
CS 1	1.000	1.000	1.000	1.000
CS 2	0.750	1.000	1.000	1.000
CS 3	1.000	0.800	1.000	1.000
CS 4	0.954	1.000	0.889	1.000
CS 5	1.000	1.000	1.000	0.652
CS 6	0.904	0.906	0.903	1.000
CS 7	0.690	0.421	0.827	0.541
CS 8	0.713	0.408	0.765	0.580

so the coverage is poor. Similarly, candidate summary 3 has two noise SUs in the head and end, so the conciseness is poor. Candidate summary 4 is generated by dropping 20% frames at the beginning of each SU and 20% at the end of each SU; therefore, it leads to incoherence. In candidate summary 5, the SU sequence has the wrong order, so the score of context is low. Candidate summary 6 is a retake of the reference summary, so it has good performance in all four criteria. Candidate summary 7 is one baseline summary of TRECVID 2007, and candidate summary 8 is the summary from one participant. These two candidate summaries are generated by automatic multimedia content analysis algorithms. Obviously, their performances are not as good as the artificially generated summaries, and the problems of quality are more complicated.

To further validate the effectiveness of the 4C assessment algorithm, we carry out a user study on the whole dataset. We explain the 4C criteria to the evaluators for five minutes before the manual evaluation. Then, each evaluator is asked to evaluate all the candidate summaries according to 4C criteria. The evaluation results in the value range from 0 to 1 with ten steps, and higher score means better performance.

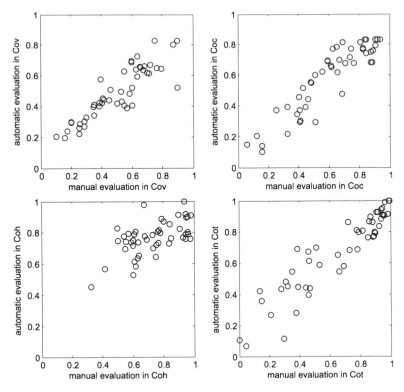

Fig. 5 Comparison of manual evaluation results and automatic assessment results according to 4C criteria on the test data

Table 5 Performance of automatic 4C assessment on the test data		s_{Cov}	s_{Coc}	s_{Coh}	s_{Cot}
	MAE	0.064	0.083	0.107	0.085
	CC	0.897	0.915	0.626	0.926

Figure 5 shows a comparison between the manual evaluation results and the automatic assessment results according to 4C criteria on the test data. Table 5 shows the MAE of the automatic 4C assessment results and their correlation coefficients (CC) to the manual evaluation results. It shows high correlation in coverage, conciseness, and context between the manual evaluation results and automatic assessment results. The results in coherence show weaker correlation, since the evaluators usually hardly give very accurate judgments to the intensity and frequency of incoherence in evaluation.

6.2 Validation of Incremental User Interaction

In this subsection, we present the feasibility of incremental user interaction. We select the human-like criteria in TRECVID 2007 rushes summarization task as the required criteria, including IN, EA, and RE [22].

Since the provided scores of IN, EA, and RE in TRECVID 2007 are given to the summaries of the total rushes but not the typical shots, we ask the ten evaluators to evaluate the candidate summaries with the proposed user interaction approach in Sect. 5. The scores used in evaluation are in five levels, i.e., from 1 to 5.

Using the transformation model generation algorithm in Table 2, we generate the transformation model from 4C assessment scores to the required evaluation results on the training data. We initially build a subset with 40% size of the training data (20 candidate summaries) and incrementally add 10 candidate summaries every time. Table 6 shows the generated weight coefficient matrix in each step. We can find that the criteria directly correlated to 4C criteria, such as IN and RE, can reach the stable weight coefficients rapidly, and the criteria with more complex correlation to the 4C assessment scores, such as EA, require more training data to adjust the corresponding transformation models.

In our experiments, we use 0.1 as the threshold to measure the mean absolute error on the training data. Hence, only the manual evaluation in EA is carried out on the whole training data, and the manual evaluation in IN and RE is stopped after the evaluation on the initial subset with 40% size. It shows that the proposed incremental approach can reduce the labor cost in user interaction.

Table 6 Weight coefficient matrix in incremental user interaction

λ_{ji}		x_0	x_1	x_2	x_3	x_4	MAE
$k = 40\%$	y_1	**0.073**	**0.985**	**0.007**	**0.009**	**0.018**	**0.083**
	y_2	0.058	0.381	0.042	0.028	0.524	0.137
	y_3	**0.025**	**0.009**	**0.967**	**0.023**	**0.004**	**0.091**
$k = 60\%$	y_1	0.135	0.962	0.016	0.007	0.002	0.084
	y_2	0.039	0.363	0.071	0.032	0.513	0.162
	y_3	0.047	0.006	0.953	0.016	0.005	0.083
$k = 80\%$	y_1	0.064	0.971	0.021	0.008	0.009	0.086
	y_2	0.048	0.337	0.076	0.061	0.540	0.131
	y_3	0.053	0.012	0.957	0.014	0.003	0.095
$k = 100\%$	y_1	0.079	0.976	0.013	0.003	0.006	0.085
	y_2	**0.061**	**0.344**	**0.051**	**0.019**	**0.541**	**0.107**
	y_3	0.052	0.018	0.968	0.009	0.007	0.092

6.3 Validation of Evaluation Result Transformation

In this subsection, we will show how to transform the 4C assessment scores to satisfy various evaluation requirements.

Based on incremental user interaction and the transformation generation algorithm in Table 2, we can calculate the weight coefficient matrix to transform the 4C
assessment scores. Table 7 gives the weight coefficient values for IN, EA, and RE.
From Table 7 we can find that coverage and conciseness dominate the IN and RE
scores, respectively, while coverage and context dominate the EA score together. It
is consonant with the definition of IN, EA, RE in TRECVID 2007 [22].

We generate the automatic evaluation results in IN, EA, RE by weighted sum of
the 4C assessment scores. Figure 6 shows the comparison between the automatic
evaluation results and manual evaluation results in IN, EA, RE on the test data.
Table 8 shows the MAEs of the automatic evaluation results and their correlation
coefficients to the manual evaluation results. It is obvious that the proposed automatic evaluation techniques can fit manual evaluation very well.

We further calculate the sum of coefficients in each column as the total weight
of the corresponding criterion in 4C criteria (Table 2). It can be used to assess the
criteria used in video summary quality evaluation. It shows that coverage and conciseness are fully considered in the evaluation criteria including IN, EA, RE, but the
coherence is ignored.

Table 7 Weight coefficient matrix for individual evaluation results generation

λ_{ji}	$x_0 = 1$	s_{Cov}	s_{Coc}	s_{Coh}	s_{Cot}
g_{IN}	0.073	0.985	0.007	0.009	0.018
g_{EA}	0.061	0.344	0.051	0.019	0.541
g_{RE}	0.025	0.009	0.967	0.023	0.004
total weight		1.338	1.025	0.051	0.563

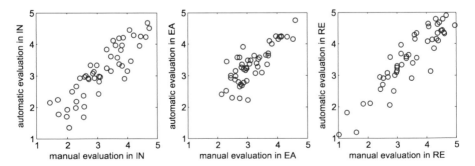

Fig. 6 Comparison of manual evaluation results and automatic evaluation results in IN, EA, RE
on the test data

Table 8 Performance of automatic IN, EA, RE evaluation on the test data

	g_{IN}	g_{EA}	g_{RE}
MAE	0.349	0.467	0.328
CC	0.875	0.813	0.906

7 Conclusions

This chapter presents a novel framework to evaluate the quality of the video summary according to various user requirements. The framework replies on three underlying algorithms that are well adapted to the characteristics of video summary evaluation: frame alignment-based summary unit matching, similarity-based automatic 4C assessment, and incremental user interaction-based individual evaluation. Together, they provide a complete evaluation framework that well satisfies the user requirements in video summary quality evaluation. We have illustrated the performance of proposed techniques on the standard dataset of rushes summarization in TRECVID 2007.

Further work will be explored from two aspects. First, we intend to seek the quality evaluation method without the requirement of a perfect reference summary, i.e., nonreference or reduced-reference evaluation for video summary. Second, current transformation model is based on linear combination of 4C assessment scores. We will consider the possibility of other models and compare the evaluation performance with the weighted sum model.

Acknowledgements   We would like to thank the volunteers for their work in manual evaluation. This work is supported by the National Natural Science Foundation of China (60721002, 60975043) and Hong Kong General Research Fund PolyU 5204/09E.

References

1. Agnihotri, L., Dimitrova, N., Kender, J.R.: Design and evaluation of a music video summarization system. In: IEEE International Conference on Multimedia and Expo, Taipei (2004)
2. Das, D., Martins, A.F.T.: A survey on automatic text summarization. CMU Course (2007). http://www.cs.cmu.edu/dipanjan/pubs/summarization. Accessed 20 February 2010
3. Du, Y., Shao, L.: Video shots retrieval using local invariant features. In: International Workshop on Interactive Multimedia for Consumer Electronics, Beijing (2009)
4. Dumont, E., Mérialdo, B.: Rushes video summarization and evaluation. Multimed. Tools Appl. (2009). doi:10.1007/s1104200903749
5. Gong, Y., Liu, X.: Summarizing video by minimizing visual content redundancies. In: IEEE International Conference on Multimedia and Expo, Tokyo (2001)
6. He, L., Sanocki, E., Gupta, A., Grudin, J.: Auto-summarization of audio-video presentations. In: ACM International Conference on Multimedia, Florida (1999)
7. Hua, X.S., Liu, W., Zhang, H.J.: An automatic performance evaluation protocol for video text detection algorithms. IEEE Trans. Circuits Syst. Video Technol. **14**(4), 498–507 (2004)
8. Huang, M., Mahajan, A.B., DeMenthon, D.F.: Automatic performance evaluation for video summarization. Technique Report of Maryland University, Maryland (2004)

9. Knoche, H., De Meer, H.G., Kirsh, D.: Utility curves: mean opinion scores considered biased. In: International Workshop Quality of Service, London (1999)
10. Kusuma, T.M., Zepernick, H.J.: A reduced-reference perceptual quality metric for in-service image quality assessment. In: Mobile Future and Symposium Trends in Communications, Bratislava (2003)
11. Law-To, J., Chen, L., Joly, A., Laptev, I., Buisson, O., Gouet-Brunet, V., Boujemaa, N., Stentiford, F.: Video copy detection: a comparative study. In: International Conference on Image and Video Retrieval, Amsterdam (2007)
12. Li, Y., Zhang, T., Tretter, D.: An overview of video abstraction techniques. HP Technique Report (2001)
13. Lienhart, R., Effelsberg, W., Jain, R.: VisualGREP: a systematic method to compare and retrieve video sequences. Multimed. Tools Appl. **10**(1), 47–72 (2000)
14. Liu, T., Zhang, H.J., Qi, F.: A novel video key-frame extraction algorithm based on perceived motion energy model. IEEE Trans. Circuits Syst. Video Technol. **13**(10), 1006–1013 (2003)
15. Liu, Y., Zhang, Y., Sun, M., Li, W.: Full-reference quality diagnosis for video summary. In: IEEE International Conference Multimedia and Expo, Hannover (2008)
16. Lowe, D.G.: Object recognition from local scale-invariant features. In: IEEE International Conference on Computer Vision, Kerkyra (1999)
17. Ma, Y.F., Lu, L., Zhang, H.J., Li, M.: A user attention model for video summarization. In: ACM International Conference on Multimedia, Juan les Pins (2002)
18. Manjunath, B.S., Ohm, J.R., Vasudevan, V.V., Yamada, A.: Color and texture descriptors. IEEE Trans. Circuits Syst. Video Technol. **11**(6), 703–715 (2001)
19. Naphide, H.R., Huang, T.S.: A probabilistic framework for semantic video indexing, filtering, and retrieval. IEEE Trans. Multimed. **3**(1), 141–151 (2001)
20. Naturel, X., Gros, P.: A fast shot matching strategy for detecting duplicate sequences in a television stream. In: International Workshop on Computer Vision Meets Databases, Maryland (2005)
21. Needleman, S., Wunsch, C.: A general method applicable to the search for similarities in the amino acid sequence of two proteins. J. Mol. Biol. **48**(3), 443–453 (1970)
22. Over, P., Smeaton, A.F., Kelly, P.: The TRECVid 2007 BBC rushes summarization evaluation pilot. In: ACM International Workshop on TRECVid Video Summarization, Maryland (2007)
23. Over, P., Smeaton, A.F., Awad, G.: The TRECVid 2008 BBC rushes summarization evaluation. In: ACM International the Workshop on TRECVid Video Summarization, Vancouver (2008)
24. Ren, T., Liu, Y., Wu, G.: Full-reference quality assessment for video summary. In: International Workshop on Video Mining, Pisa (2008)
25. Sheikh, H.R., Wang, Z., Cormack, L., Bovik, A.C.: Blind quality assessment for JPEG2000 compressed images. In: International Conference on Signals, Systems and Computers, California (2002)
26. Shen, H.T., Ooi, B.C., Zhou, X.: Towards effective indexing for very large video sequence database. In: ACM International Conference on Management of Data, Maryland (2005)
27. Silva, G.C., Yamasaki, T., Aizawa, K.: Evaluation of video summarization for a large number of cameras in ubiquitous home. In: ACM International Conference on Multimedia, Singapore (2005)
28. Taskiran, C.M.: Evaluation of automatic video summarization systems. In: International Conference on Multimedia Content Analysis, Management, and Retrieval, California (2006)
29. Truong, B.T., Venkatesh, S.: Video abstraction: a systematic review and classification. ACM Trans. Multimed. Comput. Commun. Appl. **3**(1), 1–37 (2007)
30. Uchihashi, S., Foote, J., Girgensohn, A., Boreczky, J.: Video Manga: generating semantically meaningful video summaries. In: ACM International Conference on Multimedia, Florida (1999)

31. Wang, Z., Bovik, A.C., Sheikh, H.R., Simoncelli, E.P.: Image quality assessment: from error visibility to structural similarity. IEEE Trans. Image Process. **13**(4), 600–612 (2004)
32. Yahiaoui, I., Merialdo, B., Huet, B.: Comparison of multiepisode video summarization algorithms. EURASIP J. Appl. Signal Process. **2003**(1), 48–55 (2003)
33. Zhang, H.J., Kankanhalli, A., Smoliar, S.W.: Automatic partitioning of full-motion video. In: Jeffay, K., Zhang, H.J. (eds.) Readings in Multimedia Computing and Networking, 1st edn. Morgan Kaufmann, San Francisco (2001)

Multimedia Experience on Web-Connected CE Devices

Dan Tretter, Jerry Liu, Xuemei Zhang, Yuli Gao, Brian Atkins, Hui Chao, Jun Xiao, Peng Wu, and Qian Lin

Abstract Consumer electronics (CE) are changing from stand-alone single-function devices to products with increasing connectivity, convergence of functionality, and a focus on customer experience. We discuss the features that characterize the new generation of CE and illustrate this new paradigm through an examination of how web services can be integrated with CE products to deliver an improved user experience. In particular, we focus on one aspect of the CE segment, digital photography. We introduce AutoPhotobook, an automatic photobook creation service and provide a detailed look at how it addresses the complexity of photobook authoring through a portfolio of automatic photo analysis and composition technologies. We then show how this collection of technologies is integrated into a larger ecosystem

D. Tretter (✉) · J. Liu · X. Zhang · Y. Gao · B. Atkins · H. Chao · J. Xiao · P. Wu · Q. Lin
Hewlett-Packard Laboratories, 1501 Page Mill Road, Palo Alto, CA 94304, USA
e-mail: dan.tretter@hp.com

J. Liu
e-mail: jerry.liu@hp.com

X. Zhang
e-mail: xuemei.zhang@hp.com

Y. Gao
e-mail: yuli.gao@hp.com

B. Atkins
e-mail: brian.atkins2@hp.com

H. Chao
e-mail: hui.chao@hp.com

J. Xiao
e-mail: jun.xiao@hp.com

P. Wu
e-mail: peng.wu@hp.com

Q. Lin
e-mail: qian.lin@hp.com

L. Shao et al. (eds.), *Multimedia Interaction and Intelligent User Interfaces,*
Advances in Pattern Recognition,
DOI 10.1007/978-1-84996-507-1_11, © Springer-Verlag London Limited 2010

with other web services and web-connected CE devices to deliver an enhanced user experience.

1 Introduction

The consumer electronics industry is undergoing a transformation. Despite the word "electronics" in its name, consumer electronics devices are increasingly differentiated not by the electronics within them, but by the breadth of functionality that these devices provide. These functionalities often consist, at least in part, of applications and services that rely on a connected infrastructure. Most major consumer electronics categories, such as smart phones, televisions, set-top boxes, game consoles, Blu-ray players, DVRs, digital photo frames, and printers, have associated services and content that can be accessed or streamed from the internet.

In fact, consumer electronics are no longer stand-alone devices that perform a single function but can often grow and change depending on the installed applications. Common applications and services include content services (videos, photos, music, podcast, news, weather, or sports), social networks (Twitter, Facebook, or MySpace), games, and productivity tools. The line between content services and applications is also becoming blurrier. Content owners now often provide client applications that adapt content, and interfaces to navigate within that content, to device-specific screen size and capabilities. These cloud-based applications and services are, in many cases, driving the growth of the consumer electronics industry, creating entirely new categories of devices while reinventing many existing categories.

A number of recent publications have introduced various aspects of the transformation in the consumer electronics industry. MIT Professor Henry Holtzman has labeled the next generation of consumer electronic as "Consumer Electronics 2.0" (CE 2.0) and characterizes it as "internet of things" [1]. Ken Wirt of Cisco believes that connectivity will become the major impetus of consumer electronics [2]. In our view, there are a number of factors that characterize the evolution to CE 2.0 from CE 1.0.

One factor is the allocation of development resources. The development resources for traditional consumer electronic devices used to be very hardware centric, with the software or firmware portions playing a minor role of enabling the hardware. In contrast, in CE 2.0, the hardware tends to be based on off-the-shelf components, with software development occupying the dominant share of the development costs. Along the same vein, CE 1.0 products are differentiated by their product specifications. The feature list on the product box tends to be along the lines of clock speed of the processor or the size of the memory it contains. With CE 2.0 products, the differentiation comes from the look and feel of the product.

CE 2.0 products are also characterized by their increasing connectedness. Whereas CE 1.0 devices are stand-alone devices designed to operate by themselves, CE 2.0 products are designed to be placed on a network, whether through WiFi, cellular data, or cabled Ethernet, and are expected to be part of a larger ecosystem.

Table 1 Cameras exhibit increasing connectivity and convergence of functionality over time

	Capture	View	Share	Create/Edit	Connectedness
Analog camera	X				None
1st Generation digital camera	X	X			None
Current digital cameras	X	X	x	x	Low
Smartphones	X	X	X	X	High

Once on the network, CE 2.0 devices can connect to larger data stores, dynamic pools of applications, other devices, and, through these devices, other people. CE 2.0 devices are also much more context-aware. CE 1.0 products tend to be passive devices that operate based only on direct user input, with little knowledge of their environment. In contrast, CE 2.0 products, through embedded sensors and network connectivity, have the capability to find out about their environment and take action to improve their own functionality. A simple example is the Wii gaming console, which is capable of checking online for new versions of the system software and updating itself as appropriate.

The flexibility of these devices leads to a convergence of functionality, a move from special purpose devices to more general-purpose PC-like devices. For digital photography, this is captured well by looking at the evolution of cameras.

One of the boons of convergence is that it allows consumers to move seamlessly among the different experiences that are associated with an ecosystem. In the case of digital photography, this means the user can capture a photo, view it instantly, edit it, and then share it via a variety of sharing mechanisms in a matter of minutes. Of course, this same benefit is true in other ecosystems as well. In the case of movies, for example, consumers can research movie reviews, select a film, watch it, and rate or recommend it without ever moving from their seat. Convergence and connectedness go hand in hand in CE 2.0 devices, giving access to ever-larger content libraries while simultaneously allowing the consumer to interact more richly with the content than ever before. One downside to increasing connectedness, however, is in the difficulty of navigating these large content libraries. As connectedness grows, the need for organization and visualization tools grows as well.

What all of these changes lead to, fundamentally, is a shift from a focus on consumer *electronics* to a focus on consumer *experience*. This shift is perhaps best illustrated by Apple's successful smartphone, the iPhone. Contrary to how most vendors promote their products, with specifications of processor clock speed or other numerical measures, Apple differentiates the iPhone from its competitors based on its software and look and feel. The device knows the user's environment (time, location, orientation) and usage habits, enables users to connect with friends and content anytime, anywhere, while the applications in the App Store keep up with the user's lifestyle changes. Table 1 shows that cameras exhibit increasing connectivity and convergence of functionality over time.

As the consumer electronics industry shifts focus from devices to connected experiences, there are a number of implications for multimedia research. Innovation opportunities now span an ecosystem of home and mobile devices, and web-based services. Multimedia content transformation between devices and web services can provide unique differentiations for consumer electronics products. Research topics can be found in new architecture for distributed media processing, content and metadata organization, storage, and distribution, as well as user interaction models. In addition, web technologies can be used to create compelling research prototypes.

In this paper, we explore the implications for multimedia research in the context of Consumer Electronics 2.0. As a case study, we focus on one aspect of the consumer electronic ecosystem, digital photography. We set the context by discussing the current trends and research challenges in digital photography. We then introduce AutoPhotobook, a photobook creation service that addresses one of the common problems in digital photography, and highlight its novel features. We show how the service can play a part within a larger ecosystem containing various consumer electronic devices to provide them with the breadth of functionality expected of CE 2.0 products. Within this narrative, we also describe a number of research areas in the intelligent creation of multimedia content, and the deployment of content creation web services.

2 Digital Photography Ecosystem

In this section, we discuss one example of consumer electronics ecosystem, digital photography. The digital photography ecosystem supports five main consumer needs centered around photos: capture, storage, viewing, sharing, and editing/product creation. The ecosystem started with cameras, computers, and home printers. Over the years, more and more devices and services have joined this ecosystem. Today, photos are captured by mobile phones and cameras, and stored in personal computers, phones, laptops, home media servers, online photo sharing services, and social networks. People further create photo products such as calendars, photobooks, greeting cards, etc., and print them at home, or order through websites and at retail. In addition, digital photo frames are becoming increasingly popular and are used to display photos at home. Figure 1 shows a high-level depiction of the digital photography ecosystem.

Consumers face many challenges in dealing with the digital photography ecosystem. Of the five consumer needs mentioned above, capture, storage, and simple viewing are all fairly well supported by the current mix of devices and services, but sharing and editing/product creation are more challenging, since they often involve selection of appropriate photos from a large archive. People snap large numbers of photos to capture events in their lives. According to Lyra Research, consumers will capture more than 500 billion photos in 2010. More than half of them will be captured by phone cameras. Of these photos, only a very small fraction is tagged. Most people do not have time to organize and tag their photos. Yet, they desire simple ways to browse and find their photos, and to interact with them to express their creativity.

These trends pose a number of research challenges. Primarily, they are in the area of semantic understanding of photos, and image management and composition to generate creative output.

Services   Connected Devices

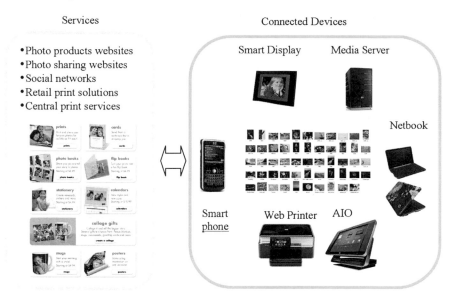

Fig. 1 Example multimedia experience—digital photography ecosystem

(1) Semantic understanding. A lot of research is being conducted to understand what a photo is about. The research falls into several categories.

- Object detection: this answers the question of what is in a photo. For example, are there people in the photo? How many people are in the photo? Are there pets, cars, houses?
- Event detection: there is also a lot of interest in finding out the type of events depicted by a photo collection. For example, are these photos taken during a birthday party, on a beach, during a ski trip?
- People recognition: this addresses the question of who is in a photo. Often using face recognition as the base algorithm, one can analyze an image collection and find out answers to questions such as "How many images have John?", "Who appears in the same images with John?", etc.
- Image quality assessment: this can include metrics such as image sharpness, brightness and contrast, eye open/close detection, etc.

This information is often augmented by timestamps and possibly location information, which are provided by the capture devices.

(2) Image management and composition for creative output. Research in this area explores the organization, browsing, search, enhancement, and composition aspects of digital photo collections.

- Organization, search, and browsing: as digital photo collections expand, more and more people are encountering the problem of how to find a certain photo or class of photos. Automatic image tagging using object detection and event detection often does not provide a complete solution. Visual browsing interfaces and multiple search mechanisms can be combined to provide a more powerful solution.

- Image enhancement: early image enhancement algorithms focused on brightness and contrast enhancement. As research in this area evolved, more sophisticated enhancement algorithms can correct redeyes automatically and even beautify a face.
- Image composition: using a combination of image segmentation and layout algorithms, there is a huge opportunity in generating interesting image collages.

Much progress has been made to address these challenges in recent years. Given the importance of people as subjects in consumer photography, face analysis and recognition is used to automatically group photos according to people and tagged, so that it is easier to browse and navigate photo collections according to people [3]. Contextual information such as time and location are also used to annotate and classify photos [4, 5]. While automatic image tagging with arbitrary objects remains an unsolved problem, progress has been made on a semi-automatic approach where a subset of photos are manually tagged and the tags are propagated to the rest of the album [6].

With new generative image composition technologies such as Blocked Recursive Image Composition [7], it is possible to create flexible image layouts with good aesthetics in real time. In comparison with more common layout techniques based on a library of fixed templates, algorithms like BRIC can accommodate a larger variety of photo shapes and sizes on a wider range of pages, since layouts are generated on the fly as needed and do not have to be created in advance. Also, generative approaches have the potential to support more seamless user editing actions, since compositions can be quickly altered or updated in response to user actions. Coupled with new user interaction models such as Mixed Initiative Collage Authoring [8], it becomes relatively easy for ordinary people without special graphical design skills to tell their stories from photo collections. In addition, web content can be added to make the story-telling more compelling [9]. The experience of preserving and sharing memories on paper can be enhanced by linking with digital content [10].

In the next section, we will describe the AutoPhotobook system, which uses advanced techniques in image processing to move digital story-telling to the next level.

3 AutoPhotobook System

One example of an application that could benefit greatly from advances in semantic understanding of photos and image composition is photobook creation. Studies have shown that while photobooks have the highest appeal among all photo merchandise categories, people are deterred by the time and effort involved in making such artifacts. A 2008 PMA survey showed that 47.7% of people who started a photobook and did not finish said the reason they did not finish is that the process took too long or was too difficult [11], as illustrated in Fig. 2.

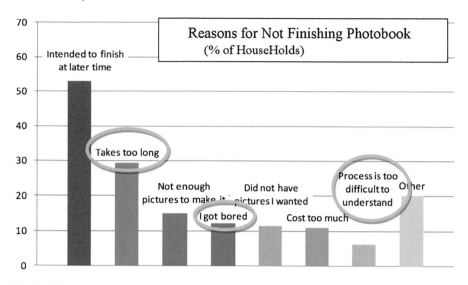

Fig. 2 47.7% of households who did not finish a photobook abandoned it because it was too hard, too boring, or simply took too long

When it comes to computer-assisted photobook creation, users want simplicity, quality, customizability, and speed. However, conventional solutions leave a lot to be desired, typically trading these four characteristics off against one another, sacrificing simplicity for customizability, or speed for quality. On one hand, the limited options of page layout templates and associated artwork hamper true customizability. All too often the difference between what the author would like to present, and what actually ends up being printed, is a disappointing force-fit. On the other hand, essential difficulties associated with storytelling through personalized photobooks remain; these include photo selection, photo grouping into pages, image cropping, page layout, and background selection, all of which can be time-consuming and difficult to optimize. Effective solutions must utilize knowledge of good design practice to present proposed albums that both tell the underlying story and are aesthetically pleasing.

Today's auto build functionalities are a good start toward resolving some of these difficulties. Considerable recent work has addressed image selection. For example, an automatic photobook generation system was developed in [13] using content-based and context-based image analysis; a scalable image selection system was presented in [12]; and a personal photo management system with the capability to remove undesirable low-quality images was described in [15]. Pagination and layout is another major pain point in the conventional photobook creation experience, but most existing solutions are template based, and few explore the possibility of dynamic page layout and background artwork adjustment. Finally, the issue of how to expose all these capabilities in a unified, intuitive user interface remains largely unsolved.

Thus, photobook creation is one of the most technically challenging workflows for solution and service providers, and the workflow from photo collection to fi-

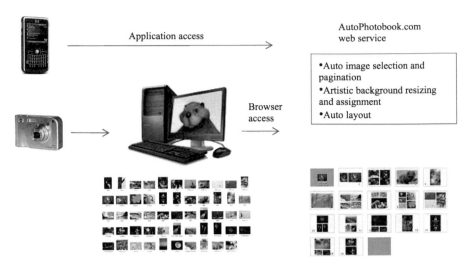

Fig. 3 Automatic photobook creation

nal photobook tends to be fragmented and time-consuming. These problems are only magnified when the authoring platform is expanded beyond PCs to other consumer electronics platforms. The HP Labs AutoPhotobook system uses core imaging algorithms to streamline the workflow and automate many of the more cumbersome steps, which both simplifies the creation process on PCs and makes it more amenable to other authoring platforms. This system and its component technologies will serve as a good example of some of the research challenges and approaches to addressing the needs of CE 2.0 products and systems.

Figure 3 shows how the AutoPhotobook system fits into the CE 2.0 environment. Photos captured by digital cameras are typically stored in a computer. A user can access AutoPhotobook through a web browser. Alternatively, a user can also access the system through a thin client on a smart phone, or other mobile computing devices. The AutoPhotobook system performs automatic image selection and pagination, smart artistic background resizing and assignment, and automatic layout. We will discuss in detail how this workflow can enable automatic creation of photobooks, as well as supporting interactive editing, if the user chooses to make additional changes, in the rest of this section. We will discuss how AutoPhotobook can be linked to additional web services such as social networking sites in the next section.

The AutoPhotobook system addresses the complexities of photobook authoring with advances over prior solutions in the following areas: automatic image selection and theme-based image grouping; dynamic page layout; automatic cropping; automatic background selection; design-preserving background artwork transformation; and a simple yet powerful user interface for personalization. Our overall approach is to create a high-quality candidate photobook automatically and then allow the user to easily edit and customize the photobook to meet their preferences. We leverage both design knowledge and image understanding algorithms to auto-

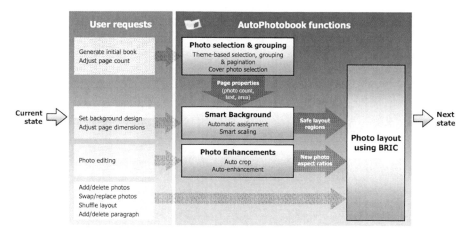

Fig. 4 AutoPhotobook system. Note that any user request can be made at any point in the creation process

mate time-consuming tasks like image selection, grouping, cropping, and layout. This streamlines the initial creation phase, so the user is never stuck staring at a blank page wondering where to begin. Our composition engine then allows users to easily edit the book: adding, swapping or moving photos, exploring different page layouts and themes, and even dynamically adjusting the aspect ratio of the final book. All of these technologies are delivered through a rich internet application, so the compute-intensive photo analysis algorithms can be carried out in the cloud, and the interface and interaction mechanisms can be run locally on devices with modest computation capabilities.

The block diagram in Fig. 4 shows the main components and workflow of AutoPhotobook. Image content analysis is done on the fly through parallel processing when users upload their photos to the system. After photo upload is complete, an automatically generated photobook is presented to the user, along with a simple yet powerful user interface for personalization.

Content analysis results are first used to select and group photos to produce a structured representation that helps to tell the story behind the photos. These algorithms are explained in more detail in Sect. 3.1. We then use our Structured Art technology to select and adapt designed backgrounds to the pages of the book, adapting to the size and shape of the book while creating style-consistent page spreads. This technology is covered in Sect. 3.2. Finally, our BRIC layout engine is used to dynamically create custom layout templates for each page that accommodate the book size and the number and shapes of photos assigned to that page. We discuss this technology in Sect. 3.3.

The user is then presented with a finished book for editing and fine-tuning. Photo selection, page assignments, and layouts can all be adjusted with simple drag and drop functionality, which can be supported on a variety of devices. Users can edit individual photos with a single touch or click of the mouse, using toggle buttons to auto-crop and auto-enhance photos as desired. For the auto-crop functionality, we use the HP Labs auto-crop algorithm described in [16], and for auto-enhance, we use HP's HIPIE algorithm [15]. The user interface and interaction mechanisms are designed to allow users to quickly explore photobook variants and converge to a desired customized version. We discuss the user interactions and flow in more detail in Sect. 3.4 below. The final result is a photobook creation system that adapts automatically and intelligently to user photos and editing actions.

3.1 Design-Driven Photo Selection and Pagination

In order to autogenerate photobooks that serve as good starting points for users, we have conducted experiments with graphic designers to better understand photobook creation and design principles. According to insights from these experiments, we then developed an algorithm that proceeds as follows: First, discard any image that is too blurry or obviously "bad." Second, discard any image that is near duplicate [21] to, but of lower quality than, another image in the collection. Third, divide the remaining photos into pages using "themes," as inferred from time clusters, color, detected faces, and detected locations.

3.1.1 Blurry Image Removal

In consumer image collections, it is not uncommon to find blurry images. In practice, designers tend to remove these images from further consideration because they generally do not look good in a photobook. To achieve this goal, we have designed a sharpness metric to identify these blurry images.

Blur in images is often caused by camera motion or out of focus. In either case, blur weakens the major edges in images. For example, in Fig. 5, the edge strength histograms are shown for two very similar images, one blurry and the other nonblurry. Observe that the edge strength histogram of the blurry image is flatter in shape and smaller in range than the nonblurry one due to the smoothing effect from out-of-focus blur. This observation leads us to the formulation of a simple sharpness score as the following:

$$Q = \frac{\text{strength}(e)}{\text{entropy}(h)}$$

where strength(e) is the average edge strength of the top 10% strongest edges, and entropy(h) is the entropy of the normalized edge strength histogram. Intuitively, nonblur images have stronger edges and more peaky edge strength distribution, which leads to large strength(e) and smaller entropy(h), resulting in a larger Q value. We simply threshold this Q value to remove blurry images.

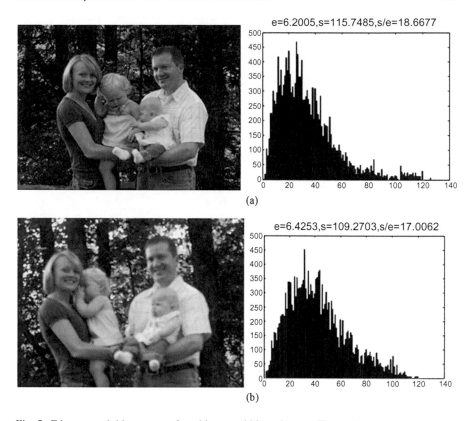

Fig. 5 Edge strength histograms of nonblurry and blurry images. The nonblurry image shown in (**a**) has a 18.7 Q score vs. the 17.0 Q score of the blurry image shown in (**b**)

3.1.2 Duplicate Photo Detection

Removing near-duplicate photos is generally desirable as users often take multiple shots of the same scene/people only to keep the best one. However, the meaning of "near duplicates" varies depending on the problem domain. In this work, we use the following definition:

Two images are a "near-duplicate pair" (NDP) when they are two snapshots of the same scene, i.e., they are 2D projective transforms of the same 3D scene under the same camera internal parameters but different external parameters. We allow subjects in the 3D scene to have slight nonrigid motions between two shots. Examples of NDPs are shown in Fig. 6, where camera rotation, zoom, perspective change, and subject motions are observed between the NDP pairs. If an image pair is not an NDP, it is labeled as a "distinct pair" (DP).

One popular solution to this detection problem is to use local feature-based image matching such as SIFT [17], because it has been proven to be much more accurate compared to global features such as color histogram. However, local features are computationally expensive to detect and match, and this approach is too slow for a

Fig. 6 Examples of image pairs labeled as near duplicates

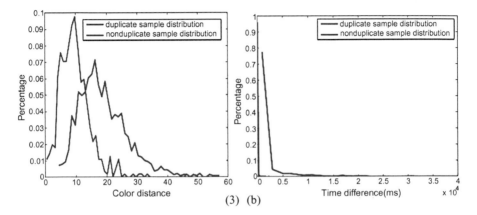

Fig. 7 Distributions of picture-taking time difference and color distance for NDPs vs. DPs

lot of practical multimedia applications where real-time processing of large image collections is required. We want to address this performance issue without sacrificing matching accuracy. In this work, we develop a novel computation-sensitive cascade framework to tackle this problem.

Near duplicates are "rare events," and most of the image pairs can be easily be classified as "distinct pairs" (DP) using simple features like color histogram. Although this is a good idea in general, it is hard to determine the optimal number of bins as an effective color representation; therefore we use adaptive color histogram instead as our global image representation, where the number of bins and their quantization are determined by adaptively clustering image pixels in LAB color space. To measure the dissimilarity between two variable-length color histograms, we use the well-studied Earth Mover Distance [18]. Color distance distributions between NDPs and DPs are plotted in Fig. 7(a). It can be observed that a large number of DPs can be correctly classified without too many false alarms with a large threshold in color distance.

Modern digital cameras record, in each photo's EXIF header, a rich set of metadata such as camera model, shot parameters, and image properties. Intuitively, if two photos are near duplicates, their EXIF metadata should be fairly similar to each other. In Fig. 7(b), we plot out the distribution of the difference in picture-taking time for both NDPs and DPs, and it can be seen that, similar to color distance, this feature clearly has discriminative power to identify true DPs with a large time difference threshold without many false alarms.

Obviously, these three types of image features (local feature, color histogram, and EXIF) are very different in their discriminative power and the cost of extraction. Generally speaking, features with higher discriminative power require higher computational cost. Most prior work assumes features are preextracted, stored, and indexed in a database. In many online applications, however, extracting all the features is simply too slow. Therefore we adopt a minimalist principle, where we only extract features that are absolutely necessary for accurate classification. Since NDPs are rare events compared to DPs, this "on-demand" feature extraction scheme should result in significant saving in computational cost.

In their seminal paper [19], Viola and Jones proposed a cascade classifier learning framework to quickly reject image patches that are nonface like. They use Haar-like features along with integral images, making the cost of extracting different Haar-like features essentially constant. In our case, however, we have features that are widely different in computational cost. The basic idea is to use cheap features as much as possible to classify image pairs, and to only extract the more expensive features when those cheap features cannot determine if they are duplicates. Building on Viola and Jones' original work, we extend their cascade training algorithm to be "computation-sensitive" as follows:

Formally, given a set of training samples $X = \{X^+, X^-\}$, where X^+ are positive samples, and X^- are negative samples, represented in a feature space $F = \{f_1, f_2, \ldots, f_n\}$,

1. Cluster features based on their computational cost into m categories, i.e., $F = \{f^{(1)}, f^{(2)}, \ldots, f^{(m)}\}$, where $f^{(i)} = \{f_{i1}, f_{i2}, \ldots, f_{ij}\}$, and $\forall f_{ij} \in f^{(i)}$ has similar computational cost. Note that feature clusters are ranked, so that the cost of computing $f^{(u)}$ is cheaper than $f^{(v)}$, if $u < v$;
2. For $i = 1 : k$
   a. Bootstrap X to $\{X_t^+, X_t^-\} \cup \{X_v^+, X_v^-\}$ and train a stage boosting classifier C_i using feature set $f^{(1)} \cup \cdots \cup f^{(i)}$ on training set $X_t^+ \cup X_t^-$.
   b. Set threshold T_i for C_i such that the recall rate of $C_i(T_i)$ on the validation set $X_v^+ \cup X_v^-$ is over a preset level R close to 1 (this is to enforce the final classifier has a high recall).
   c. Remove from X the samples that are classified by $C_i(T_i)$ as negative.
3. The final classifier C is the cascade of all stage classifiers $C_i(T_i)$, $i = 1, \ldots, k$.

Note that stage classifiers are trained on progressively more expensive, yet more powerful feature spaces. At test time, if a test sample is rejected by cheap stage classifier $C_i(T_i)$, none of the more complex stage classifiers $C_j(T_j)$, $j > i$, will be triggered, therefore avoiding the extraction of more expensive features.

In order to evaluate the performance of the cascade learning, we randomly downloaded 975 image pairs of personal photo collections from Picasaweb and manually labeled them as Near-Duplicate Pairs (NDP) or Distinct Pairs (DP). We split the dataset into the training set with 475 image pairs and testing set with 500 image pairs. The features are ranked according to their computational cost as: EXIF fea-

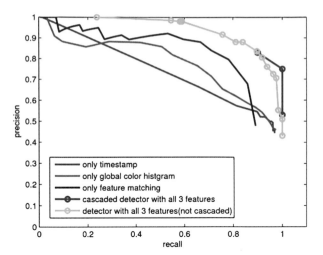

Fig. 8 Comparison of the classification precision and recall between computation-sensitive cascade (*red*); each individual feature (*blue*, *magenta*, and *black*) and regular boosting but without cascade (*cyan*)

ture, global color histogram, and local feature matching score. They correspond to the three stage classifier in our detector.

As a test of the efficiency of our approach, we ran the 500 test samples over our trained computation-sensitive cascade classifier and observed that only 419 samples extracted color histogram feature and 297 samples extracted the most expensive local features. On average, computing EXIF features takes about 0.0001 s, the global histogram feature takes about 0.49 s, and the structured local feature matching takes about 1.16 s; thus the total time for classifying all 500 samples using our cascade classifier is about $500 \cdot 0.0001 + 0.49 \cdot 415 + 1.16 \cdot 297 = 455.145$ s, compared to $500 \cdot 0.0001 + 0.49 + 1.16 = 825.05$ s if all features are extracted for all images. This is almost a $2\times$ speed up. Notice that the speed improvement is affected by several factors, for example, the number of true duplicates in the dataset, the similarity between image content, etc. The more NDPs in the dataset, the more computation is needed, because duplicates need to go through all the cascade stages before a correct prediction can be made. Considering that in real applications, the ratio between NDPs and DPs is far lower than our experimental setup (<30% of random image pairs are NDPs); the speed up therefore should be much larger in practice.

The precision/recall metrics of our approach are also measured and shown in Fig. 8. We compare the computation-sensitive cascade's performance against (a) noncascade boosting classifier with all features and (b) with each individual feature alone. As can be observed in the figure, our computation-sensitive cascade gives much better performance than using only each single feature. Compared to regular boosting with all features, it gives a similar classification accuracy, while at the same being much more computationally efficient.

3.1.3 Theme-Based Pagination and Layout

Once the low-quality images and duplicates are removed, we then try to cluster the remaining images by "themes." Time-based photo clustering algorithms have been extensively studied in literature [20]. Our algorithm goes beyond that and takes advantage of additional high-level semantic features for better image grouping. The themes concept is used frequently by graphics designers when they create artifacts from image collections, which generally means certain similarities in dimensions such as time, color, people, and places. We capture these dimensions using the following functions:

(1) Time distance function $Dt(x, y)$, defined as the absolute difference between the photo-taking time of image x and y.
(2) Color distance function $Dc(x, y)$, defined as the Earth Mover Distance [18] between the color clusters extracted from image x and y.
(3) Face distance function $F(x, y)$, defined as the average distance between faces detected in image x and y.

Due to the variety of similarities, one can measure between images, simply computing all metrics on all possible pairs of images in the sequence could lead to a very high computational cost. To reduce the cost, we take advantage of the following locality assumption: images that were taken closer in time are more likely to be grouped into a page than images that were taken further apart in time. This locality property motivates us to restrict the expensive theme-based clustering process within a certain time window, therefore reducing the computational cost significantly. We describe our theme-based clustering algorithm as the following:

(1) Partition the image sequence into nonoverlapping image subsequences using a predefined time gap T.
(2) Within each image subsequence, a theme graph is constructed by treating all images as nodes, and edges between nodes represent their thematic distance, measured by a linear combination of $Dt(x, y)$, $Dc(x, y)$, and $F(x, y)$.
(3) The graph is then pruned by removing edges whose distances are over a tunable threshold, which is set by the end user to control the number of output pages.
(4) Finding theme clusters is then cast as finding nontrivial cliques in these theme graphs.

Once the theme clusters are found, we simply map each cluster into a photo page. The resulted pages are then fed into the BRIC layout engine with relative weights to reflect their "importance" in the group, and the BRIC engine will determine the size of the photos according to their importance scores.

3.2 Artistic Background Resizing and Assignment

Graphical artwork is increasingly used to enhance the photo layout and provide a theme to the event or story told in a photobook. It is an important part of high-quality photobook solutions. Such artworks are usually prepared only for a fixed page dimension by graphic artists. Even though multiple versions of the same design may be prepared manually for several "standard" page sizes, it is a time consuming task, and difficulty arises when the user's desired page size is not one of the standards. This limits the use of the artwork. In addition, for each theme, there is usually a set of related artwork, and when applying them to a photobook, challenges arise in managing the consistent, harmonic, and interesting appearance of designs across facing pages and the whole book. To this end, we propose a method that addresses some of the challenges: it automatically resizes the artwork to different paper sizes; it orchestrates relative positioning of design elements with the photo placement by computing a new allowable photo layout region for each page; at book level, a theme grammar specifies usage constraints of each background artwork.

3.2.1 STArt Design for Automatic Resizable Artwork

There have been some prior works on automatic image retargeting for different display or page size. The seam-carving technique described in [22–24] was able to automatically resize images to different aspect ratios by removing low-energy paths. This approach works well for resizing natural scene photographic images. However, because background art often contains patterned graphic elements with strong regularity and symmetry, directly applying this technique to the whole image could introduce severe and obvious distortion and artifacts. Other proposed resizing methods [25] also do not address some of the more complex graphic objects in background art images, where page resizing sometimes not only requires the scaling of the graphic objects but could also require addition, abstraction, or synthesis of new graphic objects.

Motivated by various theme art samples created by graphic artists, Birkhoff's original aesthetic order [26] and general aesthetic measure [27] in document layout, we have developed a Structured Art (STArt) design method. It allows automatic transformation of the background art to new aspect ratio while preserving the original aesthetics by preserving the semantics, symmetry, alignment, continuity, connectivity, uniformity, regularity, and the relative positions and size of the elements on the page and to other objects in the original design. This method is facilitated through a design language and an associated transformation algorithm.

The design language is an XML description of the artwork in the form of a list of design elements as its semantic structure. For each element, there is a content object and an array of attributes, such as type, geometric layout position, style, and alignment. The content of the element is usually an illustration in the format of an image or another STArt design. For each element, its type can be "stretchable", "nonstretchable", or "repeating". The position attribute can be one of the ten locations as "top", "bottom", "left", "right", "middle", "area", "topLeft", "topRight", "bottomLeft", and "bottomRight". The "style" and "alignment" attributes describe how the "repeating" patterns are placed on the page. For example, a repeating element in "perfectFit" style draws an integer number of patterns within the described region and along indicated alignment direction, and an element in "texture" or "looseFit" style draws patterns repetitively until it runs out of space; in this case a pattern can be partially drawn. A detailed description of the language and structure can be found in the references [28, 29].

Transformation Algorithm The transformation algorithm takes elements' attributes into consideration and dictates how each element should be scaled and translated on a page during resizing. Symmetry and alignment are observed by keeping the relative positions of design elements to the edges of references indicated by their location attributes. For example, a "topLeft" positioned element keeps its relative distance to both top and left edges of the page; a "left" positioned element keeps its relative distance to the left edge in horizontal direction while preserving the distances (for stretchable) or ratio of the distances (for nonstretchable element) to the top and bottom edge in vertical direction; and a middle-positioned element preserves the distances (for stretchable element) or ratio of distances (for nonstretchable) in both horizontal and vertical directions. Therefore a corner element always stays in the corner; and an element that was symmetrically placed in the middle of the page will stay in the middle. Elements aligned in the same direction as their position attributes stay aligned. Continuity and connectivity are also preserved with similar mechanism and with different types of elements. For a stretchable element, it is the distance to the referenced edge in one direction and distances to the other two edges in the other direction are preserved with the same scaling factor as the nonstretchable elements on the page. Therefore, for example, for a stretchable "top" positioned element, when page resizing stretches more in horizontal direction, its width scales up. Its distances to the left and right edge and its height are scaled proportionally as the page scaling in vertical direction (the smaller page scaling factor). Therefore, if this element is originally connected with a "topRight" or "topLeft" nonstretchable corner element, which, during resizing, also scales proportionally as the page in the vertical direction with a locked aspect ratio, after page resizing, it remains connected with the corner element. Uniformity and regularity are achieved through repeating pattern. As a page is resized, the number of patterns appearing on the page can be recalculated to preserve the style.

Examples are shown in Fig. 9. A sample design file is shown in Fig. 9(a). It includes various stretchable, nonstretchable, and repeating elements. The artwork described by the design file is shown in Fig. 9(b). Shown in Fig. 9(c) is a more complex repeating design, where integer numbers of stripes are placed in the horizontal direction, and stripes can continuously grown or shrink in the vertical direction.

A user study was performed using 18 designs which have been laid out for two different aspect ratios by graphic artists, a square layout and a landscape layout of 11.25×8.5. Based on the square layouts, we created XML descriptions of the designs and automatically resized them to the landscape layouts based on our method. Ten users rate the autoresized layouts and the artist-resized layouts based on visual appearance and usability. The "no-difference" trials were evenly split between the "artist-better"and the "auto-better" groups. The proportion of "artist-better" trials were 0.48, slightly lower than the "auto-better" group, but the difference is not significant (two-sided binomial test, 180 trials from 10 subjects and 18 designs, $p > 0.05$). Therefore, the autoresized theme art images give comparable results to manually resized ones.

```xml
<?xml version="1.0" encoding="UTF-8"?>
<BACKGROUND x="0.0" y="0.0" width="523.0" height="380" leftMargin="54.605" rightMargin="128.98798"
            topMargin="70" bottomMargin="105" >
  <Element type="stretchable" position="top" x="0" y="0" width="380" height="65">
    <image source="bluefabric.jpg" height="50.0" width="100.0"/>
  </Element>
  <Element type="repeating" position="middle" alignment="both" style="texture" x="0" y="65" width="379" height="221">
    <image source="quilted.png" height="112.0" width="72.0"/>
  </Element>
  <Element type="repeating" position="bottom" alignment="" style="looseFit" x="0" y="287" width="379" height="91">
    <image source="bluestitch.jpg" height="204.0" width="130.0"/>
  </Element>
  <Element type="repeating" position="top" alignment="H" style="looseFit" x="0" y="58.948" width="380" height="13.824" >
    <image source="sm_dots.png" width="30" height="13" />
  </Element>
  <Element type="repeating" position="bottom" style="looseFit" alignment="H" x="0" y="270" width="379" height="32" >
    <image source="crochet.png" width="18" height="32.399" />
  </Element>
  <Element type="non-stretchable" position="topRight" x="243" y="85" height="136" width="136">
    <image source="stamppad.png" height="136" width="136"/>
  </Element>
  <Element type="non-stretchable" position="topRight" x="266" y="106" width="93" height="93" >
    <image source="elephant.png" width="93" height="93" />
  </Element>
  <Element type="non-stretchable" position="bottomLeft" x="10" y="285" width="94" height="94">
    <image source="safetypin.png" width="94" height="94" />
  </Element>
</BACKGROUND>
```

(a)

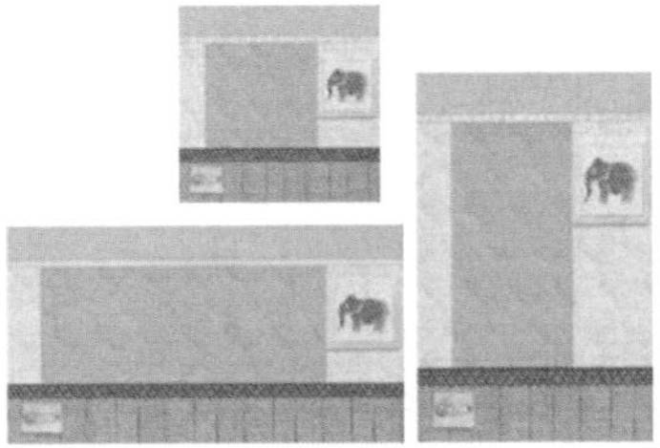

(b)

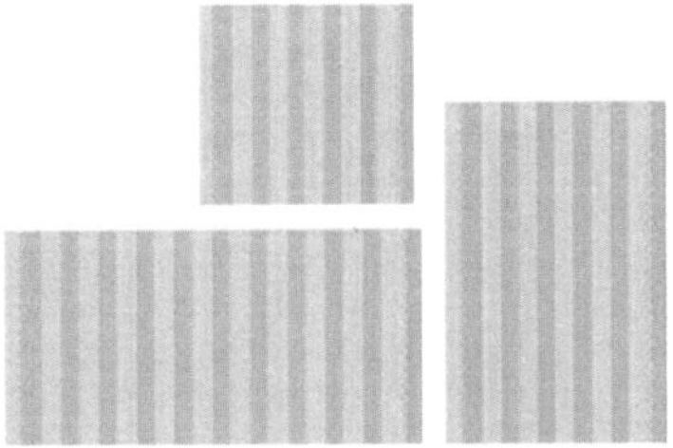

(c)

Fig. 9 Example of the STArt designs. A sample XML design file is shown in (**a**). The artwork described by (**a**) is shown with different aspect ratios in (**b**). The shaded areas shown in (**b**) are the allowable photo layout regions. An artwork in (**c**) shows a repeating pattern

Fig. 10 Example of automatic background assignment according to theme grammar

3.2.2 Dynamic Photo Layout Region on the Page

As the artwork resizes, STArt design computes a new allowable photo layout region according to the new page dimensions. This area is computed in two ways. It is first computed by scaling the margin proportionally to the smaller one of the horizontal and vertical scaling factors. It is then further modified based on the bounding boxes of the elements labeled as margin pushers. The content of the margin pusher attribute of the element indicates which margin it influences. In 4(b), the shaded region in the middle shows the allowable photo region for difference page sizes.

3.2.3 Theme Grammar for Photobook

The design language is also extended to describe design themes containing multiple related backgrounds. The theme grammar specifies usage constraints of each background, such as suitability for text display or multiple-photo layout, appropriate text color, left or right side, and which backgrounds are compatible with each other on facing pages. These constraints ensure the consistent and harmonic appearance of the photobook. For each background, there are usually a few candidates for its facing page. The final selection of the facing page is a random selection among the choices. This random process makes the facing page more interesting. Backgrounds can be automatically assigned according to these constraints with a single click. Figure 10 shows an example of a small photobook with automatic background artwork assignment with a user-selected theme. Facing pages (pairs in black rectangular frames) have been assigned matching background designs. Users can override each selection easily, but the automatic assignment allows them to quickly change the design theme of a book with minimal effort.

3.3 Automatic Layout

In most photobook authoring solutions, the user is provided with templates, each having fixed regions into which photos and text may be inserted. However, in AutoPhotobook there is no template library. Instead, a module called a "layout engine" creates and edits page layouts in response to commands from the user. The layout engine is based on a photo layout method called Blocked Recursive Image Composition, or BRIC, which is introduced in [7]. The use of BRIC as a collage layout engine is documented in [8]. AutoPhotobook borrows most of its creation and editing functionality from [8] directly, but one difference is that AutoPhotobook supports placement of a text block on the page. Aspects of text including typeface, point size, and line spacing are all regarded as fixed, although as discussed below, alternative presentations of a text block usually differ in how the text is broken into lines.

3.3.1 Prior Related Work

As mentioned above, most photobook authoring solutions rely on templates. Templates are usually generated by graphic artists and as such may offer some guarantee of aesthetic quality. However, template libraries can be costly to generate and manage. If a template library is too big, then it may be burdensome for the user to navigate. If it is too small, there may be instances where the user wishes to present a certain set of content, but the available templates are inappropriate with respect to one or more of the following: number of photos; photo aspect ratios; photo sizes and positions; whether text is allowed; and the maximum length of inserted text. This suggests that there is a need for more automated methods that support the creation and editing of such composites.

Some prior work in automated *photo* layout is reviewed in [7] and [8]. Other recent work includes the automatic method of [30], which uses a Bayesian formulation to optimize layout such that a visually important subset of each photo is visible, and the photo layout optimization techniques of [31]. There is also significant prior work in automated creation and editing of *mixed-content* layouts, which we define as including both text and images. We are not aware of any other work specifically geared toward composites with one text block and any number of photos. However, a generally related area is that of automatic document layout; a recent survey is given in [32]. Much of this work focuses on pages that are primarily textual. In AutoPhotobook pages that have text *at all* tend to have a much greater proportion of image content. Moreover, many document layout and adjustment techniques rely on the premise that the content will respect some prescribed structure, such as a column of a certain width, or a given tabular arrangement. In AutoPhotobook, there is no such specifically prescribed structure. Within these restrictions, there are a few potentially relevant approaches including some based on genetic algorithms [33–35] and others introduced by de Oliveira [36]. However, from published accounts it is not clear whether any of them would be suitable for an interactive experience as described here.

3.3.2 The AutoPhotobook Layout Engine

As mentioned above, the AutoPhotobook layout engine is based on BRIC [7] as used in [8], with the novel development that the user is free to add a text block of virtually any size. In this subsection, we provide a brief overview of BRIC, and we illustrate how the AutoPhotobook layout engine supports inclusion of a text block.

BRIC is an algorithm for arranging virtually any number of photos on a rectangular canvas having any dimensions [7]. In contrast to other photo layout methods, BRIC satisfies the following two criteria: First, photo aspect ratios are respected, so that all of each photo remains visible in the composite; and second, the space between adjacent photos is precisely controlled. Formally, the layout is characterized as a binary tree that corresponds to a recursive partition of the page. Each of the terminal nodes in the tree is associated with a photo, and each interior node corresponds to a rectangular bounding box. In any actual layout, the area of each photo is determined by its position relative to the other photos (i.e., the tree structure), taken together with the canvas dimensions and with the constraints on space between adjacent photos.

Many of the editing mechanisms introduced in [8] and used in AutoPhotobook follow the procedure of first modifying the tree (in a manner prescribed by the editing command), then "reflowing the page" or computing an updated layout based on the modified tree. For example, to swap two photos, we swap the respective terminal nodes in the tree and then reflow the page. AutoPhotobook uses this procedure to support the operations of swapping objects; replacing an object (with a photo or text block as allowed subject to the maximum of one text block); cropping a photo; and editing a text block. (To add an object to the page, or to delete an object, we simply generate a new layout.)

To implement text support in AutoPhotobook, we characterize a text block as having has multiple presentations, where each presentation is fixed in both aspect ratio *and* area. Each presentation is defined by a specific set of dimensions, (i.e., a (height, width) pair); and all presentations are regarded as equally acceptable. During layout creation, or when reflowing the page, we generate a different set of candidate layouts for each presentation; and the candidate having the highest score is used.

3.3.3 Results Illustrating Text Support

Figure 11 shows alternate layouts of four photos and a text block. As described in [8], to generate alternate layouts, we run separate instances of the layout engine, with each instance based on a different set of suggested relative areas for photos. In a majority of instances, as illustrated in Fig. 11, each of the alternate layouts uses a different presentation of the text block. This is not deliberate, and we attribute it to use of different suggested relative area assignments.

Although the AutoPhotobook layout engine strives to respect photo aspect ratios, text presentations are regarded as fixed, and in some cases photos are cropped as a last resort. To illustrate, Fig. 12 shows four layouts that differ only in text block length. Layout (b) was generated first. In this result photos are either not cropped, or cropped minimally. To create Layouts (c) and (d), we only added text to their respective precursors; and to create Layout (a), we deleted text from Layout (b). Note that in Layout (d) photos have been cropped considerably to make room for text.

Fig. 11 Alternate layouts of a content set. Note the use of different text block presentations

| Layout (a): Result of deleting text from the text block in Layout (b). | Layout (b): Initial arrangement generated by layout engine. | Layout (c): result of adding text to the text block in Layout (b). | Layout (d): result of adding text to the text block in Layout (c). |

Fig. 12 Layouts resulting from editing the text block

3.4 User Interface Design

In developing the user interface (UI), we strove for a minimalist design that still retains full advantage of the features themselves as our previous work [14]. Our goal is to avoid restraining the user to the prescribed steps, but to seek synergies between focusing solely on user control or computer automation.

AutoPhotobook anticipates users' needs with contextual UI controls appearing in two views: index view (overview of all pages of a photobook) and book view (close-up view of a single two-page spread). At any of the creation, editing, and reviewing stages, the user can switch between the two views that offer both context and detail on demand. All user interactions are in-place, without opening up new editing or preview windows, so that users only need to get familiar with two views.

When a user first opens an album to create a book, the automatically generated book is presented in index view (Fig. 13), which offers an overview of all pages in the book with their layout. In this view, users can easily swap or move photos between pages and add or delete pages, as well as perform editing actions on individual pages to shuffle, add/delete photos, swap photo locations, and replace a photo on the page.

For finer-scale editing on each page, users can switch to the book view (and back to index view) via a single button click. This brings up a single two-page spread with flip-enabled pages, so users can easily flip to other pages in the book for editing or preview (Fig. 14). In this view, users can add a text block to the page, edit the text content, or perform auto-crop and auto-enhance on photos. Shuffle, add/delete, swap, and replace photos are also enabled in this view.

Each page has at most two button controls that become visible only when the user moves the mouse onto that page. Clicking the shuffle button scrambles the layout

Fig. 13 Index view in AutoPhotobook. Between-page editing, as well as most page-level editing actions, can be done in this view

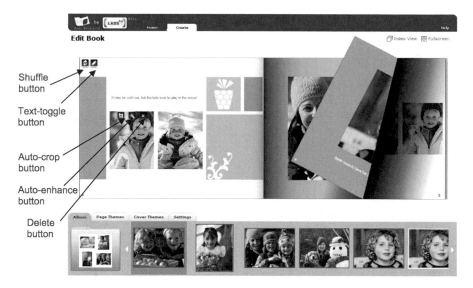

Fig. 14 Book view in AutoPhotobook. Photo-level editing and text editing can be done in this view, in addition to other page-level editing actions

on the page, so users can easily preview different layout choices. On the cover page, the shuffle button serves a slightly different role. It toggles through all candidate

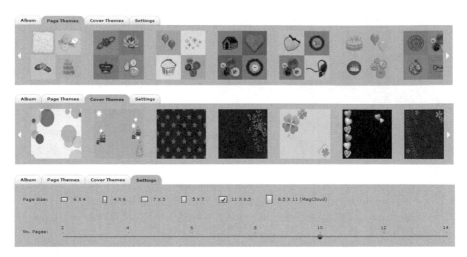

Fig. 15 Page Theme, Cover Theme, and Settings view of AutoPhotobook control tabs

cover photos selected by the automatic algorithm if there is only one photo on that page. There is also a text button that toggles the text block on a page. Other editing actions such as swapping, replacing, and adding photos are done by drag-and-drop operations.

There are up to three button controls on each photo on a page. One toggles auto-crop on and off, another toggles auto-enhance on and off, and the third one is the delete button. The auto-crop and auto-enhance functions give users some flexibility in photo-level editing while keeping the editing UI minimal and easy to learn. The one-click crop and enhance toggle buttons make it easy for the users to preview and decide whether they want to keep the auto-crop and auto-enhance results.

Resources and controls used at book-level are organized into four tabs on the bottom of the screen (Fig. 15). The "Album" tab lists all available photo collections uploaded by the user. The user clicks on an album icon to open it and then scroll through the photo strip to browse and select photos if they wish to modify the selection done by the automatic pagination algorithm (see Fig. 14). The "Page Themes" tab lists all page designs available to choose. Clicking on any of the design will update the entire photobook to that design, by assigning specific backgrounds to each page automatically and adjusting all page layouts accordingly. The "Cover Themes" tab lists all photobook cover designs. Our pilot test indicated that users prefer to have cover design selection independent from page design selection, hence the decision to separate these two design lists. Finally, the "Settings" tab is used to adjust number of pages in the photobook and page dimensions. When the users mark the selection or drag the slider to make changes, the selection of the photos, pagination, page layout, and the artwork sizing are all adjusted automatically in real time to accommodate the changes. Again, all changes appear in-place with context, without opening up new windows.

Much of the editing flexibility we provide through this UI was enabled by the powerful automatic processing algorithms such as scalable pagination algorithm, structured art framework, and automatic layout generation algorithm. The ability to make significant changes to the book pagination and layout with a few simple clicks, without leaving the book editing environment, gives a natural and effortless feel to the photobook tool. The user interface described herein is well suited for devices that have reasonably large displays that support drag and drop as well as clickable actions either through touch screens or computer mouse actions. Some creative product authoring might also be done using devices with smaller displays or more limited interactions. For these, the approach we take of automatically creating an initial photobook and then allowing the user to edit as desired can easily be adapted to a target device. The automatic creation step will still work for any networked device, since all of the computation is done in the cloud. Interactive editing options can then be customized to fit the capabilities of the device. Some devices might not support drag and drop functionality and instead only allow the user to shuffle among the automatically created page alternatives. Image enhancement and auto-crop might be automatically used for all images on some devices, and page designs might be more basic if the device does not support high-quality color or high resolution. Overall, we believe that our approach can be readily adapted across a wide range of networked devices, making it ideal for a CE 2.0 world.

4 Powering CE 2.0 with AutoPhotobook

AutoPhotobook is a full-function web destination that is accessed using a standard web browser. We can increase its effectiveness and reach by incorporating AutoPhotobook within a larger ecosystem that makes use of functionalities from other sources, as well providing photobook creation services to other clients. This integration allows users to build solutions where the AutoPhotobook capability is one component among many others within a software stack. For instance, we may create photobooks using photos stored on Flickr, a popular photo storage web site. We may also provide users not using a standard web browser the capability to create photobooks using AutoPhotobook. This latter use case is particularly pertinent to consumer electronics as few CE devices incorporate standard web browsers. In this section, we will describe how this integration is done and show how the AutoPhotobook features are delivered to devices as part of a broader customer solution.

AutoPhotobook can consume the services and import content from other web sites. It also can allow clients to control various steps in the AutoPhotobook creation process and export final photobooks to other destinations programmatically, without the use of a human-driven interactive interface. The most popular style of web services communication is REST (Representational State Transfer) [37], a simple protocol commonly implemented on the ubiquitous HTTP protocol. Many Web 2.0 sites, such as Flickr or Facebook, provide a REST API to allow clients access to the stored content. AutoPhotobook is equipped with a number of REST client modules to access the services from these sites.

There are two primary categories of services that AutoPhotobook integrates with: Web 2.0 social community services with large amounts of media content and fulfillment services. Social community sites, including sites such as Flickr, Blogger, or

Facebook, are popular content sharing sites capable of archiving large amounts of data. As AutoPhotobook is primarily a photobook creation site, rather than replicating functionality found in existing services, we simply reuse their functionalities. Thus, it is possible for an AutoPhotobook user to import her photo collections from one of these popular photo sharing sites into AutoPhotobook and create a photobook from these pictures.

Another class of web services used by AutoPhotobook is related to print fulfillment. After creating a photobook online, users often want a physical copy of the book as a keepsake. Although AutoPhotobook provides a PDF for users to download and print at home, print fulfillment providers can produce photobooks on higher-quality material and binding which may be more suitable for a keepsake book. Currently, AutoPhotobook can submit photobooks to print fulfillment sites such as HP's MagCloud print-on-demand service, although this capability can be extended easily to any site that provides a REST interface for clients.

By using web services provided by the media sharing and print fulfillment sites, the AutoPhotobook system expands from a site specializing in photobook creation to a customer solution that truly spans the workflow from photo collections to finished books. Depending on the end user application, it is possible to integrate the current solution with additional services to address niche offerings. For instance, by integrating AutoPhotobook with a travel review site and importing location descriptions and photos, it would be possible to publish travel photobooks as a travel guide book.

One aspect of integrating into a network of services and devices is to create more complex solutions; the other aspect of this integration is to make this solution available to more clients. Although the most visible part of AutoPhotobook is the standard web page interface for web browsers, the services and content from AutoPhotobook are also available via web services using a REST programming interface. A number of the algorithms that operate on a single photo, such as auto-crop or photo enhancements, are structured as web services. Many of the operations which map to user actions, such as uploading photos, shuffling photos within a page, or moving a photo from one page to another, are also exposed as web services. In fact, the standard user interface in AutoPhotobook, which is implemented with Adobe Flex, is simply a client that knows how to invoke the AutoPhotobook REST interfaces. The server itself does not know, nor care, the origin of the client requests. Thus, it is possible to develop multiple client front-ends for AutoPhotobook. Figure 16 shows how the components come together to form a number of different solution.

It is the exposure of the AutoPhotobook functionalities as programmatically invokable web services which makes it possible to use these same services to augment the functionalities found in consumer electronic devices. The consumer electronic device is a client no different than the standard Flash client on the AutoPhotobook web site. One obvious consumer electronic platform for integration is the camera-equipped smartphone. A service such as AutoPhotobook, when integrated into the smartphone software environment via an application, can transform the camera phone from a picture taking device into a photobook creation device, with the end

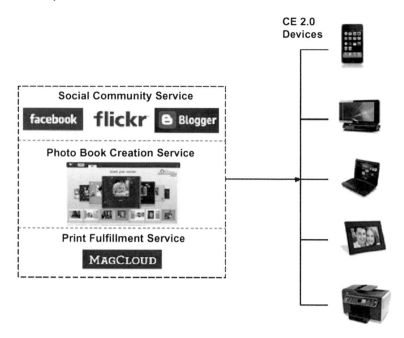

Fig. 16 The extended AutoPhotobook ecosystem

product being not just a digital photograph, but potentially a physical photobook as well.

Figure 17 shows an example of a photobook application running on an iPhone. Note that in this case, the user interface on the phone looks nothing like the actual web site but has been designed and customized for the consumer electronics device itself. When a consumer electronics device is enhanced with web services, the additional service functionality is integrated into the device, but user interfaces are typically custom created to best leverage the specific capabilities and characteristics of the device.

This pattern of augmenting devices with web services can be extended to other consumer electronics devices besides the smart phone. Another example is the digital photo frame. In addition to displaying the photo collections in different slideshow format, by connecting to AutoPhotobook service, the digital frame can be enhanced to display photobooks as well, with no additional hardware. As many digital photo frames now download the source photos from photo sharing sites, AutoPhotobook can be used to import the photos from those sites and export finished photobooks to the digital frame as well. Another viable candidate for enhancement is the home printer. When a user inserts the memory card into the printer for photo printing, the printer can use the AutoPhotobook service to create photobooks to provide additional product alternatives for the user. In terms of CE 2.0 products' ability to grow and adapt to the users' needs, enhancing their capabilities through connections with web services is an effective method that is growing in popularity.

Fig. 17 iPhone client
connected to the
AutoPhotobook creation
service

5 Conclusion

Consumer electronics products are increasing differentiated by software and services rather than by hardware specifications. Many new research challenges come up that require consideration of not only single products but a combination of products and services in an ecosystem. In the AutoPhotobook system as an example, intelligent image analysis and composition are core technologies that are used in multiple implementation paradigms targeted at creating a seamless multimedia experience.

Acknowledgements The authors would like to thank Phil Cheatle, David Slatter, Chris Willis, Andrew Carter, and Roland Penny for technology contributions and many helpful discussions on the Autophotobook application. We would also like to thank HP's Global Delivery China Center team members, lead by Hua Zhang, for their dedicated efforts in building the Autophotobook.com site described in this paper: Tonghai Duan, Fei Ma, Zhidong Mao, Zeshuo Yin, and Yue Yuan.

References

1. MacManus, R.: Consumer Electronics 2.0: MIT's Henry Holtzman on the Internet of Things. ReadWriteWeb (2009)
2. Yoshida, J.: What Cisco's 'CE 2.0' challenge means to consumer electronics market. EE Times (2009)

3. Zhang, T., et al.: Face based image navigation and search. In: Proceedings of the 17th ACM International Conference on Multimedia (2009)
4. Gallagher, A.C., et al.: Image annotation using personal calendars as context. In: Proceedings of the 16th ACM International Conference on Multimedia (2008)
5. Yuan, J., et al.: Mining GPS traces and visual words for event classification. In: Proceedings of the 16th ACM International Conference on Multimedia (2008)
6. Dong, L., et al.: Smart batch tagging of photo albums. In: Proceedings of the 17th ACM International Conference on Multimedia (2009)
7. Atkins, C.B.: Blocked recursive image composition. In: Proceedings of the 16th ACM International Conference on Multimedia (2008)
8. Xiao, J., Zhang, X., Cheatle, P., Gao, Y., Atkins, C.B.: Mixed-initiative photo collage authoring. In: Proceeding of the 16th ACM International Conference on Multimedia, pp. 509–518. ACM, New York (2008)
9. Boll, S., et al.: Semantics, content, and structure of many for the creation of personal photo albums. In: Proceedings of the 16th ACM International Conference on Multimedia (2008)
10. Henze, N., et al.: Snap and share your photobooks. In: Proceedings of the 16th ACM International Conference on Multimedia (2008)
11. PMA Marketing Research. In: 2008 PMA Camera/Camcorder and Digital Imaging Survey (2008)
12. Obrador, P., Moroney, N., MacDowell, I., O'Brien-Strain, E.: Image collection taxonomies for photo-book auto-population with intuitive interaction. In: Proceeding of the Eighth ACM Symposium on Document Engineering, pp. 102–103. ACM, New York (2008)
13. Sandhaus, P., Thieme, S., Boll, S.: Processes of photo book production. Multimedia Syst. **14**(6), 351–357 (2008)
14. Yu, M., Liang, Y., Lee, K., Chen, B., Ouhyoung, M.: Smart album: photo filtering by effect detections. In: ACM SIGGRAPH 2008 Posters. ACM, New York (2008)
15. Keshet, R., Staelin, C., Oicherman, B., Fischer, M., Kisilev, P., Schein, S., Shaked, D., Vans, M., Nachlieli, H., Bergman, R., Maurer, R., Aharon, M., Berkovich, A., Waidman, R., Bengigi, O., Amit, G., Harush, S., Asher, A., Chao, H., Greig, D., Gaubatz, M., Simske, S.J.: Automatic photo enhancement server (HIPIE 2). In: International Symposium on Technologies for Digital Fulfillment, Las Vegas, NE (2009)
16. Cheatle, P.: Automatic image cropping for republishing. In: Imaging and Printing in a Web 2.0 World. Proceedings of SPIE, vol. 7540A (2010)
17. Lowe, D.: Distinctive image features from scale-invariant keypoints. Int. J. Comput. Vis. **60**(2), 91–110 (2004)
18. Rubner, Y., Tomasi, C., Guibas, L.: The earth mover distance as a metric for image retrieval. Int. J. Comput. Vis. **40**(2) (2000)
19. Viola, P., Jones, M.: Rapid object detection using a boosted cascade of simple features. In: CVPR (2001)
20. Graham, A., Garcia-Molina, H., Paepcke, A., Winograd, T.: Time as essence for photo browsing through personal digital libraries. In: JCDL (2002)
21. Tang, F., Gao, Y.: Fast near duplicate detection for personal image collections. In: Proceedings of the 17th ACM International Conference on Multimedia (2009)
22. Avidan, S., Shamir, A.: Seam carving for content-aware image resizing. ACM Trans. Graph. (2007)
23. Rubinstein, M., Shamir, A., Avidan, S.: Improved seam carving for video retargeting. ACM Trans. Graph. (2008)
24. Wang, Y., Tai, C., Sorkine, O., Lee, T.: Optimized scale-and-stretch for image resizing. ACM Trans. Graph. (2008)
25. Dragicevic, P., Chatty, S., Thevenin, D., Vinot, J.L.: Artistic resizing: a technique for rich scale-sensitive vector graphics. In: Proceedings of the 18th Annual ACM Symposium on User Interface Software and Technology (2005)
26. Birkhoff, G.D.: Aesthetic Measure. Harvard University Press, Harvard (1933)
27. Harrington, S.J., Naveda, J.F., et al.: Aesthetic measures for automated document layout. In: Proceedings of the ACM Symposium on Document Engineering (2000)

28. Chao, H., Gabbur, P., Wiley, A.: Preserving the aesthetics during non-fixed aspect ratio scaling of the digital border. In: Proceedings of the 2007 ACM Symposium on Document Engineering, pp. 144–146. ACM, New York (2007)

29. Chao, H., Zhang, X., Tretter, D.: Structured layout for resizable background art. In: Proceedings of the ACMMM Associated Workshop on Interactive Multimedia on Consumer Electronics (ICME) (2009)

30. Wang, J., Sun, J., Quan, L., Tang, X., Shum, H.-Y.: Picture Collage. In: Proceedings of Computer Vision and Pattern Recognition (CVPR) (2006)

31. Wei, Y., Matsushita, Y., Yang, Y.: Efficient optimization of photo collage. Technical Report, Microsoft Research, MSR-TR-2009-59, May 2009

32. Hurst, N., Li, W., Marriott, K.: Review of automatic document formatting. In: Proceedings of the 9th ACM Symposium on Document Engineering (DocEng '09), pp. 99–108 (2009)

33. Goldenberg, E.: Automatic Layout of Variable-Content Print Data. MS thesis, University of Sussex, Brighton, UK (2002)

34. Purvis, L.: A genetic algorithm approach to automated custom document assembly. In: Proceedings of the 2nd International Conference on Intelligent Systems Design and Applications (ISDA'02), Atlanta, GA, August 2002

35. Purvis, L., Harrington, S., O'Sullivan, B., Freuder, E.: Creating personalized documents: an optimization approach. In: Proceedings of the ACM Symposium on Document Engineering, Grenoble, France (2003)

36. de Oliveira, J.B.: Two algorithms for automatic document page layout. In: Proceedings of the Eighth ACM Symposium on Document Engineering (DocEng '08), Sao Paulo, Brazil, 16–19 September, pp. 141–149 (2008)

37. Fielding, R.: Architectural styles and the design of network-based software architectures. PhD thesis, University of California, Irvine (2000)

Index